# Rewriting Literacy

## Critical Studies in Education and Culture Series

Education under Seige: The Conservative, Liberal and Radical Debate over Schooling
*Stanley Aronowitz and Henry A. Giroux*

Literacy: Reading the Word and the World
*Paulo Freire and Donaldo Macedo*

The Moral and Spiritual Crisis in Education: A Curriculum for Justice and Compassion
*David Purpel*

The Politics of Education: Culture, Power and Liberation
*Paulo Freire*

Popular Culture, Schooling and the Language of Everyday Life
*Henry A. Giroux and Roger I. Simon*

Teachers As Intellectuals: Toward a Critical Pedagogy of Learning
*Henry A. Giroux*

Women Teaching for Change: Gender, Class and Power
*Kathleen Weiler*

Between Capitalism and Democracy: Educational Policy and the Crisis of the Welfare State
*Svi Shapiro*

Critical Psychology and Pedagogy: Interpretation of the Personal World
*Edmund Sullivan*

Pedagogy and the Struggle for Voice
*Catherine E. Walsh*

Learning Work: A Critical Pedagogy of Work Education
*Roger I. Simon, Don Dippo, and Arleen Schenke*

Voices in Architectural Education: Cultural Politics and Pedagogy
*Edited by Thomas P. Dutton*

Educational Leadership: A Critical Pragmatic Perspective
*Spencer J. Maxcy*

Culture and Power in the Classroom: A Critical Foundation for Bicultural Education
*Antonia Darder*

Cultural Pedagogy: Art/Education/Politics
*David Trend*

Teaching Against the Grain: A Pedagogy of Possibility
*Roger I. Simon*

# Rewriting Literacy

## Culture and the Discourse of the Other

Edited by
Candace Mitchell
and
Kathleen Weiler

Critical Studies in Education and Culture Series
Edited by Henry A. Giroux and Paulo Freire

**BERGIN & GARVEY**
New York • Westport, Connecticut • London

Library of Congress Cataloging-in-Publication Data

Rewriting literacy: culture and the discourse of the other / edited
   by Candace Mitchell and Kathleen Weiler.
      p.    cm.—(Critical studies in education and culture)
   Includes bibliographical references and index.
   ISBN 0–89789–225–9 (alk. paper)
   ISBN 0–89789–228–3 (pbk. : alk. paper)
   1. Literacy.  2. Sociolinguistics.  3. Pluralism.  4. Educational
sociology.  5. Educational anthropology.  I. Mitchell, Candace.
II. Weiler, Kathleen.   III. Series: Critical studies in education &
culture.
   LC149.R48   1991
   302.2'244—dc20          91–15503

British Library Cataloguing in Publication Data is available.

Library of Congress Catalog Card Number: 91–15503
ISBN: 0–89789–225–9
        0–89789–228–3 (pbk.)

First published in 1991

Bergin & Garvey, One Madison Avenue, New York, NY 10010
An imprint of Greenwood Publishing Group, Inc.

Printed in the United States of America

The paper used in this book complies with the
Permanent Paper Standard issued by the National
Information Standards Organization (Z39.48-1984).

10 9 8 7 6 5 4 3 2 1

Copyright Acknowledgment

Chapters in Parts I-IV of this volume originally appeared in the *Journal of Education*, and are
reprinted here with the permission of the *Journal*.

For Our Mothers

# CONTENTS

# SERIES INTRODUCTION: LITERACY, DIFFERENCE, AND THE POLITICS OF BORDER CROSSING

All of the authors in this book perform a valuable theoretical service. They analyze some central questions relevant to the debate that is increasingly being waged around the relationship between literacy, culture, and difference in education. They discuss what it means to restructure school curricula in order to address the needs of those groups who traditionally have been generally excluded within the dominant discourse of schooling. The authors in their respective interventions raise a number of important questions about the importance of redefining literacy as a form of cultural politics, a redefinition that would provide the conditions for subordinate groups to learn the knowledge and skills necessary for self and social empowerment. Everyone needs to be able to live in a society in which everyone has the opportunity to govern and shape history rather than be consigned to its margins.

Literacy in its varied versions, many of which are discussed in detail both in Candace Mitchell's excellent preface and demonstrated by the authors included in the book, is about the practice of representation as a means of organizing, inscribing, and containing meaning. It is also about practices of representation that disrupt or rupture existing textual, epistemological, and ideological systems. In this sense, literacy becomes critical to the degree that it makes problematic the very structure and practice of representation; that is, it focuses attention on the importance of acknowledging that meaning is not fixed, and that to be literate is to undertake a dialogue with others who speak from different histories, locations, and experiences. Literacy is a discursive practice in which difference becomes crucial for understanding not simply how to read, write, or develop aural skills, but also to recognize that the identities of "others" matter as part of a broader set of politics and practices aimed at the reconstruction of democratic public life. Literacy as part of a broader politics of difference and democracy points, at the very least, to two important considerations. First, it makes visible the historically and socially constructed strengths and limitations of those places and borders we inherit that frame our discourses and social relations. Second, literacy is a form of ethical address that structures how we construct relationships between ourselves and others. It marks out the boundaries of difference and inscribes them in borders that "define the places that are safe and unsafe, [that] distinguish *us* from *them*."[1] Borders signal in the metaphorical and literal sense how power is inscribed differently on the body, culture, history, space, land, and psyche. When literacy is defined in monolithic terms, from the center, within a linear logic that erases uncertainty, it only recognizes the borders of privilege and domination. What is crucial here is that the discourse of literacy cannot be abstracted from the language of difference and power. As such, literacy cannot be viewed as merely an epistemological or procedural issue, but must be defined primarily in political and ethical terms. It is political in that how we "read" the world is always implicated in relations of power. Literacy is ethical in that people "read" the world differently depending, for instance, on circumstances of class, gender, race, and politics. They also read the world in spaces and social relationships constructed between themselves and others that demand actions based on judgments and choices about how one is to act in the face of ideologies, values, and experiences that are the mark of "others," of "otherness." It is these shifting relations of knowing and identity that frame our "different modes of response to the other (e.g. between those that transfigure and those that disfigure, those that care for the other in his / her otherness and those that do not)."[2]

If a politics of difference is to be fashioned in emancipatory rather than oppressive practices, literacy must be rewritten in terms that articulate difference with the principles of equality, justice, and freedom rather than with those interests supportive of hierarchies, oppression, and exploitation. In this case, literacy as an emancipatory practice requires people to write, speak, and listen in the language of difference, a language in which meaning becomes multi-accentual, dispersed, and resists permanent closure. This is a language in which one speaks *with* rather than *for* Others. Put differently, the discourse of critical literacy is one that signals the need to challenge and redefine the substance and effects of cultural borders, the need to create opportunities for students to be border crossers in order to understand otherness on its own terms, and the need to create borderlands in which diverse cultural resources allow for the fashioning of new identities within existing configurations of power.[3]

In what follows, I want to take up these issues briefly to highlight what I call a postmodern discourse of literacy and difference. The emphasis here will be on the importance of the relationship between literacy and difference rather than on the specific substance and effects of the various approaches to literacy that are examined both in the introduction and the various chapters of the book. However, before I take up these issues, I think it is important to address briefly the broader political context in which the debates over cultural difference and literacy have been framed during the last decade. It is to this issue that I will now turn.

## CULTURAL LITERACY AS EUROCENTRISM

The ideological parameters of the current debate over culture and difference took shape during the Reagan era. During the last decade, the terms of this debate have been principally set by conservatives such as Allan Bloom, Diane Ravitch, Chester Finn, and E.D. Hirsch, Jr.[4] All of these critics have presented in different ways an agenda and purpose for shaping public schooling and higher education under the terms of a cultural discourse in which the concept of difference is seen as a threat to what is labeled as Western culture. Within this discourse, the issue of culture and schooling is taken up primarily in terms aimed at overcoming or erasing difference, rather than incorporating it as part of an ongoing democratic and pedagogical project. The conservative position has arisen from the recognition by some of its followers that the United States is in the midst of a cultural crisis that can be traced to the broader ideological tenets of the radical social movements that emerged during the 1960s, along with the more recent emergence and influence of diverse forms: postmodern, feminist, and poststructuralist theory. The villains include among others: those who hold that intellectuals should engage public life in oppositional terms; those who reject universal reason as a foundation for human affairs; those who oppose totalizing narratives; those who refuse to accept Eurocentric notions of Western culture as being synonymous with the very notion of civilization; those who argue that student experience should qualify as a legitimate form of knowledge; and those who claim that racial, class, gender, and ethnic differences extend, rather than threaten the most basic principles of a democratic society.

In response to these developments, neo-conservatives have attempted to reduce the politics of difference and schooling to forms of character education in which the call to pluralism becomes a euphemism for educating students to learn how to follow the rules and to adapt rather than critically engage the values that reproduce existing structures of power. In this view, the concept of cultural difference, especially racial difference, is seen as threatening to the integrative character of the American polity, a threat to the merits of individualism, and disrespectful of the "high culture" of the West.

Removed from the language of social justice, difference is associated with a notion of literacy in which a critique of Eurocentrism, racism, or cultural domination is dismissed as merely an instance of a vile form of particularism that threatens to undermine the basis of what is unproblematically labeled as Western civilization. Related to this perspective, there is a general tendency to view "otherness" as threatening to the notion of equality and tolerance central to the neo-conservative view of national unity and security. The call to literacy has become a powerful weapon used by neo-conservatives in their fight against the diverse groups attempting to rewrite the cultural, political, and social codes of the dominant society. Fearful of the threat to its physical (immigration), linguistic (bilingualism), academic (curriculum and canon), and racial (segregation) borders, neo-conservatives have constructed a notion of cultural literacy that abstracts equity from difference while framing educational policies in a language that represents a new form of nativism. Consequently, literacy is often defined by the pedagogical imperative to learn knowledge, skills, and values that transcend the difficulties of race, color, ethnicity, language, and religion. Within this view, Diane Ravitch, for example, attacks those who analyze how cultural differences have been structured in forms of dominance and subordination as particularists and separatists who have not learned how to treat her notion of literacy and the "common culture" with reverence and respect.[5]

In my mind, this approach to difference, literacy, and schooling raises a fundamental challenge to how educators and others might view the role of educating students for critical citizenship in a democratic society. At risk in this debate is neither the "tradition" of Western culture as it is represented in school curricula nor the issue of whether subordinate students will be given the appropriate skills to function adequately in the labor market. Of course, these are important issues, but they should not be the concerns that define the purpose and meaning of literacy and schooling in this country. That is, the purpose and meaning of schooling extend beyond the function of a museum safeguarding the treasures of cultural tradition or the needs of the corporate state for more literate workers.

What is at stake in this debate is the status of literacy defined in relation to the radical responsibility of ethics, a responsibility that takes seriously educating students with the knowledge, skills, and values necessary for establishing relations between the self and others that refuse acts of violence, aggression, and subjugation. In question are those democratic values that provide the possibility for drawing attention to the languages, histories, and voices of those groups who have been traditionally excluded or marginalized from the discourse and citadels of power. More specifically, the importance of the debate on literacy, difference, and schooling raises important questions about the fragile nature of democracy itself. This suggests that any debate about schooling and difference is inseparable from a wider concern with the reconstruction of democratic public life.

## REWRITING THE DISCOURSE OF LITERACY AND DIFFERENCE

In opposition to the emerging neo-conservative view, which defines democracy against cultural difference and literacy as a politics of equity, justice, and representation, I want to develop a rationale along with some pedagogical principles for developing a politics of difference responsive to the imperatives of a critical democracy. In doing so, I want to emphasize that public schools and institutions of higher learning cannot be viewed simply as instructional sites; they must be more broadly defined as contradictory agencies engaged in specific forms of moral and political regulation. That is, they produce knowledge, and they provide students with a sense of place, worth, and identity. In doing so, they offer students selected representations, skills, social relations, and values that presuppose particular histories and ways of being in the world. The moral and political dimension at work here is revealed in the question: Whose history, story, and experience prevail in the school setting? In other words, who speaks for whom, under what conditions, and for what purpose? As such, educational institutions and the processes in which they engage are not innocent. Simply stated, schools are not neutral institutions designed for either providing students with work skills or with the privileged tools of culture. Instead, they are deeply implicated in forms of inclusion and exclusion that produce particular moral truths and values. In effect, they both produce and legitimate cultural differences as part of their broader project of constructing particular knowledge/power relations and producing specific notions of citizenship. To some, this may sound commonsensical and a bit tiresome, but I think it is imperative to locate all levels of education within a moral and social context in order to asses how a politics and pedagogy of difference might be engaged as part of a discourse fundamental to the reconstruction of a critical democracy.

The problems facing education around the issue of difference in the United States need to be reformulated as a crisis in citizenship and ethics. This suggests that the solution to these problems lies ultimately in the realms of values and politics, not in simplistic calls for the creation of a common culture, a monolithic notion of cultural literacy, or a pluralism divorced from the issues of power and struggle. What is at stake is not the semantic difference between pluralism and particularism, but the creation of a democratic society in which differences are affirmed and interrogated, rather than dismissed as essentialist or disruptive. It is no small irony that many conservatives who oppose a politics of difference to the discourse of pluralism are also arguing for measuring citizenship competencies through standardized cultural literacy tests and dismissing the voices of those who have been left out of dominant versions of academic discourse by suggesting that they are incapable of being more than self-referential and doctrinaire. Within this formulation, justice is subordinated to a plea for academic balance, while at the same time the school curriculum (canon) is defended as being representative of a version of Western history that is self-righteously equated with the meaning of civilization itself. There is something ironic in the charge by those in power (white academic males), especially in higher education, that they have been pushed to the margins as a result of their defense of a Eurocentric-based curriculum. In the face of an upsurge of racism across the country, this type of logic translates into the self-indulging act of mistaking the call to defend one's views as a form of aggression. So much for the spirit of critical inquiry. The sentiment echoes what the dominant curriculum suggests, and blacks, women, and other subordinate groups generally accept as a given: it is only the voices of white males that count.

At the risk of overstating this issue, the crisis of literacy in this country must be framed as part of a politics of difference that provides students with the opportunity to engage in a deeper understanding of the importance of democratic culture, while developing classroom relations that prioritize the importance of diversity, equality, and social justice. The ethical imperative that links difference, schooling, and democracy in institutions of public and higher education should educate students primarily for the responsibilities of learning how to govern. This means organizing curricula in ways that enable students to make judgments about how society is historically and socially constructed, how existing social practices are implicated in relations of equality and justice, as well as how they structure inequalities around racism, sexism, and other forms of oppression. It also means offering students the possibilities for being able to make judgments about what society might be, and what is possible or desirable outside existing configurations of power.

Students need more than information about what it means to get a job or pass standardized tests that purport to measure cultural literacy; they need to be able to assess critically dominant and subordinate traditions so as to engage their strengths and weaknesses. What they do not need is to treat history as a closed, singular narrative that simply has to be revered and memorized. Educating for difference, democracy, and ethical responsibility is not about creating passive citizens. It is about providing students with the knowledge, capacities, and opportunities to be noisy, irreverent, and vibrant. Central to this concern is the need for students to understand how cultural, ethnic, racial, and ideological differences enhance the possibility for dialogue, trust, and solidarity. Within this perspective, difference can be analyzed and constructed within pedagogical contexts that promote compassion and tolerance rather than envy, hatred, and bigotry. The pedagogical and ethical practice that I am emphasizing is one that offers opportunities for students to be border crossers; as border crossers, students not only refigure the boundaries of academic subjects in order to engage in new forms of critical inquiry, but they also are offered the opportunities to engage the multiple references that construct different cultural codes, experiences, and histories. In this context, a pedagogy of difference provides the basis for students to cross over into diverse cultural zones that offer a critical resource for rethinking how the relations between dominant and subordinate groups are organized, how they are implicated and often structured in dominance, and how such relations might be transformed in order to promote a democratic and just society. Difference in this case does not become a marker for deficit, inferiority, chauvinism, or inequality; on the contrary, it opens the possibilities for constructing pedagogical practices that deepen forms of cultural democracy that serve to enlarge our moral vision.

As many of the authors in this book suggest, it is crucial for educators to link a politics of literacy and difference to a theory of social welfare and cultural democracy. At the very least, this means that educators can work to insert the idea of difference into the curriculum as part of an attempt to rearticulate the ideas of justice and equality. A politics of literacy and difference not only offers students the opportunity for raising questions about how the categories of race, class, and gender are shaped within the margins and center of power, but it also provides a new way of reading history as a way of reclaiming power and identity. This is no small matter for those students who have generally been either marginalized or silenced by the dominant ideologies and practices of public schooling. Educators need to acknowledge that the radical responsibility of a politics of literacy and difference necessitates an ongoing analysis by students of the contradictions in American society between the meaning of freedom, the demands of social justice, the obligations of citizenship, on the one hand, and the accumulated suffering, domination, force, and violence that permeates all aspects of everyday life on the other. Such an analysis necessitates forms of literacy grounded in the ethical imperative to both challenge the prevailing social order while simultaneously providing the basis for students to deepen the intellectual, civic, and moral understanding of their role as agents of public formation.

This means that the debate over the politics of literacy, difference, and culture might be reconstructed to engage the broader issue of how learning that goes on in American education is truly attentive to the problems and histories that construct the actual experiences students face in their everyday lives. A pedagogy of literacy and difference is not based merely on providing students with conflicting paradigms or the dispassionate skills of rhetorical persuasion; on the contrary, it points to pedagogical practices that offer students the knowledge, skills, and values they will need to critically negotiate and transform the world in which they find themselves. The politics of critical literacy and cultural difference engages rather than retreats from those problems that make democracy messy, vibrant, and noisy. Of course, literacy and difference when defined in these terms appear dangerous to neo-conservatives and others who believe that social criticism and social justice are inimical to both the meaning of American education and the lived experience of democratic public life. This is precisely why educators cannot let the politics of literacy and difference be subordinated to cleansing and comforting self-righteous appeals made in the name of a common culture or the false equality of a pluralism devoid of the trappings of struggle, empowerment, and possibility. Our students do not deserve an education constrained by the smothering dictates of a monolithic and totalizing view of culture, literacy, and citizenship; they deserve an education that acknowledges its role in the preparation of critical political subjects and that prepares them to be agents capable of locating themselves in history while simultaneously being able to shape it.

*Rewriting Literacy* is an important book providing readers with diverse elements of a critical approach to literacy that ruptures universal versions of reason and linear notions of history; this is a book that points to decentering margins as spaces that offer the opportunity for other voices to speak and be heard. Literacy as it is developed here is not bogged down in a stifling regime of knowledge that refuses to recognize its own partiality, but in a view of uncertainty that makes dialogue and debate possible. At the same time, the call for literacies rather than literacy does more than displace regimes of certainty; it also, as Iain Chambers points out in a different context, "suggests an ecological frame in which the other continues to simultaneously exist apart from us and yet be part of us in a shared responsibility for living in difference, for being responsible, just as we are for ourselves and the ethics that sustain such a relationship."[6] This points to a view of literacy that extends rather than cuts off the possibilities of acknowledging a world forged in differences that matter, and that addresses the memories, traces, and voices of those who think and act in the struggle for an extension of human dignity. This is a pedagogy of literacy in which "differences are recognized, exchanged and mixed in identities that break down but are not lost, that connect but remain diverse."[7] It is a literacy that both affirms and disrupts in the name of hope committed to the radical responsibility of politics and ethics that informs the struggle for a better future.

—Henry A. Giroux

## NOTES

1. Gloria Anzaldua. *Borderlands / La frontera: The new mestiza.* San Francisco: Spinsters / Aunt Lute, 1987, p. 3.

2. Richard Kearney. *The wake of imagination.* Minneapolis: University of Minnesota Press, 1988, p. 369.

3. These themes are developed extensively in: Stanley Aronowitz and Henry A. Giroux. *Postmodern education: Politics, culture, and social criticism.* Minneapolis: University of Minnesota Press, 1991.

4. Allan Bloom. *The closing of the American mind.* New York: Simon & Schuster, 1987; E. D. Hirsch, Jr. *Cultural literacy: What every American needs to know.* Boston: Houghton Mifflin, 1987; Chester Finn and Diane Ravitch. *What do our 17-year olds know?* New York: Harper and Row, 1987.

5. Diane Ravitch. What's at stake with multicultural education? *Clipboard* 4 (February 15, 1990), pp. 1–2. Ravitch has played a prominent role arguing a neo-conservative position around the relationship between culture and school knowledge. She played most recently a key prominent role in the textbook debates in California and is also responsible for organizing a protest against the New York report on minority representation in school curricula.

6. Iain Chambers. *Border dialogues: Journeys in postmodernity.* New York: Routledge, 1990, p. 115.

7. Ibid., p. 114.

# PREFACE

Candace Mitchell

*Rewriting Literacy* is a book that seeks to do just what the title suggests. It strives to move beyond the dominant discourse of the day, a discourse of literacy steeped in paranoia, discomfort, and fear. This is a discourse that focuses not on literacy, but rather on illiteracy. In so doing, it focuses not on the positive end of this imposed dichotomy, but rather on the negative. This focus emerges as a result of the fixing of polar extremes, and leads, in turn, to the implicit classification of those who are "literate" as good and of those who are "illiterate" as somehow bad. The discourse of which I write is illustrated in the following comments taken from a Boston Globe article by Mike Barnicle, "Illiteracy: the enemy within" (September 25, 1990. p. 15). Barnicle writes of a young 17-year-old man seated outside a Boston courtroom as he waits for arraignment on a drug possession charge. The young man, the reader learns, is the father of a 10-month-old whose mother is 16. Although the mother can read, the young man cannot. Not so implicit in Barnicle's scenario is the assumption that illiteracy is the root cause of the young man's "frustration and lawlessness." It is the young man's inability to read and write that has led him to a life of crime, to teenage parenthood, and to this courtroom lobby where he is being charged with illegal possession. In order to break this trend toward "illiteracy and hopelessness," Barnicle suggests, we have, as a nation, to spend more on public education and stop throwing "an army of the poor out on to the street every single morning and then scratch our heads and express shock about all the drugs, crime and shootings." I agree with Barnicle: literacy is an economic issue. Certainly more money is needed for education, much more. At the same time, however, I suggest that educators as well as the public need to rethink what it means to be literate and how one acquires literacy. To spend more while remaining ensconced in present-day ideological perspectives that view literacy and illiteracy as monolithic, polar opposites will lead, I would suggest, to but a continuation of the present state of affairs, a status quo marked by minority disenfranchisement, a high drop-out rate, and a continuation of what I would characterize as an exclusionary literacy.

What is an exclusionary literacy? An exclusionary literacy seeks itself as the model for what should be. Embedded in a modernist ideology, an exclusionary literacy "claims transcendental and transhistorical status" (Giroux, 1988). Situated centrally, an exclusionary literacy views itself as a universal form of reading, writing, and language use. Discourse forms situated at the boundaries of this centrally located form are designated as deviant, as lacking in rationality, and as in need of eradication. Those situated outside the confines of the monolithic, exclusionary literacy are designated as the Other, alien and troubled, lawless and frustrated, and marked by an inherent failure to learn to read and write, and an inability to use language appropriately. Also, although many do step beyond blaming the individual for this failure, as does Barnicle, and move to a recognition that institutions and institutional policies serve to perpetuate the socalled literacy problem, few move beyond this level of critique and truly problematize the very nature of literacy itself and, in turn, problematize how literacy is acquired. An exclusionary literacy still designates the literacy problem as one that, in the words of James Paul Gee, "resides within individuals" (1989, p. 5). As a result, the solution to the literacy problem is sought "in terms of what is going on inside individuals' minds, what skills they have failed to obtain, and how they can acquire them." What we need to do then, as a society, according to Barnicle and others, is simply teach people to read and write, and of course, to use language appropriately. Literacy is then viewed as the decoding and encoding of language, a skill, decontextualized from a historical, social, and cultural context. This decontextualized, unproblematized view of literacy does not question what is to be read, what forms writing will take, and what language or dialect will be used in the process. Nor does this decontextualized, unproblematized view of literacy consider the issue of student voice. A multiplicity of voices—those of women, men, girls, and boys, working, lower, middle, and upper classes, Blacks, Asians, Hispanics, and Native Americans, among others—need to be heard in order for individuals to participate fully in the process of acquiring and, with hope, reshaping literacy.

By reorienting the focus of discussion from differences in individual performance, that is, the inability to read and write, to a concern for the social / cultural / historical context of literacy, those involved in reconceptualizing and rewriting literacy move away from the assumption that individual performance is related to individual talent, and turn instead to the recognition that success or lack of success in school and the "failure" to learn to read and write may be more directly related to the distance the learner's own discourse community is from the discourse of the school, a discourse reflective of middle- and upper-

class ways of using language. Students from middle- and upper-class backgrounds come to schools already well versed in the discourse structures expected in schools, whereas students from nonmainstream backgrounds, Black
working-class and lower-class students, and many nonnative speakers of English, for example, enter educational institutions well versed in the discourse
structures of their communities. These structures have been found to differ in
fundamental ways from those of the mainstream (Heath, 1982; Michaels,
1981). Those who fail in schools are those who fail to master the genres of
schooling: that is, they fail to master the ways of structuring and of dealing
with experience that schools value in varying ways (Heath, 1982). Though
now supported by ethnographic research and careful linguistic analysis (Gee,
1989; Gumperz, 1982; Michaels, 1981), this notion of mismatch (and the ram-
ifications of the mismatch) is not a new conception. Antonio Gramsci (1971),
for example, wrote early in the century,

> In a whole series of families, especially in the intellectual strata, the children find
> in their family life a preparation, a prolongation and a completion of school life;
> they breathe in, as the expression goes, a whole quantity of notions and attitudes
> which facilitate the educational process properly speaking. (p. 31)

Pierre Bourdieu's (1977) notion of cultural capital speaks to the same issue.
Bourdieu writes:

> Indeed, one can put forward the hypothesis that the specific productivity of all
> pedagogic work other than the pedagogic work accomplished by the family is a
> function of the distance between the habitus it tends to inculcate (in this context,
> scholarly mastery of scholarly language) and the habitus inculcated by all previ-
> ous forms of pedagogic work and, ultimately, by the family (i.e. in this case, prac-
> tical mastery of the mother tongue). (p. 72)

Unfortunately, this mismatch often leads to the erroneous reaction on the part
of individuals in authority in educational institutions that students from non-
mainstream backgrounds are not making sense, when, in fact, they are. What
is occurring is that the sense making is embodied in structures alien to individuals outside the group. The fact that they are perhaps alien does not mean,
however, that they are impenetrable (Gee, 1985; Gumperz, 1982; Michaels,
1981).

*Rewriting Literacy* situates discussions of literacy and the nature of literacy
in the social, cultural, and historical context, while at the same time considering issues of student voice. Each chapter brings to light important concerns regarding literacy, concerns that are often ignored by the more traditionally
oriented educationalist. To the more traditionally oriented, literacy is but reading and writing, or but the decoding and encoding of an unproblematic entity:
language. In contrast, the authors contributing to *Rewriting Literacy* view liter-

acy as embedded in a historical, social, and cultural context. To do so problematizes the very nature of what it means to be literate. Each piece highlights either implicitly or explicitly the highly political nature of literacy, and in so doing, approaches the study of literacy from a critical perspective.

Contributors to the book come from a variety of fields, including linguistics, sociolinguistics, anthropology, education, English as a second language, and reading and writing theory. *Rewriting Literacy* makes a profound contribution to the developing field of literacy studies since it is the first book that seeks to link such a variety of fields. All but a few of the authors report on their own highly original, primary research. Methodological approaches employed by the various authors include classroom ethnography, case study, and discourse analysis, as well as historical research. *Rewriting Literacy* will be of interest to researchers, theorists, and practitioners in each of the fields mentioned above. Overall, the body of work presented in *Rewriting Literacy* is relevant not only to individuals whose main focus is in the area of literacy studies, but to all those who are concerned about minority disenfranchisement, institutional inequity, and the political, cultural, and social dimensions of education.

*Rewriting Literacy* is organized into four sections: "Literacy, Discourse, and Power," "Multiple Ways of Constructing Reality," "The Politics of Reading and Writing," and "Literacy, History, and Ideology." In what follows, I will touch upon the main themes presented in each of the chapters of the book.

The first section of *Rewriting Literacy* contains four chapters that discuss literacy practices, discourse practices, and the fundamental relationship of the two to issues of power in society. In "What Is Literacy?" James Paul Gee defines literacy. In so doing, he immediately breaks down the notion of literacy as monolithic and instead analyzes varieties of discourse practices, each of which he characterizes as a form of literacy. Thus literacy, in Gee's analysis, becomes pluralized as it is embedded in the social context. All then who engage in the social use of language are literate. This reconceptualization of literacy as pluralized immediately discards the negative extreme: illiteracy. Gee recognizes, however, that all forms of literacy are not the same. Gee characterizes the varieties of forms in terms of their dominance and power, as well as in terms of their relationship to home-based and community-based ways of using language.

The second chapter in this section, "Discourses of Power, the Dialectics of Understanding, the Power of Literacy" by Adrian Bennett, also critiques a monolithic, mainstream definition of literacy, as well as offers an alternative view of literacy. Bennett does so by comparing his oral "reading" of a picture story to that of the story as told by a young student named Carlos. Drawing on a linguistic analysis of the two narratives, Bennett provides evidence for his argument that his own, more "literate" telling pales in comparison to Carlos's narrative, despite the fact that Carlos's narrative does not conform to forms associated with essayist literacy (Scollon & Scollon, 1981). Bennett's analysis and subsequent critique of the notion of essayist, or school-based, literacy as good or better than other forms of language practice contribute to the rewriting of what it means to be literate.

In the third chapter of the first section, "The Struggle for Voice: Narrative, Literacy, and Consciousness in an East Harlem School," Adrian Bennett and Michèle Solá report on their ethnographic study of three junior high school classrooms in East Harlem. The authors examine both the oral and written discourse produced by Black and Puerto Rican students, and discuss how the students use language to state who they are in relationship to the school. At times, the student discourse was observed to be at odds with the expectations of the school, yet this was not always the case. The students' "struggle for voice," the authors argue, is representative of the greater struggle of a disenfranchised minority. Thus the dynamics involved in the struggle of these particular students to express their own lived experiences, rather than merely creating the discourse expected by the school, reflects the larger quest among the lower classes to achieve autonomy. The authors conclude by questioning who should define the "basic skills" of literacy, thus once again problematizing the nature of literacy.

Finally, Perry Gilmore argues in "'Gimme Room': School Resistance, Attitude, and Access to Literacy" that, although the young, Black elementary school-aged (grades 4–6) girls she studied for three years were adept at displaying extensive literacy and language-related skills outside the academic context, they were in school judged negatively. The young girls' teachers did not view them as literate because, argues Gilmore, the girls' literate practices were embedded in a cultural and social context that was perceived of as extremely negative by the teachers. In her study, Gilmore isolates two recurring events for analysis: steps and stylized sulking. Both were viewed as aspects of Black communicative behavior, and both were also viewed by the school as bad. However, Gilmore's analysis reveals that sulking and steps reflect a particular ethnic style and socio-economic class, and are not reflective, by any means, of negative character traits. In fact, the young girls who engaged in these two behaviors displayed some of the very "literacy skills" teachers sought to teach students in their classes. What Gilmore uncovers is that "social alignment with the school is usually interpreted as literacy achievement while social resistance is often understood as literacy skill deficiency."

The second section of *Rewriting Literacy* contains two chapters by James Paul Gee and one by Sarah Michaels. The two authors examine the ways in which nonmainstream students structure experience. In so doing, both provide evidence for a rational structuring of experience that differs from mainstream ways. An essayist, school-based literacy requires, among other things, that the narrator or writer order events linearly, emphasize one main point, rely primarily on syntactic devices to make the text cohere, and so forth. Both Gee and Michaels demonstrate that, despite the fact that the student texts they examined did not conform to essayist-based texts, they were nonetheless logical. This logic was embedded in different discourse strategies, strategies that conformed to the students' own discourse communities.

Gee in "The Narrativization of Experience in the Oral Style" analyzes a story told by a Black second grader during sharing time (show and tell) in school. The young girl's teacher found her story to be rambling, incoherent, and lacking in cohesion. In fact, as a result not only of this story, but of others produced by this young girl, the teacher recommended her for special education classes. The teacher made this recommendation because she felt the girl was not able to order her experiences in a logical manner. In contrast, Gee found the girl's narrative to be a "tour de force," a story rich in such techniques as "parallelism, repetition, sound play, foregrounding, showing rather than telling," techniques highly regarded in literature. The form and techniques used by the young girl are reflective of her own cultural background, and are not reflective of the forms of language expected in the school context.

Sarah Michaels, as does Gee, focuses in her chapter, "Hearing the Connections in Children's Oral and Written Language," specifically on the inability of teachers, despite good intentions, to interpret texts produced by young people from outside mainstream, middle-class culture. Michaels looks at two texts: one produced orally by a Black girl in first grade during sharing time and a written text produced by a sixth grader who displayed, though classified as white by a teacher, many of the linguistic features of Black English Vernacular as well as features of urban working-class speech. Michaels argues that the two students' attempts to construct texts were met first with confusion and then with an effort on the part of both teachers to constrain and limit the young people's texts to one narrowly defined topic. In so doing, both teachers discounted, and in fact, appeared not to understand more complex connections and issues both students were attempting to sort through. The inability of teachers to comprehend and negotiate meaning with students whose discourse structures fall outside of mainstream ways with words often leads to what Michaels refers to as a "differential treatment of the student." Such differential treatment and a subsequent lowering of expectations in turn lead to a context in which students are restricted from access to school-based literacy.

In the final chapter in this section, "Discourse Systems and Aspirin Bottles: On Literacy," Gee contributes further to his argument that, in order to understand the diverse uses that society makes of language, we need an expanded definition of literacy. Rather than defining literacy narrowly as the mere decoding and encoding of print, Gee expands on the definition of literacy presented in "What Is Literacy?" He argues that reading and writing need not play a central role in the definition of literacy at all. For Gee, a definition of literacy must include elements not only of reference and contextualization, but also of ideology. The three constitute what Gee refers to as a discourse system. Such systems, argues Gee, are "ultimately about the ways in which people situate themselves in the world." Gee grounds his argument in the comparative analysis of actual instances of language use. He first analyzes the responses by

Black and white teenagers to the classroom statement of a moral dilemma. He then makes the same analytical use of different kinds of language elicited in a job interview. Gee's argument does much to advance a theory of literacy with the explanatory power to serve more than the dominant class.

All the chapters in the third section consider the relationship between literacy and political as well as social and cultural issues. Also, overall the chapters consider issues of practice more directly than do chapters in the other three sections of the book. This section begins with a chapter entitled, "The Importance of the Act of Reading," by Paulo Freire in which he recounts his memories of learning to read, a process he contextualizes and characterizes as learning to read the world. Freire links his own experience to that of teaching adults to read and write. Although Freire uses the term "illiterate" in his discussion of adult nonreaders of print, he attributes to these same adults the ability to read their world. The process of moving from reading the world to reading the word is, to Freire, a dynamic and transformative one—transformative in that it is to stem from a critical reading of reality, a reality emerging from the student's own context, not the teacher's.

Like Freire, Donaldo Macedo, in his chapter, "The Politics of an Emancipatory Literacy in Cape Verde," argues that literacy needs to be seen as "an integral part of the way in which people produce, transform, and reproduce meaning." He focuses his discussion on the political context of choices made regarding the use of language in institutional contexts in postcolonial Cape Verde. In his chapter, Macedo summarizes four traditional models of reading: the Academic Approach, the Utilitarian Approach, the Cognitive Approach, and the Romantic Approach, and argues in turn for what he characterizes as an Emancipatory Approach to literacy. An emancipatory literacy would not tie learners to mechanical aspects of the language, but rather have as its goal for learners the ability to comprehend texts critically so that the oppressed would become "equipped with the necessary tools to reappropriate their history, culture, and language practices." Paradoxically, despite the fact that many educators in Cape Verde embraced the revolution that freed them from Portuguese colonization, they have not yet been able, argues Macedo, to free themselves from the oppressive use of Portuguese rather than Capeverdean in the educational, as well as other institutional contexts.

Linda Brodkey in her chapter "Tropics of Literacy" also embeds literacy in the political and social context. She argues that the prevalent conception linking adult illiteracy with poverty, unemployment, and crime serves to obscure other variables that have a greater impact on an individual's status and actions within society. Further, she argues forcefully that "literacy tropes invariably project a social relationship between the illiterate and literate." Many of those in a position of power, the literate, advocate adult literacy programs that are functional in nature. These programs work to create a populace geared to serving bureaucracy and to functioning efficiently in the workplace. Instead, literacy programs, argues Brodkey, should be designed with "the self-determined

objective of adult learners in mind" and with "the goals of political empowerment advocated by Freire."

Jan Nespor in "The Construction of School Knowledge: A Case Study" examines the way in which reading is taught at the community college level.
Nespor situates the concept of knowledge in the work of Pierre Bourdieu and
argues that indeed, despite assumptions on the part of schools, school knowledge is not neutral. Rather, school knowledge and its valued forms are tied to
those of the dominant classes. In his case study of a community college reading
class, Nespor uncovers a view of reading decontextualized from social context,
one in which teachers convey in word and act the notion that a text holds
meaning and the reader is to encode this static meaning. In his study, Nespor
observed that students were not encouraged to draw personal meaning from
the truncated passages they read in class, nor were they encouraged to challenge and interpret texts. On the contrary, students were led through a process
of completing decontextualized exercises in search of an elusive main idea that
corresponded to the teacher's conceptions of what this should be.

Finally, the last two chapters in this section, one by Jonathan Kozol and the
other by Pat Rigg, examine the context for teaching literacy to adult learners.
In "Benjamin's Story," Kozol considers the way in which reading and writing
are taught in the military, and Rigg, in "Petra: Learning to Read at 45," examines the case of one adult woman, a migrant worker engaged in the process of
learning to read. Kozol notes that, often for the young men and women who
enter the military, the service represents one of the few job options available.
Job-skills training and opportunities for educational advancement are two of
the promises the military offers its recruits. In a moving narrative, Kozol explicates the inherent horror underlying these promises. Kozol writes of the fragmented skill instruction with which the military seeks to make its recruits
useful. Kozol argues that such training, particularly the literacy training in the
military, serves to create functionaries of the most dangerous sort. This mechanistic approach to education is exactly what a critical pedagogy argues against.
Once again, the impact social, cultural, and economic factors have on access to
literacy is clearly presented in Pat Rigg's case study of Petra, a 45-year-old migrant worker. Petra's attempts to learn to read and write are not met with success. She, however, is not presented as a failure, for she is not. Rather, it is
society that has failed Petra. Further, it is her instructors, suggests Rigg, who
have failed by not entering, in the Freirian sense, into a dialogue with Petra as
an equally knowing subject.

The last section of *Rewriting Literacy* contains three chapters that consider
the historical construction of ideologies of literacy and the subsequent impact
these social constructions have had, and continue to have, on pedagogical practices. In "How Illiteracy Became a Problem (and Literacy Stopped Being
One)", James Donald examines the 18th- and 19th-century social and political
context in England in which the literacy practices of the working class were
reconstituted in such a way that they came to be perceived as illiterate prac-

tices. This reconstitution in ideology led to the casting of illiteracy as a problem that was to be dealt with in state-provided educational institutions. Donald argues that, during the 18th and 19th centuries, literacy practices were widespread among the emerging working class, and that this widespread ability to read and write in conjunction with access to small popular presses resulted in the rapid dissemination of politically radical materials. At the same time, in response to this movement came coercive measures instituted by conservative members of the ruling classes. These coercive measures included such things as the regulating and disciplining of language practices, and a conception of literacy that called for the ability to read instructions and biblical passages. Donald interrogates the historical processes and rationale for the establishment of national, standard linguistic forms. He connects the increasing imposition of the language practices of the middle and upper classes during this period of time to the construction of a new ideology of language and power that, in many ways, situates the working class and poor outside the boundaries of what it means to be human. Thus, we see the insinuation of one group's ways of using language and perceptions of what counts as knowledge into universalized conceptions that, in turn, take on the attributes of natural formations. What is in fact socially and historically constructed emerges in perception as natural.

In his chapter, "Hegemonic Practice: Literacy and Standard Language in Public Education," James Collins traces briefly the historical development of public education and related ideologies of literacy in England and the United States, and then links this discussion to the context of teaching literacy skills, in particular the teaching of reading, to working- and lower-class students in public schools today. He situates his discussion in the work of Michel Foucault, Antonio Gramsci, and Pierre Bourdieu in an effort to illuminate ways in which discursive practices have been shaped by dominant institutions as a means of social control. Collins argues that embedded within a "literate tradition" lie concealed biases against nonstandard discursive practices, and the subsequent teaching to the standard within public institutions today leads to the attempt on the part of educators to eradicate nonstandard features of student language. Drawing upon specific examples of classroom language, Collins illustrates how this emphasis on molding to the standard leads to a limiting of educational opportunity for nonmainstream students.

Although Collins links his historical analysis most specifically to strategies for teaching reading, John Willinsky, in his chapter, "Popular Literacy and the Roots of the New Writing," situates his historical survey, focusing as do the other two authors in this section on the 17th, 18th, and 19th centuries, in a discussion of writing practices and present-day theories of teaching writing that incorporate a process approach. In so doing, Willinsky considers both the social and political implications of a popular literacy, a literacy that has its basis in nonstandard language practices. What emerges from Willinsky's discussion is the recognition that a popular literacy works to give voice to those who may previously have been silenced, a silencing that occurs most specifically in the context of schooling.

In many ways, *Rewriting Literacy* heightens our awareness of that which we know: The world we inhabit is replete with horrific inequalities. Clearly, the young father of whom Mike Barnicle writes is a social product of this inequality. Maxine Greene (1986) deals with this very issue in the following:

> The world we inhabit is palpably deficient: There are unwarranted inequities, shattered communities, unfulfilled lives. We can not help but hunger for traces of utopian visions, of critical or dialectical engagements with social and economic realities. And yet, when we reach out, we experience a kind of blankness. . . . How are we to . . . break with the given, the taken for granted—to move towards what might be, what is not yet? (p. 440)

Greene comments not only on the inequity in society, but also on the need to break, as she writes, "with the given, the taken for granted," in order to "move towards what might be, what is not yet." *Rewriting Literacy* is meant to provide an impetus to move beyond present-day restrictive notions of the nature of literacy and, in so doing, provide, in turn, possibilities for the "what might be, what is not yet." *Rewriting Literacy* seeks to do so by challenging universal truths surrounding traditional views of literacy, and in turn offering alternatives to mainstream views of literacy, thus opening positive avenues for change. Such change would, with hope, transform present-day exclusionary ideologies of literacy into an ideology of literacies that would be truly inclusionary.

## REFERENCES

Barnicle, M. (September 25, 1990). Illiteracy: the enemy within. The Boston Globe, 15.

Bourdieu, P. (1977). The economics of linguistic exchanges. Social Science Information, (16) 6, 45–68.

Gee, J. P. (1985). "The Narrativization of Experience in the Oral Style," *Journal of Education*, (167) 1:9–35.

Gee, J. P. (1989). "Discourses, socio-culturally situated educational theory, and the failure problem," ms. University of Southern California.

Giroux, H. A. (1988). "Postmodernism and the Discourse of Educational Criticism," *Journal of Education*, (170) 3:5–30.

Gramsci, A. (1971). *Prison notebooks*. Trans. Quentin Hoare and Geoffrey Smith. N.Y.: International.

Greene, M. (Nov., 1986). In search of a critical pedagogy. Harvard Educational Review, (56) 4, 427–441.

Gumperz, J. (1982). *Discourse strategies*. N.Y.: Cambridge University Press.

Heath, S. B. (1983). *Ways with words: Language, life and work in communities and classrooms*. Cambridge: Cambridge University Press.

Heath, S. B. (1982). What no bedtime story means: Narrative skills at home and school. Language in Society, 11, 49–76.

Michaels, S. (1981). Sharing time: Children's narrative styles and differential access to literacy. Language in Society, 10, 423–442.

Scollon, R. & S. B. K. Scollon (1981). *Narrative, literacy and face in interethnic communication*. Norwood, N.J.: Ablex Publishing Corporation.

# ACKNOWLEDGMENTS

We would like to take this opportunity to thank the numerous individuals who have in various ways contributed to this book. The chapters included all originally appeared in the *Journal of Education*, which is located at the School of Education at Boston University. Thus we would first like to thank Joan Dee, Associate Dean of the School of Education at BU, for her generous support of the *Journal* over the years. In addition we want to thank Jim O'Brien, who has contributed a great deal more than his formal position as copy editor of the *Journal* might indicate. His insight and critical engagement with the issues raised in these chapters, as well as his considerable talents as an editor, have been invaluable.

For more than a decade the *Journal of Education* has been a leading voice in the critical study of education. This commitment is due in large part to the encouragement and support of Henry Giroux, who first became involved with the *Journal* when he joined the faculty of the School of Education at Boston University in 1978. His energy and high standards of scholarship, as well as his support of a generation of graduate students, provided leadership and direction to the editorial board and established the *Journal* as an international forum for the exploration of critical issues in education. Now the recipient of the first endowed chair in secondary education in the United States, the Waterbury Chair in Secondary Education at Pennsylvania State University, Henry Giroux continues his association with the *Journal* as a member of its consulting editorial board.

We also would like to thank James Paul Gee, who worked actively with the editorial board of the *Journal* during his tenure at the School of Education at

Boston University. Now Professor of Linguistics at the University of Southern California, Jim Gee continues his association and support of the *Journal* through his participation as a member of the consulting editorial board.

We thank as well consulting board member Donaldo Macedo from the University of Massachusetts at Boston who has provided support and encouragement to the board through the years, particularly in the area of critical literacy.

We also want to recognize the contributions of those who have served as editorial board members of the *Journal*. The success of the *Journal* over the years has rested on the commitment and involvement of this editorial board, which is composed for the most part of graduate students at Boston University.

Finally, we want to thank Sophy Craze, our editor at Bergin & Garvey, who has kindly supported this project from its inception.

—Candace Mitchell
and Kathleen Weiler

# Part I

---

## LITERACY, DISCOURSE, AND POWER

# 1

# WHAT IS LITERACY?

## James Paul Gee

It is a piece of folk wisdom that part of what linguists do is define words. In over a decade as a linguist, however, no one, until now, has asked me to define a word. So my first try: what does "literacy" mean? It won't surprise you that we have to define some other words first. So let me begin by giving a technical meaning to an old term which, unfortunately, already has a variety of other meanings. The term is "discourse." I will use the word as a count term ("a discourse," "discourses," "many discourses"), not as a mass term ("discourse," "much discourse"). By "a discourse" I will mean:

> a socially accepted association among ways of using language, of thinking, and of acting that can be used to identify oneself as a member of a socially meaningful group or "social network."

Think of a discourse as an "identity kit" which comes complete with the appropriate costume and instructions on how to act and talk so as to take on a particular role that others will recognize. Let me give an example: Being "trained" as a linguist meant that I learned to speak, think, and act like a linguist, and to recognize others when they do so. Now actually matters are not that simple: the larger discourse of linguistics contains many subdiscourses, different socially accepted ways of being a linguist. But the master discourse is not just the sum of its parts, it is something also over and above them. Every act

This chapter was prepared for the Mailman Foundation Conference on Families and Literacy, Harvard Graduate School of Education, March 6–7, 1987.

of speaking, writing, and behaving a linguist does as a linguist is meaningful only against the background of the whole social institution of linguistics. And that institution is made up of concrete things like people, books, and buildings; abstract things like bodies of knowledge, values, norms, and beliefs; mixtures of concrete and abstract things like universities, journals, and publishers; as well as a shared history and shared stories. Some other examples of discourses: being an American or a Russian, being a man or a woman, being a member of a certain socio-economic class, being a factory worker or a boardroom executive, being a doctor or a hospital patient, being a teacher, an administrator, or a student, being a member of a sewing circle, a club, a street gang, a lunchtime social gathering, or a regular at a local watering hole.

There are a number of important points that one can make about discourses. None of them, for some reason, are very popular with Americans, though they seem to be commonplace in European social theory (Belsey, 1980; Eagleton, 1983; Jameson, 1981; Macdonell, 1986; Thompson, 1984):

1. Discourses are inherently "ideological." They crucially involve a set of values and viewpoints in terms of which one must speak and act, at least while being in the discourse; otherwise one doesn't count as being in it.

2. Discourses are resistant to internal criticism and self-scrutiny since uttering viewpoints that seriously undermine them defines one as being outside them. The discourse itself defines what counts as acceptable criticism. Of course, one can criticize a particular discourse from the viewpoint of another one (e.g., psychology criticizing linguistics). But what one cannot do is stand outside all discourse and criticize any one or all of them—that would be like trying to repair a jet in flight by stepping outside it.

3. Discourse-defined positions from which to speak and behave are not, however, just defined internal to a discourse, but also as standpoints taken up by the discourse in its relation to other, ultimately opposing, discourses. The discourse of managers in an industry is partly defined as a set of views, norms, and standpoints defined by their opposition to analogous points in the discourse of workers (Macdonell, 1986, pp. 1–7). The discourse we identify with being a feminist is radically changed if all male discourses disappear.

4. Any discourse concerns itself with certain objects and puts forward certain concepts, viewpoints, and values at the expense of others. In doing so it will marginalize viewpoints and values central to other discourses (Macdonell, 1986, pp. 1–7). In fact, a discourse can call for one to accept values in conflict with other discourses one is a member of, for example, the discourse used in literature departments used to marginalize popular literature and women's writings. Further, women readers of Hemingway, for instance, when acting as "acceptable readers" by the standards of the discourse of literary criticism, might find themselves complicit with values which conflict with those of various other discourses they belong to as women (Culler, 1982, pp. 43–64).

5. Finally, discourses are intimately related to the distribution of social

power and hierarchical structure in society. Control over certain discourses can lead to the acquisition of social goods (money, power, status) in a society. These discourses empower those groups who have the fewest conflicts with their other discourses when they use them. For example, many academic, legalistic, and bureaucratic discourses in our society contain a moral subdiscourse that sees "right" as what is derivable from general abstract principles. This can conflict to a degree with a discourse about morality—one that appears to be more often associated with women than men—in which "wrong" is seen as the disruption of social networks, and "right" as the repair of those networks (Gilligan, 1982). Or, to take another example, the discourse of literary criticism was a standard route to success as a professor of literature. Since it conflicted less with the other discourses of white, middle-class men than it did with those of women, men were empowered by it. Women were not, as they were often at cross-purposes when engaging in it. Let us call discourses that lead to social goods in a society "dominant discourses" and let us refer to those groups that have the fewest conflicts when using them as "dominant groups." Obviously these are both matters of degree and change to a certain extent in different contexts.

It is sometimes helpful to say that individuals do not speak and act, but that historically and socially defined discourses speak to each other through individuals. Individuals instantiate, give body to, a discourse every time they act or speak; thus they carry it (and ultimately change it) through time. Americans tend to focus on the individual, and thus often miss the fact that the individual is simply the meeting point of many, sometimes conflicting discourses that are socially and historically defined.

The crucial question is: how does one come by the discourses that he or she controls? And here it is necessary, before answering the question, to make an important distinction. It is a distinction that does not exist in nontechnical parlance but nevertheless is important to a linguist: the distinction between "acquisition" and "learning" (Krashen, 1982, 1985; Krashen & Terrell, 1983). I will distinguish these two as follows:

*Acquisition* is a process of acquiring something subconsciously by exposure to models and a process of trial and error, without a process of formal teaching. It happens in natural settings which are meaningful and functional in the sense that the acquirers know that they need to acquire something in order to function and they in fact want to so function. This is how most people come to control their first language.

*Learning* is a process that involves conscious knowledge gained through teaching, though not necessarily from someone officially designated a teacher. This teaching involves explanation and analysis, that is, breaking down the thing to be learned into its analytic parts. It inherently involves attaining, along with the matter being taught, some degree of meta-knowledge about the matter.

Much of what we come by in life, after our initial enculturation, involves a mixture of acquisition and learning. However, the balance between the two can be quite different in different cases and different at different stages in the process. For instance, I initially learned to drive a car by instruction, but thereafter acquired, rather than learned, most of what I know. Some cultures highly value acquisition and so tend simply to expose children to adults modeling some activity and eventually the child picks it up, picks it up as a gestalt rather than as a series of analytic bits (Heath, 1983; Scollon & Scollon, 1981). Other cultural groups highly value teaching and thus break down what is to be mastered into sequential steps and analytic parts and engage in explicit explanation. There is an up side and a down side to both that can be expressed as follows: "we are better at what we acquire, but we consciously know more about what we have learned." For most of us, playing a musical instrument, or dancing, or using a second language are skills we attained by some mixture of acquisition and learning. But it is a safe bet that, over the same amount of time, people are better at these activities if acquisition predominated during that time. The point can be made using second language as the example: most people aren't very good at attaining functional use of a second language through formal instruction in a classroom. That's why teaching grammar is not a very good way of getting people to control a language. However, people who have acquired a second language in a natural setting don't thereby make good linguists, and some good linguists can't speak the languages they learned in a classroom. What is said here about second languages is true, I believe, of all of what I will later refer to as "secondary discourses": acquisition is good for performance, learning is good for meta-level knowledge (cf. Scribner & Cole, 1981). Acquisition and learning are differential sources of power: acquirers usually beat learners at performance, while learners usually beat acquirers at talking about it, that is, at explication, explanation, analysis, and criticism.

Now what has this got to do with literacy? First, let me point out that it renders the common-sense understanding of literacy very problematic. Take the notion of a "reading class." I don't know if they are still prevalent, but when I was in grammar school we had a special time set aside each day for "reading class" where we would learn to read. Reading is at the very least the ability to interpret print (surely not just the ability to call out the names of letters), but an interpretation of print is just a viewpoint on a set of symbols, and viewpoints are always embedded in a discourse. Thus, while many different discourses use reading, even in opposing ways, and while there could well be classes devoted to these discourses, reading outside such a discourse or class would be truly "in a vacuum," much like our repairman above trying to repair the jet in flight by jumping out the door. Learning to read is always learning some aspect of some discourse.

One can trivialize this insight to a certain degree by trivializing the notion of interpretation (of printed words), until one gets to reading as calling out the names of letters. Analogously, one can deepen the insight by taking successively deeper views of what interpretation means. But there is also the problem that a "reading class" stresses learning and not acquisition. To the extent that reading as both decoding and interpretation is a performance, learning stresses the production of poor performers. If we wanted to stress acquisition we would have to expose children to reading, and this would always be to expose them to a discourse whose name would never be "Reading" (at least until the student went to the university and earned a degree called "Reading"). To the extent that it is important to gain meta-level language skills, reading class as a place of learning rather than of acquisition might facilitate this, but it would hardly be the most effective means. Traditional reading classes like mine encapsulated the common-sense notion of literacy as "the ability to read and write" (intransitively), a notion that is nowhere near as coherent as it at first sounds.

Now I will approach a more positive connection between a viable notion of literacy and the concepts we have dealt with above. All humans, barring serious disorder, get one form of discourse free, so to speak, and this through acquisition. This is our socio-culturally determined way of using our native language in face-to-face communication with intimates (intimates are people with whom we share a great deal of knowledge because of a great deal of contact and similar experiences). This is sometimes referred to as "the oral mode" (Gee, 1986a & b). It is the birthright of every human and comes through primary socialization within the family as this is defined within a given culture. Some small, so-called "primitive," cultures function almost like extended families (though never completely so) in that this type of discourse is usable in a very wide array of social contacts. This is due to the fact that these cultures are small enough to function as a "society of intimates" (Givon, 1979). In modern technological and urban societies which function as a "society of strangers," the oral mode is more narrowly useful. Let us refer then to this oral mode, developed in the primary process of enculturation, as the "primary discourse." It is important to realize that even among speakers of English there are socio-culturally different primary discourses. For example, lower socio-economic black children use English to make sense of their experience differently than do middle-class children; they have a different primary discourse (Gee, 1985; 1986d; Michaels, 1981, 1985). And this is not due merely to the fact that they have a different dialect of English. So-called Black Vernacular English is, on structural grounds, only trivially different from Standard English by the norms of linguists accustomed to dialect differences around the world (Labov, 1972). Rather, these children use language, behavior, values, and beliefs to give a different shape to their experience.

Beyond the primary discourse, however, are other discourses which crucially involve social institutions beyond the family (or the primary socialization group as defined by the culture), no matter how much they also involve the family. These institutions all require one to communicate with non-intimates (or to treat intimates as if they were not intimates). Let us refer to these as "secondary institutions" (such as schools, workplaces, stores, government offices, businesses, or churches). Discourses beyond the primary discourse are developed in association with and by having access to and practice with these secondary institutions. Thus, we will refer to them as "secondary discourses." These secondary discourses all build on, and extend, the uses of language we acquired as part of our primary discourse, and they are more or less compatible with the primary discourses of different social groups. It is of course a great advantage when the secondary discourse is compatible with your primary one. But all these secondary discourses involve uses of language, whether written or oral or both, that go beyond our primary discourse no matter what group we belong to. Let's call those uses "secondary uses of language." Telling your mother you love her is a primary use of language; telling your teacher you don't have your homework is a secondary use. It can be noted, however, that sometimes people must fall back on their primary uses of language in inappropriate circumstances when they fail to control the requisite secondary use.

Now we can get to what I believe is a useful definition of literacy:

*Literacy* is control of secondary uses of language (i.e. uses of language in secondary discourses).

Thus, there are as many applications of the word "literacy" as there are secondary discourses, which is many. We can define various types of literacy as follows:

*Dominant literacy* is control of a secondary use of language used in what I called above a "dominant discourse."

*Powerful literacy* is control of a secondary use of language used in a secondary discourse that can serve as a meta-discourse to critique the primary discourse or other secondary discourses, including dominant discourses.

What do I mean by "control" in the above definitions? I mean some degree of being able to "use," to "function" with, so "control" is a matter of degree. "Mastery" I define as "full and effortless control." In these terms I will state a principle having to do with acquisition which I believe is true:

Any discourse (primary or secondary) is for most people most of the time only mastered through acquisition, not learning. Thus, literacy is mastered through acquisition, not learning, that is, it requires exposure to models in natural, meaningful, and functional settings, and teaching is not liable to be very successful—it may even initially get in the way. Time spent on learning and not acquisition is time not well spent if the goal is mastery in performance.

There is also a principle having to do with learning that I think true:

> One cannot critique one discourse with another one (which is the only way to seriously criticize and thus change a discourse) unless one has meta-level knowledge in both discourses. And this meta-knowledge is best developed through learning, even when one has to a certain extent already acquired that discourse. Thus, powerful literacy, as defined above, almost always involves learning, and not just acquisition.

The point is that acquisition and learning are means to quite different goals, though in our culture we very often confuse these means and thus don't get what we thought and hoped we would.

Let me just briefly mention some practical connections of the above remarks. Mainstream middle-class children often look as if they are *learning* literacy (of various sorts) in school. But in fact I believe much research shows they are *acquiring* these literacies through experiences in the home both before and during school, as well as by the opportunities school gives them to practice what they are acquiring (Wells, 1985, 1986a, 1986b). The learning they are doing, provided it is tied to good teaching, is giving them not the literacies, but meta-level cognitive and linguistic skills that they can use to critique various discourses throughout their lives. However, we all know that teaching is by no means always that good—though it should be one of our goals to ensure that it is. Children from non-mainstream homes often do not get the opportunities to acquire dominant secondary discourses—including those connected with the school—in their homes, due to their parents' lack of access to these discourses. At school they cannot practice what they haven't yet got and they are exposed mostly to a process of learning and not acquisition. Therefore, little acquisition goes on. They often cannot use this learning-teaching to develop meta-level skills, which require some control of secondary discourses to use in the critical process. Research also shows that many school-based secondary discourses conflict with the values and viewpoints in some non-mainstream children's primary discourses and in other community-based secondary discourses (e.g., stemming from religious institutions) (Cook-Gumperz, 1986; Gumperz, 1982; Heath, 1983).

While the above remarks may all seem rather theoretical, they do in fact lead to some obvious practical suggestions for directions future research and intervention efforts ought to take. As far as I can see some of these are as follows:

1. Settings which focus on acquisition, not learning, should be stressed if the goal is to help non-mainstream children attain mastery of literacies. These are not likely to be traditional classroom settings (let alone my "reading class"), but rather natural and functional environments which may or may not happen to be inside a school.

2. We should realize that teaching and learning are connected with the development of meta-level cognitive and linguistic skills. They will work better

if we explicitly realize this and build the realization into our curricula. Further, they must be carefully ordered and integrated with acquisition if they are to have any effect other than obstruction.

3. Mainstream children are actually using much of the classroom teaching-learning not to *learn* but to *acquire,* by practicing developing skills. We should honor this practice effect directly and build on it, rather than leave it as a surreptitious and indirect byproduct of teaching-learning.

4. Learning should enable all children—mainstream and non-mainstream—to critique their primary and secondary discourses, including dominant secondary discourses. This requires exposing children to a variety of alternative primary and secondary discourses (not necessarily so that they acquire them, but so that they learn about them). It also requires realizing that this is what good teaching and learning are good at. We rarely realize that this is where we fail mainstream children just as much as non-mainstream ones.

5. We must take seriously that no matter how good our schools become, both as environments where acquisition can go on (so involving meaningful and functional settings) and where learning can go on, non-mainstream children will always have more conflicts in using and thus mastering dominant secondary discourses. After all, they conflict more seriously with these children's primary discourse and their community-based secondary discourses, and (by my definitions above) this is precisely what makes them "non-mainstream." This does not mean we should give up. It also does not mean merely that research and intervention efforts must be sensitive to these conflicts, though it certainly does mean this. It also requires, I believe, that we must stress research and intervention aimed at developing a wider and more humane understanding of mastery and its connections to gatekeeping. We must remember that conflicts, while they do very often detract from standard sorts of full mastery, can give rise to new sorts of mastery. This is commonplace in the realm of art. We must make it commonplace in society at large.

## REFERENCES

Belsey, C. (1980). *Critical Practice.* London: Methuen.

Cook-Gumperz, J., Ed. (1986). *The Social Construction of Literacy.* Cambridge: Cambridge University Press.

Culler, J. (1982). *On Deconstruction: Theory and Criticism after Structuralism.* Ithaca, N.Y.: Cornell University Press.

Eagleton, T. (1983). *Literary Theory: An Introduction.* Minneapolis: University of Minnesota Press

Gee, J. P. (1985). The narrativization of experience in the oral mode, *Journal of Education,* 167, 9–35.

Gee, J. P. (1986a). Units in the production of discourse, *Discourse Processes,* 9, 391–422.

Gee, J. P. (1986b). Orality and literacy: From the *Savage Mind* to *Ways with Words,* *TESOL Quarterly,* 20, 719–746.

Gilligan, C. (1982). *In a Different Voice*. Cambridge, Mass.: Harvard University Press.

Givon, T. (1979). *On Understanding Grammar*. New York: Academic Press.

Gumperz, J. J., Ed. (1982). *Language and Social Identity*. Cambridge: Cambridge University Press.

Heath, S. B. (1983). *Ways with Words: Language, Life, and Work in Communities and Classrooms*. Cambridge: Cambridge University Press.

Jameson, F. (1981). *The Political Unconscious: Narrative as a Socially Symbolic Act*. Ithaca, N.Y.: Cornell University Press.

Krashen, S. (1982). *Principles and Practice in Second Language Acquisition*. Hayward, Ca.: Alemany Press.

Krashen, S. (1985). *Inquiries and Insights*. Hayward, Ca.: Alemany Press.

Krashen, S. & Terrell, T. (1983). *The Natural Approach: Language Acquisition in the Classroom*. Hayward, Ca.: Alemany Press.

Labov, W. (1972). *Language in the Inner City*. Philadelphia: University of Pennsylvania Press.

Macdonell, D. (1986). *Theories of Discourse: An Introduction*. Oxford: Basil Blackwell

Michaels, S. (1981). "Sharing time": Children's narrative styles and differential access to literacy, *Language in Society*, 10, 423–442.

Michaels, S. (1985). Hearing the connections in children's oral and written discourse, *Journal of Education*, 167, 36–56.

Scollon, R. & Scollon, S.B.K. (1981). *Narrative, Literacy, and Face in Interethnic Communication*. Norwood, N.J.: Ablex.

Scribner, S. & Cole, M. (1981). *The Psychology of Literacy*. Cambridge, Mass.: Harvard University Press.

Thompson, J. B. (1984). *Studies in the Theory of Ideology*. Berkeley & Los Angeles: University of California Press.

Wells, G. (1985). "Preschool literacy-related activities and success in school," in D. R. Olson, N. Torrance, & A. Hildyard, eds. *Literacy, Language, and Learning*. Cambridge: Cambridge University Press.

Wells, G. (1986a). "The language experience five-year-old children at home and at school" in J. Cook-Gumperz, ed. *The Social Construction of Literacy*. Cambridge: Cambridge University Press.

Wells, G. (1986b). *The Meaning Makers: Children Learning Language and Using Language to Learn*. Portsmouth, N.H.: Heinemann.

# 2

# DISCOURSES OF POWER, THE DIALECTICS OF UNDERSTANDING, THE POWER OF LITERACY

Adrian T. Bennett

Until fairly recently it has generally been assumed that literacy is a good thing, that in any case it is essential to active membership in modern industrial and urban societies, and that the state has a responsibility to make all its citizens literate through mass public education. Literacy is often equated in this view with the ability to decode print and/or to encode speech into written symbols. Although it is sometimes noted that these abilities can imply certain specialized modes of thinking and reasoning, not much thought is given to a critique of these modes themselves. Even less frequently considered are the constraints literacy may place on interpersonal relationships, and on cultural and personal identity. Formal education is supposed to provide each individual with the power to participate in society, so literacy, as a certain set of skills, is already associated in our minds with power. But what if we were to say that literacy is

The analysis of Carlos's narrative and the discussion of issues of language proficiency assessment are based on a research project funded by InterAmerica Research Associates and the National Institute of Education, NIE Grant No. 400-79-0042, A. T. Bennett and Helen B. Slaughter, Principal Investigators. Thanks go to our research assistants, Olivia Arrieta, Betty Garcia, and Otto Santa Ana-A. Many staff members of the Tucson Unified School District contributed much time and many good ideas, including Mary Kitagawa, who had the skill to elicit Carlos's narrative, and Chris Crowder, who coordinated all our efforts and stimulated my own thinking. Michèle Solá provided essential editorial and moral support in revising a much longer and more diffuse earlier draft. I also want to dedicate this chapter to the memory of my friend, the late Ellen Schulman, who worked closely with me in developing a framework for the analysis of discourse and provided a good deal of warmth and support while doing so. Thanks also to Carole Edelsky who provided detailed comments on an earlier draft.

associated with power in another way, that literacy is intricately tied up in the maintenance of vested interests in an already existing structure of power?

It is a commonplace that literacy skills are differentially distributed among classes and ethnic groups in U.S. society. But it might be suggested that both the forms and the social uses of literacy are intricately bound up with modes of thinking, reasoning, and understanding which help to mediate between vested political and economic interests on the one hand and the daily practices of persons on the other, with the ongoing result that unequal structures of power are rationalized and reproduced even by those who are disadvantaged by these very structures.

There is a growing body of research on literacy from the perspectives of anthropology, cognitive science, sociolinguistics, and the humanities that makes it difficult to view literacy any longer as an undiluted, unqualified good, or as a uniform cognitive skill which is neutral to the social, political, economic, and cultural conditions within which literacy takes its particular forms. Much of this research grounds itself in the historical analyses and speculations of such scholars as Havelock (1963, 1973), Ong (1967, 1971, 1977, 1978), and Goody and Watt (1972). They have argued that the way we view the world is somehow governed by the media through which we view it and talk and write about it, and that there is some essential connection between our habitual ways of understanding the world and the forms of discourse associated with the various media.

The argument of scholars that perception and thinking—and human experience generally—depend on the media of communication, or to put it more strongly, is "caused" by these media, are not always convincing. But when the forms of discourse involved with particular media are studied with attention to their social uses in particular societies, the mediation of language and thought through forms of communication appears less tenuous. Havelock's (1963) attempt to examine the relationship between the development of Greek thought and the development of writing in the context of a changing Greek society in the fifth and fourth centuries B.C. is particularly pertinent to the discussion I shall attempt here of certain aspects of the politics of understanding, literacy, and education in the United States today.

Havelock argues that writing made possible the eclipse of the concrete, individualized, idiosyncratic, formulaic, and tradition-bound thinking of the pre-Socratics. It was gradually replaced by a separation of knower from known, a raising of the known to the status of an abstract, autonomous object out of the reach of ordinary, everyday experience, a corresponding emphasis on the autonomy of the individual, and the division of knowledge into discrete, independent categories arranged hierarchically in such a way as to become the unique domain of professional specialists. Socrates and Plato, according to Havelock,

> created "knowledge" as an object and as the proper content of an educational system, divided into the areas of ethics, politics, psychology, physics, and metaphys-

ics. Man's experience of his society, of himself and of his environment was now given separate organised existence in the abstract word.

Europe still lives in their shadow, using their language, accepting their dichotomies, and submitting to their discipline of the abstract as the chief vehicle of higher education, even to this day. (p. 305)

New modes of understanding were intricately woven into a developing fabric of new forms of discourse made possible by writing. These new modes of discourse did not simply imply new cognitive styles, nor were they confined to the written text; in fact, they altered human relations in fundamental ways. For example, the dependence of the individual's thought on tradition and on an ongoing oral dialogue with others was broken, and a new form of impersonal, expository discourse emerged which eschewed metaphoric language, literary allusion, Homeric epithets, and the dramatization of speech through direct quotes. In Havelock's words, a new "syntax suitable to abstract statement," a new way of using language to make abstract systems of thought possible, was coming into being.

In *The Republic*, Havelock argues, Plato was less interested in working out a political theory than in setting up a new model of educational training in ethics and political morality. The vehicle of truth was no longer to be poetry or drama—both of which were closely associated with oral transmission, recitation, and ritual occasion—but the pure, impersonal logic of which mathematics was the highest example.

Literacy, of course, did not begin to become widespread in Western societies until the late nineteenth and early twentieth centuries, when it was associated with the rise of mass education, industrialization, and the expansion of international commerce. During this time education in literacy shifted from using classical Greek and Roman texts as models for public oratory, to the transmission of reading and writing skills for practical use in commerce and industry (Ong 1978). It is possible to see this development as an extension of certain post-Renaissance trends. Ong (1967) suggests that Peter Ramus (1515–1572) and his followers contributed to major realignments in the European educational system which deemphasized oral traditions of rhetoric grounded in formulas, epithets, proverbs, analogy, and "open-ended" thinking. Ramus substituted the "closed system" thinking of an impersonal logic and a "method which prescribed how the logic which contained it was to be organized and consequently how all thought was to be organized."

Both Olson (1977) and Fish (1972) point out that the development of the "plain style" as the model for clear thinking in the seventeenth and eighteenth centuries carried these emphases over into philosophical and scientific writing, so that idiosyncratic, personalized, metaphoric thinking, and the baroque style that Bacon had used in his *Advancement of Learning,* or Burton in his *Anatomy of Melancholy,* were discarded. "Texts were written in a new way, namely to make the meaning completely explicit, and not open to interpretation. The attempt was to create autonomous text, text in which what was said was a fully conventionalized representation of what was meant." (Olson, 1977, p. 73)

The new epistemology, associating systematic logical progression, linear order, clarity, and certainty with the plain style of impersonal, non-metaphoric, expository prose was essentially a model of understanding. Relationships between the steps of an argument and the conclusions those steps "necessarily" led to could be made available to consciousness in the form of a sequence of explicit assertions.

Sociolinguists and anthropologists have recently made important contributions to our understanding of the textual properties of various kinds of written text. For example, Scollon and Scollon (1981), in an important study of English literacy in the context of Athabaskan culture, aptly characterize the model of truth "in" the text as "essayist literacy." In the ideal text of essayist literacy, they argue, "the important relationships to be signalled are those between sentence and sentence, not those between speakers, nor those between sentence and speaker." The reader bears a "third-person relationship to the author and this consistent maintenance of the point of view is one of the hallmarks of written text" (p. 48). Similarly, both Kay (1977) and Cook-Gumperz and Gumperz (1982) note that "autonomous codes," or "culturally neutral" styles of both spoken and written discourse were developed in certain "world languages" (i.e., the languages of European colonizers) to facilitate the increased social differentiations which are an essential part of the development of industrial societies. Despite the importance of this work, simply pointing out the correlative historical development of essayist literacy, autonomous codes, and complex social differentiations in modern industrial societies is in itself not sufficiently explanatory.

An important characteristic of the essayist model of discourse is that the discovery of truth is placed in an essentially non-negotiable context. Text rules (e.g., the canons of formal logic and general principles of "empirical" validation) provide the basis for choosing what is to be accepted, believed, and understood as true, rather than situated negotiations of intent and understanding by means of which participants jointly tie particular truths to particular contexts. It is not my purpose to examine the ideology of essayist literacy. However, the standardization of certain kinds of "literate" discourse (both oral and written), and the tieing of truth criteria to text and underlying systems of logic seem to me to have important implications. The discourse of "culturally neutral styles" is not necessarily politically neutral since standardization and the removal of truth from the personalized subject may provide the basis for strategies of domination, by allowing individuals to be treated as interchangeable recipients of the truths embedded in particular texts. That is, individuals can be held accountable to the logic of the text, since the truths communicated therein are the same truths for everyone. I am not suggesting that this is an automatic outcome of training people to be readers of essayist literary texts, or to use "culturally-neutral" styles of speech. I would suggest, however, that the socialization of children into the standards of essayist literacy is part of a more general process of the incorporation of individuals into particular positions and functions which serve to maintain current relations of production. A full critical exploration of this hypothesis would require attention to several levels of analysis, including an examination of relations of production, ownership, and consumption, as well as of the relationship between education and corporate interests. But analysis of those interests which are beyond the direct control of particular individuals is not enough to show us how these interests influence the lives of individuals. A consideration of how cultural modes mediate between individual and "external" forces is needed as well (Willis, 1978). As part of this latter investigation I will concentrate here on how forms of discourse are used to constitute forms of thinking and understanding, focusing in particular on what might be considered an alternative to the discourse of essayist literacy.

## THE DIALECTICS OF UNDERSTANDING

What possibilities of understanding are available to us, and how do the acquisition and uses of particular forms of literacy affect these possibilities? The view of understanding we take will no doubt affect our answers to these questions. I want to consider here some of the views set forth in recent phenomenological and hermeneutic studies to see what they can contribute to an approach to such questions. The views I have in mind characterize understanding as a dialectical play between self and other, past and present, structure and process, expectation and contingency, event and meaning, text and self. I will explicate this dialectic briefly and then return to the question of literacy by attempting to apply this model of understanding to the interpretation of a short text produced by an eleven-year-old child.

I begin with what will no doubt seem to many a rather obscure text from Heidegger's *Being and Time* (1962):

> As understanding, Dasein projects its Being upon possibilities. This *Being-towards-possibilities* which understands is itself a potentiality-for-Being, and it is so because of the way these possibilities, as disclosed, exert their counter-thrust upon Dasein. (p. 188)

Dasein (literally "being-there") is Heidegger's technical term for "human being," and his concern is to show that *as* human beings, or in our capacity as *human*, we always exist in some state of possibility which is lived through time and is thereby always in flux. We always have some kind of understanding which "projects" us toward certain possibilities (some of which we grasp explicitly, some of which we are only vaguely aware of, some of which are inherent in our situation but unseen by us). There is not only a flow to the movement but direction, point, and meaning which also "belong to" the movement through time. For Heidegger, understanding is "primordial": not something we occasionally arrive at, but something always there with us as part of, or rather as equivalent to, our situation. He gives the example of the carpenter in the workshop. When he is using tools, such as a hammer, in the usual way, the carpenter "understands" the tool because he knows how to use it in a particular context, for particular purposes. His is a skilled understanding, of course, not that of one unfamiliar with such tools. The feel of the hammer in the palm of the hand, its weight and texture, the light shock of contact when pounding in a nail and the sharp sound this makes, the greater resistance encountered once the nail is fully in and the change in timbre of the accompanying sound—all these are elements of a particular understanding, or context.

In the passage cited above, Heidegger draws on one of the main themes of *Being and Time*, the reciprocal nature of whatever elements we can "see in" or "draw out of" the notion of context. The possibilities which the situated human being projects "exert their counter-thrust," either revealing new possibilities or preventing certain possibilities from appearing or being realized. If I see a hammer as a tool I may not be able to understand it as "found art" when I see it exhibited in a museum. But if my only experience of it is in the museum, I will certainly not have the understanding of it that a skilled carpenter has, even if I know what it is used for. At the same time, if I allow myself to enter into a new context—i.e., a new relationship—I may be able to realize these other possibilities and experience a new understanding. But in either case I will have to take time to get to know my way around in the new context, for it is only when I know my way around that I can say I understand that context and what I encounter in it. To understand the hammer as a carpenter does I must drive many different kinds and sizes of nails into different woods, both hard and soft. I also should learn the use of plane, saw, drill, chisel, and other tools. I should learn how to build something. I should *become* a carpenter. In that case I would no longer be the observer in the museum, but someone who is familiar with a workshop, the sounds of saw, hammer, chisel working on wood, the sights of different grains of wood, the different smells of green and seasoned lumber, the clear awareness that a particular task is complete, and so on. I would be a different person. I wonder if then I would be able to perceive a hammer displayed in an art museum in the same way as before.

This is exactly Heidegger's point. There is a reciprocal relation between our acts and the contexts we create, between those contexts and our understanding, between our understanding and our possibilities, between our possibilities and who we are, between who we are and what we might become. Gadamer (1970) and Ricoeur (1981) have, in somewhat different ways, further developed Heidegger's notion of understanding by relating it to discourse. Both argue that a dialectical understanding of a text involves more than receiving information, but rather "culminates in the self-interpretation of a subject who thenceforth understands himself differently, or simply begins to understand himself" (Ricoeur, 1981, p. 158).

## DISCOURSES OF POWER

If examined in relation to their uses, the ideal discourses of essayist literacy might well be found to have functions beyond a "neutral" means of transmitting and storing information. To discover whether this is in fact the case we need some way to consider discourse in terms of its political implications. This is much more than a matter of using linguistics to analyze the persuasive techniques of political and advertising rhetoric, even where the linguist is as astute an analyst as Bolinger (1980). I find Foucault's recent discussions of the relations of power, truth, and discourse suggestive in this connection. I take his discussion of "truth" to be roughly equivalent to the discussions of understanding in the works of Ricoeur and Gadamer discussed earlier. Foucault (1980) argues that

> Truth isn't outside power, or lacking in power: contrary to a myth whose history and functions would repay further study, truth isn't the reward of free spirits, the child of protracted solitude, nor the privilege of those who have succeeded in liberating themselves. Truth is a thing of this world: it is produced only by virtue of multiple forms of constraint. And it induces regular effects of power. Each society has its regime of truth, its "general politics" of truth: that is, the *types of discourse which it accepts and makes function as true;* the mechanisms and instances which enable one to distinguish true and false statements, the means by which each is sanctioned; the techniques and procedures accorded value in the acquisition of truth; the status of those who are charged with saying what counts as true. (p. 131; emphasis added)

It is interesting that the notion of truth Foucault rejects here in the opening sentence of this passage is quite Platonic, or as Havelock would argue, suggestive of certain literate standards. I have suggested that the discourses which we "accept and make function as true" in formal education today are typically those of the ideal texts of essayist literacy, and what I want to suggest now is that the constraints on truth, or understanding, associated with the discourses of essayist literacy may often act as strategies for sustaining particular relations of power. I do not mean this as an "attack" on literacy, but do want to suggest that wherever language is, there we will also find mechanisms (or better, strategies) of social control that make use of particular forms of discourse. Typically, these forms of discourse are defined by particular sets of constraints which both enable and limit the development of certain forms of understanding and social relationships, constituting thereby each human individual as a being with particular possibilities constrained in particular ways. As Foucault argues,

> In any society, there are manifold relations of power which permeate, characterize and constitute the social body, and these relations of power cannot themselves be established, consolidated nor implemented without the production, accumula-

tion, circulation and functioning of a discourse. There can be no possible exercise of power without a certain economy of discourses of truth which operates through and on the basis of this association. (1980, p. 93)

Clearly, those who take this line would want to examine the "discourses of truth" themselves. Foucault himself rarely does this, though his suggestions do provide a general perspective which tells us what to look for in such an examination and how to understand the results. In the next section I will attempt an interpretation of a piece of discourse with just this perspective in mind, with a special interest in the questions of literacy and understanding I have already raised. Consider this as an attempt to get at a small piece of "the politics of understanding" by way of penetrating "deeply enough into detail to discover something more than detail" (Geertz 1973, p. 313).

## NARRATIVE ON THE BORDER

The text I will concern myself with was elicited in strange circumstances, but according to plan, by a teacher from an eleven-year-old Mexican-American boy, whom I shall call Carlos (after the Mexican novelist Carlos Fuentes).

I say the circumstances were "strange" yet "according to plan," because the elicitation placed two people, an adult and a child completely unknown to each other, in a rather unusual situation where talk was somehow supposed to get done. The elicitation was part of a pilot project conducted in the spring and summer of 1980 by a committee of teachers, researchers, and administrators in Tucson, Arizona. This committee spent several hours in meetings developing procedures for testing the "language proficiency" of schoolchildren whose reported home language was other than English.

The process by which the committee gradually arrived at the particular format used to elicit the text I will present below is a long and interesting story. It included a good deal of argument, discussion, pilot testing, and plain old trial and error, and in my view it revealed a lot about the ideologies which constrain educators from doing what their instincts and experience tell them ought to be done. Nevertheless, it was finally agreed to elicit samples of talk from individual children, to record these samples, and then to develop ways of assessing them. While tapes are laborious, they are an excellent means of documentation, and they enable more than one evaluator to review a tape when there is some doubt as to its interpretation. The elicitation session itself may seem strange to most children but even primary-grade children are used to being pulled out of class by a strange adult and asked to do strange things—particularly children in federally funded instructional programs.

The text Carlos produced was elicited by a teacher who was part of our committee. The elicitation itself was part of the pilot project; in this case it included tasks, such as playing and then describing a board game, that were later done away with. After this task, Carlos was asked—or asked himself—to "read" a story based on a wordless picture book, *Frog Goes to Dinner,* by Mercer Mayer (1974). He produced the "reading" which is given in its entirety below.

The strangeness of the situation did not seem to bother Carlos. His performance of the narrative went some ways toward domesticating the situation, making it into something familiar both to himself and to the adult stranger. The two were sitting on different sides of the corner of a table, and when Carlos took up the book, he held it up so both he and the adult could see it, as if he were reading to her, not merely performing a task *for* her. Carlos thus set up a situation in which he played the role of Reader and invited the adult to take on the role of child or peer Listener. That is, he set up the possibility of a relationship between equals by treating the situation as if it in fact involved such a relationship. His prosody—that is, his use of variations in pitch stress or loudness, changes in tempo and rhythm, as well as in voice quality—helped to set up this kind of situation as well. He adopted a "reading" style right from the beginning. That is, listeners to the tape readily assume Carlos was reading from a printed format, rather than, say, telling a story spontaneously. In fact, one listener, who heard the tape without first being shown the book, could not believe the book had no words until I showed her a copy of it. I will have more to say about Carlos's use of prosody in the discussion below, because it is his use of vocal effects which makes his performance so distinctive, and which leads me to suspect that in many ways his narrative is typical of performed stories as found in nonliterate or preliterate societies. It is of interest, by the way, that the adult examiner did not treat the situation as if it were a relationship between equals, but maintained her adult status. For example, at the end of the reading she provided an evaluation, redefining the situation as a formal school setting.

I will provide two versions of the story side by side, Carlos's and mine. Numbers in parentheses at the left indicate divisions of the book as provided by pagination, each new number corresponding to a turn of the page. The book alternately displays a single scene on two facing pages, and new scenes on each facing page. These variations will not, however, affect the presentation of the texts or my analysis.

### *Frog Goes to Dinner*

| *Carlos's Version* | *My Version* |
|---|---|
| (1) Once upon a time there was a boy named Joshua. He looked at himself in the mirror. He had a dog named . . . a dog named, uh . . . Petey, a frog named . . . um . . . (What's her name?) . . . uh, a frog named frog, a turtle named . . . just . . . Gomer Pyle. | A little boy is looking in the mirror on his dresser, putting on his tie. A dog, frog, and turtle all sadly watch him. |

(2) (Okay). The boy said, "I'm going. I'm going, you stay here." The boy didn't know it and uh ... the frog jumped into the boy's pocket.

The boy pets his dog while pulling his jacket off the back of a chair. Unseen by the boy, the frog climbs into his jacket pocket. The boy waves goodbye to the dog and turtle, while Mom, Dad, and Little Sister wait outside the door. The frog waves goodbye too, still unseen by the boy.

(3) They went out to go ... to go eat at ... The doorman leave, let the man, lead the man, *led* the man. *(Oh yeah, they're having dinner. Oh yeah.)*

We see the family standing in front of a "Fancy Restaurant," and the Dad giving instructions to a Doorman as they leave the car.

(4) The man said, "What would you order?" "Hm," they all looked at the menu. Petey said, "I'll order ... a hamburger and french fries." The mom said, "I'll order a big steak." The dad said, "I'll order a big steak." The little girl said, "I'll order ... fish." The band kept on playing.

Seated at a table the family members read menus while a waiter stands by. A three-piece band (trumpet, drum, saxophone) plays nearby. The frog is flying through the air toward the saxophone.

(5) Something was the matter with this man's, uh *(What is it called?* Examiner: Saxophone.) Saxophone. He said, "Whatsa matter with this thing?" The other guy said, "What are you doing? You're messing up the band!"

The frog is disappearing into the saxophone. The saxophonist is blowing very hard and the others stop playing. The saxophonist looks up into the bell of the instrument. The drummer frowns and scratches his head, the trumpeter looks on with curiosity.

(6) He said, "A frog!" He said *(this guy)*, "Ah ha ha ha, ah ha." "Oh oh! A frog went into my drums." [Makes crashing sound.]

The frog falls on the saxophonist's face, who then falls backward into the drum, breaking it. The drummer throws an arm up in anger, the trumpeter laughs.

(7) He looked in the drum. The other man was mad. "Why you!" The other man was laughing so hard that he almost start to cry. The manager said, "Now look what you done! You messed the whole band up. *You're fff— ... (no, you're not fired).*

On the left-hand page the drummer talks angrily to the saxophonist, and the trumpeter bends over laughing. On the right-hand page the frog flies happily through the air, about to land in a salad being carried high on a tray by a waiter.

[gap in tape]

(8) The waiter said, "Madame, what would you order? Madame, here's your food." "Thank you, waiter." She took a bite of her food. She saw a frog. She got frightened.

The waiter serves the salad to an elderly lady. As she lifts a forkful of salad to her mouth, the frog pops up with a smile on his face.

(9) "I hate frogs!" And she fell, in [tape unclear]. The lady was screaming. The frog jumped into champagne. The manager said, "How is the m— ... How is the eating?"

The lady screams and falls backward, and the frog leaps away in fright. He lands in a glass of champagne held high by a man toasting his wife. In the background a waiter watches the frog's shenanigans as he helps the elderly lady up.

(10) "Waiter! I want that ... what *ever* that is, captured, and sent to the woods, or the *river*, or the SEWER! I don't care!" the man said. The frog interrupted his ... talking with the lady. He just squirted in his nose. He squirted out the champagne and hit him on the nose.

The elderly lady is complaining loudly to the manager, while the waiter watches the frog kiss the man with the champagne on the nose as he attempts to take a drink. The man's wife looks shocked.

(11) "Why you little creep, I'll get you!" "Hhh, oh! I'm sick! Take me home!"

The waiter pounces on the frog, who is waving goodbye to the distraught couple as they stagger away from the table. The husband supports the wife who appears dizzy and ill.

(12) "I got you, you little froggie you!" "Wait! Wait!" said Peter. "That's my frog! Come back with that!"

The waiter, having caught the frog, carries him dangling upside down by his hind legs towards the fire exit. The boy points open-mouthed at them.

(13) "Nope. I am going to throw him out."
"Say, what?"
"Yes, I am going to throw him out."
"No you ain't. Dad! Dad!"
"I'll get 'im."
"Thank you, Daddy. How you doing froggie?"
"Nice."

The whole family confronts the waiter. The waiter "shows them the door," i.e., throws them out. Boy and frog are happily reunited.

(14) They rode home, and the mom and dad and sister were *very* angry. The sister said, "Why you, I oughta slap you once!"

Riding home in the car, everyone is angry at boy and frog, both of whom look very dismayed.

(15) The father say, "Go to your room." "Yeah, go to your room." The dog and Gomer Pyle were very ... were very very sad.

The father sends the boy and frog to their room. Little Sister sticks her tongue out at the retreating figures. Dog and turtle peek out of the boy's room.

(16) That night they all ... the frog and Petey had so much fun laughing at what the frog had done ... what the *frog* had done. The dog and Gomer Pyle didn't even understand why they were laughing. They thought they were crazy.

Boy and frog roll on the floor, laughing. Dog and turtle watch them, somewhat dismayed and puzzled.

Examiner: Very good! You did a terrific job.

If we ask whether Carlos' version can stand by itself as autonomous text we can easily find problems with it. For one thing, he sometimes leaves out crucial, or at least salient, information. For example, he does not mention the frog waving goodbye in (2), or the frog leaping through the air in (4). These examples involve information that is salient since they concern actions which help characterize the central figure in the story. However, they are not essential to following the sequence of those events which make up, from a structural point of view, the backbone of the plot because they provide those essential relations of cause and effect which impel the action forward. The frog's disappearing into the saxophone in (5) is such an event, since it is necessary to know the frog is in the saxophone to understand succeeding events.

There are other "problems" as well. For example, Carlos is not always consistent. He names the dog "Petey," in (1), but switches to using this name for the boy in (4), although he had originally called the boy "Joshua." We are provided with no warning of this switch, although once the boy is called "Petey," that name is used for him throughout. In contrast to this, Carlos is sometimes remarkably consistent. He calls the turtle "Gomer Pyle" in (1), and again uses that name when the turtle appears much later in the story in (15). Other inconsistencies occur, however. For example, in (10) a speech is given to "the man," when it is actually spoken by the elderly lady. In (6) the drummer says, "A frog went into my drums," when it was actually the saxophonist who fell in the drums.

Certain aspects of background information which are important for understanding the meaning of the story are also left out. For example, in (9) we are told, "The frog jumped into champagne," but not that this was a glass of champagne held out by the young man. Nor are we told that a young man is there at all, let alone that he fails to see the frog jumping into the glass. Yet such information is important for understanding the events immediately following: that the man attempts to take a drink from the glass, that the frog kisses (not "hits" as Carlos tells us) the man on the nose, and that the man is naturally thereby shocked.

Carlos also seems to have some problems with syntax. In (3) he never does get the phrasing right about the Doorman's role vis-à-vis the Father. Taken by itself, the sentence "The doorman leave, let the man, lead the man, *led* the man." has not much meaning, and in connection with the storyline, perhaps less meaning. In any case, the doorman is not shown "leading" anyone anywhere, but is rather depicted standing by the car parked in front of the restaurant. Another sentence, "The man interrupted his . . . talking with the lady," while perhaps not grammatically incorrect, certainly lacks the elegance we associate with essayist prose, and might once have been taken as a sign of "linguistic interference," although that term is, I sincerely hope, going out of fashion. Another grammatical "mistake" is found in (15): "The father say . . . " Similarly, the expression given to the waiter in (4), "What would you order?," sounds less idiomatic than, say, "Would you like to order?" or "What would you like?"

We could also fault Carlos's text for a certain vagueness about the identity of the characters when they are given dialogue. For example, who says "Yeah, go to your room" in (15)? In (7) the phrase "the other man" is used twice in succession to distinguish the three band players. It works in its first use, distinguishing the drummer as "the other man" from the saxophonist. But the second time the phrase is a bit confusing, since it no longer refers to the drummer, but to the trumpeter. Of course, if one can see the picture, in which the trumpeter is bending over in laughter and the drummer is angrily addressing the saxophonist, there is no problem in identifying each speaker.

Thus we can find inaccuracy, inconsistency, misrepresentation, grammatical mistakes, incompleteness of detail, and confusion in Carlos's narrative. Judged as a text that should stand on its own it does not come off well. And this is just the way children's texts, oral and written, are often judged in the schools.

I can almost hear some readers muttering protests at such a conclusion, or at least at the implication that Carlos is not linguistically proficient. Isn't it just the point that the adult examiner to whom Carlos was telling the story—*for* whom he was "reading" it, one should say—could see the book, that he in fact made sure she could, as I indicated earlier? It is hardly fair to imply a lack of proficiency when his performance was consistent with a situation he had himself partially defined. I would in fact expect anyone who was at all sensitive to the political nature of assessing the language proficiencies of bilingual children in the schools to make such an argument. Yet, as essayist text, Carlos's version is inferior to my own. This is of course a rather insidious comparison to make, but I submit that such comparisons are implicitly made more frequently than we might care to admit in public education (for recently documented examples see Erickson & Schultz, 1981; McDermott & Gospodinoff, 1981; and Michaels, 1981). I will have more to say about this in a moment, but first want to turn my attention to certain other features of Carlos's story.

Someone familiar with the nature of children's storybooks might point out that Carlos makes use of a number of devices that he is very likely to have gotten from reading such books, or from having them read to him. He was actually chosen by his teacher as a likely subject for our pilot study because she viewed him as advanced in reading. Consider his use of devices such as the formulaic expression "Once upon a time" to begin the story, and other formulaic devices such as naming the characters at the beginning one by one, using a "round" in (4) where he has each family member order a meal by beginning with "I'll order . . ." and the use of the three-part refrain in (10): " . . . and sent to the woods, or the *river,* or the SEWER!" These devices are characteristic of children's literature. However, some of the other devices Carlos uses, while they sometimes occur in children's books, are also found in the most sophisticated fiction for adults. One such device is the placement of speaker identification *after* the quoted speech, as in (10) and (11).

Even more sophisticated, perhaps, is the device of leaving out any references to speakers at all, as in all of the dialogue in (13). Although I know of no studies that attend to this device in oral narratives, I believe it may not be common there, except of certain rather skillful oral performers, a few of whom I have had occasion to observe myself. But this device is much favored in written narrative, being especially highly developed by certain modern novelists such as Hemingway and Henry Green. In Carlos's story, the content of each bit of dialogue in (13) gives clues as to speaker identity, *if* one already knows which characters are taking part in this scene—the waiter who catches the frog, Peter, his Dad, and the frog. At the same time, the identification of certain characters, particularly the waiter, might be difficult, since we are never explicitly told he was trying to catch the frog, that he has caught it, or that he is heading toward the fire exit with it. These events occur in (11) and (12) and must be inferred from the speeches given to the waiter, speeches which are not identified as his: "Why you little creep, I'll get you!" "I got you, you little froggie, you!".

Of course to point this out leads us back to the argument that much of what Carlos does is clear enough to anyone who has the book to refer to. But to say this is to point away from the influence of literacy and literature on Carlos's telling, and to refer back to its characteristics as oral performance. It is impossible to convey in print the importance of prosody in Carlos's representations of dialogue. Every character is provided a characteristic tempo, intonation, rhythm, and voice quality. These prosodic devices sharply delineate both character and situation, providing a basis for a listener to make rather complex inferences about the role of the character in the situation, the character's attitude toward the situation and toward other characters, and the character's relationships to other characters, relationships which are hardly inferrable from the pictures themselves.

For example, in (11) the waiter is given a low-pitched, somewhat "gravelly" voice quality, while the "sick" wife is given a high-pitched, almost "whispered" voice, a voice that sounds weak. The waiter's speech in this scene is delivered in regularly spaced rhythmic beats, with equal and rather heavy stress placed on each of the syllables italicized here: *"Why you lit*tle *creep, I'll get you!"* Each of the vowels in these syllables is also elongated. The resulting effect is of someone expressing a strong determination to carry out a threat. But the wife's voice is provided with tones that rise quite high and glide back down on the words "sick" and "home," so that she is made to sound quite distraught.

Another interesting example is the sister's "Yeah, go to your room" in (15), which is spoken in exactly the same phrasing, tone, tempo, and rhythm as the father's prior, identical speech. Such effects can only be weakly conveyed in print, by such devices as "he said angrily," or "in imitation of her father, the little sister said . . ."

While prosodic devices can only be roughly indicated in writing, lexical choices and syntactic constructions can be fully replicated. And Carlos does not rely solely on prosody, but also provides characters with appropriate vo-cabulary and grammar. In most of the dialogue it would be difficult to say whether the lexico-grammatical or the prosodic is "primary" in importance, since they are in fact nicely balanced and mutually supportive. An interesting example is the wife's "I'm sick! Take me home!" in (11). First of all, note that it is given as a direct, unmitigated order. A mitigated request might, by con-trast, be phrased as, "Well, ready to go home now?" or "I'm getting tired," both of which would of course be inappropriate to the situation. In this situa-tion, *because* she is highly distraught, a direct order is most appropriate. Yet it is given in a high-pitched, "weak" tone of voice that emphasizes her feminine dependency on her husband. This dependency can also be inferred from the necessity of telling him to "take" her home. That is, some women might these days say something like, "I'm going home," rather than utter any such request.

The lexical and grammatical form of the waiters' speeches are also revealing of their characters. When they address the customers, they are very polite, as can be seen in (4), (8), and (9). It is true that sentences like "What would you order?" are not quite what a sophisticated waiter might say, yet the contrast in politeness is clear enough when compared to speeches like "Why you little creep you, I'll get you!" in (11). The same waiter who utters this last speech gets pretty dignified when he tells Peter in (13) "Yes, I am going to throw him out." In this speech he does not use contractions, as he does in the speech in (11), and he speaks in what can only be characterized here as a superior tone, with rising tones on "going" and "throw" and a falling tone on "out."

The blend of effects that can be captured in print and effects that are spe-cific to oral performance can be found in expository sections of the narrative as well. As indicated earlier, Carlos adopts from the outset a "reading style" for these passages which makes them sound as if he is actually reading from a printed book. He is perfectly consistent throughout in his use of this style for all the expository passages, so that a contrast with the dialogic passages is thereby set up. A change of voice is thereby effected, from the narrator's to the characters' voices. But the lexical and syntactic properties of the expository passages are also characteristic in that they sometimes reflect properties com-mon to children's books. I have already mentioned the use of formulas in both exposition and dialogue. Other formulas, somewhat less noticed in the re-search literature on children's books, also occur, such as the repetition of "very" in (15) ("very very sad") and the use of the phrase "so much" in (16) ("the frog and Petey had so much fun").

I have stressed the "border-like" quality of Carlos's narrative in its use of both literate and oral strategies for building up a text that, as we have already seen, depends to some extent on the listener's presence, a listener whose role is defined by the performance itself. I want to turn now to an examination of the richness of implication and meaning of Carlos's narrative by way of com-parison with my own. I am quite certain that, even if a trained actor performed my version, it would be difficult to convey the kind of variety, richness, and complexity of meaning that Carlos's version has.

Consider, for example, the sister's role in (14) and (15). Until now her role has been confined to taking part in the "round" of ordering dinner in (4). In (14) she threatens Peter, and in (15) she exactly reproduces the father's command, "Go to your room." She thereby aligns herself with him against Peter. Would it be too much to say that this little piece of "side business," as it is called in the theater, is a nice evocation of the theme of sibling rivalry? It is almost as if the sister is seizing here the chance provided by Peter's guilt—a guilt by association with the crimes of the frog—to "get her digs in." Like a glimpse through a door left accidentally open, we get a hint of the private life of the family here, a life that is apparently in many respects representative. Of course from our adult perspective the sister is perhaps merely cute, but from her own perspective this seems to be a serious game. She certainly does not *sound* in Carlos's rendition like someone who does not mean to be taken seriously.

My version of (14)–(15) is by comparison rather pale, I think, though it cannot be faulted for accuracy. The theme of sibling rivalry could still be safely inferred from that version, but nothing would justify further inferences that the sister is using particular linguistic and prosodic strategies, and that these strategies support a social strategy of aligning herself with an authority figure to score a point in the sibling rivalry wars. My version is constructed on canons of essayist literacy. Inferences that go beyond the text in this way can be questioned. In fact, to the extent that the canons of explicitness and clarity—as modelled in essayist literacy—are adhered to, it may not be possible to draw inferences from the text in the way I have drawn them from Carlos's performed text. I could, of course, get the "same" meanings across by making them explicit, thus justifying the reader in drawing certain conclusions. I could say something like, "Exactly imitating her father's tone of voice and expression, the Little Sister said . . ." I could go on to explain, "Thus did she cleverly employ a strategy of aligning herself with the father figure to score a point," and so on. But notice that in doing this I would not be doing what Carlos did. Instead of creating a text from which certain inferences *might* be drawn, I would be drawing those inferences *for* the reader. If I follow the canons of essayist literacy I *must* draw a distinct line between what can justly be concluded from the text, and what cannot.

This is quite different from the experience of meaning one can get from listening to Carlos's version. My suggestion that a theme of sibling rivalry is "evoked" in Carlos's version was couched in the form of a question because, although I think a case can be made for this assertion and the interpretations I clustered around it, I cannot point to anything in the text that justifies saying, "See, the author tells us this right here." The fact is, Carlos never tells the listener how to interpret his text. Some inferences can be more easily drawn and supported than others. We can pretty easily infer that it is the sister who says, "Yeah, go to your room," *if* we have the book in front of us (the mother cannot have said it, because she is smilingly trying to restrain the father in his anger). But whether we are supposed to think about sibling rivalry or not, whether we are supposed to notice the sister's spontaneous ability to seize an opportunity or not, Carlos does not tell us. What he *does* do is speak the sister's dialogue in such a way that it parallels exactly the father's. Are we supposed to notice this parallelism, and what would we mean by "noticing" in asking such a question? That we hear it is most likely; that we can describe what we have heard is much less likely, unless we are trained observers and linguists.

But this brings me to a most crucial aspect of Carlos's performed text as it contrasts with my own written one. It is an issue I find extremely difficult to talk about and still adhere to the canons of explicitness and precision of essayist literacy. There may be aspects of the meaning of Carlos's version that cannot be put into the form of explicit assertions. I realize that in saying this I may be leaving myself open to a charge of "mysticism" or some equally distasteful pejorative. However, I believe it is of the essence of Carlos's text that, while rich lines of inference and interpretation can be opened up by it, the boundary between inferences justified by the text and inferences which exceed the text is very vague indeed, shifting, nebulous, and undefined. Carlos never tells us in words what we are supposed to make of the world projected by his text, or to what extent we are to fill in that world with details not spoken by the text itself.

The meanings that can be drawn out of, or that hover around, Carlos's text (one finds oneself wanting to resort to metaphor here) are to some extent qualitatively different from those of the ideal essayist text, certainly qualitatively different than those derivable from my rather flat version. Or perhaps I should say, the difference lies in differences in the qualities of experience that can be evoked by each text. Like a Proppian analysis my version gives an accurate rendition of the plot structure (Propp 1968). Knowing my version you would know, and know better than you can know from Carlos's version taken by itself, what happens. But, just as Propp's analysis of Russian fairy tales gives little sense of their meaningfulness for those who told them and preserved them over many centuries, my version is without particular significance. On the other hand, Carlos's version is, I believe, capable of meanings that may go well beyond what Mercer Mayer had himself envisioned when he created his story.

The qualitative difference I am trying to elucidate here is like the difference some people claim to find between the verbal and nonverbal arts. Clearly there is some sense in which it is appropriate to say that dance, painting, music, and the like "have meaning," but just as clearly this meaning cannot be wholly translated into words. It must be "felt" or "lived" or "experienced"; it cannot be said.

When Carlos gives the sister's "Yeah, go to your room" the same prosodic contours as the father's command, we hear, and we may *feel* or *experience* significance, meaningfulness, the "filling-in of a world," without anyone— including ourselves—having first expressed in words the nature of that world.

And I would insist that, although I have focused on one small example, this quality of a filled-in world where everything that happens is permeated with significance, is found everywhere in Carlos's narrative. Without analyzing them here I will merely mention the characterization, largely through dialogue, of the chaos the band is thrown into in (5), (6), and (7); the elderly lady's severely put demand in (10); the confrontation in (13) between Peter and the waiter, his calling Dad to the rescue, and the frog's one-word response of "nice" when asked how it is doing.

• In each of these cases relatively complex paths of inference are laid out more or less entirely through strategies of implication. And the qualitative nature of the meanings, or experience of meaningfulness, that is evoked is dependent, I would add, on these strategies of implication. By withholding comment, by not providing explicit *guidelines* regarding where the inference process is to be cut off, Carlos creates a text that leaves up to the listener the decision whether to follow paths of implication which are indicated by the telling. He makes it possible to experience a created world which is replete with implication, a world whose boundaries are undetermined, a world where lines of force, as it were, extend beyond our horizons and yet confront us with the familiar. Carlos's storytelling strategies transcend the criteria of definiteness, explicitness, and precision. He is not here so much oriented to the standards of essayist literacy as to those of what Plato called, in Havelock's (1963) rendering, the "dramatic-mimetic mode" of creating a strong illusion of a "rich and unpredictable flux of experience."

Put negatively, Carlos created a text which has no signposts telling us to proceed no further in our inferences. Put more positively, his text invites us to saturate ourselves with the meanings of a projected world, a world originally designed by Mercer Mayer but transformed by Carlos. Saturation of this kind means taking time to roam around in that world, to find the meaningful by finding where it gives us "room to maneuver," to borrow a phrase from Heidegger (1962). I do not think I need belabor the point that this is what Ricoeur and Gadamer are talking about when they discuss "dialectical understanding." I think Carlos's narrative invites such understanding, and in this sense it is again "on the border": it brings us into contact with a new world, changing our old one, thereby changing us—*if* we engage in an act of appropriation. I am not of course claiming that Carlos's narrative is on the level of "great literature," but merely that it has qualities which may be antithetical to those canonized in the traditions of essayist literacy. Carlos's virtuosity is certainly in the traditions of oral storytelling. His narrative persona is almost Homeric. It appears everywhere, like a chameleon, in the guise of the presented characters, bringing with it a sparkling array of variations in mood, attitude, and perspective. This narrator is certainly a fictionalized self, but, far from being anonymous in the way the author of the modern scientific essay is supposed to be, he appears as a rather mysterious but strong presence behind all that is presented.

## THE POWER OF LITERACY

In at least some Western societies the growth of literacy seems to have been contemporaneous with a decline of oral narrative performance. Lord certainly thought this was so:

> When writing is introduced and begins to be used for the same purposes as the oral narrative song, when it is employed for telling stories and is widespread enough to find an audience capable of reading, this audience seeks its entertainment and instruction in books rather than the living songs of men, and the older art gradually disappears. (1958, p. 20)

It is arguable as to whether this is the whole story; the point was made earlier that the effects of literacy in various societies cannot be understood simply as matters of new technologies of communication. Historical, economic, and political developments must be kept in mind when attempting explanations of the effects of literacy. However, arguments like Lord's are valuable because they help us to raise questions about our own practices. For one thing, I cannot help wondering whether the schools, in their efforts to foster (enforce?) essayist literacy and its associated constraints on personal interaction, presentation of self, thinking, reasoning, and understanding, will do anything to promote Carlos's already considerable skills in oral narrative performance. His invitation to a relationship of equality between himself and his adult listener, his creation of an open-ended narrative that invites appropriation and dialectical understanding, his power to perform a narrative self that is at once impersonal and uniquely determining—all these seem to me to go against much of what is encountered in the effort to promote "universal literacy," an effort that goes unquestioned in what are otherwise highly intelligent discussions of the issues (Akinaso, 1981).

Literacy, it has been persuasively argued, promotes analytic linear thinking and can be used, as it has certainly been in Western societies, to break with traditions that impede change, or to break up traditions by subjecting them to analytic scrutiny. Through writing, at least in the powerful forms of essayist literacy promoted early on by scientific societies like the Royal Academy of London, we may have found a means to separate knower from known and thereby to free the mind for scientific inquiry. Throughout this chapter I have questioned the way in which essayist literacy has been so taken for granted in most discussions, and I want to suggest that certain forms of literacy are susceptible to association with an anonymity, an anomie, and an alienation from certain forms of dialectical understanding that we might do well to recover, if it is true that we have lost them.

Whatever forms literacy takes it will be associated with certain powers of understanding and consciousness, because wherever language is used, constraints on its use necessarily will exist also. The constraints of essayist literacy supply it with certain very powerful forms of understanding, but thereby may deprive us of others. The question ought not to be whether literacy should be spread around the globe, but rather: What do we mean by literacy? Whom does literacy serve? An examination of these questions in educational circles is much needed. It can only be carried out successfully by an act of imagination which can encompass both a consideration of the discourses of literacy in school and society, and a continually renewed questioning of the nature of our own understanding.

## REFERENCES

Akinaso, F. The consequences of literacy in pragmatic and theoretical perspectives. *Journal of Anthropology and Education*, 1981, 12, 163–200.

Bolinger, D. *Language—the loaded weapon: The use and abuse of language today.* London: Longman, 1980.

Cook-Gumperz, J., & Gumperz, J. J. From oral to written culture: The transition to literacy. In M. F. Whiteman (Ed.), *Variation in Writing.* New York: Lawrence Erlbaum, 1982.

Erickson, F., & Schultz, J. *The counselor as gatekeeper: Social interaction in interviews.* New York: Academic Press, 1981.

Fish, S. *Self-consuming artifacts.* Berkeley: University of California Press, 1972.

Foucault, M. *Power/knowledge: Selected interviews and other writings* (C. Gordon, Ed.). New York: Pantheon Books, 1980.

Gadamer, H. G. *Truth and method.* New York: The Seabury Press, 1970.          .

Geertz, C. *The interpretation of cultures.* New York: Basic Books, 1973.

Goody, J., & Watt, I. The consequences of literacy. In P. P. Giglioli (Ed.), *Language and social context.* London: Penguin Books, 1972.

Havelock, E. A. *Preface to Plato.* Cambridge, Mass.: Harvard University Press, 1963.

Havelock, E. A. *Prologue to Greek literacy.* Cincinnati: University of Oklahoma Press for the University of Cincinnati Press, 1973.

Heidegger, M. *[Being and time]* (J. Macquarrie & E. Robinson, trans.). New York: Harper and Row, 1962.

Kay, P. Language evolution and speech style. In B. Blount & M. Sanches (Eds.), *Socio-cultural dimensions of language change.* New York: Academic Press, 1977.

Lord, A. B. *The singer of tales.* Cambridge, Mass.: Harvard University Press, 1958.

Mayer, M. *Frog goes to dinner.* New York: Dial Press, 1974.

McDermott, R., & Gospodinoff, K. Social contexts for ethnic borders and school failure. In H. T. Trueba, C. Pung Guthrie, & K. Hu-Pei Au (Eds.), *Culture and the bilingual classroom.* Rowley, Mass.: Newbury House, 1981.

Michaels, S. "Sharing time": Children's narrative styles and differential access to literacy. *Language in Society,* 1981, *10,* 423–442.

Olson, D. The languages of instruction: The literate bias of schooling. In R. C. Anderson, R. Spiro, & W. E. Mantague (Eds.), *Schooling and the acquisition of knowledge.* Hillsdale, N.J.: Lawrence Erlbaum, 1977.

Ong, W. *The presence of the word.* New Haven: Yale University Press, 1967.

Ong, W. *Rhetoric, romance and technology.* Ithaca: Cornell University Press, 1971.

Ong, W. *Interfaces of the word.* Ithaca: Cornell University Press, 1977.

Ong, W. Literacy and orality in our times. *ADE Bulletin*, no. 58, September 1978.

Propp, V. *Morphology of the folktale*. Austin: University of Texas Press, 1968.

Ricoeur, P. *Hermeneutics and the human sciences*. London: Cambridge University Press, 1981.

Scollon, R., & Scollon, S. B. *Narrative, literacy and face in interethnic communication*. Norwood, N.J.: Ablex Publishing Co., 1981.

Willis, P. *Learning to labour: How working-class kids get working-class jobs*. Westmead, England: Saxon House, 1978.

# 3

# THE STRUGGLE FOR VOICE: NARRATIVE, LITERACY, AND CONSCIOUSNESS IN AN EAST HARLEM SCHOOL

Michèle Solá and Adrian T. Bennett

In her* illuminating discussion of the printed book and popular culture in 16th-century France, Natalie Zemon Davis considers "the printed book not merely as a source for ideas and images, but as a carrier of relationships." Davis shows how "social structure and values" channeled "the uses of literacy and printing" in 16th-century France, and how printing helped to establish "new relations ... among people and among hitherto isolated cultural traditions" (Davis, 1975, p. 192). Similarly, we would argue, the written texts children are taught to produce in U.S. schools today are used to carry certain kinds of social relationships and to construct certain kinds of cultural knowledge. Schools use writing instruction not only to inculcate certain skills, but to shape their students into particular kinds of social beings.

A number of studies of the writing done in schools have focused on the internal organization of information in the written texts, emphasizing the linguistic, textual and cognitive structures that, as all the "crisis in education" reports agree, every student must learn (Frawley, 1982; Michaels, 1981; Tannen, 1982). In the crisis reports themselves we often find statements to the effect that "Clear writing leads to clear thinking; clear thinking is the basis of clear writing" (Boyer, 1983, p. 90). Such statements reify both the kind of thinking and the kind of writing that schools teach, without questioning the nature of the cultural and social relationships that written texts in school are made to carry.

*Funding for this research was provided under a contract with the National Institute of Education and the National Center for Bilingual Research.

Rather than approach school writing from this point of view, we will consider how particular forms of written texts produced in classrooms are made to carry certain kinds of relationships by the participants involved in producing them. This approach will take the focus away from "skills" considered as value-neutral entities whose influence on the social and cultural reality of those who are supposed to acquire them can be considered negligible, to direct our attention to how writing instruction in school is used to establish "relations . . . among people and . . . cultural traditions." In particular, we will explore how the relationships carried by written texts produced in East Harlem junior high school classrooms by working-class Puerto Rican students can be understood as pieces of a more encompassing relationship between schooling and an ethnic minority community whose students have traditionally not been well served by the public schools.

Our interest in the social production of these written texts is stimulated in part by a number of recent studies that indicate an important role played by narratives in the verbal life of the East Harlem community in New York City. Alvarez (1983), Bennett (1984), Bennett and Pedraza (1984), and Sola (1984) have begun to show that in oral discourse, personal narratives are crucial to establishing relationships between speakers and in carrying on the daily social and cultural life of the community. These studies also suggest that the specific ways in which narratives are used to construct social relationships may reflect members' experience and history in the Puerto Rican community. The way people use narratives and the more performative features of their discourse may be related to how much contact they have maintained with Puerto Rico itself, the age at which they migrated to the mainland, and how successfully they have negotiated the limiting economic conditions that confront them (see Bonilla and Campos, 1981, for a discussion of these conditions). Literacy, interpreted in the broad sense as a collection of cultural and communicative practices associated with particular uses of both written and spoken forms among specific social groups (Cook-Gumperz & Gumperz, 1981; Heath, 1981) is clearly central to the Puerto Rican community, as it is for all those living in modern urban environments. Hence our interest in looking more closely at the relationship between literacy instruction in the school—an institution which enlists virtually all members of the community for an extended period of social participation—and the social and cultural environments within which the school is embedded.

The "crisis" facing the Puerto Rican child in the schools is rather more drastic than that described in the most publicized of the crisis reports, which complain, for example, that our high school graduates cannot produce a simple, clearly written paragraph, or read anything as "complex" as the *New York Times* (e.g., NCEE, 1983). The most dramatic statistic is the 79.2% dropout rate of Puerto Ricans in New York who begin high school (ASPIRA, 1983). Although scores on standardized tests which are administered every year in New York City to the third, sixth and eighth grades, have improved recently for the district in which the junior high school of our study is situated, they are still well below the norm for the city as a whole, and even further below those achieved in schools with predominantly middle-class populations. In our study, Bennett was present the day the eighth graders received their responses to their applications to high school. Many of them had applied to alternative high schools, which require high performance in school and, in some cases, on standardized tests. Not one was admitted. There were many looks of morose disappointment and anger on the students' faces that day, and many tears. One girl, considered by the students to be the most intelligent in the class, could be heard sobbing uncontrollably for a good part of that afternoon in the stairwell that led to the fifth-floor classrooms of the junior high grades.

The study on which our discussion will be based was conducted in the winter of 1984 by Bennett using ethnographic methods and an anthropological perspective informed by recent work in discourse analysis (Gumperz, 1982), classroom ethnography (Spindler, 1982), and language philosophy (Bakhtin, 1968, 1981; Volosinov/Bakhtin, 1973), as well as by anthropological studies of literacy in its social contexts (Goody, 1968; Heath, 1983). The junior high school program which was the focus of the study was a small, alternative program designed to serve children living in the neighborhood of the school and who had attended the same school in the primary grades. About 80% of these students were Puerto Rican, the rest black. They were all of working-class origin. The program was limited to one seventh and one eighth grade group in order to provide more individualized attention and to allow students to maintain contact with the cohesive peer groups they had formed in the earlier years. The program was not limited to "high achieving" students, as is the case with so many alternative programs in the New York City schools, but purposely included a range of academic achievers. The principal, who had instituted the program in 1978 out of an awareness of the special needs of these students, noted that he looked for students who needed to remain in close association with their friends, who could use the special attention that the program could give them (unlike the large junior high school of several hundred students most of them would otherwise have gone to), and who could themselves contribute to the development of a vibrant school program that all could take pride in. He placed a special emphasis on writing in the program, encouraging all his junior high teachers to incorporate as much writing as possible into their curricula. He had created a special class in composition as well, a rare feature in city junior high schools, seeing to it that one of his experienced teachers received the special training offered to school districts by the New York City Writing Project. Observations soon showed that all of the teachers in the three classrooms which were observed over a three-month period—composition, social studies, and language arts—were taking their mandate very seriously. Selection of these classrooms for intensive study was in fact based on the fact that considerable writing and discussion of writing were taking place in them.

## DIALOGUE AND DISSONANCE

As Todorov notes in his study of Bakhtin, culture can be thought of as consisting of "the discourses retained by collective memory . . . discourses in relation to which every uttering subject must situate himself" (1984, p. x). For Bakhtin, though, culture was not simply a set of acquired discourse patterns, communicative rules, or language games (Wittgenstein, 1953), although this is the way ethnographers of communication and sociolinguists have in fact tended to portray both culture and communication. For Bakhtin the discourses which social groups construct and reify to achieve particular ends are in constant flux and tension between the homogeneous and the heterogeneous, between that which makes people uniform and that which separates them and pulls them apart, sometimes to create new forms, sometimes to destroy:

> Such is the fleeting language of a day, of an epoch, a social group, a genre, a school and so forth. It is possible to give a concrete and detailed analysis of any utterance as a contradiction-ridden, tension-filled unity of two embattled tendencies in the life of language. (Bakhtin, 1981, p. 272)

Unlike that other post-revolutionary Russian who has so captured the attention of American students of language, L. S. Vygotsky, Bakhtin was not a specialist in child language development. However, one can infer from the many statements he made regarding individuals' consciousness that he saw growing up in any society, encountering its many different "ways with words" (Heath, 1983) in which people conduct their daily business, as less akin to learning a set of rules than to feeling one's way through a forest with tracks veering off in every direction. In this forest, all ways are equally obscure or equally clear.

> Language is not a neutral medium that passes freely and easily into the private property of the speaker's intentions; it is populated—overpopulated—with the intentions of others. Expropriating it, forcing it to submit to one's own intentions and accents, is a difficult and complicated process. (Bakhtin, 1981, p. 294)

Dialogue and community are always possible, given a certain sharing of knowledge, ways, and purposes. But conflict is also always possible, and always present, at least implicitly:

> Our ideological development is . . . an intense struggle within us for hegemony among various available verbal and ideological points of view, approaches, directions and values (Bakhtin, 1981, p. 346).

Nowhere is this rough and tumble of exchange and conflict so evident as when cultures come into contact with each other, which is why Bakhtin chose to produce one of his most ambitious works on Rabelais, who marked for him the beginning of the end of the common people's culture, or at least of its legitimate public expression (Bakhtin, 1968).

## THE PLAY OF DISCOURSES IN THE SCHOOL

Although it is something of a simplification, a convenient way to think about the discourse in the school to be discussed here is to see it as divided between two "streams" of communication, an official and an unofficial stream, an overt discourse governed by teachers and administrators and a more covert form constructed by the students. Gilmore refers to the latter as "sub rosa" discourse (1983, p. 236). In the classrooms in the East Harlem school, sub rosa discourse could take many forms and could involve nonverbal (winks, grimaces, stares, gestures, body posture, and orientation) as well as verbal channels. It could involve oral as well as written messages, very loud speech as well as whispering. It could also include students passing each other, often surreptitiously, a variety of materials that anthropologists would call "cultural artifacts": comic books, teen magazines, combs, "walkman" radios, white gloves in the style affected by Michael Jackson, hand-held computer games, and the like. These objects were sometimes confiscated by teachers, with or without comment.

Meanwhile, "above" this rich, multilayered, and shifting stream of sub rosa discourse, teachers conducted their own models of classroom interaction. In fact, it became clear during the observations that one of the attributes of a skilled teacher is the ability to deal satisfactorily with the inevitable undercurrents of sub rosa discourse while at the same time maintaining instructional discourse and personal composure.

Some ethnographers of schools, notably Willis (1977) and Everhart (1983) have characterized peer discourse in terms of resistance to the authoritative discourse of the school. This is a useful way to think of it, if only to counter the influence of the school's view that it is illegitimate. In our own research, there was clearly a continuous interplay between the two streams of official and sub rosa discourse, such that it might almost be said that they mutually defined and constrained each other. Their relationship was more subtle, more of a mixture, than either Willis's or Everhart's analysis implies.

Gilmore suggests that certain aspects of the sub rosa discourse of the student peer groups she observed not only violated certain norms, but operated on rather different principles, values, and genre expectations. They represented different ways with words, different ways of constructing meanings, and were the medium for qualitatively different kinds of social relationships. The studies of Puerto Rican adults' discourse cited above suggest the further implication that sub rosa discourse is created out of different needs than those defined by the school—and the social groups that govern schooling in this country—as legitimate. In looking at both the oral and written discourse produced in the three classrooms in our study, we asked these questions: What social conditions is the students' discourse responding to? How does the interplay of official and sub rosa discourse affect the students' acquisition of writing, literacy, information gathering, and thinking skills? How does this play of discourses define their understanding of the uses to which these skills can be put, and shape their developing awareness of who they are, or might be, in relation to community, school, and society?

## DISCOURSE IN THE COMPOSITION CLASS

"Mr. C," the composition teacher, was schooled through New York City Writing Project workshops on the "writing as a process" model and uses some of the procedures associated with this method in his teaching (Emig, 1983; Graves, 1983; Moffett, 1968). In addition, the pattern of *elicitation / student response / teacher evaluation* that Mehan (1979) and Sinclair and Coulthard (1975) have found to be a basic pattern of classroom discourse is a familiar one in his classroom. Very often, he begins a class with a review of some points covered in the previous class and follows up with a discussion of some new aspect of writing. This discussion begins with his dictating some rules which the students copy down. One day in the eighth grade he focused on rules for revision and the discussion proceeded as follows:

*Mr. C:* I'm going to dictate to you a specific list of things to look for. Copy it down. Number one: "When you have finished your draft comma allow some time comma preferably."
*Student:* (Interrupting) What?
*Mr. C:* "Preferably at least a day comma before you start revision." Ricardo read it back please?
*Ricardo:* When you have finished your draft comma allow some time preferably at least a day comma before you start revision.
*Mr. C:* Very good, Richard.

Mr. C goes on dictating and in between each rule conducts a short discussion of what the rule means, what the technical terms mean, and why these rules are helpful to the writer.

While this interaction could be thought of as belonging to the official discourse stream, and both the teacher and the student appear to be engaged in it, the description is deceivingly simple. For instance, as Mr. C reads the fourth rule, the discourse goes as follows:

*Mr. C:* Number four: "Read through again looking particularly for unity and organization."
*Student:* Can you repeat that?
*Mr. C:* Sure. "Read through again looking particularly for unity and organization." I

would venture to say that most of us after we fix the spelling, and the punctuation and change a *word* or two, leave it at that. What is organization?

*Student:* Order.

*Mr. C:* Okay—outline—what else?

*Student:* The ideas tied together.

*Mr. C:* Very good. Arcadio, you hear that?

*Arcadio:* Can he say it again?

*Mr. C:* He can but he wouldn't have to if you listened the first time.

From this and other transcripts and field notes we can see that students in Mr. C's classroom have learned how to engage in the kind of oral interactions that are generally supported in school. They show evidence of this by copying rules down when directed to do so, by requesting clarification of something they did not catch the first time through, by repeating back the rules so exactly that they include Mr. C's dictated punctuation marks, and by answering content questions. But some of the students are talking to each other in the back of the room. Mr. C singles out Arcadio in this example, and chastises him for being engaged in some kind of interaction with his peers. This does not necessarily mean that the interaction in question is unconnected to the official discourse stream, as Arcadio could just as easily have been asking a classmate for clarification as engaging in sub rosa discourse meant to subvert the official lesson. In this classroom there is a great deal of interplay between the two streams of discourse, and it is impossible to separate the streams on the basis of the form of the language. This becomes apparent in Arcadio's response to the teacher's query. Arcadio's "Can he say it again?" is not so unlike a previous question addressed to the teacher by another student, "Can you repeat that?" Yet the teacher's responses to these two questions are entirely different. In the context of Arcadio's interaction with another student, his question is treated as what Gilmore calls an "interference" with official discourse and is subsequently "thwarted, suppressed and punished."

At this point, Mr. C goes on dictating a few more rules for revision. When he has completed the list he asks a student to repeat back the whole set of seven rules, appears satisfied with the result, and suggests the following exercise:

*Mr. C:* Okay . . . I think the most likely follow-up for this is to look over your work and revise it . . . Do you have any suggestions?

Not getting any, he directs the students to go to their writing folders, pick out a piece of writing, and revise it using the rules he has just dictated. Another possibility he suggests is revising someone else's writing. Most of the students go to their folders and read either their own or someone else's composition. Some start rewriting and others do not. Ricardo, who complied so precisely with the discourse rules in the dictation earlier, gets up and walks over to three girls and plays a game over whether he will keep a pen he has borrowed from one of them, then walks over to Jack and talks for quite a long time. Mr. C finally looks up from his desk where he is working with two girls on their papers and asks, "What is the matter, Ricardo?" Ricardo says, "Nothing," and sits down. He continues to talk to the girls across the room and eventually shifts his attention to Juan, who is sitting next to him. A couple of other boys in the front are lobbing wadded pieces of paper into a wastebasket, glancing over their shoulders at Mr. C, who does not see them. Many students talk among themselves, at first quietly, but gradually louder. Half of them seem to be talking about the assignment, and half do not. Some kind of resistance to the writing assignment seems to be taking place, but it is not particularly organized and does not involve the entire class as it has on other occasions. And even Ricardo, who seems to be engaging in resistance, is minimally complying with the assignment. As the class is nearing a close Ricardo hands Juan his corrected paper and comments: "Instead of 'everyone' you should have wrote 'anyone.'" Mr. C ends the class by saying: "The paper you're correcting is your revision—put it in your folder."

This attempt to connect the oral discourse with a written assignment was quite typical of the classes conducted by Mr. C. In an interview, he stated that he sees himself, not as teaching specific writing skills, but as trying to get students to connect writing with something that interests and excites them, to make it fun somehow. He also stated that he occasionally likes to give free writing, as sometimes the students produce interesting texts. While Mr. C may have the eventual goal of making writing meaningful and interesting for students, he knew that there is considerable pressure from the district office to teach the so-called basic skills of writing and that he is chiefly responsible for seeing that the students master such skills. During the time his class was being observed, Mr. C had the students produce quite a variety of writing genres, including speeches, compositions, and plays. Each of these exercises was preceded by a discussion of rules for constructing these genres. Yet there always seemed to be some sort of tension between the official assignment and the students' rendition of it.

Perhaps the most graphic example of a conflict between official and unofficial discourse in the composition class was revealed when the seventh-grade students worked in small groups writing plays. From Mr. C's point of view, or from the point of view of the official discourse, the assignment was an exercise in producing dramatic scripts in which characters disagreed with each other and argued their opposing positions in "a convincing way." Several days of class time were devoted to this project and Mr. C continually told the students to make their characters' arguments as convincing as possible. He seemed to be looking for dialogue in which characters used formal logic to be convincing. The students showed a great deal of enthusiasm for the assignment. They devised their own dramatic subjects and wrote out the dialogue in a script format. While one or two students in each group usually ended up with the major responsibility for writing down the scripts, everyone participated actively in the discussions about what actions to portray and what the characters should say. For the students, one of the most important elements in producing the play was how the performance of it would look. They engaged in much acting out of parts, banter, laughing, mimicry, teasing, and joking in the process of the collaborative writing. The other element that seemed to be of utmost importance to the students was a focus on a conflict that has meaning for them in their own lives. The three groups produced plays which focused on teenage pregnancy, a young girl getting caught sneaking out of the house to attend a party, and an involved set of social relationships that is set up at a weekend party in a lakeside cabin.

Mr. C had each group perform its play for the class and the students took a great deal of pleasure in performing for each other. The performers exuberantly took on their roles, and the audience was totally engrossed in the plays. They showed their appreciation by laughing, pounding on the desks, and offering comments to the actors and to other members of the audience throughout the performance. While Mr. C obviously enjoyed the students' performances he was still dissatisfied with the students' attempts to resolve the central conflict of the play via a "persuasive argument." He also remarked to the researcher that he was tired of themes like teenage pregnancy that come up every year. His two concerns obscure the fact that the students demonstrated obvious skills with dramatic form, particularly in the economical use of dialogue and other dramatic devices to set the scene, portray character, and move the action along. They were also skilled in using humor and irony to manipulate their audience's reactions to the dialogue. Bennett and Sola (1984) suggest that much of the students' awareness of how to construct such plays may have their roots in television soap operas, situation comedies, and other popular dramatic forms.

This play-writing event raises the question of how students who are so involved in the writing process can produce texts so unsatisfactory to Mr. C, whose expressed objective is for students to enjoy writing. If we think of these students as using the play scripts and performances as a vehicle for establishing relationships with other students in the class, we may have part of the answer. The students' enthusiasm for and involvement in writing these plays may have stemmed from the opportunities that plays provide to establish relationships to each other through performance. Earlier studies have shown that performance is an important element of discourse in the Puerto Rican community, and in this play-writing event students tried to legitimately bring performance into the classroom. Through the performance, the selection of themes relevant to adolescent lives, and the expropriation of discourses from widely popular soap operas and situation comedies, these students were perhaps creating a community within the classroom. Mr. C did not seem to value these elements of the students' plays, and was never able to get the students to engage the skill lesson he was trying to teach them. The struggle that ensued as Mr. C attempted to make the official assignment the primary focus of the students' attention is one that occurred over and over again in this classroom.

## DISCOURSE IN THE SOCIAL STUDIES CLASS

"Ms. S," the social studies teacher, teaches both American History and Civics, which includes some discussion of current events. She is a competent, intelligent and committed teacher. Her comments in interviews on the history and status of the working-class Puerto Rican community showed much awareness and sensitivity. She seems to recognize that the community is politically and economically oppressed and wants to help students understand this. During some of the civics lessons she often tries to bring these understandings into the content of the lessons and this sometimes resulted in the sub rosa stream of discourse "taking over" the classroom interaction. One discussion where this complex process became obvious involved a lesson on neighborhood vandalism. Ms. S handed out xeroxed copies of pages from a text developed by the New York City Board of Education. The text moved from defining vandalism to a consideration of its illegality and the threat of arrest, and then to the property damage and harm that vandalism can cause. The technique was to interpolate questions and pictures, leaving room for students to fill in blank spaces with answers.

Ms. S followed the format of the text, but rephrased and repeated questions and topics for oral discussion, gradually eliciting more and more student opinion, and moving thereby away from the constraints of the test into more open discussion. Most of the students paid attention and tried to answer her questions when called on. When Ms. S. asked the following question the discussion quickly became more and more animated.

*Ms. S:* When would you break a law for your friends? What do you really owe them?

In asking this question, Ms. S is building on prior responses of students who had said they might (or might not) commit acts of vandalism if their friends urged them to, but they wouldn't tell on their friends in any case. Several students give answers to her question. Then David says,

*David:* I expect my friends to be loyal like if my friend said he'd be there, I'd expect him to be there. I might help him cheat on a test.
*Ms. S:* Okay, that's a common thing. How many of you would do that?

Several students raise their hands. When they put them down in this "hand vote" several are still holding them up, waving frantically to get Ms. S's attention. Robert, for example, like several other students, is leaning across his desk, half standing, making loud sounds with his mouth closed, moving his hand, arm, and upper body in rapid back-and-forth motions. Ms. S calls on Ellie:

*Ellie:* I don't owe them anything. Like I didn't ask my mother to bring me into this world. It depends on the situation.

At this point, the discussion gets very animated and proceeds much faster. Several students are talking at once. The teacher is trying to call on those with hands raised, and for a while she tries to summarize, and mediate between, points made by different students. For example, she says more than once, "Wait a minute, wait a minute! There's not as much difference between what Ellie is saying and the rest of you as you think," following this (when the students allow her) with an explanation and summary of points different students have offered. But more and more students shout out short responses to Ellie, who sticks to her original point (which may not be well understood by everyone, but it is an open question of how much the precise argument mattered to each of the students). Students confer with each other in loud overtones, giving each other their own viewpoints. They give the impression that they are too eager to say something to wait to be called on. Some bang hands or books on desks when someone else makes a particularly funny joke or a salient or controversial point. They sometimes mimic disgust with someone's expressed view, sometimes support it with a nod and a "right on!"

The students are clearly excited about the argument and are very eager to participate. But this is no longer a performance *for* the teacher, but a real exchange of views between the students. Ms. S finally stops attempting to intervene (it is difficult to get the floor in all the uproar), and lets the students compete freely for turns at talk, which results in a lot of simultaneous turn-taking and use of both verbal and nonverbal strategies for getting a chance to be heard by others. When the bell signals the end of the period, the students continue to argue, shout, and laugh as they file out of the room, still focused on the issue of what one owes one's friends.

The teacher's reaction to this session was revealing of her own sense of being caught between two poles of peer and school discourse. The students had been genuinely interested in the topic and had actively participated in their own ways. However, Ms. S felt that it was all right to "let them go" like that only once in a while—allow them to let off steam, but not too often. She said she used to encourage students to do this more in her first couple of years of teaching, but then she became concerned that they were not learning enough of the "skills" they would need later. It was fine to let them express themselves, but to do it all the time was, in her words, too "touchy-feely." We assume that the "skills" she referred to were those related to essayist or school literacy in the broad sense. When the researcher asked her how one can make a connection between what the students could get excited about and these "skills," she pointed to the writing assignment on the board: "What responsibilities does the President have?" She said, "I will probably get them to talk about who the President is responsible to, his immediate acquaintances, his friends, people he doesn't know, and so forth." This raises an interesting question about how Ms. S actually brings her understanding of the Puerto Rican community to bear in the classroom. On the one hand, she is sometimes open to straying from the official discourse embodied in the civics text on vandalism, and students obviously enjoy these opportunities to express their own opinions. On the other hand, Ms. S's distinction between "touchy-feely" and skills lessons raises a question about how legitimate she actually feels their opinions to be, or how she feels their opinions and experiences are related to the economic and political status of their community she explicates so well. The writing assignment she has given provides a partial answer, and points out something about the way information is organized in official discourse as well. Students are asked to draw analogies between their own and someone else's experience; they are supposed to become aware of the general nature of one person's responsibility to another, and in this way arrive at an understanding of vandalism in the abstract.

A similar process took place in the oral discussion we just described. It provides an implicit comment on Ms. S's expressed views. As she summarized students' arguments she changed their form. The Puerto Rican students usually provided a hypothetical narrative to support their points, and made these more and more personalized as the argument grew more and more heated. For example, they might say something like, "If a friend of mine got in a fight, and asked me to help, I would do it. But if he didn't ask me, I might not." Later, in the more heated part of the argument, they might personalize by referring directly to people they knew—such as their friends and relatives—or to people everyone in the class knew, such as specific students in the class. "If Robert got in a fight, and he asked me to help. . . ." Ms. S, on the other hand, would paraphrase the logic and generalize the point: "Okay, you believe in helping your friends when they ask you to, but you wouldn't volunteer to get in trouble with them." Although she used this pattern several times to show students that they did not disagree as much as they thought, they did not follow her example in formulating their own arguments. Two hypotheses suggest themselves here, which future research might consider. One is that the students simply did not understand the form of her paraphrases, or that she intended them as an example of how to develop an argument in a discussion. Another is that, although they may have understood what she was doing, they chose not to follow her lead because they wanted to "play out" the open debate. Their reliance on hypothetical narrative to make points, and their dramatizations of their attitudes through body movements and shouting of approval and disapproval show an interesting parallel with previously mentioned studies of adult Puerto Rican discourse. Bennett and Pedraza (1984) and Bennett and Sola (1984) suggest that using such narratives and performative forms may tell us something about the ways community members construct particular forms of consciousness through their ongoing daily communications with each other. Further, they suggest that such forms can help us understand how that consciousness, in its variability, provides members with responses to particular socio-historical conditions as they experience them. What we may be seeing here, then, are students in this East Harlem junior high school in the process of creating a sense of a Puerto Rican community within the classroom. They may be using the resources available to them in the larger community to make some statement about who they are vis-à-vis the official institution of schooling.

## DISCOURSE IN THE LANGUAGE ARTS CLASS

"Ms. L," the language arts teacher, is a black woman who grew up in East Harlem, though she does not live there at present. Her ethnicity is an important part of her background. She manages to incorporate certain aspects of black culture and communicative practices into her teaching and these are an essential ingredient in her success in eliciting oral participation of students. In particular, she shows a genuine appreciation of performance before an audience as a value in itself and as a source for achieving rapport and solidarity with students. She is an able performer herself, and encourages students to "take the floor" and perform as well. This includes having students perform pantomimes of scenes demonstrating dramatic irony; having students read about their own written work, creating situations where students have to "think on their feet," as she expresses it; and performing (not merely reading) written works of literature herself. Her style of "dialoguing" with the class also often has elements of drama built into it, as we will explain below.

Closely related to her implicit valuing of dramatic aspects of oral discourse is Ms. L's use of personal narrative. She consistently attempts to get students to see the relevance of assigned reading to their own lives by eliciting narratives of personal experience from them in both oral and written forms. Most importantly, she reciprocates by providing personal narratives of her own, making them relevant to readings and topics current in the class.

Although during the three-month period in which this study took place, Ms. L exposed the seventh- and eighth-grade students to classical myths, fables, short stories, and poems, our discussion will focus on the material presented in February, which had been designated Black History Month. Ms. L took the opportunity to augment the regular texts with selections of literature written by Langston Hughes, Richard Wright, Nikki Giovanni, and Gwendolyn Brooks, among others. She clearly enjoyed making dramatic presentations of these works, yet did not confine herself to oral presentation and discussion of them. Through various skillful means she converted them into writing exercises of various kinds. We have chosen to present an example of the oral and written discourse that took place around a chapter of Langston Hughes's autobiography, *The Big Sea* (1940), but it should be made clear that the kinds of things we are about to describe also happened when Ms. L presented authors and genres that were much more remote from these students' personal experiences. Ms. L's overall philosophy of teaching is one of making literature in all of its forms in some way relevant to the students' lives and we will try to show how she went about doing so.

*The Big Sea* is the first installment of Hughes's autobiography and provides the reader with a series of glimpses of his first three decades of life, during which he decided to make writing his profession. Many of the chapters read like closed narratives, more or less complete within themselves. This is the case with the chapter entitled "Salvation," which tells of his experience in being "saved" when he was 12. The opening paragraph sets the scene:

> I was saved from sin when I was going on thirteen. But not really saved. It happened like this. There was a big revival at my Auntie Reed's church. Every night for weeks there had been much preaching, singing, praying, and shouting, and some very hardened sinners had been brought to Christ, and the membership of the Church had grown by leaps and bounds. Then just before the revival ended, they held a special meeting for children, "to bring the young lambs to the fold." My aunt spoke of it for days ahead. That night I was escorted to the front row and placed on the mourners' bench with all the other young sinners, who had not yet been brought to Jesus. (p. 18)

From Ms. L's reading of this passage, her students may get an impression of a stronger and blacker voice speaking than most readers would. Yet, in many ways, Hughes's style is constituted by a matter-of-fact restraint and understatement. These qualities are manifest particularly in his presentation of conflict and of contradictions to which that conflict is a response. In church in "Salvation" the twelve-year-old boy is the last one still sitting on the mourners' bench. All the other children have joined the "saved" and are all standing by the altar. Even Langston's friend Westley has finally given in, saying, 'God damn! I'm tired o' sitting here. Let's get up and be saved.' So he got up and was saved." Langston presents the conflicts in his mind in this way:

> Now it was really getting late. I began to be ashamed of myself, holding everything up so long. I began to wonder what God thought about Westley, who certainly hadn't seen Jesus either, but who was sitting proudly on the platform, swinging his knickerbockered legs and grinning down at me, surrounded by deacons and old women on their knees praying. God had not struck Westley dead for taking his name in vain or for lying in the temple. So I decided that maybe to save further trouble, I'd better lie, too, and say that Jesus had come, and get up and be saved. So I got up. (p. 20)

Focus here is not on the emotional response to the conflict, nor on the pain that conflict is inflicting on Langston except the one mention of being "ashamed." Instead our attention is focused on his observations and his reasoning that finally led to resolution of the conflict, if not of the contradiction. Nor is the contradiction analyzed, or even discussed. It is only implied when later that night Langston is crying in bed. His aunt wakes up and tells his

> uncle I was crying because the Holy Ghost had come into my life, and because I had seen Jesus. But I was really crying because I couldn't bear to tell her that I had lied, that I had deceived everybody in the church, that I hadn't seen Jesus, and that now I didn't believe there was a Jesus any more, since he didn't come to help me. (p. 21)

The same church that has been an important historical force for unity, solidarity and resistance for Afro-Americans, at the very same time can act as a force dividing a family, and challenging a boy's allegiance *to* that family. This is the kind of analysis that Hughes shuns. We get the point, but we may not recognize the power of the voice that presents it.

Ms. L picks up on the black language that is embedded or sometimes only hinted at in Hughes's language. While Hughes may be read, and has certainly read his own works for recording, as "almost white," with very moderate inflections of pitch, rhythm and tempo, Ms. L turns the reading into an effective evocation of the revival meeting and thereby conveys much of the intensity of the experience that casual readers might well miss if left to their own devices. Ms. L creates an "evangelical" tone in her reading. She uses sharp contrasts of stress, pitch, tempo, vowel length, and pitch contours which are clearly modeled on black preaching styles, as described by Gumperz (1982), Kochman (1983) and others.

About a third of the way through the three-page narrative the students begin to shout out responses, as the elders that Hughes describes do. Truman, a Puerto Rican student, was a leader in this, the first to shout out an appropriate "revival-style" response: "Hallelujah!" Some students laugh, Ms. L interrupts her reading to respond, "Hallelujah!," and she then goes on with the reading. When Ms. L reads, "Then he said: 'Won't you come? Won't you come to Jesus? Young lambs, won't you come?'" Truman responds with, "Yeess, come to the Lord, Come to Jesus!" Other students are chiming in, so that by the middle of the story, when Ms. L reads the following passage, several of the students are calling out similar responses: "Langston, why don't you come? Why don't you come and be saved? Oh, Lamb of God! Why don't you come?" Ms. L reads this with great drama. The students are calling out: "Come to Jesus." "Hallelujah!" "Come and be saved!" "Why don't you come?"

After the reading there is a brief discussion about revival meetings, what they are for, when they happen and where, and Ms. L tells of her own personal experience of them. She asks them the meaning of "salvation," its denotation and connotation. After some discussion, she gives them an impromptu writing assignment. They are to write a poem on the theme of "salvation." This is an in-class assignment and they will get to read them aloud to the class. Truman is so excited he can hardly sit still in his seat. He gets up to check the door, near where his table stands, shuffles his books and papers, sends sudden grins to people, raises and waves his arms frantically, and meanwhile produces odd excited utterances. Truman's excitement becomes more irrepressible when Ms. L says they can read their poems aloud to the class. He begins to say things like "Oh boy! I wanna read mine, I wanna read mine," as he gets down to work. Less than five minutes later he is waving his hand and muttering to attract Ms. L's attention. He has two poems ready of about ten or twelve lines each.

Ms. L can hardly ignore him. Even before he finishes she promises him he can read his poem aloud first and, yes, he can come up to the front of the room. Once he gets there, Truman doesn't simply stand there and read his poem in a soft monotone. He spreads his legs wide apart to get a solid footing, he arches his body backward, thrusts his chest out, raises his chin ready to expostulate. He swings stiffly back and forth, swaggers, adjusts his thick glasses, and stares wide-eyed out over his audience, his "congregation." A grin flicks over his face repeatedly, and he sometimes glances down when he smiles in an "Aw shucks" pose. He seems very aware of and appreciative of his own performance. Ms. L always conveys a sense of her own enjoyment when she performs her readings, but Truman is almost ecstatic. He never stops moving, gyrating, swinging an arm, or even raising both arms straight out to either side, hands opened palm outward toward his "congregation" in a Martin Luther King–style "embrace." He delivers his reading in a deep, loud tone, exaggerating the evangelical preaching style. This is his first poem:

> Lord help me in this time of need
> I need your salvation quick,
> Help me Lord in the sins of the
> past. I need your salvation quick,
> Lord help Lord help me. We
> know you're all mighty but Lord
> help me in the time of need.

After reading this poem, Truman begs to be allowed to read his second promising it will be short: "See, see, Ms. L," he cried, holding out his paper it's only, let's see, um" (and he counts the lines), "only nine lines short."

Although not all of the students show Truman's excitement, many of them volunteer to read their poems aloud. Ms. L asks as many as she can, trying to give everyone a chance. This reflects her goal of creating opportunities for the students to express themselves, to be spontaneous, and to "think on their feet." Their creations show they have caught and can reproduce in their own writing certain characteristic features of black preaching styles and genres. Truman's performance of course brought out many features having to do with the use of body and vocal modulations. Many of the written poems show a sensitivity to certain characteristic images (e.g. light / dark, good / evil, sin / holiness, damnation / redemption, suffering / salvation, devil / angel). They make sharp contrasts of theme, idea, image, and setting, and use structural repetition to link themes or make contrasts. They use invocations to "the Lord" and "Jesus," and they position the poem's speaker in the role of supplicant. Consider, for example, a poem produced by Francine, a Puerto Rican girl:

Come! Come! Come oh Lord!
Come and save me.
I have lived my life as a
sinner.
I have been put through
sin and misery.
I need your salvation!
I need the light!
O Lord come save me!

Francine has produced a highly articulated structure, built on contrast, repetition, and parallelism. In her poem, the speaker invokes the "Lord," relying on repetition ("Come! Come! Come oh Lord!"), and on sharp, simple contrasts ("sin" and "misery" vs. "salvation" and "light"). The speaker is cast in the role of supplicant, confessing to sinfulness and begging for "salvation" and "light." The last line is a repetition, with variation, of the opening invocation in lines 1 and 2. This shows a certain subtlety of technique. The poem is framed by the vocative plea ("oh Lord, come save me") found in the opening and closing lines. Sandwiched in between is a middle section which divides neatly into two parts: lines 3–6 use two sentences to foreground the "my life as a sinner" theme; lines 7–8 use two sentences to foreground the speaker's "need." Each of these two parts also divides neatly into two subparts. For example, "I have lived my life as a sinner" implies someone making choices, an active agent. But "I have been put through sin and misery" implies conditions not chosen but given. Contrasts of this nature capture the sense of Langston Hughes's "Salvation" in poetic verse.

We make no claim that Francine is aware of this structure, or even that she could reproduce it at will. That she can *produce* it, however, is evident. It would be interesting to know more about how she learned these ways with words, and about how Ms. L's reading, and general presentation of literature selections, influence Francine's writing and understanding of particular genres of both writing and speaking.

## CONCLUSION

The students in these classrooms used written texts and spoken language to carry relationships in varied, complex, and subtle ways. The discourses they constructed were "channeled," though not totally determined, by the "social structure and values" of their cultural milieu. They began, as everyone must, with the discourse that surrounded them, discourses "overpopulated with the intentions of others." They sometimes managed, as we have seen, to make these discourses submit to their own intentions, and in doing so created a voice that was neither wholly of the school nor of the community, but a *bricolage* of their own creation that met particular needs in specific situations. Ricardo handled a piece of school discourse—Mr. C's dictation of rules for revision—with such facility that his performance bordered on parody. The seventh graders' plays gave them an opportunity to comment on, through performance, situations and issues of interest to them but not to the official discourse of the composition class. The eighth graders, in their dramatization of a heated debate in the social studies class, took a piece of school discourse—the "discussion"—and turned it into an opportunity to take all control of topic-comment, evaluation, questioning, and turntaking into their own hands. At the same time, their discussion was more serious and concerned than any other witnessed in that class. In the language arts class the students and teacher worked together to construct a discourse in which a communal voice became strongly resonant, accomplishing along the way some of the teacher's instructional objectives.

Thus, sometimes the students' discourse was at odds with the purposes of school discourse, sometimes peer and school discourse seemed to merge, and sometimes the students expanded a piece of school discourse beyond its usual limits to accomplish their own ends. As we have seen, the responses of the three teachers to this ebb and flow of language and intentions were rather varied. Mr. C struggled hard to bring the students around to the ways of school discourse, but encountered considerable frustration along the way. Ms. S had a good understanding of the oppressive social conditions under which the Puerto Rican community struggles, but was baffled by the discourse in her classroom that so clearly erupted out of that struggle. Ms. L, on the other hand, having considerable facility herself with some of the key features of the community discourse—narrative, performance, dramatization—was often (though not always) able to accommodate the school official discourse to the peer-community ways with words. In so doing, she legitimated the discourse of the community and the students, and elicited a quite different mode of participation than they were able to offer in the other two classes.

But we would not want to suggest that the answer to the struggles of these students (who are members of a social group rejecting schooling in impressive numbers) is simply to tolerate, or even to utilize, their own ways with words. Partial legitimation of their peer discourse is clearly possible, as in Ms. L's classroom, but that does not mean that schools could let peer discourse dominate the school environment. If they did, their structure, their policy, their purpose, their whole cultural milieu would have to be drastically changed. The solution to the dropout problem—if it is a problem—does not lie merely in training more teachers to be like Ms. L, or teaching prospective teachers more about the "cultural ways" of Puerto Ricans and blacks. Not that this would be a bad thing to do—in fact, it ought to be considered a minimum of teacher training, at least for teachers who will teach these students. But to train teachers in this way, useful as it might be, would not change the basic organizational structure of schooling in U.S. society which puts all teachers of these populations of students into positions of major conflict and contradiction.

No matter how well teachers are trained, no matter how much knowledge researchers gather about the variable cultural ways of different subgroups in our society, the fact remains that ethnic minority communities like East Harlem have historically been politically and economically marginalized. The symptoms of this marginalization are well known: high unemployment, low income, high disease rates, low educational attainments. These are the social conditions in which schools like the one discussed here are embedded. At least in practice, for most community members the schools remain major progenitors of unequal opportunity. And failure in school is used to justify rejection in the job market later on. As long as such conditions exist, schools remain in a contradictory position, covertly undermining what they overtly intend.

What is almost amazing is the ingenuity with which students like those in our study created solutions to this contradiction as they experienced it in school. They readily seized opportunities to create their own voice in response to the conditions they found themselves in. Their spontaneous ability to accomplish this testifies to the viability of their community's culture. But to the extent that the schools—and other key institutions—fail to listen to that voice, or attempt to transform that voice into something alien, "failure" is almost predetermined.

There are many ways to reject schooling, dropping out being only one. But schools cannot easily offer ethnic minority students something meaningful, because that would require those who govern the schools to acknowledge the marginality of minority communities, as well as the political and economic reasons for that marginality. The answer does not lie in formulating ever new versions of policy. Rather, we suggest that the processes of schooling need to be examined on a very specific and concrete level, as we have tried to do here, and interpreted in the light of the social, political and economic realities which form their context.

We have tried to adumbrate in our examples the pull and push of various discourses that inhabit a particular environment, the struggle for voice. What we believe we have seen is an important piece of a larger struggle between a minority community and the classes that rest on the labor of the community. This is the struggle for hegemony over the productive processes of consciousness formation—or ideology in Bakhtin's terminology. Against this backdrop, the concern with so-called basic skills becomes only one more piece of the struggle for consciousness. Questions remain: Who will define these "skills"? Who is to say what is "basic"? Whose purposes will it serve that particular "skills" be learned, not by everyone, but by a select few? Whatever policy makers decide, students like those in this study will go on constructing their own voices in response to the conditions they find in community, school and the rest of the world. If we learn to understand and acknowledge these cultural processes, we might even learn to facilitate them instead of frustrating them.

## REFERENCES

Alvarez, C. (1983, October) *Narrative performance in conversational interaction.* Paper presented in Spanish in the U.S. Conference, Hunter College, New York City.

ASPIRA. (1983). *Racial and ethnic high school dropout rates in New York City: A summary report.* New York: ASPIRA of New York.

Bakhtin, M. M. (1968). *Rabelais and his world.* H. Iswolsky, Trans. Bloomington: Indiana University Press.

Bakhtin, M. M. (1981). *The dialogic imagination.* C. Emerson & M. Holquist, Trans. Austin: University of Texas Press.

Bennett, A. T. (1984). *Literate discourse and the Puerto Rican child.* Report to the National Center for Bilingual Research.

Bennett, A. T. & Pedraza, P. (1984). *Political dimensions of discourse, consciousness and literacy in a Puerto Rican neighborhood in East Harlem.* In M. O'Barr, C. Kramara, & M. Schultz (Eds.), *Language and power: Linguistic resources against discrimination.* Beverly Hills, CA: Sage.

Bennett, A. T. & Sola, M. (1984, October). *Writing, voice and school: Literacy and consciousness in an East Harlem junior high school.* Paper presented at Fourth Annual Bilingual/ESL Conference, William Paterson College, Wayne, NJ.

Bonilla, F. & Campos, R. (1981). A wealth of poor: Puerto Ricans in the new economic order. *Daedalus,* 110(2), 133–176.

Boyer, E. L. (1983). *High school: A report on secondary education in America.* New York: Harper and Row.

Cook-Gumperz J. & Gumperz, J. (1981). From oral to written discourse: The transition to literacy. In M. F. Whiteman (Ed.), *Variation in writing.* Hillsdale, NJ: Lawrence Erlbaum.

Davis, N. Z. (1975) *Society and culture in early modern France.* Cambridge: Harvard University Press.

Emig, J. (1983) *The web of meaning: Essays on writing, teaching, learning, and thinking.* Upper Montclair, NJ: Boynton/Cook.

Everhart, R. (1983). *Reading, writing and resistance: Adolescence and labor in a junior high school.* Boston: Routledge and Kegan Paul.

Frawley, W. (Ed.) (1982). *Linguistics and literacy.* New York: Plenum.

Gilmore, P. (1983). Spelling "Mississippi": Recontextualizing a literacy-related speech event. *Anthropology and Education Quarterly, 14,* 235–255.

Goody, J. (Ed.) (1968). *Literacy in traditional societies.* Cambridge: Cambridge University Press.

Graves, D. (1983). *Writing: Teachers and children at work.* Exeter, NH: Heinemann.

Gumperz, J. (Ed.) (1982). *Language and social identity.* London: Cambridge University Press.

Heath, S. B. (1981). Toward an ethnohistory of writing in American education. In M. F. Whiteman (Ed.), *Variation in writing.* Hillsdale, NJ: Lawrence Erlbaum.

Heath, S. B. (1983). *Ways with words: Language, life and work in communities and classrooms.* London: Cambridge University Press.

Hughes, L. (1940). *The big sea*. NY: Hill and Wang.

Kochman, T. (1983). *Black and white styles in conflict*. Chicago: University of Chicago Press.

Mehan, H. (1979). *Learning lessons*. Cambridge: Harvard University Press.

Michaels, S. (1981). "Sharing time:" Children's narrative styles and differential access to literacy. *Language in Society, 10*, 423–442.

Moffett, J. (1968). *Teaching the universe of discourse*. Boston: Houghton Mifflin.

NCEE (National Commission on Excellence in Education). (1983, April). *A nation at risk: The imperative for educational reform*. Washington, DC: Government Printing Office.

Sinclair, J. & Coulthard, R. M. (1975). *Towards an analysis of discourse*. Oxford: Oxford University Press.

Sola, M. (1984, May). *Coherence, contradiction and resistance in child discourse*. Paper presented at New York Child Language Group, New York City.

Spindler, G. (Ed.). (1982). *Doing the ethnography of schooling*. New York: Holt, Rinehart and Winston.

Tannen, D. (1982). The oral / literate continuum in discourse. In D. Tannen (Ed.), *Spoken and written language*. Norwood, NJ: Ablex.

Todorov, T. (1984). *Mikhail Bakhtin: The dialogical principle*. Minneapolis: University of Minnesota Press.

Volosinov, V. N. (M. Bakhtin). (1973). *Marxism and the philosophy of language*. New York: Seminar Press.

Willis, P. (1977). *Learning to labour*. Farnborough, England: Saxon House.

Wittgenstein, L. (1953). *Philosophical investigations*. New York: Macmillan.

# 4

# "GIMME ROOM": SCHOOL RESISTANCE, ATTITUDE, AND ACCESS TO LITERACY

Perry Gilmore

This chapter is based on a three-year study which was conducted in a predominantly low-income black urban community and its elementary school (grades 4–6). A central focus in the initial phase of the research was to identify school- and community-perceived problems concerning literacy achievement. The problems seen as important by the participants and voiced within the setting then guided the direction of the subsequent investigation (for fuller discussion of this research, see Gilmore, 1982, 1985a, b).

The major concerns expressed by the administrators, faculty, parents, and students were much less focused on reading and writing skills per se than might have been expected. Instead, the community members' most frequently articulated concerns about literacy achievement were focused on *social* rather than cognitive dimensions of behavior. Thus a study begun with a direct focus on literacy skill achievement took a slight detour.

The major literacy achievement problem identified and voiced repeatedly by teachers, parents, administrators, and even the children was "attitude." A "good attitude" seemed to be the central and significant factor in students' general academic success and literacy achievement in school. Indeed, in this particular setting, talk about "attitude" was dramatically more prominent than talk about intelligence or reading and writing ability. It was clear to staff and parents as well as students, that in cases of tracking and / or selection for honors or special academic preference, "attitude" outweighed academic achievement or IQ test performance. In particular, a "good attitude" appeared to be central to inclusion in special high-track classes referred to as the Academics Plus Program.

The Academics Plus Program is described by staff as a rigorous "back to basics" curriculum in which academic achievement is the primary goal. To qualify, a student not only has to be working at a certain grade level, but also to display a "cooperative attitude." The program is in effect a tracking procedure for attitude as well as academic achievement. Teachers sometimes talk about the process as one of "weeding out bad attitudes." A student working at a relatively low grade level might be admitted to the program if his or her behavior indicated a desire to work and be cooperative. In such a case, a "good attitude" outweighs limited academic achievement. In other reported instances, a bright child who might be achieving academically, but whose behavior is characteristic of a "bad attitude," would not be admitted. In such a case, "attitude" again outweighs academic achievement.

The staff often expressed pride and identification when talking about the school and its students, especially the Academics Plus students, referring to "our kids" in a proud and affectionate tone. One teacher, attempting to illustrate the exceptional attitude and reputation of the students, asked, "Have you seen our sixth-grade Academics Plus students? They're cultured. They're not street kids. Have you seen the way they carry themselves?" The reference to the way the students "carry themselves" suggests demeanor and propriety. In this particular urban black low-income community and school, where upward mobility and success in middle-class society are expressed goals, "attitude" rather than reading ability or intelligence is the means for assigning stable stratified social ranks among students.

Less than a third of the population in each intermediate grade level (3–6) was selected for the special academic program. It was clear to the staff, the children, and the parents that although the participation in the Academics Plus Program did not guarantee literacy success and general academic achievement, it certainly maximized the chances for it. It created an elite. It stratified the students. It made mothers cry with their children when they were rejected. And the key factor for admission was something everyone called a "good attitude."

In order to unravel the meaning of "attitude" in this school community, the study focused on discrete social and linguistic behaviors. The object was to discover how attitudes were communicated, understood, and interpreted. The functions and uses of the concept as it was constructed in this particular context were considered.

Two key behavioral events were observed which provided data for the analysis of the enactment of attitude. Correspondences and contrasts in the way people *talked* about attitude and the way people actually *behaved* with regard to attitude were detailed. Both behavioral events stood out as behaviors that were readily noticed, controversial, and problematic for the teachers at school. Both key behaviors were counted as inappropriate, as representative of bad or deteriorating attitudes. Both were performances that stood out and received attention from the staff.

The first key behavioral event is a characteristic response in face-to-face clashes of will between student and teacher. These were conventional displays of emotion that appeared regularly in my field notes and were prominent and noticeable in classroom interactions. These displays of *stylized sulking* were usually nonverbal and often highly choreographed performances which seemed, in the teachers' words, to convey "rebellion," "anger," and a stance of "uncooperativeness." The displays were themselves discrete pieces of behavior which conveyed information. They were dramatic portrayals of an attitude. They were postures that told a story to the teacher and to onlooking peers. They were portraits of resistance. They were face-saving dances. And they were black: they were regularly interpreted as part of black communicative repertoire and style. Students who frequently used the displays were also students who were identified as having bad attitudes. (See Gilmore, 1984 for fuller discussion of this event.)

The second key behavioral event that will be analyzed is the performance of a distinctive genre of street rhymes which seems to have grown out of the tradition of drills and cheers. The genre is locally referred to as "steps" (or "doin' steps") and it involves chorally chanted rhymes punctuated with foot steps and hand claps which set up a background of rhythm. It is performed by groups of girls and, consistent with tradition in children's folklore (Bauman, 1982), it is full of taboo breaking and sexual innuendo in both the verbal and nonverbal modes of its performance. The dances were striking, the chants full of verbal virtuosity. They turned passersby into audiences. They were polished. But they were also "nasty," seen as representing defiance and "deteriorating attitudes." They were seen as black. They were banned from the school. (See Gilmore, 1983 for fuller discussion of this event.)

The two behavioral events, stylized sulking and doing steps, provide windows through which we can look at underlying cultural themes. Both communicative events detail concrete and specific aspects of behavior that can be analyzed as to their relation to attitude. Both events were seen as part of black communicative style and both were interpreted as conveying "bad attitudes." It was no surprise that students who were viewed as having good attitudes were also viewed as being good kids. The label became a part of the constitution and indicative of one's worth. Yet when the behaviors subsumed under the "attitude" were examined they consisted largely of a set of linguistic, paralinguistic, and kinesic communicative adornments which are associated with a particular ethnic style and socio-economic class rather than a set of character traits reflecting the nature of individuals. Both key behaviors communicated resistance to the school's carefully articulated rules for proper demeanor.

In the following two sections a brief analysis of each of the key behavioral events will be presented. Stylized sulking and doing steps will be considered in terms of the immediate shape of their performances, their functions and uses, the metaphoric nature they suggested, and the social meanings they held for the participants. The final section of this chapter will discuss the data as they relate to attitude assessment and its effects on literacy achievement.

## STYLIZED SULKING

Although recent years have witnessed a steadily growing body of ethnographic data concerning classrooms, the realm of emotions has largely been ignored. The sociolinguistic emphasis in classroom research has been primarily focused on verbal aspects of communicative (Hymes, 1962) or interactional (Mehan, et al., 1976) competence (see, for example, Cazden, John, & Hymes, 1972; Edwards & Furlong, 1978; Gilmore & Glatthorn, 1982; McDermott, 1976; Mehan, 1979). This body of ethnographic literature illustrates that beyond academic competence students need to demonstrate interactional competence in social settings in order to do well in school. These studies have primarily demonstrated that a student must not only possess academic knowledge, but must also know when and how to display it according to socially acceptable rules of classroom interaction.

Though this sociolinguistic research has certainly enriched the study of schooling and expanded our awareness of important dimensions of the interactions surrounding learning events in school, it has somehow failed to address some of the most essential aspects of classroom life. One frequently overlooked aspect is that urban classrooms are often scenes of clashes of will. Many of the most crucial social interactions in school settings are highly charged with emotion and regularly interpreted with regard to "attitude." The ways in which these confrontations are interpreted and treated by teachers and students will strongly affect the nature of the attitudes conveyed as well as any learning which takes place in classrooms.

All situations carry with them a sense of what feelings are appropriate to have. Hochschild (1979) addresses this issue when she discusses *emotion work,* which she describes as "the act of evoking or shaping as well as suppressing feeling in oneself" (p. 552). Hochschild suggests that there are *feeling rules* which are learned and used as baselines in social exchanges. Classrooms provide an excellent setting in which to capture the pedagogy involved in emotion work and the teaching and learning discourse that surrounds feeling rules. In classrooms such rules are frequently articulated.

Consider the emotion work embedded in this brief classroom interaction taken from my field notes:

> There is a loud chatting and calling out and several students are out of their seats while the teacher is trying to explain how to do the assignment. The teacher suddenly shouts in a loud and angry voice, "Sit down, sit up . . . (more softly) and don't look surprised or hurt cause we've gone over this before."

The teacher first shows anger, shouting at the class to "sit down" and "sit up" (i.e., get in your seats and sit tall at attention). When several students portray looks of "hurt" or "surprise," she tells them it is not acceptable to feel or, more accurately, to look as if they feel that way. In this particular instance the teacher may have been mediating her expression of emotion by telling the class that it wasn't a serious enough emotion to be hurt by. The teacher reminds the students that they know the rules they were breaking (e.g., calling out, walking around the room while she was talking to them as a class, side-chatting loudly). This reminder is conveyed in the phrase "we've gone over this before." Therefore she is able to justify her own angry response while instructing the class on the appropriate emotional response she expects them to *have* and—even more significant—to *show*.

Thus a three-part lesson is being learned by the students: (a) there is an appropriate set of feelings to have in a given context; (b) there are conventional ways (e.g., postures, facial expressions, and the like) that are used to express your feelings to the other participants in the setting; and (c) even if you are *not* actually feeling the appropriate feelings in a given situation, you can, and are in fact expected to, enact the conventionally accepted bodily and facial configurations that correspond with the approved emotion. *Emotional masquerading,* knowing when and how to disguise inappropriate feelings, is an essential aspect of classroom survival.

Silence and nonverbal behavior are particularly important in classroom interactions because much of student emotional communications must take place without talk. The traditional classrooms I observed support the generalization that most of the talk is by the teacher (Anderson, 1977) and that "children's time is spent overwhelmingly in listening and reading" (Cazden, 1979a). "Silent communication" was frequent between students and teachers. My classroom observation specifically focused on interactional silences, that is, the features and boundaries of silence in face-to-face interactions other than pauses for thought. (This excluded, for example, the silence which may have occurred while doing independent assigned seatwork such as reading or writing exercises.)

In Examples 4.1 and 4.2 generated from my field notes, each student replies to the teacher's question with silence. In one case the silence is acceptable, in the other it is not.

These two examples suggest that it is not merely the silence that is or is not appropriate, but the way in which the silent performance is adorned with bodily configuration and gestures. In the first example the gestural adornment was interpreted by the teacher, and by the student's peers, as both a public confession and a public apology. The teacher was allowed to remain in authority and the social structure was not disrupted. In the second example, however, the nonverbal postures and facial expressions were interpreted quite differently. This assorted package of bodily signals was seen as defiant, a public resistance and challenge to the teacher's authority. The child was sent to the principal's office a few minutes later.

**Example 4.1**
**Acceptable Silence**

| Example 1 | (Acceptable Silence) | |
|---|---|---|
| Speaker | Utterance | Gestural Adornment |
| Teacher: | What were you doing? | |
| Student No.1: | (silence) | Looks up at teacher with slightly bowed head, eyebrows turned up with slightly quizzical look, shrugs shoulders, raising arms with elbows bent and palms up |
| Teacher: | Okay. But don't do it again. | |

Ritual displays have been described as behaviors which provide a "readily readable expression of [an individual's] situation, specifically his intent" as well as "evidence of the actor's alignment in the situation" (Goffman, 1976, p. 69). It seems reasonable then to view as *silence displays* the behaviors described under the label "gestural adornments" in the examples above. These silent responses are, in fact, conventionalized acts which are choreographed predictably and perfunctorily in portraying alignments and attitudes. The reader can, no doubt, make an accurate guess as to which of the two students above would be designated as having a "bad attitude."

**Example 4.2**
**Unacceptable Silence**

| Example 2 | (Unacceptable Silence) | |
|---|---|---|
| Speaker | Utterance | Gestural Adornment |
| Teacher: | What were you doing? | |
| Student No. 2: | (silence) | Chin up, lower lip pushed forward, eyebrows in a tight scowl, downward side glance to teacher, left hand on her hip which is thrust slightly forward |
| Teacher: | Answer me. | |
| Student No. 2: | (silence) | same |
| Teacher: | I asked you a question...Answer me....I said answer me! | walks toward student |

The student communicative silences that are most visible occur in teacher-student confrontations such as those shown in examples 1 and 2 above. Usually these encounters are ones in which the student is being reprimanded, and they often take place in front of other class members. In these cases I have observed two kinds of student silence displays, which can be called *submissive subordinate* and *nonsubmissive subordinate*. The first, submissive subordinate, is only observed in interactions with the teacher or another adult authority, never with peers. This display is marked with gestures such as a bowed head, quizzical expression around the eyes, a smile, a serious but relaxed facial expression, or, if the offense is not too serious, even a giggle.

By contrast, the nonsubmissive subordinate display of silence, which I have chosen to label *stylized sulking*, carries with it a very different bodily configuration (recall Example 2).

Stylized sulking differs for boys and girls. Girls will frequently pose with their chins up, closing their eyelids for long periods and casting downward side glances, and often turning their heads markedly sidewards as well as upwards. A girl also will rest her chin on her hand with her elbow supported by the desk. Striking or getting into the pose is usually performed with an abrupt movement that will sometimes be marked with a sound, either the elbow striking the desk or a verbal marker like "humpf." Since silence displays can easily go unnoticed, it is necessary to draw some attention to the silence and with the girls it seems to be primarily with a flourish of getting into the pose.

Boys usually display somewhat differently. Their stylized sulking is usually characterized by head downward, arms crossed at the chest, legs spread wide, and usually desk pushed away. Often they will mark the silence by knocking over a chair or pushing loudly on their desk, assuring that others hear and see the performance. Another noticeable characteristic of the boys' performance is that they sit down, deeply slumped in their chairs. This is a clear violation of the constant reminder in classrooms to "sit up" and "sit up tall."

The behavioral event of stylized sulking is a characteristic response in face-to-face clashes of will between student and teacher. Students who frequently used the displays were often students who were also identified as having "bad attitudes" and as a result were tracked out of academic programs.

Stylized sulking as a school problem seems age-related. Though these displays were not performed exclusively by students in the intermediate grades (4–6) they were significantly more prominent then. Sulking was primarily performed in a silent channel and an angry key. It seems, in fact, a last holding place to express defiance. For those students who do cross the line, the predictable verbal accompaniment transforms the crime from one of "bad attitude" to one of insolence and insubordination. These latter labels usually are associated with treatments more extreme than low-track classes (e.g., suspension, psychological guidance, and the like).

Stylized sulking was usually performed to an authority figure. The individual sulker is subordinate in status to the receiver of the display. Though the display, which is often used as a face-saving device, is certainly meant to be seen by onlooking peers, the primary audience is the adult in control. Sulking generally appeared in settings where an authority figure was in control and usually in direct conflict with the performer. Classrooms, hallways, lunchrooms, and the like are predictable settings for this kind of display. Further, the behavior appeared more in classes which have not "weeded out bad attitudes." In settings where propriety had been selected for, such as Academics Plus classes, few, if any sulking events were observed (even for the few students who had been observed sulking in the heterogeneous classes the year before). Certain agreed-upon expectations of attitude and behavior in the Academics Plus classes changed the classroom context in a way that made sulking no longer adaptive. The resistant demeanor was no longer appropriate for the teacher or the peer group in the setting. Though the act of sulking itself was rarely, if ever, mentioned, and was almost never consciously a part of the assessment of a student's attitude, students who repeatedly sulked had negative characteristics attributed to them as a result. Stylized sulking was selected out—not consciously, but nonetheless quite effectively—in the process of identifying "good attitudes."

Another concern focuses on how stylized sulking was treated in this community. The behavior seemed to be seen as a "cultural" variation of expression and communication. Sulking, in the highly stylized way it was performed by many of the students, was viewed by both black and white teachers as part of a stereotypic communicative style of blacks.

In addition to expressing emotion, displays provide evidence of an actor's alignment. Sulking displays therefore must also be considered in this latter regard. In general, sulking displays can function as face-saving devices which maintain dignity through individual autonomy when confronted by an authority in control. The display indicates the actor's refusal to align him or herself with the authority figure. The stylized sulking characteristic of black communicative repertoire further seems to be interpreted as a statement of alignment with the student's own ethnicity and socio-economic class, and as a statement of resistance to the school ethos.

## STEPS

I noticed steps early in the spring of my first year of fieldwork. Girls would almost burst out of the hall at recess onto the playground, form lines and begin "doin' steps." These are chorally chanted rhymes similar to, yet distinct from, drills and cheers. The chanted talk is punctuated by a steady alternating rhythm of foot stepping and hand clapping. The steppers line up and perform in chorus as well as individually down the line. There are numerous rhymes, each with its own choreography and rhythm. Entire recess periods were spent "doin' steps," and it was often difficult for students to stop when they went back to their classrooms. Girls would chant or "step" in the room and be told to "stop" or "settle down." The "steps" were not unique to this school and in fact one could see the same performances in parks and driveways and on front steps all over the city, through the spring and summer months and until the cold weather came in the fall.

Within the community, challenges and competitions were held in which different neighborhood blocks would perform the rhymes for judging. Groups often had captains, who were in charge, and formal names, like "Stars" or "Bad Girls." In some cases groups had uniforms paid for by churches or community groups.

The staff and administration turned attention to the performance that spring also. The "dances" were labeled as "lewd," "fresh," "inappropriate for school," "disrespectful," and simply "too sexual." The principal banned the "dances" from the school in a formal announcement over the public address system one morning, saying "Nice girls don't do that." The genre was viewed as representing "deteriorating attitudes." It broke norms of propriety which were of central importance in the school ethos.

One of the stepping street rhymes, "Mississippi," seemed to be not only related to matters of propriety and attitude in general, but to literacy in particular. "Mississippi" is performed in a variety of ways, each version having its own choreography and rhythm to accompany and accent the verbal alternations. Each version has as its core the spelling of the word *Mississippi*. These variations include description of and metaphorical references to the letters and ongoing narratives which play with the letters as beginnings of utterances.

The performance of "Mississippi" is an intersection of visual and verbal codes. Steppers use the body dramatically as an iconic sign for the letters. The most prominent, noticeable, and controversial use of bodily representation of the letters is the formation of the letter *s*, or "crooked letter." The transformation of the body into the letter *s* is demonstrated in a limbo-like dancing movement with one arm forming a crook at the shoulder. It is not uncommon to find an elementary school teacher asking students to make their bodies shape a letter. Yet, in this case, although the steppers successfully perform such bodily letter representation, it was interpreted negatively. The iconic sign was viewed as being dressed with too sexual a body idiom for school, and, often family contexts.

It appears that few observers actually associated the dance movement with the words or letters. The performances were not studied but only casually observed, if observed at all, by most of the staff. The range of teacher responses to the dance movements in "Mississippi" ranged from "You have to be an adult to know it was suggestive," to "It's like an orgasm." Other examples were "It's like nothing I've ever seen before"; "It could be a nice kid, then all of the sudden it just comes over her"; "It's like an epileptic fit"; "It's bad"; and "Nasty."

## "MISSISSIPPI": A DISPLAY OF
## LITERACY-RELATED COMPETENCIES

In informal interviews and discussions, teachers regularly commented that their students lacked necessary language and literacy skills. They were concerned that students had deficiencies in *word analysis skills* such as rhyming, syllabification, and identifying initial and medial blends. They said their students lacked *comprehension skills* such as being able to identify main ideas, develop narrative themes, recognize semantic differences in homonyms, and so on. Finally, they were concerned that their students lacked the *good citizenship skills* that were necessary for school instruction in language arts and literacy—listening to or cooperating with each other, getting organized, or working in groups. Bearing these teachers' concerns in mind, let us consider the following description of one of the most popular steps. Several versions are presented below. These examples of oral group performances provide strong evidence that both the citizenship skills and the language skills identified by teachers as deficiencies for this population were demonstrated regularly in peer group contexts.

| *Oral Performance* | *Description* |
| --- | --- |
| 1. MISSISSIPPI | A straight spelling, reciting each letter in rhythmic, patterned clusters, the most concrete form of the rhyme. |
| 2. MI crooked letter, crooked letter, I, crooked letter, crooked letter I, hump back, hump back, I | A spelling that includes a description or metaphorical reference to the physical features of some of the letters. In this version, "Crooked letter" refers to S and "hump back" to P. The children sometimes refer to the entire genre of steps as "Kookelater (crooked letter) Dances." The children perform the S in a limbo-like dance movement with one arm forming a crook at the shoulder. |
| 3. M for the money<br>I if ya give it to me<br>S sock it (to me)<br>S sock it (to me)<br>I if I buy it from ya<br>S sock it<br>S sock it<br>I if I take it from ya<br>P pump it<br>P pump it<br>I | This version is often followed by version 2 with a smooth transition. The spelling uses the letters of Mississippi to produce the first word of each line in an ongoing narrative. |

4. Hey (name), yo
   You wanted on the phone.
   Who is it? Your nigger.
   I bet he wants my lips,
   my tits, my butt, my smut.
   My crooked letter, crooked
   letter, I.

A controversial narrative that is only punctuated with parts of the spelling. The play with the narrative rather than the orthography dominates the verbal content. The "crooked letter" by its position in a series of "wants" take on an ambiguous sexual meaning, especially as the letter is being adorned in dance.

5. He, Deede, yo
   Spell Mississippi
   Spell Mississippi right now
   You take my hands up high
   You take my feet down low
   I cross my legs with that gigolo
   If you don't like that
   Throw it in the thrash
   And then I'm bustin out
   With that Jordache
   Look in the sky
   With that Calvin Klein
   I'm gonna lay in the dirt
   With that Sergiert (Sergio
   Valente)
   I'm gonna bust a balloon
   With that Sassoon
   Gonna be ready
   With that Teddy
   I'm gonna be on the rail
   With that Vanderbail
   With the is-M is-I
   Crooked letter crooked letter I

This version of Mississippi was performed by fewer individuals and was viewed as an accomplished recitation by peers. The jeans theme made it a favored version of the narrative performance.

Each girl took a turn for an individual performance, stepping out of the line with an expression such as "Gimme room." Each was expected to have her own style within the conventions and boundaries of the performance, using embellishments and markers of individuality. The degree of oral composing varied, but performers who were creative were recognized for their virtuosity and often became captains, organizing and instructing the others.

While teachers and parents had heard and seen the steps performed enough to notice and ban them, most had never really listened enough to be aware of the general content. Instead, they were aware of isolated words (see, e.g., Example 4) or dance movements (e.g., the performance of the "crooked letter") that were considered too sexual or improper. Although stepping performances were public and prominent, the melodic prosody of the chants made the words and meaning almost unintelligible. Once the "sirens" lured a listener in, the taboo words could be heard with an assaulting clarity.

Stepping, like stylized sulking, seemed to be seen as a "cultural" variation of expression and communication. "Doin' steps" was something that black girls do. The musical chants and movements were referred to by several white and black teachers as "ethnic type dances," reminiscent of "African music" and "Caribbean music."

The particular community in which my observations were conducted might be characterized as being extremely responsive to the expressed norms of the school. Many parents who initially allowed the dances, once hearing that the school banned them, enforced the ban at home. One student who had been a stepping captain the year before told me the following fall that she no longer did steps because her mother wanted her to get into the Academics Plus program.

## "MISSISSIPPI" CONVEYS SOCIAL MESSAGES

The performance of "Mississippi" can be examined as an "instructional routine." In many ways the routine sounds like what one might expect in a school classroom. Directions are called to an individual to spell a word: *Mississippi*, a difficult word to spell at that. Yet there are several aspects of the instruction that seem to break with expected norms of speech and politeness and with predictable co-occurrence rules of classrooms.

First, instead of a single teacher's voice, the entire group of steppers chant the request in loud chorus. This is the reverse of the stereotypic model of an individual teacher request followed by an entire class's choral response. The request itself has marked characteristics that countered expectations of what a classroom teacher would say.

Hey, (Wendy). Spell Mississippi.
Spell Mississippi, right now!

The request sounds more like a challenge or a dare. Consider some of the linguistic markers that run counter to expectations of co-occurrence rules. The use of the word "hey" is informal, is usually considered inappropriate for school, and has a slightly threatening quality—as if one is being "called out" rather than "called on." Further, there is an impatient tone to the demand as a result of the quick repetition "Spell Mississippi" and the conclusion "right now!" It has been pointed out that teachers tend to use politeness forms frequently in order to modify the power and control they have. These forms soften acts of instruction that might be interpreted as face-threatening to students (see Cazden, 1979b). The teacher request in "Mississippi" seems to do exactly the opposite.

The stepper who is called on to perform the spelling task usually utters a quick phrase like "Gimme room" or "No sweat" as she jumps forward out of the line to begin her routine. These utterances indicate the stepper's willingness to take on the dare and the stepper's confidence that the performance is fully within the range of her competencies. Thus the instructional routine sets up an aggressive and suspicious teacher command and a student stepper who takes on the challenge with a sexual swagger and obvious confidence about her spelling prowess.

A spelling exercise, ordinarily practiced in the classroom, is transformed through linguistic play and dance with a market shift in ownership. By reframing the instructional exchange the literacy-related behaviors are recontextualized—taken from the school's mode of literacy instruction and made a part of the children's own world. Interpretive frames are created that signal to onlookers that this particular performance of literacy-related behaviors does not belong to or count for school.

The syncopation of this spelling lesson allows children, as subordinates, to mock school instruction. In much the same way skits and jokes present concrete formulations of an abstract cultural symbol, the images conveyed in the "Mississippi" performance can be seen as containing the children's symbolic social portraits of the dynamics of schooling.

Thus the message conveyed by these students through the performance of "Mississippi" can seem quite a poignant one. It is not merely defiant; it is not merely black. It can easily be seen as face-saving, a way of maintaining dignity through collective autonomy when confronted with the school's undermining doubt in their ability. At the end of "Mississippi" the entire group does the spelling performance in a striking flourish, declaring, for all to see, their excellence as literate spellers, as dancers, and as kids. When the steppers call out "Gimme room" they are asking for room to be seen, trusted, and evaluated as skilled language users—as individuals who have the right to instructional circumstances where pride and ownership are the central features of learning.

## ATTITUDE, EXPECTATIONS, AND INSTRUCTION

In the case of assessing attitudes in the study site, in Bateson's (1972) terms, the "nip" becomes the "bite" rather than denoting it. The sign is read as the act rather than a suggestion of it. These narrow restrictions, born out of stereotyped fears and sensitivity, seriously limit teacher expectations and classroom instruction. Attitude and not literacy becomes the primary instructional focus. Though a good attitude was seen as a means to an end (i.e., literacy achievement), the focus was so intense and exclusive that instructional interaction simply got stuck there. Consider the effects of this ethos in the following example.

A teacher in one Academics Plus class was going over a list of homework vocabulary words with the class. The word they were doing next was *dismal*. She asked someone to use *dismal* in a sentence. One girl volunteered, "The clouds were *dismal*, dark and gloomy." The teacher answered, "No. Dismal *means* dark and gloomy. That's like saying 'repeat again.' Now a good sentence for *dismal* would be, 'The clouds are dismal today.'"

Assuming the teacher is not stupid—which she is not—why would she reject the student's sentence of somewhat literary prose in favor of the rather bland and nonliterary one she herself offers. Consider first what the teacher is doing. She is testing her students to see if they know the meaning of the vocabulary words, which she likely assumes are new to their experience. The sentence will put the word in context so that the students can *prove* they understand the meaning. It might even be seen as cheating to use synonyms with the new word to disguise the fact that the word is not fully understood. Another sub-skill rule, to avoid redundancy, dominates the literary sense and poetic cadence. If the teacher believed the student could easily understand the word *dismal*, she might have been able to listen differently to the response. Only the suspicion that it hides ignorance registered. Seen in this light the teacher's sentence may have been offered more as an example of how to be honest (not hiding behind dictionary synonyms) than as an example of good prose and composition. This narrow pedagogy, driven by mistrust, will not provide the *room* for which the steppers have pleaded—the room which is required in order for them to demonstrate their competence.

## CONCLUSION

Expressive forms such as stylized sulking or doing steps can essentially be viewed as metaphors for the human condition. The expressive forms used by the students can be seen as a message of individual (in the case of stylized sulking) or collective (in the case of "Mississippi") autonomy in the face of authority. The behaviors discussed here are both face-saving devices which allow for pride and ownership in circumstances where opportunities for such prizes are scarce.

Both sulking and stepping seem to be associated with a certain set of black communicative displays that have typically been a class marker for failure in our society. Like nonstandard vernacular, these "street" behaviors will tend to close rather than open doors for black children who are trying to be upwardly mobile in our society. No matter how legitimate a linguistic or behavioral analysis of such behavior is, the key factor of legitimacy is how these behaviors are interpreted in the social world in which they are performed. For the children in the study site, most of their parents and teachers agree that the cost is too high. Symbols of black "street" behavior such as stylized sulking and stepping are seen as ethnic and class markers which interfere with success and may, as the discussion has shown, even limit access to socially valued commodities such as literacy.

Since fear about and focus on good attitudes made community members especially sensitive to any markers associated with black vernacular "street" culture, little latitude was allowed for any displays concerning sex (particularly for girls) or aggression (particularly for boys). For example, sexual ambiguity in stepping dances was interpreted quickly as an indicator of the performer's sexual experience. The disgruntled looks and postures associated with stylized sulking were read as threats of violence and potential aggression.

One of the original concerns of this research was to identify problems that teachers saw as interfering with student achievement in literacy and language arts. "Attitude" was repeatedly offered as a major concern in the teaching of literacy skills. The research problem was to find out exactly what the label "attitude" meant in this community and how the term and concepts it encompassed functioned in relation to literacy achievement. How was "attitude" communicated, interpreted, and understood? This was the question which guided the study. The focus of the investigation was on two specific social and linguistic behaviors that proved significant to the research. The ritual display of emotion which I have termed "stylized sulking" and the speech event of "doin' steps" were examined as metaphors for the everyday life of these children's social world. Through the use of these metaphors it became apparent that a "bad attitude" was closely associated with a conveyed message of alignment with black vernacular culture.

When I shared my findings with one of the mothers in the community, she commented on the fact that these two events appeared so prominent in the observations. Agreeing with the observations, she offered a dramatic parallel to sulking and stepping that struck her. She recalled that portrayals of black slaves in American history frequently depicted them as either *sullen* or *dancing*. The images of *sulking* and *stepping* youngsters suggest that we may not have come very far in our own brand of modern-day racism. Young students show their resistance to the authority in control through sulking facial gestures and body language, though they may go through the motions of their expected behaviors. Steps are reminiscent of some of the slave songs, sung almost in code, so that slave masters would not be able to comprehend the real content of their messages (e.g., songs such as "Follow the Drinking Gourd" and others associated with the Underground Railroad).

A study of attitude and literacy proved more to be a study of alignment and socio-economic status. The key factor for success in this school community seems to be demonstration of alignment with, if not allegiance to, the school's ethos—which in turn is compatible with, if not reflective of, the dominant ethos of the community.

Unfortunately there is a subtle confusion in the labeling process that has dramatic and lasting effects. Social alignment with the school is usually interpreted as literacy achievement while social resistance is often understood as literacy skill deficiency. The results are powerful and tragic. Stephen Jay Gould (1981) well describes them in the following way:

> We pass through this world but once. Few tragedies can be more extensive than the stunting of life, few injustices deeper than the denial of an opportunity to

strive or even hope, by a limit imposed from without, but falsely identified as lying within.

As educators and researchers concerned with literacy our professional responsibility demands that we allow ourselves the room to see beyond the limiting and arbitrary boundaries of how we have traditionally defined the world of reading and writing. By examining literacy within its socio-cultural context we are in a much stronger position to understand the dynamics of its nature, acquisition, and development.

## REFERENCES

Anderson, E. S. Learning to Speak with Style: A Study of the Sociolinguistic Skills of Children. Doctoral Dissertation: Stanford University, 1977.

Bateson, G. (1972). In *Steps to an ecology of mind.* New York: Ballantine Books.

Bauman, R. (1982). Ethnography of children's folklore. In P. Gilmore & A. Glatthorn (Eds.), *Children in and out of school.* Washington, DC: Center for Applied Linguistics.

Cazden, C. (1979a). Language in education variation in the teacher talk register. In *Language in Public Life.* Washington, DC: 30th Annual Georgetown University Round Table, 1979.

Cazden, C. (1979b). Peekaboo as an instructional model: Discourse development at home and at school. Unpublished manuscript, Harvard University, 1979.

Cazden, C. (1982). Four comments. In Gilmore & A. Glatthorn (Eds.), *Children in and out of school.* Washington, DC: Center for Applied Linguistics, 1982.

Cazden, C., John, V., & Hymes, D. (Eds.). (1972). *Functions of language in the classroom.* New York: Teachers College Press.

Edwards, A. & Furlong, V. (1978). *The language of teaching.* London: Heineman, 1978.

Gilmore, P. (1982). *Gimme room: A cultural approach to the study of attitudes and admission to literacy.* Unpublished doctoral dissertation, University of Pennsylvania.

Gilmore, P. (1983). Spelling Mississippi: Recontextualizing a literacy-related speech event. *Anthropology and Educational Quarterly, 14*(4), Winter. 235–255.

Gilmore, P. (1984). Silence and sulking: Emotional displays in the classroom. In D. Tannen & M. Saville-Troike (Eds.), *Perspectives on silence.* 139–162. Norwood, NJ: Ablex.

Gilmore, P. (1986). Sub-rosa literacy: Peers, play and ownership in literacy acquisition. In B.B. Schieffelin & P. Gilmore (Eds.), *The acquisition of literacy: Ethnographic perspectives.* Norwood, NJ: Ablex, 1985b (in press)

Gilmore, P. (1987). Sulking, stepping and tracking: The effects of attitude assessment on access to literacy. In D. Bloome (Ed.), *Literacy and schooling.* Norwood, NJ: Ablex.

Gilmore, P. & Glatthorn, A. (Eds.) (1982). *Children in and out of school.* Washington, DC: Center for Applied Linguistics.

Goffman, E. (1976). Gender advertisements. *Studies in the Anthropology of Visual Communication, 3*(2),

Gould, S. J. *The Mismeasure of Man.* New York: W. W. Norton & Co., 1981.

Hochschild, Arlie. (1979). Emotion Work, feeling rules and social structure. *American Journal of Sociology* 85 (3): 551–575.

Hymes, D. H. (1962). The ethnography of speaking. In T. Gladwin & W. C. Sturtevant (Eds.), *Anthropology and Human Behavior,* Washington, DC: Anthropological Society of Washington, 1962.

McDermott, R. P. (1976). Kids make sense: An ethnographic account of the interactional management of success and failure in one first grade classroom. Unpublished doctoral dissertation, Stanford University.

Mehan, H. (1979). *Learning lessons: The social organization of classroom behavior.* Cambridge: Harvard University Press.

Mehan, H., Cazden, C., Coles, L., Fisher, S., & Maroules, N. (1976). *The social organization of classroom lessons.* San Diego: Center for Human Information Processing, University of California.

# Part II

---

## MULTIPLE WAYS OF
## CONSTRUCTING REALITY

# 5

# THE NARRATIVIZATION OF EXPERIENCE
# IN THE ORAL STYLE

## James Paul Gee

Children from different socio-cultural groups in the United States develop, from the earliest ages, different communicative strategies (Cook-Gumperz & Gumperz, 1981; Edwards, 1976; Heath, 1982, 1983; Hill & Varenne, 1981; Michaels, 1981; Michaels & Collins, 1984; Michaels & Cook-Gumperz, 1979; Reed, 1981). These strategies may go hand in hand with different approaches to problem solving, social interaction, and conceptualizing. They are, thus, of great significance in understanding how different groups of people make sense of experience (Goody, 1977; Hall, Cole, Reder, & Dowley, 1977; Labov, 1970, 1972; Ong, 1982; Scollon & Scollon, 1979, 1981, 1984; Scribner, 1979). These different sorts of communicative strategies can be ranged along a continuum (Tannen, 1981, 1982b). Toward one end of the continuum are what have been called "orally based" or "oral" strategies. Such strategies, perhaps, reach their purest form in "oral cultures" with rich traditions of oral narrative and poetry (Finnegan, 1977; Goody, 1977; Havelock,

I am indebted first and foremost to Sarah Michaels (Harvard University), who generously shared with me a recording and transcript of L's story. Sarah's papers, as well as discussion with her, have greatly influenced me. I am also indebted to David Dickinson (Tufts University) and Barbara Gomes (San Diego State), both of whom have shaped my thought in this area. Finally, I am indebted to Dell Hymes (University of Pennsylvania) for very helpful comments on an earlier version of this chapter. Of course, none of them is responsible for, nor would they necessarily agree with, the direction their influence has taken in this chapter. This chapter is half of a two-part study (Gee, 1984), which argues for the narrative structures discussed here on somewhat more technical grounds, looking at two narratives by the child studied here and comparing them to the narrative style of an elderly white middle-class retired schoolteacher.

1963; Hymes, 1981; Pattison, 1982; Sherzer, 1983; Tedlock, 1983). Toward the other end are what have been referred to as "literate-based" or "literate" strategies, perhaps reaching their purest form in the essay and in speech that is heavily influenced by so-called essayist literacy (Bennett, 1982; Scollon & Scollon, 1979, 1981). In reality, each of us has control over a certain range of the continuum, moving closer to one end or the other as the context and task demand. However, some groups of people can extend farther than others toward one end or the other. People without full access to the essayist literacy of the schools may not be able to extend as far, in speech or writing, toward the literate strategy end of the continuum as those who have had full access. On the other hand, people who no longer have rich ties to a tradition of oral storytelling may not be able to extend as far toward the oral strategy end of the continuum as those who do. It is now a common claim that young lower- and working-class black children often come to school with a command over the oral strategy end of the continuum, but without much mastery of the literate side (Heath, 1982; Michaels, 1981; Michaels & Collins, 1984). Middle-class children, even though they cannot yet write, often come to school with the beginnings of mastery of literate style communication, presumably due to the presence of certain language practices in the home. To the extent that this is true, these two sets of strategies are in part class-based. Full access to literate strategies has been denied the poor and many minority groups. For its part, the middle class has seen the breakdown of the small, closely knit, cultural-group structure that may well be necessary to sustain oral strategies in their richest form. In fact, Givon (1979) has suggested that literate styles of speaking are characteristic of a "society of strangers," while oral styles are more characteristic of a "society of intimates."

There are many characterizations of differences between oral-based styles and literate-based styles (Bernstein, 1971; Chafe, 1980, 1982; Cook-Gumperz & Gumperz, 1981; Goody, 1977, 1982; Goody & Watt, 1963; Gumperz, 1982; Gumperz, Kaltman, & O'Connor, 1984; Havelock, 1963, 1982; Olson, 1977; Ong, 1982; Michaels, 1981; Michaels & Collins, 1984; Pattison, 1982; Poole & Field, 1976; Scollon & Scollon, 1979, 1981; Scribner & Cole, 1981; Smith, 1975; Tannen, 1980, 1982a, 1982b, 1984). Unfortunately, the oral style is often characterized negatively in terms of what it lacks that the literate style has. (It is inexplicit where the literate style is explicit; it is less well integrated than the literate style, less syntatically complex, and so on.) This only reflects, at the academic level, the literate bias of our culture (Scollon & Scollon, 1981, 1984) and the negative attitude at the school level that translates into outright prejudice. The oral style has an aesthetic aspect to it that renders it in some ways quite autonomous from the literate style (I mean the term "aesthetic" in a quite technical sense, as will become clear below), and closer, perhaps, to the "literary" style of literature (see Tannen, 1982a). After all, the oral style was the basis of both Homer and the Bible, and probably even of the classical Greek stage—and these were some of the high points of the human attempt to communicate (Alter, 1981; Habel, 1971; Havelock, 1963, 1982; Pattison, 1982; Sternberg, 1978). We can in fact see the oral style in its richest form if we turn to narrative (Bennett, 1982).

One of the primary ways—probably *the* primary way—human beings make sense of their experience is by casting it in a narrative form: "This happened and so that happened" (Forster, 1927; Hymes, 1982; Scholes & Kellogg, 1966; White, 1981). This is an ability that develops early and rapidly in children, without explicit training or instruction. Because language is acquired early and rapidly, without training or instruction, linguists argue that human beings are biologically equipped to develop language, given the appropriate triggering experiences (Chomsky, 1965; Hornstein & Lightfoot, 1981; Piattelli-Palmarini, 1980). I would suggest that the same model can be applied to the human ability to narrativize experience. Thus, no human, under normal conditions, fails to make sense when narrativizing his or her experience. And just as the common core of human language is expressed differently in different languages, so the common core of human narrative is expressed differently in different cultures. To understand these differences, and ultimately the commonalities behind them, we have to look in great detail at the ways in which different people make sense of their experience through narrative. Rather than listing global properties of the oral-based style, then, I will look very closely at one narrative of one child, a child who appears to use the oral style.

The narrative I will study here is by a 7-year-old black girl, whom I will refer to as "L." It was told as part of a sharing time exercise in school and comes from a corpus of such stories collected by Michaels and her colleagues (Michaels, 1981; Michaels & Collins, 1984; Michaels & Cook-Gumperz, 1979). Michaels has compared the sharing time stories told by middle-class white children and poorer black children in the first and second grades. The white children tell what Michaels calls "topic centered stories," while a significant number of the stories told by many black children are what she calls "topic associating stories." Michaels and her associates characterize the two sorts of stories as shown in Table 5.1 below. The topic centered story is immediately recognizable: it is middle-class speech that finds its epitome in expository writing (e.g. the essay) and not in narrative. In fact, sharing time functions as a device to give early training in literacy, before the child can engage in real expository speaking or writing. The topic associating style is less recognizable. In fact, the characterization in Table 1 is almost entirely relative to the characterization of the topic centered style, and is rather negative. It sounds a poor try at coherence. The situation is ripe for the application of a "deficit model": these children tell these sorts of stories because they don't know any better; their homes have not equipped them to do it "right." And indeed, such stories, when heard live, can be almost inexplicable to someone who does not have the necessary interpretive keys to decode them. Children who tell such stories at sharing time are often interrupted by the teacher in ways that show little understanding, and are often told to sit down before they are finished

**Table 5.1**
**Two Types of Sharing Time Stories as Characterized by Michaels (1981)**

| *Literate-Strategy Narratives* | *Oral-Strategy Narratives* |
| --- | --- |
| TOPIC CENTERED | TOPIC ASSOCIATING |
| • Tightly structured discourse on single topic or series of closely related topics | • A series of associated segments that may seem anecdotal in character, linked implicitly to particular topical event or theme, but with no explicit statement of an overall theme or point |
| • Lexically explicit referential, temporal, and spatial relationships | |
| • No major shifts in perspective, temporal orientation or thematic focus | • While these stories start with time, person, and place, temporal orientation, location, and focus often shift across segments—these shifts are marked by shifts in pitch contours and tempo, often accompanied by a formulaic time marker |
| • High degree of thematic coherence and a clear thematic progression | |
| • Begin with temporal grounding, a statement of focus, introducing key agents, and some indication of spatial grounding | • Relationship between parts of the narrative have to be inferred by the listener |
| • Orientation is followed by elaboration on the topic | • Temporal indicators (yesterday, last night, tomorrow) occur more than once |
| • The child marks syntactically complete, independent clauses with special sharing time intonation (high rising tone with vowel elongation) that means "more to come" and demarcates the clause as an information unit | • The special sharing time intonation is used not to mark continuity, but to highlight discontinuity, marking the separation of narrative segments and shifts in temporal orientation, location, or focus |
| • Finishes with a punch-line sort of resolution, signaled by a markedly lower pitch or falling tone | • The stories may give the impression to those who have no control over the style of having no beginning, no middle, no end—thus no point |
| • Stories tend to be short and concise | • Tend to be longer and seem to be not very concise |

(Michaels, 1981). The teacher feels the child is not talking about "one important thing" (a key goal of sharing time exercises) and is just rambling on in a
perversely incoherent and ill-organized way. However, once we accept the assumption that all human beings are equipped to narrate experience, such can
hardly be the case. We need, then, to look closely at such stories to see *how*
these children are making sense, with the assurance that they are.

L's sharing time narrative ("Puppy-1") is printed in the Appendix to this article. Before asking what this text might mean, we have to be aware of its structure, since this structure will give us some insight into possible meanings or
ways of understanding the text. There is a characteristic prosodic pattern in
L's style that can serve as an initial cue into the structures behind her narrative
performance. Her speech appears to be made up of a series of relatively short
sequences of words, each sequence having a single continuous intonational
contour. Most of these sequences end on a nonfalling pitch glide, often also
with some other indication of juncture (e.g., a brief pause or hesitation or a
lengthening of the final syllable). After several of these sequences we finally
get a sequence that ends on a falling contour. In the Puppy-1, I have numbered
each of these sequences and placed each on a separate line. Sequences that end
on a falling contour have the symbol "//" at the end of the line. In middle-class
more or less literate speech, falling contours (roughly speaking) mark the ends
of sentences. This is clearly not the case in L's speech, however. For example,
the opening of Puppy-1 is 17 sequences long before it gets to a falling contour,
and this material does not under any syntactic description (even correcting for
hesitations and false starts) constitute a sentence. In fact, the falling contours
in L's speech have discourse-level functions, not syntactic ones. (These functions are not fully understood at this point—they appear, for one thing, to
mark the ends of episodes, not the ends of sentences; see Michaels, 1981, and
Michaels & Collins, 1984, for a fuller description of the prosody of these sorts
of texts.)

Each of the numbered units in Puppy-1 is what Chafe (1980) calls an "idea
unit." L's idea units are, for the most part one clause long, with one piece of
new information toward the end of the clause. The new information bears the
major pitch movement (glide) in the clause (for more information on the relationship between pitch glides and focus, see Bolinger, 1972; Brazil &
Coulthard, 1980; Ladd, 1980; Selkirk, 1984). It is only when the subject of a
clause, or an adverbial element, is new information, being introduced for the
first time, that it constitutes an idea unit by itself. Once the agent or an adverbial element has been introduced as an idea unit, it can then be incorporated as
old information in the succeeding idea unit(s). Thus, it appears that L is aiming
at a series of short clauses as her ideal idea units. Furthermore, each of these
clauses is marked by an opening "and," some other conjunction (though "and"
is the overwhelming favorite), or a verb of saying. If we remove obvious false
starts and repairs from the text and collapse the few subject nouns or noun
phrases that are idea units by themselves into the clauses they belong to, we get

an ideal realization of the text, which is given in "Puppy-2" in the Appendix. Once we have gotten to the basic clauses or "lines" that L is aiming at, it becomes apparent that L groups her lines together into series of lines—often four lines long—that have parallel structure and match each other either in content or topic. I will call these groups of lines "stanzas." Furthermore, prosodically, these lines sound as if they go together, both by tending to be said at the same rate and by having little hesitation between lines. (Scollon & Scollon, 1981, found the same thing for narratives by Athabaskan children and adults telling stories, whether in their Athabaskan language, or in English.) They are separated by space in Puppy-2. Stanzas sometimes show intricate structure and patterning, taking on some of the properties of stanzas in poetry. In the thematic analysis of the text below I will display a good bit of this parallelism and how it functions semantically.

The overall structure of the text becomes clear once we see the stanza structure, and in turn gives us evidence for these stanzas. Note, in consulting Puppy-2, that the story has three parts: the first is set in the home, the second takes place going to school, and the third is set in the hospital. Each part is divided into two sub-parts. Part 1A is the opening scene involving the hook at the top of the stairs; this is separated into two four-line stanzas. Part 1B introduces the puppy and father in a paired contrast. First we get "an' then my puppy came" followed by four actions, then "an' my father came" followed by four sayings; thus, once again we have two four-line stanzas. Part 2 involves going places outside the home and being followed by the puppy. Part 2A involves going to school and being followed by the puppy and is, again, made up of two four-line stanzas (with an aside in the middle of one of them). Part 2B is an interruption of the narrative line, a series of nonnarrative, expository lines about habitually going outside the house and being followed by the puppy (these lines involve not an event in the story, but habitual happenings, a whole series of events). Finally, part 3 is set at the hospital. It is made up of two four-line stanzas (part 3a) that give us the last episode of the story, followed by two lines (part 3B) that conclude the text. The overall structure of the story then is something like:

Part 1: At Home

    Part 1A: Opening Scene: Breakfast and the Hook
        Stanza 1: four lines
        Stanza 2: four lines

    Part 1B: The Puppy and the Father
        Stanza 3: four lines
        Stanza 4: four lines

Part 2: Going Places

    Part 2A: Going to School
        Stanza 5: four lines
        Stanza 6: four lines

Part 2B: Nonnarrative section on going places
    Stanza 7: four lines (?)

Part 3: The Hospital

Part 3A: The Hospital
    Stanza 8: four lines
    Stanza 9: four lines

Part 3B: Ending
    Stanza 10: Concluding couplet

Notice that the nonnarrative section in part 2B deviates from the basic structure of the text (we would have expected two four-line stanzas). Furthermore it
is rather different linguistically from the rest of the text. The language is more
complicated syntactically, and these lines do not really fit our four-line pattern
as tightly as other lines in the text. It appears that L's language is somewhat different when she breaks out of the narrative mode. Furthermore, these lines
stop the flow of the narrative just before the final episode. Thus, these lines are
foregrounded in the text. I will argue below that they serve a purpose similar to
what Labov (1972) has called the "evaluation" in a narrative (and they appear
in the same place where Labov argues the evaluation often occurs in the narratives of black teenagers).

Given this structural description of the story, we will now turn to a
thematic / semantic analysis of the text. To start we will translate the structural
diagram above into story grammar terms. The story structure fits nearly perfectly the structures Labov (1972) attributes to the stories told by black
teenagers he studied. In the story diagram below I use terms from Labov
(1972):

Part 1: INTRODUCTION
    Part 1A: Setting
    Part 1B: Catalyst

Part 2: CRISIS
    Part 2A: Complicating Actions (Episodes)
    Part 2B: Nonnarrative Section (Evaluation)

Part 3: RESOLUTION
    Part 3A: Concluding Episodes
    Part 3B: Coda

The story starts with the general temporal marker "last yesterday," which
means, in L's dialect, "recent past." It is a temporal marker for the narrative as
a whole and also marks the fact that we are starting a narrative, a story. It thus
serves as a boundary marker that we are in the narrative world and in narrative
time. We will see that at the end of the story L uses this temporal marker to
exit us from the narrative proper and place us back in the here and now of the
"real world."

Part 1A is the Setting of the story as a whole. Part 1B is the Catalyst for the main crisis that is to follow. Together, these two episodes constitute the Introduction to the story. Both the Setting and the Catalyst are prefaced by a general time or sequence marker: "when, in the morning" in part 1A and "and then" in part 1B. (It is important to know that "and then," as opposed to "and," often marks a significant break in the thematic progression in oral style narratives).

The Setting, introduces a time ("in the morning") and a place (in her house) and highlights a personal, family relationship—a common strategy used in story openings by black children. L uses a typical oral strategy device to introduce the topic of this episode. She places the noun phrase "my father" out in front of the information that follows, thus jutting it out at us, foregrounding it. The vivid situation with the hook and the breakfast stresses the constraining discipline of the home. The father comes immediately to represent the authority of the adult world and of the home (we will later realize that just as L is constrained by the hook because she wants to go out, so the puppy will be chained up because he wants to go free). Thus, L sets from the beginning the crucial equation: home=constraint=authority=father. This becomes the crucial background motif of the story, in terms of which L ultimately makes sense of her problem. Many literate hearers are fooled here. Expecting a topic centered narrative (much like a mini-essay), they try to take the father as the main protagonist and the topic of the story as a whole, instead of seeing (as they would if they were using their literary tools) that L has used the setting to create an interpretive framework against which the main problem can be solved. It serves much the same purpose as a ground does in a figure–ground relation. Further, many literate hearers worry about the "truth value" of the hook. This is an absolutely irrelevant concern: "last yesterday" has placed us in the narrative world where we are supposed to be worrying about the *point* of the story, not the accuracy of its details. (Exactly the same applies to large stretches of the Bible.) Finally, before leaving this brilliant opening gambit, let me just point to two stylistic devices L uses throughout to give cohesion to her text, as well as to create meaning. First, she sets up contrasts. Note for instance, the contrast of the positive and *up*-ward lines 4–7 ("*top* of the stairway," "pickin me *up*," "*up* there") versus the negative and *down*-ward lines 8–11 ("had*n't* had," "would*n't* take me *down*," "did*n't* like"). L's story will be, in fact, a network of contrasts, because it is trying to work out, at a deeper level, some very fundamental dichotomies facing all children (and adults), as we will see below. Second, L will repeatedly use various sound and rythmical devices to give cohesion to her text and to support her meaning. Here, for example, we find:

there was a hoo*k*
*to*'p of the *sta*'irway
*pi*'ckin me u*p*
stu'c*k* on the hoo*k*

Part 1B is the Catalyst for the crisis to come. It introduces the main protagonist (the puppy), showing (not telling) the essential problem, and sowing the seeds of its resolution. Through a neat parallelism, a device common both to oral strategies (note again the Bible) and to literature, L sets up an initial, problematic contrast between *home* (in terms of the equation already given, i.e., home=constraint=authority=father) and *puppy*. Note also the sound effects (the *r*'s, *p*'s, and *d*'s) used for the entrance of the puppy and the chaos he causes. Note also the use of the *up* ("tried to get up") and *down* ("dropped the oatmeal") contrast again:

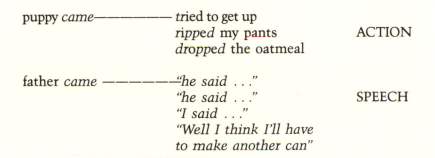

(Note the verb of obligation in the father's remark, i.e., "I'll have to," we will see later that L uses verbs of obligation as a motif of the human / adult world.) Verbs like "come" are verbs of "appearance" or "coming on the scene" and are typically used to introduce new characters. Here L uses this verb to introduce the puppy and line him up in direct contrast with the father. Father and puppy are in structural contrast, inviting us to an interpretive leap which is the function of such parallelism: Just as father represents home, authority, constraint, and the adult world, the puppy perhaps represents opposed values, the outdoors, freedom, exuberance, and youth. L invites this inference, and then confirms it for us in the following episodes. Note also the contrast, which will be utilized again, between ACTION (what the puppy does) and SPEECH (what the adult world does).

The *Crisis*, the main body of the story, is introduced by the logical connective and sequence marker "and so," marking a major break. It means: "From the foregoing material which you have just heard (i.e., the Introduction), the following material which you are about to hear (i.e., the Crisis or Body of the story) follows as a consequence." It thus becomes our job as hearers to draw the inference, that is, the connection between the Introduction and the Crisis, or the way in which the latter follows from the former. The Crisis is made up of a series of episodes that represent progressive stages of crisis: leaving the house, being followed by the puppy, having the father say the puppy can't go, being followed anyway, having to go back, and then being followed and going back repeatedly. These stages are developed in a very suspenseful and artful way (delaying information and creating suspense is often a hallmark of oral strategy narrative). For instance, note the way she uses time references to create tension and suspense: "I didn't leave *until seven*" starts the Crisis, "*by that time* it was 7:30" is inserted as an aside in the second stanza of the Crisis (we feel it getting later), and then she says the problem keeps happening over and over, but no longer mentions the time (leaving the implication that it is now *really late*). We feel the press of time as L faces the danger of getting into trouble with another constraining representative of the adult world, the school. From a linguistic point of view, L handles the development of the various stages of the Crisis quite nicely. Some of L's techniques are as follows:

In the opening stanza of the *Crisis* L uses a marker from Black English Vernacular to an interpretive end that is reminiscent of literary narrative (Fasold, 1972). She intercalates a habitual aspect statement in the midst of her narrative line:

I didn't leave till seven /
an' I took the bus /
an' / my puppy / he always be following me /
my father said . . . [the puppy] can't go / /

The habitual "be" in Black English Vernacular means that the puppy's behavior of following is something that has gone on for a long time and is part of the puppy's character or nature. The word is not "missing" its tense—it is not meant to have one in the dialect. Placed in the midst of the action, it invites us to interpret that action as a concrete exemplification of a generic situation, not as isolated events. It is not placed there by mistake, either: Note the syntactic form "my puppy, he . . . ," a form used in oral narratives to signal that the topic has momentarily switched. Notice also the sound effect of the repeated "ee" sound which highlights this line (my puppy, h*e* always b*e* following m*e*). We are thus encouraged to ask ourselves what further general truths we can draw from these concrete events—especially in terms of the interpretive matrix of father / home versus puppy / outdoors she has initiated and is further developing here. The puppy must stay in the house to avoid contaminating L's world of discipline and duty (by causing her to be late for school, for example), despite his need for freedom and fun. Notice, in this regard, a motif that will now recur throughout the narrative. Negatives are associated with people when they are engaged in carrying out duties or imposing them on others ("I *didn't* leave till seven," "you *can't* go"). We have here in fact the negative of verbs of *go*-ing. These negative verbs associated with L and her father are opposed to the positive habitual of the puppy ("always be following"). L is constrained, just as the puppy must ultimately be, and she too cannot go free, despite the likely urges of her character as a child. Finally, let us note that once again, we have a contrast of parental speech and youthful action, as the father negates through speech the going of the puppy ("my father said / um / 'he—you can't go'").

In the opening of the second stanza of the Crisis L uses contrasting verbs to bring home to us the fundamental contrasts she is working on, and once again she uses a neat parallelism to achieve an effect:

| [puppy] | followed me | *all the way* | to |
|---------|-------------|---------------|-----|
| [L] | hadda go | *all the way* | back |

Here we get a contrast between the puppy's positive, trusting, forward movement ("to") and L's verb of obligation ("hadda go") and movement backwards ("back"). Another essential aspect of the contrast is between freely chosen submission ("follow") versus constrained submission under obligation ("hadda go"). L is caught in the adult world of the home and school, and she must deny her own longings and those of the puppy in turn, so he will not disrupt the discipline of that world. We are beginning to see that in the narrative world L is counterpoised between the world of the puppy and the adult world.

L interrupts the second stanza of the Crisis by her temporal remark "by that time it was 7:30" and reiterates in the last two lines of the stanza exactly the meaning of the first two lines. Appropriately then, these lines are in the "iterative aspect" ("keep doing X"). L once again exploits parallelism, while the iterative aspect ("happening over and over again") helps us to feel the growing lateness and her growing frustration. The iterative aspect also takes us one step back toward the habitual, which will recur immediately at the opening of the Resolution. It also tells us that the *Crisis* is at its high point and calls for, while it suspensefully delays, a resolution. Of course, the literate listener who is not doing his or her share of interpretive work may feel that L is "repeating herself" or not being "concise."

| he | *kept* | followin' me | *back* an' forth |
|-----|--------|--------------|------------------|
| I hadda | *keep* | coming | *back* |

This is L's most complex piece of syntactic parallelism. Once again the puppy is following and going forth, urging L to do likewise. And once again L is associated with a verb of obligation ("hadda keep coming back"—one can feel its weight in the row of stresses and the row of stop consonants, *d, k, p, c, g, b, k*) and with going back (not forth). But now we are told that the contrast is incessant, keeps happening, as we would expect if it follows from the nature of the puppy and the contrast between that nature and the nature of the home / school / father / adult world, and must be resolved.

We should note the dexterous use L makes of aspect marking throughout the *Crisis* to develop her narrative line and at the same time to give it coherence and cohesion (line numbers are for Puppy-2 in Apendix B):

| *line* | | *aspect* |
|---|---|---|
| 21 | he always be following me | HABITUAL |
| 23 | he followed me all the way | ACTIONAL |
| 24 | I hadda go all the way back | ACTIONAL |
| 26 | he kept followin' me back and forth | ITERATIVE |
| 27 | I hadda keep coming back | ITERATIVE |
| 28 | an' he always be followin' me | HABITUAL |

L is actually using a form of crosscutting syntactic and aspectual anaphora across a significant stretch of her discourse, a tropic device that would have done a medieval rhetorician proud.

Just prior to entering the Resolution, then, given the story as a whole so far, we are prepared (if we have been doing our interpretive duties) with a set of contrasts. These contrasts serve as an interpretive matrix and a statement of the problem that needs resolving:

| *father* | *puppy* |
|---|---|
| home/school | outdoors |
| obligation | freedom |
| constraint | exuberance |
| negation | positive |
| going back | going forth |
| constrained submission | willful submission |
| lead | follow |
| adult | youth |

### L (wish?)

Before we get to the Resolution, however, L delays the narrative line. The second part of the Crisis section in the text is a nonnarrative, habitual-aspect "mediation." First, L repeats the habitual statement that occurred in the opening of the *Crisis* ("an' he always be followin' me"—line 28), reminding us that the actional details are in the service of more general truths, and bracketing off the now finished main line of the body of the story. L then continues with further habitual aspect statements that constitute a small habitual mode meditation, occurring at the crucial juncture between the main narrative line and the final resolution to come: "he wants . . . he could not go . . . he have t'be chained up." What he wants he cannot have. The puppy is at last fully implicated in the negative world of constraint, and ends up "chained" physically, as L is chained (constrained) by her duties in the adult human world (remember the hook is the opening episode). This habitual aspect meditation in lines 28–31 is extremely well constructed. L repeatedly uses the word "go" together with "could" ("go," "go," "could not go," "could go" "could go") uniting her thematic concerns of wanting to go forth free and the nature of ability, constraint, and obligation. The whole thing issues in the ultimate denial of *go*-ing through obligation: "he *have to* be *chained up*," which leaves us finally with an identification of constraint and obligation (notice in fact the English idiom "to be under an obligation," which also identifies constraint and obligation). It is interesting that L does not mention the *Agent*, the one who is obliged to chain up the puppy. The name of this Agent is suppressed: thus, the obligation is removed from the Agent and internalized in the puppy, at the same time the Agent remains faceless and anonymous. One of the deeper themes of the narrative is the way in which obligation / duty / constraint is eventually internalized in the individual, having as its source beyond the individual only institutional abstractions of the home / school / hospital of the adult world. Father / teacher / doctor can "stand" for, epitomize, or represent these sources of obligation, but do not exhaust them. In fact, father and doctor themselves act under obligations that they themselves are seemingly not the source of: "I think I'll have t'make another can" (father), "[the doctor] thought he wasn't gonna be able t'let [the puppy] go" (compare to the puppy's "he have t'be chained up").

The habitual aspect used in these lines about the puppy wanting to go free, but having to be chained up, tells us that this is the *norm*, which follows from the nature of the case and the nature of the puppy. But what about L's nature? The human cannot go back to the world of the puppy. Notice the way in which "I," which L has used throughout the text until now, finally becomes "we" ("when *I* go anywhere"—"where *we* could go"). L is set apart from the puppy as a member of the human group; she must grow up to take on the responsibilities of the adult world. But at the same time she is like the puppy in that her youthful desires to go free must be restrained and she must be chained up (constrained). The literate hearer may be tempted to see this habitual mode meditation (lines 28–31) as failing to get to the point. Yet such delaying and lingering—especially right before the denouement we anxiously await—was seen as a nearly definitional aspect of aesthetic foregrounding by the Russian formalists, a major force in 20th-century literary criticism. The Russian formalist movement in fact got much of its impetus from the study of "folk literature" (Erlich, 1955; Stacy, 1977).

After this habitual mode meditation, we get the Resolution. The Resolution starts, in the first stanza of part 3A, with an action in a completely different setting and time. This shift foregrounds the episode as a possible ending, a place where the previous actions will be explicated. Since the previous actions were (as we know from L's habitual aspect statements) merely concrete exemplifications of the puppy's nature or character, this final action must resolve the conflict in terms relevant to that character and to the interpretive matrix L has set up. At a lower level, the conflict is the puppy's nature versus the nature of the home; at a deeper level, it is the whole set of contrasts delineated above. At a yet deeper level, it is the conflict between wanting to remain a child and wanting to grow up, of wanting to go free and of taking on responsibility and the constraints that this implies.

We are now in another adult institution of constraint—a hospital. L says, "We took him to the emergency an' see what was wrong with him." "Took" implies that the puppy goes, but not under his own choice or power (compare to "follow"). "Wrong" ostensibly stands for an illness, but we know in a deep sense that it means "what is wrong with the character or nature of the puppy that causes it to stand in conflict with the adult world of the home." Note, then, that "wrong" is interpreted medically and internalized in the puppy. L is in fact appealing to one of the most pervasive and powerful epistemic models in our culture, the "medical model" (Woodward, 1982; Foucault, 1973). *If someone or something* is deviant, then *something* is organically wrong with *them* and *they* need to be treated by the medical profession (this mode has been applied to poor people, ethnic groups, deaf people, criminals, children, homosexuals, women, and so on). The hospital treats the puppy (he gets a shot). Then, in the second stanza of part 3A, L repeats the general narrative time marker "last yesterday," and then says "now," the time of the speaker / audience in the here and now of the "real world" (lines 48 and 49). This device neatly exits us—like an act of magic—from the narrative world. L brings us "up to the minute" and tells us (what, if we have done our job, we already know at a deeper level) the resolution. First, she tells us "they put him asleep." At line 10 the puppy had come out of sleep to play, causing disruption. Now he goes back to sleep, but a very different sleep. The image is powerful and moving, and ties L's narrative tautly together (long-distance cohesion of the most aesthetic sort). Then the doctor, an adult authority figure, says that the puppy "was nervous about my home," giving official recognition that there is an irremediable conflict between the nature of the puppy and that of the home. The text then ends on a couplet where the doctor says (note again *speech* in the adult world) that he, the doctor, is *not* (note again the negative associated with the adult carrying out or dictating obligations) *able* (is constrained) *to let* (=allow, a verb of obligation) the puppy *go* (free, the puppy is associated with a positive verb of going forth). Every one of L's leitmotifs is brought into this finale. The verb of obligation here, "wasn't gonna be able," is a beautiful one in the context—the doctor isn't doing it, he is constrained, unable to do otherwise—as obligation once again emanates from a faceless abstract world beyond single individuals. In the end, the home world takes precedence over the puppy's world under the reign of duty and obligation. When we realize that a puppy is a young animal, and a little girl is a young human, and take the hints of the story as a whole, we can sense the tacit equation of "L = the puppy" in this last line. Notice, in this regard, that at line 22 L makes a mistake with a pronoun: She says, "My father said he [the puppy] . . . you [L?, puppy?]

can't go"—an inspired mistake. It is important to note also how the doctor's words ("he thought he wasn't gonna be able t'let him go") hark back to and parallel these words of the father ("You can't go"), as well as the father's words in the second stanza of the Catalyst ("I think I'll have t'make another can"). Compare in fact the father's "I think I'll have to" with the doctor's "he thought he wasn't gonna be able to." This is, again, long-distance cohesion of the most aesthetic sort.

Through narrative, L is making sense of her world: why she doesn't have her puppy, why he didn't work out, and ultimately why she must belong to the world of home and school, a universal problem for children (and adults). She works out the problems in a quite sophisticated way, in terms of a conflict of natures (the Greeks, an oral society that ultimately gave birth to Western literacy, would have understood this perfectly). She carries it out with a full utilization of prosody, time and sequence markers, an intricate aspect system (actional, habitual, iterative), and parallelism and repetition, and as suspenseful thematic development. The story is in fact, from start to finish, a tour de force.

And yet L's story was not at all well received by her teacher. She was interrupted at the end by questions that showed the teacher did not understand her story. She was finally told to sit down, the teacher having found her story incoherent. Her story was felt to be inconsistent, disconnected, and rambling. Eventually, L was sent, on the basis of stories like this one, to the school psychologist.[1] We are thus faced with two questions. First, how could a 7-year-old have produced such a remarkable narrative? And second, how could she in producing it have nonetheless failed?

There are several answers to the question of why she failed. Sharing time is an exercise that is meant to lay the foundations of the literate style of speech and ultimately of the essay style of writing. The child is meant to organize his or her text around a single topic in a style that is lexically (word choice) and syntactically explicit, i.e., that does not invite the hearer to draw inferences and fill in information on the basis of shared knowledge and clues in the text (Michaels, 1981). In terms familiar from literary criticism, the child is supposed to *tell* ("say so in so many words"), not *show* (let actions and dialogue "speak for themselves"). Meaning is to be explicitly conveyed, not left to the constructive processes of the hearer. The hearer is to be an "audience," not a partner; is to be a (pretend) stranger, not an intimate. The text is meant to convey information and to be organized in a logical way, not to engage in rhetorical techniques or aesthetic devices that might impede or supersede this sort of organization. All of these factors imply, in particular, that aspects of language that are solely germane to the spoken medium and to language as personal social interaction should be downplayed—for example, any rich use of prosody, rather than words and syntax, to organize the text. Such a use of sound and prosody is of course a hallmark of L's text.

In this regard, then, we might view sharing time as a rather problematic exercise. It asks the child to ignore the evidence of her senses and to essentially pretend that the "audience" does not share a lot of common knowledge with her, is not a set of well-known peers, and is not physically present before the speaker, but rather distanced and so must be told everything (and not, for instance, have things pointed to). It looks as if one is talking to a group of peers about a personally important topic, when what one is really doing is creating a form of relatively decontextualized speech (actually a form of speech-writing) to a group of pretend strangers, for the purpose of displaying and / or learning academic literacy skills. Middle-class children evidently often have early experiences in the home that key them into the fact that the sort of enterprise that sharing time represents is somewhat misleading (Heath, 1983; Scollon & Scollon, 1981). Sharing time appears in fact to trade on typically middle-class home experiences for success, thereby excluding working- and lower-class children from an enterprise that is meant to teach the literate style to those who do not already have the foundations of that style. L failed, then, because she took the situation at face value and gave a real narrative to a group of peers, a narrative meant to give meaning to a problematic experience (the primary role of narrative, I would argue), not convey cut-and-dried facts (something for which narrative is rather ill suited). L uses language full tilt, with prosody, parallelism, rhetoric, and audience participation all contributing, together with lexical choice and syntax, to the communication of message, emotion, and entertainment. In this she is not far removed in spirit from literature, another use of words to shape and understand experience; but she is removed from a mode of exposition of facts for their own sake.

Let's look, then, at the question of how L constructs meaning. Meaning in L's text is in large part a matter of an open set of contrasting and relating themes, themes which develop through time but which eventually take on the character of a set of intricately related points held in tension in a multidimensional space: constraint, freedom; adult, youth; leading, following; indoors, outdoors; speech, action; authority, submission. This set of contrasts resides in an almost endlessly proliferating way in the concrete contrast between father and puppy that L starts with. This is in fact a good example of how the sensual and concrete give entrance into the abstract (see Levi-Strauss, 1978). These themes, entering into a limitless set of interconnected multidimensional contrasts and relations, give an overall coherence and structure to the text, while allowing meaning to proliferate without ever being exhausted. Exactly the same method is put to aesthetic use by Virginia Woolf, for instance in her novels *Mrs. Dalloway* or *To the Lighthouse*.

The technical devices that L uses to achieve her result are repetition, parallelism, sound play, juxtaposition, foregrounding, delaying, and showing rather than telling. These are hallmarks of spoken language in its most oral mode, reaching its peak in the poetry, narratives, and epics of oral cultures (Hymes, 1981; Lord, 1960; Sherzer, 1983; Tedlock, 1978, 1983) and of certain types of literature—not only folk literature but also, for example, much modern and "modernist" literature in Europe and the United States. Any number of important literary and aesthetic theories in the 20th century have made several or all of these devices crucial to their very definition of the aesthetic in literature or art generally, e.g. Pound and the Imagists (Kenner, 1971), the Russian Formalists (Erlich, 1955), Jakobson and the Prague Circle (Jakobson, 1978), Frank and Spatialization (Frank, 1963), and so forth. But the deeper question, and one not yet squarely confronted by linguists or anthropologists is this: Why is there so much similarity between oral poetry and narrative in oral cultures (whether early Hebrew poetry, Greek epic, American Indian narratives, or African poems and stories), folk art (e.g., fairy tales and folktales), myths, and certain types of "high literature," and what some black children and adults can do when telling a story? The answer, it seems to me, is that it is in these cases that we see the fullest, richest, and least "marked" expression of our human biological capacity for language, narrative, and sense making generally.

Let me close by saying that this ability to narrate experience that we all share is by no means an innocent one. As a way of organizing experience it often appeals to pervasive, culturally shared, and unquestioned myths. L, in fact, appeals, as we saw above, to two of them as organizing devices. One is her appeal to the "medical model" (deviance=organically wrong=medical treatment=authority of the doctors=cure or removal from "normal" society). The other is a model whereby duty and obligation float free from individuals who impose them or who freely accept them (impose them on themselves) and become internalized in individuals as coercive forces with anonymous sources outside themselves, perhaps in abstract institutions. This model is very similar to the process whereby lower-class people unconsciously internalize the norms of the middle class and apply them against themselves, thereby cooperating in their own oppression. These myths are, of course, not part of black culture per se, but rather are operative in the larger culture as well. Lest one think that literacy saves us from this use of myth as organizing device, let me point out that sharing time, as a literacy building activity, is based solidly on such a myth: the view of language (deeply embedded in our language and our culture) that meaning is something that is packaged in nice little bundles (words and sentences) and conveyed down a little tube-like channel to someone else who simply undoes the package and takes out the morsel of meaning (Lakoff & Johnson, 1980; Reddy, 1979). In fact, language is always something that is actively constructed in a context, physically present or imagined, by both speaker / writer and hearer / reader through a complex process of inferencing that is guided by, but never fully determined by, the structural properties of the language. Finally, schools and society at large are organized by another, yet more pervasive myth, the myth of better and worse: the belief that in all activities human beings can be measured, ranged from better (the winners) to worse (the losers), and rewarded appropriately (Gould, 1980, see ch. 4). We often go on to equate human worth with such measurements. Humans do show quite different capabilities in regard to some skills, e.g., playing a musical instrument, learning theoretical physics, playing chess or sports, and so forth. But even in regard to these skills it is somewhat silly to reward "merit" given that such individual differences are often traceable to different biological endowments, matters over which we had no control (much as it would be silly to attribute merit to people for being tall). However, reward and merit in these cases are reasonable to the extent that it often takes a good deal of dedication, time, and effort to develop these skills from their biological bases. But more importantly there are some things that all human beings, barring rather severe handicaps, are quite good at. One of these is mastering a native language. The linguistic knowledge of a 5 year old is astounding and keeps us linguists in business. It is simply perverse to say that one native speaker has mastered the grammar better than another. Similarly, though this is less well recognized, all human beings are masters of making sense of experience and the world through narrative. Most people agree, upon spending some time on L's narratives, that she is a master. She is, however, not unique in that. We all are given this gift in virtue of our humanness, though in some of us it may be atrophying under an avalanche of rational nonsense.

## NOTE

1. There are important cultural differences between middle-class whites, working-class whites, and working-class blacks on the nature and function of fiction and fictionalization. Some of these are discussed in Heath (1982) and in Scollon and Scollon (1981). The issue deserves much deeper attention. Part of the question is how much allegiance does one have to the construction of narrative worlds (and the internal structuring of narratives) as sense making devices. Many writers share with L a deep allegiance in this regard. The school sometimes gives lip service to such allegiance in literature classes, perhaps, but I suspect has very little such allegiance in any real sense. The school, like much academic culture at large, believes for the most part in the transparency of language to fact, a view epitomized by many academic views of essay writing, though not much championed by philosophers or literary critics any more. In fact, it is probably true that many great expository writers had a deep allegiance to the internal structuring of the essay as a sense making device in its own right, rather than holding any facile belief that language was a window onto the world—despite what has been handed down in schools for hundreds of years.

## REFERENCES

Alter, R. (1981). *The art of biblical narrative.* New York: Basic Books.

Bennett, A. T. (1982). Discourses of power, the dialectics of understanding, the power of literacy. *Journal of Education, 165,* 53–74.

Bernstein, B. B. (1971). *Class, codes and control* (Vol. 1). London: Routledge & Kegan Paul.

Bolinger, D. L. (Ed.). (1972). *Intonation*. Harmondsworth, Middlesex: Penguin Books.

Brazil, D. & Coulthard, M. (1980). *Discourse intonation and language teaching*. London: Longman.

Chafe, W. L. (Ed.) (1980). *The pear stories*. Norwood, NJ: Ablex.

Chafe, W. L. (1982). Integration and involvement in speaking, writing, and oral literature. In D. Tannen (Ed.), *Spoken and written language 35–54*. Norwood, New Jersey: Ablex.

Chomsky, N. (1965). *Aspects of the theory of syntax*. Cambridge: M.I.T. Press.

Cook-Gumperz, J., & Gumperz, J. (1981). From oral to written: The transition to literacy. In M. F. Whiteman (Ed.), *Variation in writing*. Hillsdale, NJ: Lawrence Erlbaum.

Edwards, A. D. (1976). Speech codes and speech variants: Social class and task differences in children's speech. *Journal of Child Language, 3*, 247–265.

Erlich, V. (1955). *Russian formalism: history—doctrine*. New Haven: Yale University Press.

Fasold, R. W. (1972). *Tense marking in black English: A linguistic and social analysis*. Arlington, VA: Center for Applied Linguistics.

Finnegan, R. (1977). *Oral poetry*. Cambridge: Cambridge University Press.

Forster, E. M. (1927). *Aspects of the novel*. New York: Harcourt, Brace & World.

Foucault, M. (1973). *The birth of the clinic: An archaeology of medical perception*. New York: Vintage Books.

Frank, J. (1963). *The widening gyre: Crisis and mastery in modern literature*. Bloomington: Indiana University Press.

Gee, J. P. (1984). Units in the production of narrative discourse. Unpublished manuscript, Program in Applied Psycholinguistics, Boston University.

Givon, T. (1979). *On understanding grammar*. New York: Academic Press.

Goody, J. (1977). *The domestication of the savage mind*. Cambridge: Cambridge University Press.

Goody J., & Watt, I. (1963). The consequences of literacy. *Comparative Studies in Society and History, 5*, 304–345.

Gould, S. J. (1980). The panda's thumb: More reflections in natural history. New York: Norton.

Gumperz, J. J. (1982). *Discourse strategies*. Cambridge: Cambridge University Press.

Gumperz, J. J., Kaltman, H., & O'Connor, M. C. (1984). Cohesion in spoken and written discourse. In D. Tannen (Ed.), *Coherence in spoken and written discourse*. Norwood, NJ: Ablex.

Habel, N. (1971). *Literary criticism of the Old Testament*. Philadelphia: Fortress Press.

Hall, W. S., Cole, M., Reder, S., & Dowley, G. (1977). Variations in young children's use of language: Some effects of setting and dialect. In R. O. Freedle (Ed.), *Discourse production and comprehension*. Norwood, NJ: Ablex.

Havelock, E. A. (1963). *Preface to Plato*. Cambridge: Harvard University Press.

Havelock, E. A. (1982). *The literate revolution in Greece and its cultural consequences*. Princeton: Princeton University Press.

Heath, S. B. (1982). What no bedtime story means: Narrative skills at home and school. *Language in Society, 11*, 49–76.

Heath, S. B. (1983). *Ways with words: Language, life, and work in communities and classrooms*. Cambridge: Cambridge University Press.

Hill, C. & Varenne, H. (1981). Family language and education: The sociolinguistic model of restricted and elaborated codes. *Social Science Information, 20,* 187–227.

Hornstein, N. & Lightfoot, D. (1981). *Explanation in linguistics: The logical problem of language acquisition.* London: Longman.

Hymes, D. (1981). *"In vain I tried to tell you": Essays in Native American Ethnopoetics.* Philadelphia: University of Pennsylvania Press.

Hymes, D. (1982). Narrative form as a "grammar" of experience: Native Americans and a glimpse of English. *Journal of Education, 164,* 121–142.

Jakobson, R. (1978). *Selected writings: III. Poetry of grammar and grammar of poetry. On Verse, its masters and explorers.* Hawthorne, New York: Mouton.

Kenner, H. (1971). *The Pound era.* Berkeley: University of California Press.

Labov, W. (1970). The logic of nonstandard English. In F. Williams (Ed.), *Language and poverty.* Chicago: Markham (also in Labov, 1972).

Labov, W. (1972). *Language in the inner city.* Philadelphia: University of Pennsylvania Press.

Ladd, R. D. (1980). *Intonational meaning.* Bloomington: Indiana University Press.

Lakoff, G., & Johnson, M. (1980). *Metaphors we live by.* Chicago: University of Chicago Press.

Levi-Strauss, C. (1978). *Myth and meaning.* New York: Schocken Books.

Lord, A. B. (1960) *The singer of tales.* Cambridge: Harvard University Press.

Michaels, S. (1981). "Sharing time": Children's narrative styles and differential access to literacy. *Language in Society, 10,* 423–442.

Michaels, S., & Collins, J. (1984). Oral discourse styles: Classroom interaction and the acquisition of literacy. In D. Tannen (Ed.), *Coherence in spoken and written discourse* 219–244. Norwood, NJ: Ablex.

Michaels, S. & Cook-Gumperz, J. (1979). A study of sharing time with first-grade students: Discourse narratives in the classroom. In *Proceedings of the fifth annual meetings of the Berkeley Linguistics Society.*

Olson, D. (1977). From utterance to text: The bias of language in speech and writing. *Harvard Educational Review, 47,* 257–281.

Ong, W. J. (1982). *Orality and literacy: The technologizing of the word.* London: Methuen.

Pattison, R. (1982). *On literacy: The politics of the word from Homer to the age of Rock.* Oxford: Oxford University Press.

Piattelli-Palmarini, M. (Ed.) (1980). *Language and learning: The debate between Jean Piaget and Noam Chomsky.* Cambridge: Harvard University Press.

Poole, M. E., & Field, T. W. (1976). A comparison of oral and written code elaboration. *Language and Speech, 19,* 305–311.

Reddy, M. J. (1979). The conduit metaphor—as a case of frame conflict in our language about language. In A. Ortony (Ed.), *Metaphor and thought.* Cambridge: Cambridge University Press.

Reed, C. E. (1981). Teaching teachers about teaching writing to students from varied linguistics, social and cultural groups. In M. F. Whiteman (Ed.), *Writing: The nature, development and teaching of written communication.* Hillsdale, NJ: Lawrence Erlbaum.

Scholes, R., & Kellogg, R. (1966). *The nature of narrative.* Oxford: Oxford University Press.

Scollon, R., & Scollon, S.B.K. (1979). *Linguistic convergence: An ethnography of speaking at Fort Chipewyan, Alberta.* New York: Academic Press.

Scollon, R. & Scollon, S.B.K. (1981) Narrative, Literacy and Face in Interethnic Communication, Norwood, NJ: Ablex.

Scollon, R., & Scollon, S.B.K. (1984). Cooking it up and boiling it down: Abstracts in Athabaskan children's story retellings. In D. Tannen (Ed.), *Coherence in spoken and written discourse* 173–200. Norwood, NJ: Ablex.

Scribner, S., (1979). Modes of thinking and ways of speaking: Culture and logic reconsidered. In R. O. Freedle (Ed.), *New directions in discourse processing* (Vol. 2) Norwood, NJ: Ablex.

Scribner, S., & Cole, M. (1981). *The psychology of literacy.* Cambridge: Harvard University Press.

Selkirk, L. (1984). *Phonology and syntax: The relation between sound and structure.* Cambridge: M.I.T. Press.

Sherzer, J. (1983). *Kuna ways of speaking: An ethnographic perspective.* Austin: University of Texas Press.

Smith, F. (1975). The relations between spoken and written language. In E.H. Lenneberg & E. Lenneberg (Eds), *Foundations of language development: A multidisciplinary approach.* New York: Academic Press.

Stacy, R. H. (1977). *Defamiliarization in language and literature.* Syracuse: Syracuse University Press.

Sternberg, M. (1978). *Expositional modes and temporal ordering in fiction.* Baltimore: Johns Hopkins University Press.

Tannen, D. (1980). A comparative analysis of oral narrative strategies. In W. L. Chafe (Ed.), *The pear stories: Cognitive, cultural, and linguistic aspects of narrative production.* Norwood, NJ: Ablex.

Tannen, D. (1981). Implications of the oral / literate continuum for cross-cultural communication. In J. Alatis (Ed.), *Current issues in bilingualism: Georgetown University round table on languages and linguistics 1980.* Washington, DC: Georgetown University Press.

Tannen, D. (1982a). Oral and literate strategies in spoken and written narratives. *Language, 58,* 1–21.

Tannen, D. (Ed.) (1982b). *Spoken and written language: Exploring orality and literacy.* Norwood, NJ: Ablex.

Tannen, D. (Ed.). (1984). *Coherence in spoken and written discourse.* Norwood, NJ: Ablex.

Tedlock, D. (1978). *Finding the center: Narrative poetry of the Zuni Indians.* Lincoln: University of Nebraska Press.

Tedlock, D. (1983). *The spoken word and the work of interpretation.* Philadelphia: University of Pennsylvania Press.

White, H. (1981). The value of narrativity in the representation of reality. In W. J. T. Mitchell (Ed.), *On narrative.* Chicago: University of Chicago Press.

Woodward, J. (1982). *How you gonna get to heaven if you can't talk with Jesus: On depathologizing deafness.* Silver Spring, MD: T. J. Publishers.

## APPENDIX

Following is the text of L's story (Puppy-1). It comes from the research data of Sarah Michaels (see Michaels, 1981; Michaels & Collins, 1984; Michaels & Cook-Gumperz, 1979). Tone group boundaries are indicated as major ("//") or minor (the tone group occurs on a separate line followed by no symbol). Tone groups are segments of the text with a single continuous intonational contour. Major tone groups end with some indication of closure; minor tone groups signal "more to come" (see Brazil, Coulthard, 1980; Gumperz, 1982). While I have indicated pausing (". ." indicating a break in timing and ". . ." indicating a measurable pause) and vowel elongation (":"), I have left out other prosodic markings (marking of pitch contours and pitch levels for instance). Though these latter are crucial to any full understanding of what L is doing, they are not central to our analysis here except as they determine the boundaries marked as "//" or line ends. L uses "//" as the marker of an end of an episode, to mark change of speakers, and to mark the end of a parenthetical remark, though this mark does not appear to be obligatory. L may not have finished her text where it terminates here. She started to continue with "he's" but was interrupted by the teacher with the question "Who's in the hospital L—?" A discussion ensued about what the word "vicious" means (L had answered the teacher's question with "the dog, he vicious about my house"), followed by further questioning by the teacher. That this text did have some unity for L is indicated by the fact that in the discussion with the teacher she very briefly summarizes the entire text over again. L's remark to the teacher shows that she is well aware the story is about the conflict between the puppy and the home.

Puppy-2, which follows Puppy-1 in the Appendix, is a version of L's story that makes clear her lines and stanzas (see analysis above). I have left spaces between the stanzas in Puppy-1 as well.

### PUPPY-1

1. L:a:st
2. last
3. yesterday
4. when
5. uh
6. m' my fa:ther
7. in the morning
8. an' he
9. there was a ho:ok
10. on the top o' the stairway
11. an' my father was pickin' me up
12. an' I got stuck on the hook
13. up there

14. an' I hadn't had breakfast
15. he wouldn't take me down =
16. until I finished a:ll my breakfast=
17. cause I didn't like oatmeal either //

18. an' then my puppy came
19. he was asleep
20. an' he was — he was
21. he tried to get up
22. an' he ripped my pa:nts
23. an' he dropped the oatmeal 'all over hi:m

24. an'
25. an' my father came
26. an' he said "did you eat all the oatmeal"
27. he said "where's the bo:wl" //
28. he said "I think the do
29. I said
30. "I think the dog . . . took it" //
31. "well
32. I think I'll have t' make another can" //

33. an' so I didn't leave till seven
34. an' I took the bus
35. an'
36. my puppy
37. he always be following . me
38. he said
39. uh
40. my father said
41. um
42. "he — you can't go //

43. an' he followed me all the way to the bus stop
44. an' i hadda go all the way back
45. by that time it was seven thirty //
46. an' then he kept followin' me back and forth =
47. an' I hadda keep comin' back //
48. an' he always be followin' me =
49. when I go anywhere
50. he wants to go to the store
51. an' only he could not go t' pla:ces
52. whe:re
53. we could go
54. like
55. to:
56. like
57. t' the stores
58. he could go =
59. but he have t' be chained up

60. an' we took him to the eme:rgency
61. an' see what was wro:ng with him
62. an' he got a sho:t
63. an' then he was cry:in'

64. an' . . . la
65. last yesterda:y
66. an'
67. now
68. they put him asleep
69. an'
70. he's still in 'e ho:spital
71. an' the doctor said that he hasta
72. he got a shot because he:
73. he was
74. he was ne:rvous
75. about my home that I had

76. an' he
77. an' he could still stay but
78. he thought he wasn't gonna be a
79. he thought he wasn't gonna be able =
80. t' let him go: //

PUPPY-2

Part 1: INTRODUCTION
    Part 1A: SETTING

1. Last yesterday in the morning
2. there was a hook on the top of the stairway
3. an' my father was pickin' me up
4. an I got stuck on the hook up there

5. an' I hadn't had breakfast
6. he wouldn't take me down =
7. until I finished all my breakfast =
8. cause I didn't like oatmeal either //

Part 1B: CATALYST

9. an' then my puppy came
        10. he was asleep

11. he tried to get up
12. an' he ripped my pants
13. an' he dropped the oatmeal all over him
14. an' my father came
    15. an he said "did you eat all the oatmeal?"
    16. he said "where's the bowl?" //
    17. I said "I think the dog took it" //
    18. "Well I think I'll have t'make another bowl" //

Part 2: CRISIS
    Part 2A: COMPLICATING ACTIONS

19. an' so I didn't leave till seven
20. an' I took the bus
21. an' my puppy he always be following me
22. my father said "he — you can't go" //

23. an' he followed me all the way to the bus stop
24. an' I hadda go all the way back
    (25. by that time it was seven thirty) //
26. an' then he kept followin' me back and forth =
27. an' I hadda keep comin' back //

Part 2B: NON-NARRATIVE SECTION (EVALUATION)

28. an' he always be followin' me = when I go anywhere
29. he wants to go to the store
30. an' only he could not go to places where we could go
31. like to the stores he could go = but he have to be chained up

Part 3: RESOLUTION
    Part 3A: CONCLUDING EPISODES

32. an' we took him to the emergency
33. an' see what was wrong with him
34. an' he got a shot
35. an' then he was crying

36. an' last yesterday, an' now they put him asleep
37. an' he's still in the hospital
38. (an' the doctor said . . .) he got a shot because
39. he was nervous about my home that I had

    Part 3B: CODA
40. an' he could still stay but
41. he thought he wasn't gonna be able to let him go //

---

# 6

---

## HEARING THE CONNECTIONS
## IN CHILDREN'S ORAL AND
## WRITTEN DISCOURSE

Sarah Michaels

Recent work in discourse analysis has focused attention on the similarities and differences in the language of written and oral texts (Chafe, 1982; Redeker, 1984; Rubin, 1980; Tannen, 1982). Researchers in education have recognized the value of this work in characterizing more precisely what forms and functions of language children must master in making the transition to literacy (Cook-Gumperz & Gumperz, 1982: Danielewicz, 1984). However, much less attention has been paid to the similarities and differences in the interpretive processes at work as listeners and readers understand and respond to oral and written texts. In classroom contexts in particular, we have much still to understand about the role teachers play in interpreting, shaping, and evaluating—on the spot—the oral and written language of students, and the results this has on students' literacy development.

In this chapter, I want to begin to explore this question by looking in detail at two contrasting occasions of teacher response to students' discourse. In one case, I will analyze a first grader's oral narrative at "sharing time" (known as "show and tell" in some classrooms) and in the second case, a sixth grader's written composition and one-on-one writing conferences with the teacher. In

Work on this chapter has been supported by the Microcomputers and Literacy project, funded by the National Institute of Education (Grant #G-83-0051). John Strucker, a research assistant on this project, provided fieldnotes and tape recordings of the various phases of writing and conferencing in the sixth grade classroom. Special thanks to Mrs. Jones, Mrs. Stone, and Deena and Elliott for making this analysis possible.

each case, I will look in detail at the student's text as well as the response, shaping, and evaluation of the discourse by the teacher.

These occasions of student discourse and teacher response were observed and recorded at different times, at different grade levels, and in different parts of the country. Because this is a case study focusing on only two examples, it is necessary to specify how these texts were selected and how representative they are of regular classroom practices.[1]

First of all, it is important to note that these cases are examples of problematic interactions between teacher and child. As will be seen, each case entails some misunderstanding as well as attempts at clarification by both teacher and child. I have selected problematic examples because it is in cases of interpretive discord or breakdown that the very processes that fail become highlighted. In problematic cases, it is often easier to see the systematic nature of classroom discourse processes and the interactional work that generally goes unnoticed in smooth exchanges.

While these two cases are not representative of all sharing time turns or all writing/conferencing events, both are nonetheless fully representative of recurring patterns of interaction noted in each classroom. The sharing time example was observed and recorded in 1980 and was first analyzed as part of a study of sharing time as "oral preparation for literacy," based on recordings of over 60 sharing time sessions throughout the school year. (See Michaels, 1981, for a discussion of this example in an article focusing on children's differing narrative styles.) This particular sharing time turn was representative of the discourse of the black girls in this class and of the problems the teacher had throughout the year with the black children.

The writing/conferencing example was observed and recorded in the fall of 1984, in the context of a study of computers used for writing in an urban sixth-grade classroom. The sequence of events and exchanges that took place between student and teacher (writing / conferencing / revising) was fully typical of the procedure all students engaged in in this classroom when completing a piece of teacher-assigned writing. The particular problems evidenced in this example have been noted frequently with other students in this classroom.

Finally, both sharing time activities and writing / conferencing activities are common practices in classrooms throughout the country. They do not always occur precisely in the fashion of these cases, but these examples bear enough family resemblance to other occasions of teacher response to students' oral and written discourse to warrant contrastive analysis—as a first attempt to study similarities and differences.

In what follows, I will first present the sharing time example and then the writing example. In order to contextualize the student's discourse, I will describe briefly the classroom speech activity and the teacher's phrasing of the specific task the student was asked to perform on the occasion under consideration. Following a discussion of the examples, I will discuss similarities and differences between them and general principles emerging from this case study. I will end by raising questions about how these findings can be made useful to teachers.

## EXAMPLE 1: DEENA'S SHARING TIME TURN

In a study of an integrated first-grade classroom in northern California, "sharing time" was a whole-group activity that took place each morning.[2] It was an activity in which students were allowed to talk at some length about "out-of-school" topics—a past event or an object brought from home. Student contributions were a kind of "oral text" in the form of a monologue to the class. The teacher, however, played an active role as primary listener and responder, interjecting questions and comments. Sharing time turns thus had both a monologic (child-structured) and dialogic (primarily teacher-structured) component.

Systematic analysis of teacher / child collaboration at sharing time suggests that the teacher provided certain kinds of assistance or "scaffolding" (Cazden, 1983) through questions and comments to the sharer. The teacher's scaffold often helped the child elaborate, clarify, and make lexically explicit his or her ideas, eliciting talk that was similar to literate-like descriptive prose. In this sense, sharing time was a speech event which could serve as "oral preparation for literacy." The teacher's contributions, however, proved to be a more successful scaffold in some cases than in others. With some children, the teacher's questions and comments served to elicit more complex and lexically explicit descriptive discourse; with others the teacher's assistance seemed to "derail" the child, interrupting the sharer and eliciting fragmented responses which did not build on or extend the child's original topic. (See Michaels, 1981, and Michaels & Collins, 1984, for a summary of the California study and Michaels & Cazden, 1986, for a report on a replication of this study in the Boston area.)

The sharing time turn transcribed below was recorded during the last month of the 1979–1980 school year. Deena,* the child sharing, was a 6-year-old black girl from a working-class family. She had participated willingly and frequently at sharing time throughout the year. On the basis of her many sharing time performances, her teacher, Mrs. Jones, described Deena as a child whose sharing time talk was "long and rambling, moving from one thing to the next." She saw this as a problem of planning, saying that Deena was always "talking off the top of her head" and simply didn't take the time to "plan what she wanted to say in advance." To forestall this possibility, Mrs. Jones began this turn with very clear instructions to Deena as to what she considered an appropriate sharing time topic, saying, "Deena, I want you to share some one thing that's very important, one thing," said with emphasis on "one thing." Late in the year, when this turn was recorded, students were often asked simply to share from where they were on the rug, rather than go and stand in front of the group.

*All the teachers and students referred to in this chapter have been given pseudonyms.

**Deena's Sharing Time Turn³**

(1)    Teacher:  Deena / I want you to share some- one thing / that's very important //
(2)              one thing // from where you are // ... is that where you were? //
(3)    Deena:    No //
(4)    Teacher:  OK (chuckles) //
(5)    Deena:    um ... in the su:mme:r /
(6)              ...I mean/ ...w-when um / I go back to school/
(7)              I come back to schoo:l /
(8)              in Septe:mber /
(9)              ...I'ma ha:ve a new co:at /
(10)             and I already got it //
(11)             ...and / ...it's / ...u:m... (...)got a lot of bro:wn in it //
(12)             ...a:nd / ...when-/ um / and I got it ye:sterday /...
(13)             ...and when...I saw it / my um...my mother was...was going
                 some... where /
(14)             ...when my...when I saw it /...on the cou:ch /and I showed my
                 sister /
(15)             and I was readin' somethin' out on...on the ba:g /
(16)             and my bi:g sister said ⌈(...)
(17)    Child:                           ⌊um close the door
(18)    Deena:   my big sister said / Deena you have to keep that away / from Keisha /
(19)             'cause that's my baby sister/
(20)             and I said no//
(21)             ...and I said the plastic ba:g /
(22)             ...because/ ...um/ ...when...u:m/ ...sh-when the um..
(23)             she was u:m (with me) / wait a minute /
(24)             ...my cou:sin and ⌈her (...)
(25)    Teacher:               ⌊wait a minute // you stick with your coat now //
(26)             I s-said you could tell one thing // ...that's fair//
(27)    Deena:   this was about my ⌈coat
(28)    Teacher:                   ⌊OK/ ⌈alright / go on
(29)    Deena:                          ⌊this was-
(30)             and today/ and yesterday when I ...got my coat /
(31)             my cou:sin ran outsi:de / and he (..) ran to tried to get him /
(32)             and he / he he start- /...an' when he get in- when he got in my house /
(33)             ...he layed on the floor / and I told him to ge:t up because he was
                 cry:in //
(34)    Teacher: mm-what's that have to do with your coat? //
(35)    Deena:   ⌈h-he..becau- he wanted to go outside / but we...couldn't //
                 (exasperated)
(36)    Teacher: why?//
(37)    Deena:   'cau:se my mother s-wanted us to stay in the house //
(38)    Teacher: what does that have to do with your coat? //
(39)    Deena:   bec- it um...
(40)    Child:   (whispers)
(41)    Deena:   because /.....I don't know //
(42)    Teacher: OK (chuckles) // ⌈thank you very much Deena //
(43) Children:                    ⌊(talking)
(44)    Teacher: OK / do you understand what I am trying to do? // Deena?/
(45)             I was trying to get her to stick with one /...thing //
(46)             and she was talking about her .../
(47) Children:  coat //
(48)    Teacher: ne:w.../
(49) Children:  coat //
(50)    Teacher: coat // it sounds nice Deena //

In this example, Deena begins her turn in line 5, explaining that she has already gotten a new coat that she will be wearing when she returns to school in the fall. In lines 5–11, Deena provides a nonnarrative topic statement ("new coat") and brief description. Prosodically, her discourse is rythmically chunked, and is marked by vowel elongation and high holding pitches with no sharp intonational contours.

In line 12, her discourse changes rhythmically and prosodically into Deena's more typical narrative style (which I identified in narrative accounts during sharing time as well as in peer–peer conversations outside the classroom). As Deena shifts into narrative prosody, there is a corresponding shift in verb tense as well, from future- and present-tense verbs to simple narrative past. It appears that the early talk about her coat serves as a preamble or descriptive aside, setting the scene for a narrative account. There is further evidence that the preamble is separate from her narrative in that Deena says, "yesterday" with a marked rise–fall intonational contour in line 12. "Yesterday" with this intonational cue is used frequently by the children as a sharing time *formula* at the very beginning of a narrative account.[4] In Deena's case, however, the formula occurs in the middle of her talk, just as she begins the narrative proper.

In the narrative segment, Deena orients the action temporally and spatially (yesterday, at home), and adds the information that her "mother was goin' somewhere." She introduces her two sisters and recounts their discussion about keeping the plastic bag (presumably the one covering her new coat) away from her baby sister. It appears that the teacher hears Deena's talk about the plastic bag and her sisters as peripheral but still loosely related to the topic of her new coat. But in line 24, when Deena begins to talk about her cousin, the teacher loses the thematic thread completely and interrupts her, telling her to stick with her original topic, the new coat. This begins the dialogic segment of Deena's turn.

In line 27, Deena responds to the teacher's objections, saying that the talk about her cousin is in fact related to her coat. She even tries to make this connection explicit by saying, "and yesterday when I got my coat, my cousin ran outside." However, for Mrs. Jones, who is looking for lexically explicit talk on a single topic, a narrative listing of temporally contiguous events is inappropriate. Mrs. Jones asks two more times, "What does that have to do with your coat?" Finally in line 41, with a sigh of frustration, Deena says, "I don't know" and sits down.

For Mrs. Jones, Deena's shift from the coat to her sisters and then cousin was a violation of her sharing time expectations and instructions to "talk about one thing that's very important." In repeatedly asking Deena "What does that have to do with your coat?" she was indirectly instructing her not to include anything at all about her cousin or her sisters, but rather to stick to a simple description of her coat. She makes her intention explicit in lines 44–50, directed both at Deena and at the class at large.

The teacher, it appears, was unable to follow Deena's prosodic cues signaling a shift from preamble to narrative, and could hear no overarching connection between the coat and the anecdotal accounts of her sisters and her cousin.[5] In an interview, she indicated that she interpreted Deena's "shifts" as free associations from one topic to another, thought up on the spur of the moment so that Deena could continue talking. This impression was reinforced by Deena's inability to explain the connection between her cousin and her coat when asked point-blank to do so.

Things looked quite different from Deena's perspective. As I have discussed elsewhere (Michaels, 1981), and as Gee discusses in Chapter 7, the narrative style used by Deena and other working-class black students at sharing time entails the complex development of a theme through a series of related episodes. This "topic associating" or "episodic" style (Michaels & Cazden, 1986) allows for shifts in time, place, or characters across major episode boundaries. A thematic focus is present and thematic progression is systematically signaled prosodically and through lexical and syntactic parallelism; however, the overall point must be inferred by the listener from the series of concrete anecdotes. An important theme is developed—if one is able to "hear" the connections.

In an interview in which I played the tape for Deena, she was able to verbalize and clarify many of the unstated connections in her sharing time turn. When asked about the link between her baby sister and the coat, Deena hesitated momentarily whereupon her 10-year-old sister (also present during the interview) said, "My mama say keep plastic out of Keisha's reach, 'cause she might put it over her head." Deena promptly agreed. She explained the link between her cousin and her new coat by saying that her 3-year-old cousin was "a bad little boy, and when he came back in the house he started to put his hands on my coat, and his hands was *dirty!*" Thus it appears that Deena saw connections between the coat and the two subtopics in the narrative, her baby sister and her cousin. In one case, she was protecting a young child in her care from the coat (bag) and, in the other case, she was protecting the coat from a young, messy child.

Whether Deena could have made these links explicit had the teacher not interrupted her is of course moot. The important point is that rather than help her clarify and extend her complex rhetorical goals, the teacher's probes elicited more fragmented and less coherent discourse. At sharing time, Deena and Mrs. Jones seemed to be at cross purposes. Mrs. Jones was looking for simple, prose-like description (similar to that in the preamble) on a single topic, organized in such a way that it sounded "important." Deena, however, intended to develop the theme of her new coat through a series of personal narrative accounts, as if to highlight the importance of her new coat by showing its reflection in the experience of key family members.

Each was working with her own sharing time expectations; without a shared sense of task and a mutually shared set of narrative strategies, collaboration was unsuccessful. The teacher's "assistance" was seen by Deena as interruptive, unappreciative, and confusing. Mrs. Jones' indirect attempts at instruction were misinterpreted. (In the interview, Deena said she interpreted Mrs. Jones' question "What does that have to do with your coat?" as a request to say *more* about her cousin.) Deena's use of topic centered discourse (in the preamble) was not appreciated, nor was her discourse seen as organized and well-planned. Misevaluations such as these, on the part of both teacher and child, may explain in part why children's "topic associating" strategies at sharing time persisted over time, despite the fact that children like Deena got frequent opportunities to share and were generally able learners, as shown by their improvement over the course of the year in other literacy-related skills such as spelling.

While it is easy here to sympathize with Deena, my point is that successful collaboration between teacher and child requires both a shared goal (based on a common view of what "good" sharing time talk is) and a shared set of interpretive strategies for giving a personal descriptive account. Teachers' unquestioned and often unconscious concern with topic centered discourse leads to expectations and "ways of hearing" that put students like Deena at a disadvantage. Rather than building on the rich narrative competence of these children, teachers try to shape their complex ideas into a simple structure. And as the example with Deena suggests, these attempts are often unsuccessful. But even more unfortunate, this concern with form is often interpreted as a devaluing of the student's ideas. Deena indicated this poignantly when asked how she felt about sharing time. She responded, "Sharing time got on my nerves. She was always interruptin' me, sayin' 'that's not *important* enough,' and I hadn't hardly started talkin'!"

## EXAMPLE 2: WRITING AND CONFERENCING IN A SIXTH-GRADE CLASSROOM

The second example comes from an ongoing study of writing in a multi-ethnic sixth-grade classroom in the greater Boston area, where a computer with QUILL writing software had been introduced (Cazden, Michaels, & Watson-Gegeo, 1983). In Brenda Stone's sixth-grade classroom, there were 16 students. Most were from working-class minority backgrounds, including American and Jamaican blacks and first- and second-generation Portuguese immigrant children. Writing in this classroom was a regularly occurring series of activities. Early drafts of teacher-assigned writing were done on paper, and were edited by the teacher in a series of writing conferences. Final drafts were then entered on the computer.

Taken together, writing and conferencing in this classroom present an interesting analog to the sharing time activity described above. Students were expected to produce a written text in response to the teacher's assignment, which in most cases narrowly prescribed both topic and genre. After completing a first draft on paper, students were expected to show their compositions to the teacher, who made corrections in red ink, asked questions about the students' ideas, and made suggestions for improvement—often both orally and by writing on the paper. Thus, as in sharing time, writing / conferencing activities in this classroom involved both a monologic text and a teacher-structured dialogue, intended to clarify and structure the student's discourse. What follows is a detailed look at the production of a piece of writing in this classroom, tracing it through a series of drafts and teacher / student writing conferences.

## THE CIRCUS COMPOSITIONS

In October 1984, Brenda Stone's entire class took a field trip to the Barnum and Bailey Circus. Several students had never been to the circus before. The next school day, the students were told that they would be writing about this experience. In a pre-writing "brainstorming" session with the whole class, Mrs. Stone summarized their writing task as follows: "Whatever your favorite part of the circus would be, a particular act (pause), think of some title that would be an appropriate title for your composition." Later, as the students were beginning to write, she reiterated the task: "Right now you should be putting an act at the top of the page; that's what I want you to focus on." Still later, she reminded the students to "stick to one particular act," telling them to write "about two or three paragraphs to go with that one particular act." Just as in sharing time, where the teacher repeatedly urged students to talk about just one thing, so in this writing assignment Mrs. Stone made clear to the students that they were to write about just one thing about the circus.

## ELLIOTT'S COMPOSITION—THE PINK PANTHER ACT

Elliott Brown was described by Mrs. Stone as "the classroom bully" due to personal problems he was having at home, where he lived with a foster mother while his real mother underwent rehabilitation therapy for a drug problem. He was a tall, light brown-skinned boy who looked part Hispanic or black, but who was classified by his previous teacher as "white." His English evidenced many dialect features of urban working-class speech, and showed some influence from Black English Vernacular. Examples of topic associating strategies were evident in his written and oral discourse.

Elliott's first draft of his circus composition read as follows:[6]

Elliott Brown                                                    Oct 22, 1984
                              The Pink Panther Act
I liked the Pink Panther Act very much. Because he is my favorite character. I've seen him on T.V. cartoons and movies. Where he is not on. But there a man named Inspector Clooseau. Who is trying to catch the Pink Panther. The movies are in color as in cartoon. When he's in the circus the best act is when he is on a three wheeler and two men are chasing him on motorcycles. And they are chasing him all around the areana. I really liked the circus alot. It was amazing. [sic]

Elliott's piece begins with an evaluation of the Pink Panther act. He assumes shared knowledge on the reader's part that the act was one of many at the circus. Elliott then shifts markedly to a discussion of the Pink Panther character in another medium—specifically the Pink Panther movies, which star Peter Sellers as Inspector Clouseau. This appears to be embedded background information, explaining more about the Pink Panther character to clarify his significance in the circus or at least his significance to Elliott. Corresponding to this shift in topic, Elliott shifts from the simple past tense ("I liked the Pink Panther act very much") to past perfect and present tense description of the Pink Panther's unusual status in these movies ("where he is not on"). There is no overt marker of this shift to background information. (Elliott might have made this shift lexically explicit by saying something like, "Not only is the Pink Panther a character in the circus, I've also seen him on . . ." Alternatively, the information could have been signaled as background information graphically, through the use of parentheses).

Elliott then returns to the topic of the circus, this time signaled syntactically by the adverbial clause "When he's in the circus." However, this transition is not as clear to a reader as it would be had it been indented as the beginning of a new paragraph or if the Pink Panther had been renominalized as the focus, rather than referred to as "he." In this segment, Elliott describes the best act involving the Pink Panther in the circus, and ends with a return to simple past tense verbs and two evaluative statements, now providing evaluation of the circus as a whole.

Thus we see in this piece a shift from circus to TV and movies and a concomitant shift from the Pink Panther to Inspector Clouseau. However, transitions are not signaled graphically through paragraphing, parentheses, or redundant uses of format, punctuation, and syntax. Moreover, the rhetorical significance of the shift from the circus to the movies is never explicitly stated.

Once this draft was completed, Elliott approached Mrs. Stone's desk to be conferenced. Mrs. Stone began reading his composition, but stopped suddenly and said, "Elliott, this says, 'he's my favorite character. I've seen him on TV, cartoons, and movies, where he is not on'"? She said it with puzzlement in her voice, emphasizing "where he is not on". Elliott responded, "You know, some of the movies, he's not on and it's Inspector Clouseau . . ." Mrs. Stone interrupted with mild impatience, saying, "Then why would he be on? I don't understand. You explain it to me. It says "I've seen him on TV, cartoons, and movies where he is not on?'" (again emphasizing with questioning intonation "where he is not on").

At this point, the researcher (who had already talked to Elliott about his composition when he was asked to help spell "Inspector Clouseau") came over and attempted to intercede for Elliott. He said, "Elliott, do you mean in some of the movies they call it the Pink Panther, but they're really about Inspector Clouseau?" Elliott nodded and looked back at Mrs. Stone. At this point, Mrs. Stone paused, looked again at his paper, and then seemed to come to some understanding of the complex idea Elliott was grappling with. She tried to re-phrase it, but she herself had a hard time of it, saying, "The ones they call the Pink Panther, they're something else but they're really about the detective but he is not in it. Is that what you want to say?" Elliott nodded. She then in-structed him to take the entire part about Inspector Clouseau out and explain it "in another sentence of its own." The researcher offered a possible way of phrasing it, saying, "They show the cartoon of the Pink Panther at the begin-ning of the movie and then they go into the movie and it's about Inspector Clouseau." In addition, Mrs. Stone suggested that Elliott reorganize the com-position, explaining first about the circus and "then in your next paragraph ex-plain that you've also seen the Pink Panther on TV, cartoons, and movies, and use this as your example."

In addition to correcting the mechanics on Elliot's draft in a few places (adding commas and changing a capital "b" to a small "b"), Mrs. Stone had circled the section about Inspector Clouseau and had written directly above this in red ink, "Elliott, rewrite. Explain. Read this to yourself." At the top of the page, she also wrote, "Elliott, rewrite explaining the circled section clearly. Save this paper." Mrs. Stone asked him to do the rewrite of the con-fusing section first and then return for another conference. The field notes describing this interaction record the fact that following Mrs. Stone's in-structions, "Elliott gritted his teeth. Once back at his chair he slumped" (Field notes 10/22/84).

Back at his desk, the first thing Elliott did was to mark off with parenthe-ses the entire section about seeing the Pink Panther on TV and in movies. He then added two sentences to his original draft in the skipped lines of this sec-tion. These sentences read: "Where they show a little of him in the begin-ning but not in the movie. So the movies is named after him but not about him." As he wrote this, he inserted arrows to indicate that the text did not read from line to line, but skipped down a line (with the old text interspersed with the newly composed lines). He spent approximately 15 minutes work-ing on these lines, erasing and rewriting. He also circled the description of the Pink Panther's activities in the circus and separated off with parentheses the final sentences "I really liked the circus alot. It was amazing." It appears that these marks were made in preparation for rewriting and resequencing this information in draft.[2]

Following the writing and conferencing period, Mrs. Stone led another whole-group discussion based on her impressions of the students' writing that she had seen. She made a specific point of urging everyone to begin their com-position by telling when they saw the circus and which circus it was. In re-sponse to this, Elliott added a line between his title and his opening sentence to say, "Our class went to see the Barnum and Baily Circus."

The next day, Elliott wrote his second draft, again as a single paragraph, spending the bulk of his time working on the section about the Pink Panther in the movies. His completed draft read as follows:

Elliott Brown                                               Oct 23, 1984
### The Pink Panther Act
On October 19, 1984 Our classroom went to see the Barnum and Baily Circus it was lots of fun. I liked the Pink Panther Act very much, he was my favorite character. The best part I think is when he is on a three wheeler and two men are chasing him on dirt bikes and they are chasing him all around the areana. I've seen the Pink Panther on T.V. cartoons, and movies where it is not about him but the movie is named after him. But where they show a little of him in the beginning but not in the movie. I really liked the Circus alot. it was amazing.


Note that in this second draft, Elliott has indeed clarified his ideas about the Pink Panther's minor role in the movies. However, gone is the reference to Inspector Clouseau and, along with it, the subtle connection between the Pink Panther being chased in the circus and being chased by Inspector Clouseau in the movies. The writing conference, of course, did not focus on this connection. Rather, the issue discussed was Mrs. Stone's confusion over Elliott's sentence "I've seen him on T.V., cartoons and movies, where he is not on."

While the subtle "chase" connection between the character in the circus and in the movies was never explicitly stated in Elliott's first draft (in one case the verb "chase" appeared, in the other the verb "catch" was used), the kernel was there. It appears that neither the researcher nor the teacher noticed the implicit link when reading his first draft. In any case, neither tried to help Elliott clarify it or explain the point of such a link. (This is akin to Mrs. Jones's reaction to Deena's shift from her coat to her sisters. She did not help her clarify the implicit connection—that plastic bags on new coats can smother babies—and ultimately told her she should have stuck to a description of the coat.)

In Elliott's second draft, the information about the Pink Panther in the movies is accurate and reasonably clear to someone familiar with the Pink Panther films. However, it is not explicitly related to the circus. During Elliott's second conference with Mrs. Stone, she suggested that he take out the entire section beginning "and movies where . . ."—explaining that it takes him too far afield from the circus. She made a large red "X" through the entire movie section and replaced it with the words "and in the movies," so that the only sentence remaining read, "I've seen the Pink Panther on T.V. cartoons, and in the movies."

Aside from Mrs. Stone's "X", this draft had few red marks, and no written instructions other than the word "indent" at the beginning of the first paragraph. She corrected the spelling of "Bailey" and "arena" and broke one "and"-conjoined sentence into two independent clauses.

After copying this second draft (with Mrs. Stone's corrections) over as a final draft, Elliott entered his piece on the computer. He picked as his keywords (used in the QUILL program to identify pieces on a disk) the words "Three Wheeler." The computer printout was edited by Mrs. Stone for typographical errors (there were two) and Elliott made corrections using the computer's electronic text editing commands. The final printout read as follows:

### The Pink Panther Act

On October 19, 1984, our classroom went to see the Barnum and Bailey Circus. It was lots of fun. I liked the Pink Panther Act very much, he was my favorite character. The best part I think is when the Pink Panther is on a three wheeler and two men are chasing him on dirt bikes. They are chasing him all around the arena. I've seen the Pink Panther on T.V. cartoons, and in the movies. I really liked the Circus alot. It was amazing.

Elliott Brown

Keywords: / Three Wheeler /

Compared to his first draft, Elliott's final draft contained fewer mechanical errors (though some oddities remained, such as the "classroom" going to the circus). Structurally, the piece was short and concise, with temporal grounding in the beginning and evaluative statements at the end; structurally, in fact, it bore a striking resemblance to the rest of his classmates' pieces, in spite of the fact that they wrote about different circus acts. On any kind of holistic or primary trait scoring scheme, it would no doubt receive a higher score than his first draft would.

However, all of Elliott's knowledge about the Pink Panther's unusual role in the movies, Inspector Clouseau, and so forth was gone. The subtle but elegant parallel between the Pink Panther being chased in the circus and in the movies had been edited out. Moreover, the parallelism between the Pink Panther's unusual status in the movies (appearing only at the beginning, in cartoon form) and the Pink Panther's unusual status in the circus was never explicitly alluded to, though it might have been. For example, the Pink Panther character in the circus was not himself an "act" like the trapeze artists or the horses, but rather appeared at the beginning (as in the movies) and then again at infrequent intervals. He was not a real animal, in a circus of real animals doing human-like stunts, but a man dressed up as an animal (analogous to a cartoon character in a movie about real people). Finally, he served as the theme of the circus but was not really "in it" (just as the Pink Panther is the theme and namesake of the movie but not really "in it").

The kernels of all these ideas appeared in some form in Elliott's first draft (though this is not to say that Elliott himself was aware of the parallels). Only someone with firsthand knowledge of the movies, who in addition saw some of these connections in Elliott's very unclear first draft, could have helped him develop and clarify them. But most importantly, only someone who was willing to push for complex ideas over simplicity of form would have encouraged Elliott to say *more* about his knowledge of the movies and link this knowledge to his description of the circus. Mrs. Stone did give him a second chance to clarify his ideas about the movie character, but focused his attention only on one point of confusion (the fact that the Pink Panther is "in it" but "not in it"). By the second draft, some of the potential parallels, such as the "chase" connection, had already been edited out.

In an interview about Elliott's piece, Mrs. Stone said she saw the information about the movies as "off the topic of the assignment," and therefore felt that it was better left out. She did not see it as playing an integral role in explaining Elliott's appreciation of the Pink Panther in the circus, or as leading to interesting parallels. Even once these potential connections were pointed out, she felt that it was not really sticking to the assignment that she gave—to tell about one act in the circus. Only after much discussion did she reconsider her position and remark that there might have been a way for Elliott to bring in this information and still have it be about the circus.

But even a less constraining assignment or less concern with "sticking to the topic" might not have fundamentally altered Mrs. Stone's response to Elliott's first draft. On the spot, she couldn't see the connections to begin with and thus could not help him build on them. Her only alternative would have been to encourage him simply to talk and write more about his ideas about the Pink Panther in the movies; if that had happened, she might have had more rather than less to go on in the second draft.

When I interviewed Elliott about his composition and in particular about the section that he finally removed altogether, he had several interesting points to make. First of all, Elliott indicated that the section about the Pink Panther in the movie was important to him, because the Pink Panther was his "favorite character." He talked animatedly about how he used to draw him in the fourth grade and had seen all the Pink Panther movies. He added proudly that "It was probably showing that I knew more about the Pink Panther than everybody thought." Though Elliott didn't actually say this, there may have been some tension between how much he, the student, knew and how much Mrs. Stone, the teacher, knew. One wonders what Mrs. Stone's response would have been had the researcher not interceded in an attempt to clarify Elliott's original idea.

Second, Elliott indicated that he was "writing a lot about Inspector Clouseau but it was really about the Pink Panther." He explained that in order to really understand the Pink Panther, "you have to talk about Inspector Clouseau." Thus for Elliott, a description of the Pink Panther in the circus required information about the character itself, which, in turn, necessarily led to a discussion of the movie and Inspector Clouseau.

Third, when asked if he saw distinct parallels between the movie and the circus, he said he didn't. However, as soon as I mentioned that the Pink Panther was often being chased, he said, "The best part I think is when the Pink Panther is on the three wheeler and two men are chasing him on dirt bikes. They're chasing him all around the arena. And it's just like Inspector Clouseau is—is like a bounty hunter trying to catch him." I asked him if he had been thinking about that when he wrote his composition and he said, "Well, not really, but I know it now." Similarly, when other parallels were mentioned, he immediately picked up on them and extended them. For example, when I referred to the fact that the character appeared in cartoon form but wasn't featured in the movie, he added an additional parallel linking the Pink Panther cartoons (on Saturday morning TV) with the movie and circus. He said, "Like on the cartoon, Pinky and Panky [his sons in the cartoon], it's about Pinky and Panky and their friends but they hardly ever show the Pink Panther, sort of like the movie too." Thus Elliott was ripe for seeing connections, once encouraged to explore them.

Finally, when asked if he liked his piece better *with or without* the section about Inspector Clouseau and the movies, he said, "The teacher knows best. Miss Stone said for me to take it out 'cause it wasn't, it was like changing the subject. She's the teacher so I have to listen to her." Then he added softly, "But I think it would have made the story more interesting."

## DISCUSSION

The two examples discussed above involved teachers setting similar tasks and responding to students' attempts to carry them out. However, there are important differences between the texts produced—differences of both a linguistic and a social nature.

1. A written text is fixed in time and space. It can be read and reread if so desired. (In practice, Mrs. Stone generally gave a piece a quick read and an immediate response.) An oral text is temporally fleeting. It must be responded to on the fly, based on the hearer's moment-by-moment interpretation. There is no possibility of a second hearing, though the speaker is, of course, available for questioning.

2. Barriers to processing reflect the above differences in modality. In the case of written text, handwriting and the mechanics of spelling, punctuation, and sentence structure can create barriers to understanding by the teacher. In oral texts, on-line performance features such as false starts, hesitations, or faulty articulation can lead to processing problems. In addition, paralinguistic cues, such as rhythm, stress, and intonation, can have class- or community-specific functions. When teacher and student do not share the same discourse strategies for signaling prominence, contrast, or thematic progression, this creates further interpretive difficulties, as seen in Deena's case. In both modalities, the lack of shared cultural norms for telling a story, making a point, giving an explanation, and so forth can create barriers to understanding.

3. Finally, there is the issue of revision. Written text can undergo revision before it is finished. As we saw in Elliott's case, his composition changed significantly from first to final draft—in length, mechanics, and complexity. With written text, something of value can be salvaged from draft to draft and one is left holding a final product. In the case of oral sharing time texts, the teacher's questions can provide the student with an opportunity to continue, to

clarify a point, or to expand on the topic. This can serve as an opportunity for addition and revision of a limited sort; more text can be added *at the end.* However, as we saw in the sharing time case, in the face of the teacher's questions, Deena's discourse became increasingly fragmented and incoherent. Deena was repeatedly cut short and, in effect, *not* given a second chance. In oral discourse, one is not left with a revised finished product, only the sense that things went well or badly.

In spite of these differences due to modality, the two examples are striking in their similarities:

1. In each case, the teacher set forth a highly restricted task: to tell or write about *one* clearly specified topic.

2. Both students, in attempting to satisfy their teacher's demand, sought to integrate personal knowledge or experience into a descriptive account. In both cases, the students used topic associating strategies, which entailed shifts in time, characters, and linguistic forms, with no lexically explicit statement of the overall point of the integration or association of additional information. The relationship between personal knowledge in the form of anecdote and the initial topic had to be inferred by the listener or reader.

3. In each case, the student's discourse of personal knowledge or experience was unclear to the teacher, who was looking for discourse structured around a single topic.

4. In each case, the student was encouraged to leave out the text that the teacher found difficult to understand and difficult to connect to the initial topic. In the case of the oral text, the student was simply not allowed to continue. She was interrupted and cut short. In the case of the written text, the "inappropriate" section was crossed out by the teacher. Thus in both cases, the teacher had ultimate say over what "sticking to the topic" entailed.

As was mentioned at the outset, these two examples are not representative of all sharing turns or all writing / conferencing events. Both are cases where teacher and student had different discourse goals and understandings, as evidenced in the teacher's questions and attempts on the student's part to clarify his or her ideas. In each case, follow-up interviews with the student clarified still further the student's original intentions and the implicit logic in his or her discourse. However, because of the institutionally sanctioned power differential between teacher and child, the student's goals were subordinated to those of the teacher. As so often happens in classroom encounters, it was the teacher's agenda that prevailed.

Problematic examples such as these often provide the clearest picture of the systematic nature of discourse processes and the negotiation of meaning in classroom interactions. But aside from providing useful data for discourse analysts, these classroom encounters are cases where the negotiation of meaning is not merely a theoretical problem, but a practical problem with practical consequences as well. As Erickson (1975) has pointed out, modern life offers certain "gatekeeping" encounters which determine access to occupation, official redress, and educational opportunities. In classrooms, differences in goals or interpretive strategies for discourse organization assume great importance, because misunderstanding of student intent or overall performance frequently results in misevaluation of student ability, which in turn can lead to lowered expectations and differential treatment of the student.

## CONCLUSION

The two occasions of student discourse and teacher response discussed here were observed and recorded at different grade levels and in the context of different discourse activities. Nonetheless, I suggest that the features they share are no coincidence. An overarching concern with literacy and literate-like language is a pervasive institutionalized force in our schools, and it leads to similar tasks, practices, and evaluative mechanisms across different schools, grades, and subject areas.

This concern with literacy and the high value placed on literate-like language often lead to formal classroom activities in which teachers encourage students to speak or write clearly and concisely about a single topic, turning complex personal knowledge and experience into a simplified form of expository, descriptive prose. And while I have focused on the production of discourse—in sharing time or writing activities—the tendency to use simplified texts is characteristic as well of the early reading programs used throughout our public schools. The guiding assumption underlying teachers' assignment and use of restricted discourse texts appears to be that students first need to gain control over simple, "topic centered" forms of discourse *as a transition to literacy;* only then can they proceed to tackle more complex rhetorical and literary texts.

As these two examples illustrate, the teacher's push for explicitness and conciseness of *form* is often at the expense of students' rich personal knowledge. Students often begin with complex associative ideas which pose complicated rhetorical problems for the speaker or writer in integrating appropriate background information, description, actions, and conclusions. In collaborating over the production of a text, teachers and students are often working at cross purposes, with teachers driven by concerns about correct linguistic form and students driven by concerns about content. Teachers tend to interpret and evaluate student discourse against a narrowly defined literate "standard," whether the ideas are expressed orally or in writing.

In addition to specific concerns about literate forms, universal linguistic and cognitive processes also play a role in teachers' response to student discourse. Teachers, like all people, bring to the real-time interpretation of language their own knowledge of and experiences in the world as well as their own community-specific strategies for interpreting text or talk. Teachers' understanding of students' discourse is influenced by systematic interpretive processes, whereby teachers actively attend to linguistic cues (whether oral or written) as signals of discourse structure and thematic progression. In multi-ethnic classrooms the interpretive constraints facing teachers are particularly complex. They must respond, on the spot, to a large number of students from a variety of linguistic backgrounds.

As these examples suggest, it is often hard for teachers to see connections in students' oral or written discourse if the connections are implied, not explicitly stated, and the discourse is structured in an unfamiliar way. And where teachers, like the rest of us, cannot immediately see connections, they often fail to see the point the student is trying to make. They then cannot build on and extend their students' communicative intentions by helping them make the connections more explicit. Moreover, teachers' push for simple, standardized texts often puts minority speakers of nonstandard English at a disadvantage. Nonstandard forms or nonstandard strategies for topic development are often interpreted as inappropriate or incoherent ideas. Thus we see how teachers, even with the best of intentions, may fail to provide the kind of literacy assistance and practice that they intend to provide—to those students who most depend on their assistance.

I don't mean to imply that a concern with linguistic form is misguided and unnecessary. Teachers know better than anyone that their students will be evaluated on standardized tests and later on in formal interview situations that call for control over or displays of "correct," topic centered discourse. My concern is rather that the attention to formal "correctness" is often at the expense of students' ideas at the early stages of literacy training. I do not quibble with the ultimate goal of helping students gain control over a variety of language forms and styles. The question I raise has to do with the best means of achieving this goal.

There are no easy solutions to these institutional and interpretive problems facing teachers and students in literacy events. The ethnic and linguistic diversity of urban classrooms is here to stay and there is no evidence that teachers can be taught easily to monitor or alter their ways of speaking or ways of hearing. That is to say, it may always be difficult for teachers to hear the connections and logic in discourse that is organized differently from what they are expecting.

However, it is possible to institute writing and oral discourse activities where the students themselves have far more control over topic, genre, audience, and purpose. The work of Graves (1978, 1983) on writing and conferencing prescribes a very different role for the teacher than the one chosen in either of these examples. Ideally, the students select their own topics and the teacher serves as an honest but respectful listener, along with other classmates. It is the "author" who has final judgement and control, in response to suggestions and questions from teacher or peers. It is the student's communicative goals that drive the conferencing process, not the teacher's preconceived assignment.

The closest counterparts at sharing time to such an "author" centered writ-

ing program are occasional "kid-run" sharing time activities (see Michaels &
Foster, 1985, for an example). In a somewhat different vein, Moffett (1983)
has proposed small-group sharing time activities in which a general topic is
specified (such as "a trip I took" or "an object I made") and the teacher circu-
lates from group to group as a facilitator. The students have primary responsibility for running their groups and this format naturally generates more peer
response and less shaping of ideas by the teacher.

While much more systematic study of these various student centered discourse activities is needed, they do encourage teachers to relinquish their traditional role as primary audience, responder, shaper, and evaluator. This in
turn would reduce the institutional and interpretive burden on teachers, which
too often results in the problems described above. It seems reasonable to assume that there are many interactive paths toward literacy, some oral, some
written, some peer directed, some teacher directed. But in any case, the successful communication of complex ideas, rather than control over any particular discourse form, should be the driving force behind the early development
of literacy skills.

## NOTES

1. The cases of student texts and teacher / student interaction to be discussed came
out of different studies of classroom interaction. However, the methods employed in locating instances of classroom interaction for observation and tape recording were identical. Both studies used ethnographic methods of long-term participant observation,
interviewing, and analysis to locate recurring classroom activities which appeared to relate to students' access to literacy assistance (whether from peers or teacher). These
activities were then recorded on a systematic basis, and the oral or written discourse
subjected to fine-grained, linguistic analysis. (See Michaels, 1981, and Cazden,
Michaels, & Watson-Gegeo, 1983 for a more detailed discussion of methods and analytic framework.)

2. During sharing time, the first graders sat on the rug area in the central open space
of the classroom, while Mrs. Jones, their teacher, sat in front of the group in a chair.
When called on to share, a child went to the front of the group and stood close to Mrs.
Jones (who put her arm around the sharer). Students were allowed to bring in objects
from home to describe or to tell about past events. The only rules at sharing time were
(a) no sharing about TV or movies (because it takes too long) and (b) no sharing about
private family quarrels.

3. The methods I have used in analyzing prosody and the notations used in transcrib-
ing prosodic and paralinguistic cues were developed by Gumperz and his collaborators,
based on the work of J. Trim. In this example, to make for greater readability, I have
used a considerably simplified version of the notation. Speech initially is chunked into
tone group units (i.e., segments with a single, continuous intonational contour). These
units are then designated as major tone groups (ending with some indication of sentence closure, akin to a period in writing—indicated as //) or minor tone groups (signaling "more to come," akin to a comma—indicated as / ). Second, points of intonational
prominence are located; the primary peak of the one group is the nucleus. Third, pitch

contours are indicated on the tone group nucleus as follows: ╲ low fall; ╲ high fall; ╱ low rise; ╱ high rise; ∧ rise–fall; ∨ fall–rise;—level. Paralinguistic features are indicated as follows: (a) shift to high pitch register,⌐, or shift to low pitch register,└─ (both applying to the entire tone group); (b) pausing . , indicating a break in timing, and . . ., indicating a measurable pause; (c) vowel elongation,:, elongation, :, following the elongated syllable; (d) emphasis,—under the word or syllable receiving extra emphasis.

4. That this use of "yesterday" is formulaic, rather than a function of the fact that first graders like to tell about very recent events can be seen on the occasions when a child makes a mistake:

Bob: Yesterday, I mean, last year when I was in Arkansas . . .

Deena: Yesterday, I mean it was last night . . .

5. Moreover, even if Mrs. Jones could have "heard" the shift, she was not prepared to help Deena develop these connections further; her goal was to encourage a simpler (and certainly less artistic) form of talk rather than to clarify and build on Deena's complex narrative intentions.

6. In the writing period that followed, students wrote first drafts on yellow paper, skipping every other line—as prescribed in the writing method used by Mrs. Stone—so that they and she could make corrections of that draft.

## REFERENCES

Cazden, C. (1983). Peekaboo as an instructional model: Discourse development at school and at home. In B. Bain (Ed.), *The sociogenesis of language and human conduct: A multi-disciplinary book of readings*. New York: Plenum.

Cazden, C., Michaels, S., & Watson-Gegeo, K. (1983). Microcomputers and literacy: The impact of interactive technology on classroom organization, teacher-student interaction, and student writing. Unpublished proposal to NIE.

Chafe, W. (1982). Integration and involvement in speaking, writing and oral literature. In D. Tannen (Ed.), *Spoken and written language: Exploring orality and literacy.* Norwood, NJ: Ablex.

Cook-Gumperz, J., & Gumperz, J. (1982). From oral to written culture: The transition to literacy. In M. F. Whiteman (Ed.), *Writing: The nature, development, and teaching of written communication* (Vol. 1). New York: Lawrence Erlbaum Associates.

Danielewicz, J. (1984). The interaction between text and context: a study of how adults and children use spoken and written language in four contexts. In A. Pellegrini & T. Yawkey (Eds.) *The development of oral and written language in social contexts* (pp. 243–260). Norwood, N.J.: Ablex.

Erickson, F. (1975). Gate-keeping and the melting pot: Interaction in counseling interview. *Harvard Educational Review, 45,* 44–70.

Graves, D. (1978). *Balance the basics: Let them write.* New York: Ford Foundation.

Graves, D. (1983). *Writing: Teachers and children at work.* Exeter, NH: Heinemann.

Michaels, S. (1981). "Sharing time": Children's narrative styles and differential access to literacy. *Language in Society, 10,* 423–442.

Michaels, S., & Cazden, C. B. (1986). Teacher / child collaboration as oral preparation for literacy. In B. Schieffelin (Ed.), *Acquisition of literacy: Ethnographic perspectives.* Norwood, NJ: Ablex.

Michaels, S., & Collins, J. (1984). Oral discourse styles: Classroom interaction and the acquisition of literacy. In D. Tannen (Ed.), *Coherence in spoken and written discourse*. Norwood, NJ: Ablex.

Michaels, S., & Foster, M. (1985). Peer–peer learning: Evidence from a kid-run sharing time. In A. Jagger & M. Smith-Burke (Eds.), *Observing the language learner*. Urbana, IL: National Council of Teachers of English.

Moffett, J. (1983). *Teaching the universe of discourse* (2nd edition). Boston: Houghton-Mifflin.

Redeker, G. (1984). On differences between spoken and written language. *Discourse Processes, 7*(1), 43–55.

Rubin, A. (1980). A theoretical taxonomy of the differences between oral and written language. In R. J. Spiro, B. C. Bruce, & W. F. Brewer (Eds.), *Theoretical issues in reading comprehension*. 411–438. Hillsdale, NJ: Erlbaum.

Tannen, D. (1982). Oral and literate strategies in spoken and written narratives. *Language, 58*, 1–21.

# 7

# DISCOURSE SYSTEMS AND ASPIRIN BOTTLES: ON LITERACY

## James Paul Gee

When I first came into contact with adult literacy specialists, I was struck by the fact that there were people who worried about what it took to read the back of an aspirin bottle. I am a linguist who has, over the last few years, worried about the question "What is literacy?" from a relatively theoretical perspective (Gee, 1986a, 1986b, 1988, 1989). In addressing people interested in adult literacy, I am aware that as I take up this question once again I had better have something to say about aspirin bottles. I will; but it will take a while to get there.

Let me start with a simple (and oversimplified) view of what is involved in using language. In the process of planning speech, a speaker must ask him or herself (usually quite unconsciously) at least three questions:

a. What do I want to say? What information do I want to convey? How do I want my language to hook up to the world?

b. How do I want what I have to say contextualized, that is, how do I want it

A version of this chapter was delivered as an invited presentation to the National Reading Conference (Point-Counterpoint Session, "Defining Adult Literacy: Cognitive, Linguistic, and Cultural Perspectives," with Daniel Wagner chairing the session and Thomas Sticht serving as my fellow discussant), St. Petersburg, Florida, Dec. 5, 1987. I am indebted to M. Trika Smith-Burke for the invitation to address the conference. Though they may not wish to hear it upon reading the chapter, I am indebted to Sarah Michaels, Bea Mikulecky, Ruth Nickse, and Kristine Strand for discussion around topics germane to adult literacy. I need particularly to thank Jaime Wurzel of Boston University's School of Education for the data on "The Alligator River Story" task which I discuss in this chapter. He bears no blame for the use I make of it.

placed in the context of what has already been said, in the context of what I take the relationship between myself and my hearer(s) to be, and in the context of what I take us all to mutually share in the way of knowledge and beliefs?

c. What deeper themes, images, and ideas do I want to communicate about myself, my social group, or the world; that is, what "worldview" or "ideology" do I want to express?

I will treat these three questions as if they constituted three "systems" in the language planning process, three systems that are in turn reflected in the language used:

a. The "referential" ("literal meaning," "propositional") system, which has to do with literal meaning

b. The "contextualization" system, which has to do primarily with social relations

c. The "ideology" system, which has to do with values, beliefs, and worldview

Just as these three systems enter into the construction of language by the speaker, so too the hearer must "decode" each of them in order to get the full message. Any use of language simultaneously expresses all three; all three systems are inextricably mixed up together in any piece of language.

In order to give concrete examples of these three systems at work, I will look briefly at their operation in two oral "texts." I also want to demonstrate the way in which the use made of the three systems can differ across various socially defined groups. The following story, called "The Alligator River Story," is often used in "values clarification" tasks. Small groups of high school students were asked to discuss the story and to come to a consensus about how the characters should be ranked "from the most offensive to the least objectionable." At the end of the task, each group chose one student to give their group ranking to their teacher (who had not been part of the discussion) and to say why they had ranked the characters as they did. There are two responses, one given by the respondent for a group of black students (labeled "Black Students"), one by the respondent for a group of white students (labeled "White Students"). All the students went to a school with mainly lower- and lower-middle-class students. Each of the responses is divided into its "speech paragraphs" or, as I will call them here, "stanzas."

## THE ALLIGATOR RIVER STORY

Once upon a time there was a woman named Abigail who was in love with a man named Gregory. Gregory lived on the shore of a river. Abigail lived on the opposite shore of the river. The river which separated the two lovers was teeming with man-eating alligators. Abigail wanted to cross the river to be with Gregory. Unfortunately, the bridge had been washed out. So she went to ask Sinbad, a river boat captain, to take her across. He said he would be glad to if she would consent to go to bed with him preceding the voyage. She promptly refused and went to a friend named Ivan to explain her plight. Ivan did not want to be involved at all in the situation. Abigail felt her only alternative was to accept Sinbad's terms. Sinbad fulfilled his promise to Abigail and delivered her into the arms of Gregory.

When she told Gregory about her amorous escapade in order to cross the river, Gregory cast her aside with disdain. Heartsick and dejected, Abigail turned to Slug with her tale of woe. Slug, feeling compassion for Abigail, sought out Gregory and beat him brutally. Abigail was overjoyed at the sight of Gregory getting his due. As the sun sets on the horizon, we hear Abigail laughing at Gregory.

## BLACK STUDENT RESPONSE

All right
As a group
we decided Sinbad was the worse
because he should have never in the first place ask her to go to bed with him
*just* to get her across the water
to see *her* loved one

Then we had Gregory
because when she arrived over there
he just totally disowned her you know
like I don't want you after what you did
which is wrong

We got Slug for third
True Abigail told him to beat him up
but he didn't have to
He could have said no
and he just you know brutally beat him up

Abigail is third
because she laughed and said
(Interruption: That's four) Yeah I mean fourth Yeah
she's fourth
because she never should have told Slug to beat him up and then laughed you know

Ivan we have last
because he did the right thing by saying I don't want to be involved in the situation
He could be a friend and still not want to be involved
It's none of his business

## WHITE STUDENT RESPONSE

OK our findings were
that um the most offensive spot was Sinbad
mainly because for no other reason he just wanted to sleep with Abby
You know for his own benefit
you know kind of cheap

OK Coming in second was Gregory
mainly because he didn't really listen to a reason from her
and he kinda . . . kinda . . . tossed her aside you know without thinking
you know he might have done the same if he was put in the same position you know
for love it was why she did it

Then we put Abigail in the third spot
only because we took a vote (Laughter)
No, because we figured she didn't really do anything
She didn't I mean she didn't tell Slug to beat up Sinbad
She didn't tell Slug to beat up Gregory
so she really didn't have any bearing
She was just dejected, so

Now Slug we figured was the fourth
because his only reason for beating up Gregory was through compassion
so he wasn't really that offensive

And Ivan came in fifth
because Ivan didn't do anything
He he just kind of sat out of the way
so he offended no one

And that's that's our ranking.

The two groups of students differ only trivially on their actual rankings. But nonetheless their responses differ substantively. I will first look at the issue of contextualization. The black student, in his first stanza, uses the pronoun "her" to refer to Abigail, without having explicitly introduced her by using her name or a description for her. This makes perfect sense, since he knows that the primary addressee (his teacher) has read the story and task instructions. Therefore, no one could fail to know who "her" refers to. In fact, this strategy is used quite consistently throughout. The respondent uses a pronoun for Abigail three times in the first stanza and twice in the second before mentioning her by name in the third stanza. He uses "over there" in stanza two for the river bank, which is assumed to be mutually known, but is not explicitly introduced. He uses "him" for Gregory twice in stanza three and once in stanza four, even though Slug has replaced Gregory as the topic, assuming that the listener knows from the story that it was Gregory who was beat up by Slug. In stanza five, he quotes Ivan and says "He could be a friend," assuming the listener can infer that Ivan is addressing his friend Abigail. All these devices signal that the speaker takes himself and the hearer (the teacher) to share certain knowledge (the story and the task), which they in fact do.

The white student does not engage in the same strategy. For example, in his first stanza, he uses the name "Abby," rather than a pronoun, and in his fourth stanza he overtly mentions that it was Gregory who was beat up by Slug. This respondent overtly states information that the hearer (the teacher) already knows and which he knows she knows. This may seem strange if one thinks about it, though, of course, it sounds normal to us who share this speaker's strategy for such tasks. The black and the white students are signaling different contexts. Or, put another way, they are construing the context differently. The black student is treating the teacher as someone who shares knowledge with him and who is part of the overall task. He is also signaling that he takes the text he is orally constructing to be a continuous and integral part of the whole task starting with the reading of story and instructions, through group discussion, and ending with his summary. The white student is signaling that the teacher somehow stands outside the task. She is taken to be listening not in her role as a person who in fact shares knowledge of the story and task, but in some other role, perhaps an evaluative one. He also signals that the oral text he is constructing is autonomous (sealed off) from the rest of the overall task and the interaction it involves, and thus a pronoun cannot refer back out of the text to the earlier stages of the task and interaction.

These differences in how the speakers do or do not leave information to be inferred on the part of the hearer are matched by differences in how the speakers themselves draw inferences from the story. The black speaker says in stanza three that Abigail "told him [Slug] to beat him [Gregory] up"; the white student in his stanza three says Abigail "didn't tell Slug to beat up Gregory." The story text says "Heartsick and dejected, Abigail turned to Slug with her tale of woe." Just as the black student is willing to see the oral text he is constructing as continuous with the earlier interaction, and to see the teacher as part of the social network involved in the task, so also he is willing to make inferences that go beyond and outside the text. The white student, who treats his oral text as autonomous, sealed off from the earlier interaction and from the teacher's real knowledge, is unwilling also to go too far beyond the written story text.

We have looked at only a very small part of the contextualization system. But let's move now to the ideology system: how people structure their language to express themes, values, and a particular worldview. Once again the black and the white student differ. The black student uses terminology that we traditionally associate with morality, terms such as "right" (stanza 5) and "wrong" (stanza 2), "should" (stanzas 1 and 4), "have to" (stanza 3), and "could" (stanzas 4 and 5). He appeals to moral principles ("which is wrong," stanza 2), though without stating the source or identity of these principles. He stresses social relationships. Sinbad was wrong to ask Abigail to sleep with him "just" to get her across the river when she wanted to see "her loved one." What seems to be wrong here is that the request violates the love relationship between Gregory and Abigail. Ivan did the right thing because his social relationship of friendship does not make the problem his business. Abigail is wrong because she laughed and thus didn't take seriously the violence she was having Slug perpetrate. For this speaker, morality seems to be a matter of following moral precepts, not violating social relationships, and taking social relationships seriously.

The white speaker, somewhat surprisingly perhaps, doesn't use traditional moral terminology. Instead he uses the language of "reasons" and "reason giving." Sinbad is offensive because he didn't have a good enough reason for what he did (stanza 1). Gregory was wrong not to listen to a reason from Abigail (stanza 2). Slug wasn't that offensive because his reason (compassion) is acceptable (stanza 4). In fact, psychological states are in general mitigating, witness Abigail's dejection in stanza 3 and Slug's compassion in stanza 4. The speaker states a version of the "golden rule" in stanza two (essentially a device for computing what is rational): "he might have done the same if he was put in the same position." For this speaker, failing to act seems inherently exonerating (there appear to be only sins of commission, not of omission): Ivan is the least objectionable because he "didn't do anything" and so "offended no one," and Abigail didn't tell Slug to beat up Gregory so "she really didn't have any bearing." This speaker's "moral system" appears to be something like: an act (or an inaction) is right so long as it offends no one and the actor has a reason to do it, and psychological states (dejection, compassion) are mitigating factors. In computing reasons one should, beyond considering mitigating psychological states, consider what one would have done in the same circumstances. This is morality as rationality and psychology, not as social networks and responsibilities.

These ideological differences are reflected in the language of the two texts in another way also. The black speaker frequently construes the relationships between the characters in terms of overt social interaction and dialogue, not internal states ("asked her" in stanza 1, direct quote in stanza 2, "told him" in stanza 3, "said" in stanza 3, "laughed and said" in stanza 4, "told" in stanza 4, "laughed" in stanza 4, "saying" in stanza 5, direct quote in stanza 5). He construes the story as a set of overt social encounters. The white speaker rarely uses this device, but rather stresses internal psychological states (in stanza 1, Sinbad is offensive not because he asked Abigail to sleep with him, but because he "wants" to sleep with her; in stanza 2, Gregory tosses Abigail aside without "thinking"; in stanza 3, Abigail is "dejected" and this explains her behavior; in stanza 4, Slug is compassionate; and in stanza 5, Ivan offends no one's sensibilities). The white speaker's world is more privatized than the black speaker's, with less stress on the social and more on the psychological.

At the ideological level it becomes hard to distinguish between a speaker's reading and interpretation of the written story and his reading of the world of events like those in the story. Nor do I believe that it is important to distinguish between these two. In order not to leave the impression that the difference between white and black is paramount here, I reprint below the response of a respondent from an upper-class white group.

### UPPER-CLASS WHITE STUDENT RESPONSE

Okay see we can all sort of like come around seeing other people's point of view
but Sinbad seemed to have like a pretty pure motive
like we couldn't see any real good in what Sinbad was doing

it just seemed a pretty purely lecherous and sleazy thing to do

And then Gregory seemed second
I think just because he hit a nerve
in that here was this girl
that had you know who had done such a desperate thing for him
and he had turned [against her] with disdain
and so I think he was just ranked as an emotional reaction to the [unclear]

And Slug
we didn't like Slug's name
and to beat someone up brutally
I mean we could sort of see Gregory's point of view
and we could sort of see Slug's point of view
but they could have done something better
something to make the situation a little bit [better]

And Abigail you know
we weren't really comfortable with Abigail at all
but yeah well we could see this you know desperate attempt at love
you know we had sort of empathy with that
and you know in the end she's just embittered you know
I mean you can sort of understand her being embittered
yeah she had died for love that day

So another thing you know Ivan was just not really involved
so Ivan you know we figured
maybe Ivan was perceptive enough
to realize that these people were all really [sleazy?]

It can clearly be seen that this speaker's language reflects a different use of our three systems. And his differences from the other white group are just as significant as his differences from the black. While I cannot detail these differences here, let me simply point out that for this speaker morality seems to be a matter of "empathy" (taking someone else's point of view and seeing if one can sympathize with their internal state as a motivator or excuse for their action), as well as a matter of what effect (in terms of affect) a character has on the perceiver's internal psychological state (Gregory "hit a nerve"; "we didn't like Slug's name," "we weren't comfortable with Abigail"; note also: "Ivan was perceptive enough to realize that these people were all [sleazy?]"). Note also how the social interaction aspects of the characters' relationships to each other are here further attenuated. The characters never directly confront each other in any stanza (e.g. Abigail is never mentioned in stanza 1, becomes "this girl" in stanza 2; in stanza 3 Gregory is just "someone" Slug beat up; in stanza 4 no other character is mentioned in relation to Abigail; and in stanza 5 Ivan has an attitude to the characters as a whole, not a relationship to Abigail). The psychologized and privatized world of the previous white speaker is here carried to an absolute extreme.

Now one might say that the ideological is so apparent in the examples I have given because the speakers were dealing with morality as an overt topic. And morality seems to be naturally tied to values and worldview. However, these examples just show clearly what is always present, if less evident. Consider, in this regard, the oral texts I reprint below. These two texts are taken from an article by F. Niyi Akinnaso and Cheryl Seabrook Ajirotutu (1982). They constitute for Akinnaso and Ajirotutu a sort of "before and after" demonstration. Both texts are by women who were attending a CETA job-training program which was teaching them to interview for jobs. Akinnaso and Ajirotutu hold up the first text, by a single mother in her 20s, as a failure and the second one, by a single mother in her 30s, a woman with much more varied work experience than the other woman, as a success.

Text 1.

Q: Have you had any previous job experience that would demonstrate that you've shown initiative or been able to work independently?

1. Well / ... yes when I / ... OK / ... there's this Walgreen's Agency /
2. I worked as a microfilm operator / OK /
3. And it was a snow storm /
4. OK / and it was usually six people / workin' in a group /
5. uhum / and only me and this other girl showed up /
6. and we had quite a lot of work to do /
7. and so the man / he asked us could we / you know / do we / ... do we thinks we could finish this work /
8. so me 'n' this girl / you know / we finished it all /

Text 2.

Q: One more question was that ah, this kind of work frequently involves using your own initiative and showing sort of the ability to make independent judgment. Do you have any ... can you tell me about any previous experience which you think directly show ... demonstrates that you have these qualities?

1. Why / ... well / as far as being capable of handling an office /
2. say if I'm left on my own /
3. I feel I'm capable /
4. I had a situation where one of my employers that I've been /
5. ah previously worked for /
6. had to go on / a .. / a trip for say / ah three weeks and /
7. he was / ... / I was left alone to .. / handle the office and run it /
8. And at that time / ah I didn't really have what you would say / a lot of experience /
9. But I had enough experience to / .. deal with any situations that came up while he was gone /
10. and those that I couldn't / handle at the time /
11. if there was someone who had more experience than myself /
12. I asked questions / to find out / what procedure I would use /
13. If something came up / and if I didn't know / who to really go to /
14. I would jot it down / or write it down / on a piece of paper /

15. so that I wouldn't forget that .. /
16. if anyone that / was more qualified than myself /
17. I could ask them about it /
18. and how I would go about solving it /
19. So I feel I'm capable of handling just about any situation /
20. whether it's on my own / or under supervision

The first response is clearly a failure for all sorts of obvious reasons, including the fact that the respondent uses Black English, a perfectly good dialect of English, but not one socially acceptable on most job interviews, where Standard English is in general required. The second response is indeed a success both in terms of its referential meaning and its use of contextualization. All I mean by "success" here is that the respondent picked referential and contextualization devices and strategies that are conventionally used, accepted, and rewarded in such tasks. But at the ideological level there is a problem. The speaker appears to contradict herself, a sure sign of an ideological conflict between the ideology of her text and one that is more likely to be expected by the reader (and hearer). She claims in line 9 to have had enough experience to "deal with any situations that came up" while the boss was gone. She then immediately, in line 10, mitigates this statement by mentioning "those [situations] I couldn't handle." She goes on to mention people with more experience than her (thus taking the focus off her own expertise) and mentions asking them what procedure she should follow for problems she couldn't handle. This may not yet be a disaster, but she now goes one step further by mentioning in line 13 that there are not only problems she doesn't know how to handle, but there are even ones that she doesn't know who to ask how to handle. She writes such problems down while waiting for someone "more qualified than myself" to come by. After this extended discussion focusing on what she doesn't know, rather than on what she does know, she concludes in lines 19–20 that she feels "capable of handling just about any situation whether on my own or under supervision." The "capable of handling anything" sounds odd coming on the heels of her focus on what she didn't know and what others did; the "under supervision" leaves the suggestion that these others were in fact (or in spirit) supervising her when she was ostensibly in charge. The contradiction may be more apparent than real: the speaker may very well see showing initiative and making independent judgments as a process that involves cooperating with others as part of a social network that mutually solves problems. However, she leaves the impression that she sees being left alone on the job as just another form of supervision, in this case supervision by other people's greater knowledge and expertise. We tend not even to think of the "social network" ideology here, because most of us would have answered the question by placing more stress on ourselves as individuals and our own autonomous knowledge and expertise (in the privatized and psychologized ideology of our previous white respondents!), rather than as part of a social network that functions to get the job done. Her answer is not bad; it just conflicts with an ideology that many mainstream job sites represent, an ideology of individualism, autonomy, and self-assertion. This ideology often must be expressed even when interviewing for jobs that do not demand any very grandiose abilities or which do not in fact really allow for much independent judgment and action.

Now I want to turn to the connection between what I have discussed thus far and literacy. Any particular combination of a way of using the referential system, the contextualization system, and the ideological system I will refer to as a "discourse system." Thus, we can say that for the Alligator River task our black and white speakers used different discourse systems. Each of us by the time we are adults has control over several (perhaps a great many) discourse systems. But where do discourse systems come from? We all get at least one discourse system (for some, more than one) during our primary socialization within the family (or other primary socializing agent) early in life. This system I call a "primary discourse system." We get other discourse systems throughout life by being socialized within various other more public social institutions beyond the family. These may be local institutions (like a church, a community group, a sewing circle, a bowling team) or wider systems (like schools, businesses, government agencies). These I call "secondary discourse systems." A discourse system is a way of being, doing, and thinking in language. Our primary discourse system shapes and is shaped by our secondary ones in quite complicated ways. There may be conflicts between the uses of language our primary system draws on and those required by secondary ones (whether at the referential, the contextualization, or the ideological level). The first woman in the job interview situation above did not control an appropriate secondary discourse system for the interview. Thus, she fell back on something approximating her primary discourse system, with whatever adjustments she thought it appropriate to make. The second woman controlled an appropriate secondary discourse system as far as the referential and contextualization systems were concerned, but not as far as the ideological system was concerned. The white speaker in the Alligator River task controlled a secondary discourse system of a type that much research has shown to be connected with, and successfully rewarded by, schools (and which some mainstream people have more or less incorporated into their primary systems). The black speaker was using a discourse system that undoubtedly mixed primary and secondary elements, but which at the contextual and ideological levels failed to instantiate a typical school-based way of doing the task (there are, in fact, several acceptable school-based ways to do it, as the example from the upper-class speaker shows). In any case, we know that the black speaker's discourse style of handling the task (though in many ways more "reasonable" than the white speaker's) is not well received or judged by the school.

There is a paradox in the concept of literacy, which we can now state somewhat straightforwardly. It is this: one has to either define literacy quite narrowly as "the ability to decode (and encode) writing" or one has to define it in

such a way that reading and writing do not play a privileged role in the definition. If we demand in our view of literacy that people understand what they
read, then we perforce include in our view of literacy the interpretation people
give to the text. But this interpretation is always done in terms of some discourse system. And this discourse system will hardly ever be one that is restricted to use with written language. Rather, it will be used to encode and
decode oral language and events in the real world as well. For example, the discourse system being used by the black student had implications for how he
read the written story, how he decoded verbal interaction about the story, and
how he viewed such events in the real world. Of course, certain types of writing demand special procedures of interpretation, but then so do certain types
of speech (e.g. lectures, directions, demonstrations, speeches) and certain
types of events (e.g. court proceedings, welfare interviews, classroom interaction). Furthermore, these special procedures often themselves spill over across
the categories of print, speech, and event. For much of Western history, in
fact, church- and school-based literacy involved the ability to fluently read out
loud without comprehending at all well what was read (Gee, 1986b; Graff,
1987). Most people today (it seems) do not any longer want to call this "reading." But if we do not, then the job of a literacy teacher involves not print per
se, but discourse systems. And that is a messy business indeed, involving as it
does the world of facts, the world of social interaction and social relations, and
the world of ideology (values, norms, beliefs).

Now, at last, to the aspirin bottle. I can imagine an objection to all that I have
said, an objection that constitutes what I call "the aspirin bottle problem": all
this fancy stuff about contextualization and ideology is fine and dandy, but we
are dealing with people who can't read the back of an aspirin bottle (because it
is written at a tenth grade level or whatever) and thus could poison themselves
or their children. What have fancy theories about "discourse," "contextualization," and "ideology" got to do with the back of an aspirin bottle? Actually, I
have a fair bit of sympathy for the aspirin bottle problem, and believe that it
raises important questions. Hence, let us turn to the back of an aspirin (actually
a Tylenol) bottle:

> WARNING: Keep this and all medication out of the reach of children. As with
> any drug, if you are pregnant or nursing a baby, seek the advice of a health profes-
> sional before using this product. In the case of accidental overdosage, contact a
> physician or poison control center immediately.

Now, apart from whatever level this is written at, it is strange language indeed.
And it is strange because of its use of the contextualization and ideological levels, not because of its message about the world. First, it says it is a "warning,"
but it certainly doesn't look like a regular warning. A warning alerts one to
danger in a rather direct fashion, so the first question is why doesn't this warning read something like as follows:

> This medication, taken in any dosage, could be dangerous to children, or pregnant or nursing women; an overdosage could be dangerous to anyone. In the case of overdosage, contact a physician or poison control center immediately.

This is actually the referential content of the warning. Presumably it is not written this way because of the demands of the contextualization and ideology systems. This warning as originally written has other odd aspects. For instance, it keeps alluding to the fact that the warning applies not just to this medication, but all medication ("and all medication," "as with any drug"). The phrase "as with any drug," in particular, because of its syntactic structure and positioning, implies that the generalization "all drugs, including aspirin, are dangerous to children and pregnant women" is shared, common knowledge. The whole message in fact implies that it is meant primarily for readers who already know what it has to say. Note also the contrast between "health professional" in the case of pregnant women, but "physician" in the case of overdosage. Presumably, this contrast assumes that the reader is the sort of person who knows that the category of health providers that work with pregnant women is wider than those that deal with poisonings in emergency rooms. And then note the word "accidental" used before "overdosage": are we to assume that if someone has taken an overdose on purpose that we shouldn't call a physician or poison control? Finally, what does "immediately" mean? The dosage information on the bottle says that one should take no more than 8 pills in 24 hours. Does this mean that if I (inadvertently, of course) take 9 or 10 in 24 hours, I should at once call a doctor? Or should I wait for symptoms? If so, then I am not calling immediately.

Of course, we all realize what is going on here. The company does not want to highlight the word "dangerous" on its bottle. It wants to forestall suits by people who do things they know they shouldn't, as well as from people who are sensitive to the medicine and thus could poison themselves by a dosage that would be reasonable for others. Further, it wants to create the image that the reader is an intelligent, mainstream person living in a world in which people do not abuse drugs. Thus, the warning actually means, given its contextualization and ideological devices, something like:

> You who this warning is primarily addressed to already know you shouldn't give adult medication to children, or take medication when pregnant or nursing, or take an overdosage. You already know in fact that drugs like aspirin are potent medicine that can do harm. But if you through negligence act stupidly and so against your knowledge (as we all do) don't blame us, we warned you. If you are not this sort of person, then you probably aren't reading or at least paying attention to this label, but don't let your lawyer say in court we didn't warn you (officially speaking). If you are unluckily sensitive to this drug and even a small amount harms you, we did say anything over eight is technically speaking an overdosage, and so you were warned too. We certainly do not want you to hurt yourself, and we would like the world to be a nice mainstream sort of place: in

fact, both these things favor our selling more of this medicine, which is our primary interest.

Now what does reading the aspirin bottle mean? I think everyone will agree we must go beyond simple decoding. The way generalizations about drugs are left implicit as assumed knowledge would lead one to conclude that, at the very least, one would have to teach people these generalizations in order for them to read the bottle. That is, we would have to teach them the sorts of things which people whom this label is primarily addressed to know, or think they know, about medication in general and aspirin in particular. But how far beyond this do we go? Do we need to teach them about the ways in which contextualization devices are used to set up a particular social relationship, or the way in which these play into the ideological level to implicate a whole set of values about people and society? Do you need to know these in order to have read the bottle? I, in fact, do not have the answer. It is one that all concerned with adult literacy, or any literacy for that matter, must answer for themselves. It may depend on whether you think aspirin or the aspirin company is the more dangerous to people's well-being. If you opt for seeing literacy as a matter of discourse systems, you have opened a Pandora's box of social and political concerns. You are dealing with the root of people's identities, since discourse systems are ultimately about the ways in which people situate themselves in the world.

## REFERENCES

Akinnaso, F. N. & Ajirotutu, C. S. (1982). Performance and ethnic style in job interviews. In J. J. Gumperz (Ed.), *Language and social identity* (pp. 119–144). Cambridge: Cambridge University Press.

Gee, J. P. (1986a). Literate America on illiterate America: An essay review of *Illiterate America* by Jonathan Kozol. *Journal of Education, 168,* 126–140.

Gee, J. P. (1986b). Orality and literacy: From *The Savage Mind to Ways with Words. TESOL Quarterly, 20,* 719–746.

Gee, J. P. (1988). The legacies of literacy: From Plato to Freire through Harvey Graff. *Harvard Educational Review, 58,* 195–212.

Gee, J. P. (1989). What is literacy? *Journal of Education 171,* Number 1, pp. 18–25.

Graff, H. (1987). *The legacies of literacy: Continuities and contradictions in Western culture and society.* Bloomington, IN: Indiana University Press.

# Part III

---

# THE POLITICS OF READING
# AND WRITING

## 8

# THE IMPORTANCE OF THE
# ACT OF READING

### Paulo Freire
### Translated by Loretta Slover

In all my* years in the practice of teaching—which is political practice as well—I have rarely allowed myself the task of inaugurating or closing meetings and congresses. I have, nevertheless, agreed to speak here, though as informally as possible, about the importance of the act of reading.

In attempting to speak about the importance of reading, it is indispensable for me to say something about my preparation for being here today, something about the process I inserted myself into while writing the text I now read, a process which involved a critical understanding of the act of reading. Reading is not exhausted merely by decoding the written word or written language, but rather anticipated by and extending into knowledge of the world. Reading the world precedes reading the word, and the subsequent reading of the word cannot dispense with continually reading the world. Language and reality are dynamically intertwined. The understanding attained by critical reading of a text implies perceiving the relationship between text and context.

As I began writing about the importance of the act of reading, I felt myself drawn enthusiastically to *re-reading* essential moments in my own practice of reading whose memory I retained from the most remote experiences of childhood, from adolescence, from young manhood, when a critical understanding of the act of reading took shape in me. In writing this text, I put objective distance between myself and the different moments in which the act of reading

*This chapter was originally presented at the opening of the Brazilian Congress of Reading, Campinas, Brazil in November, 1981. It is published in Brazil in *A Importancia do Ato de Ler em Tres Artigos que se Completam* by Paulo Freire, Cortez, Sao Paulo, Brazil, 1983.

occurred in my existential experience: first, reading the world, the tiny world in which I moved; afterwards, reading the word, not always the word-world in the course of my schooling.

Recapturing distant childhood as far back as I can trust my memory, trying to understand my act of *reading* the particular world in which I moved was absolutely significant for me. Surrendering myself to this effort, I re-created and re-lived in the text I was writing, the experience I lived at a time when I did not yet read words.

I see myself then in the average Recife house where I was born, encircled by trees. Some of the trees were like persons to me, such was the intimacy between us. In their shadow I played, and in the branches susceptible to my height I experienced the small risks which prepared me for greater risks and adventures. The old house, its bedrooms, hall, attic, terrace—the setting for my mother's ferns—the back yard where the terrace was located, all this was my first world. In this world I crawled, gurgled, first stood up, took my first steps, said my first words. Truly, that special world presented itself to me as the arena of my perceptual activity, and therefore as the world of my first reading. The *texts*, the *words*, the *letters* of that context were incarnated in a series of things, objects, signs. In perceiving these, I experienced myself, and the more I experienced myself, the more my perceptual capacity increased. I learned to understand things, objects, signs through using them in relationship to my older brothers and sisters and my parents.

The *texts, words, letters* of that context were incarnated in the song of the birds—tanager, flycatcher, thrush; in the dance of boughs blown by the strong winds announcing storms; thunder and lightning; rain waters playing with geography: creating lakes, islands, rivers, streams. The *texts, words, letters* of that context were incarnated as well in the whistle of the wind, the clouds of the sky, the sky's color, its movement; in the color of foliage, the shape of leaves, the fragrance of flowers—roses, jasmine; in tree trunks; in fruit rinds: the varying color tones of the same fruit at different times—the green of a mango when the fruit is first forming, the green of a mango fully formed, the greenish yellow of the same mango ripening, the black spots of an overripe mango—the relationship among these colors, the developing fruit, its resistance to our manipulation, and its taste. It was possibly at this time, by doing it myself and seeing others do it, that I learned the meaning of the word *squashing.*

Animals were equally part of that context—the way the family cats rubbed themselves coyly against our legs, their mewing of entreaty or anger; the ill-humor of Joli, my father's old black dog, when one of the cats carelessly approached too near to where he was eating what was his. In such instances, Joli's mood was completely different from when he rather sportively chased, caught, and killed one of the many opossums responsible for the disappearance of my grandmother's fat chickens.

Part of the context of my immediate world was also the language universe of my elders, expressing their beliefs, tastes, fears, values, and which linked my world to wider contexts whose existence I could not even suspect.

In the effort at recapturing distant childhood, trying to understand my act of reading the particular world in which I moved, permit me to say again, I re-created, re-lived in the text I was writing the experience I lived at a time when I did not yet read words. And something emerged which seems relevant to the general context of these reflections. I refer to my fear of ghosts. The presence of ghosts among us was a permanent topic of grown-up conversation in the time of my childhood. Ghosts needed darkness or semi-darkness in order to appear under their various forms—wailing the pain of their guilt; laughing in mockery; asking for prayers; indicating where their cask was hidden.

Now, probably until I was seven years old, the Recife neighborhood where I was born was illuminated by gaslights lined up with a certain dignity in the streets. At nightfall, the elegant lamps gave themselves to the magic wand of the lamplighters. At the door of my house I used to accompany the thin figure of my street's lamplighter from afar as he went from lamp to lamp in a rhythmic gait, the lighting taper over his shoulder. It was a fragile light, more fragile even than the light of the lamp we had inside the house; the shadows overcame the light more than the light dispelled the shadows.

There was no better environment for ghostly pranks than that one. I remember the nights in which, enveloped by my own fears, I waited for time to pass, for the night to end, for dawn's demi-light to arrive bringing with it the song of the morning birds. In morning's light my night fears ended up by sharpening my perception of numerous noises which were lost in the brightness and bustle of daytime but mysteriously underscored in night's deep silence. As I became familiar with my world, however, as I perceived and understood it better by *reading* it, my terrors diminished.

It is important to add that *reading* my world, always basic to me, did not make me grow up prematurely, a rationalist in boy's clothing. Exercising my boy's curiosity did not distort it, nor did understanding my world cause me to scorn the enchanting mystery of that world. In this I was aided rather than discouraged by my parents.

It was precisely my parents who introduced me to reading the word at a certain moment in this rich experience of understanding my immediate world. Deciphering the word flowed naturally from *reading* my particular world; it was not something superimposed on it. I learned to read and write on the ground of the back yard of my house, in the shade of the mango trees, with words from my world rather than from the wider world of my parents. The earth was my blackboard; sticks, my chalk.

When I arrived at Eunice Vasconcellos's private school, I was already literate. Here I would like to pay heartfelt tribute to Eunice, whose recent passing away profoundly grieved me. Eunice continued and deepened my parents' work. With her, reading the word, the phrase, the sentence never entailed a break with reading the *world*. With her, reading the word meant reading the *word-world*.

A little while ago, with deep emotion, I visited the home where I was born. I stepped on the same ground on which I had first stood up, on which I first had walked, run, begun to talk, and learned to read. It was that same world which first presented itself to my understanding through my reading it. There I met again some of the trees of my childhood. I recognized them without difficulty. I almost embraced their thick trunks—young trunks in my childhood. Then, what I like to call a gentle or well-behaved nostalgia, emanating from the earth, the trees, the house, carefully enveloped me. I left the house content, feeling the joy of someone who has re-encountered loved ones.

Continuing the effort of *re-reading* fundamental moments of my childhood experience, of adolescence and young manhood—moments in which a critical understanding of the importance of the act of reading took shape in me in practice—I would like to go back to a time when I was a secondary-school student. There I gained experience in the critical interpretation of texts I read in class with the Portuguese teacher's help, which I remember to this day. Those moments did not consist of mere exercises, aimed at our simply becoming aware of the existence of the page in front of us, to be scanned, mechanically and monotonously spelled out, instead of truly read. Those moments were not *reading lessons* in the traditional sense, but rather moments in which texts were offered to our restless searching, including that of the young teacher, Jose Pessoa.

Some time afterward, as a Portuguese teacher myself in my twenties, I lived intensely the importance of the act of reading and writing—basically inseparable—with first-year high school students. I never reduced syntactical rules to charts the students had to swallow, even rules governing prepositions after certain verbs, agreement of gender and number, contractions. On the contrary, all this was proposed to the students' curiosity in a dynamic and living way, as objects to be discovered within the body of texts, whether the students' own or those of established writers, and not as something stagnant whose outline I described. The students did not have to memorize the description mechanically, but rather learn its underlying significance. Only by learning the significance could they know how to memorize it, to fix it. Mechanically memorizing the description of an object does not constitute knowing the object. That is why reading a text taken as pure description of an object (like a syntactical rule), and undertaken to memorize the description, is neither real reading, nor does it result in knowledge of the object to which the text refers.

I believe much of our insistence as teachers that students read innumerable book chapters in one semester comes from a misunderstanding we sometimes have about reading. In my wanderings throughout the world there were not a few times when young students spoke to me about their struggles with extensive bibliographies, more to be *devoured* than truly read or studied—*reading lessons* in the old-fashioned sense, submitted to the students in the name of sci-entific training, and of which they had to give an account by means of reading summaries. In some bibliographies I even read references to specific pages in this or that chapter from such and such a book which had to be read: "pages 15–37."

Insistence on a quantity of readings without due internalization of texts pro-posed for understanding rather than mechanical memorizing reveals a magical view of the written word, a view which must be superseded. From another angle, the same view is found in the writer who identifies the potential quality of his work, or lack of it, with the quantity of pages he has written. Yet, one of the most important documents we have—Marx's "Theses on Feuerbach"—is only two and a half pages long.

To avoid misinterpretation of what I'm saying, it is important to underscore that my criticism of the magical view of the word does not at all imply an irre-sponsible position on my part in relation to the obligation we all have, teachers and students, to read the classic literature in a given field of knowledge seri-ously and continually, to make the texts our own, to create the intellectual dis-cipline without which our practice as teachers and students is not viable.

To return to that very rich moment of my experience as a Portuguese teacher, I remember as vividly as if it were today rather than a remote yesterday the times I dwelled on the analysis of the texts of Gilberto Freyre, Lins do Rego, Graciliano Ramos, Jorge Amado. I used to bring the texts from home to read with the students, pointing out syntactical aspects strictly linked to the good taste of their language. To that analysis I added commentaries on the es-sential differences between the Portuguese of Portugal and the Portuguese of Brazil.

In this reflection on the importance of the act of reading, I want to make clear once again that my primary effort has been to explain how I became in-creasingly aware of its importance in my own life. It's as if I were doing the ar-chaeology of my understanding of the complex act of reading in my own existential experience. For this reason I have been speaking of certain mo-ments in my childhood, adolescence, and young manhood. I would like now to conclude by reviewing, in general terms, some aspects central to what I pro-posed a few years ago in the field of teaching adults to read and write.

First, I would like to reaffirm that I always saw teaching adults to read and write as a political act, an act of knowledge, and therefore as a creative act. I would find it impossible to be engaged in a work of mechanically memorizing vowel sounds, like in the exercises ba-be-bi-bo-bu, la-le-li-lo-lu. Nor could I reduce learning to read and write merely to learning words, syllables, or let-ters, a process of teaching in which the teacher *fills* the supposedly *empty* heads of the learners with his or her words. On the contrary, the student is the sub-ject of the process of learning to read and write as an act of knowing and a cre-ative act. The fact that he or she needs the teacher's help, as in any pedagogical situation, does not mean that the teacher's help annuls the student's creativity and responsibility for constructing his or her own written language and reading this language.

When, for instance, a teacher and a learner pick up an object in their hands, as I do now, they both feel the object, perceive the felt object, and are capable of expressing verbally what the felt and perceived object is. Like me, the illiterate person can feel the pen, perceive the pen, and say *pen*. I can, however, not only feel the pen, perceive the pen, and say *pen*, but also write *pen* and, consequently, read *pen*. Learning to read and write means creating and assembling a written expression for what can be said orally. The teacher cannot put it together for the student; that is the student's creative task.

I need go no further into what I've developed at different times in the complex process of teaching adults to read and write. I would like to return, however, to one point referred to elsewhere in this text because of its significance for the critical understanding of the act of reading and writing, and consequently for the project I am dedicated to, teaching adults to read and write.

Reading the world always precedes reading the word, and reading the word implies continually reading the world. As I suggested earlier, this movement from the world to the word and from the word to the world is always present; even the spoken word flows from our reading of the world. In a way, however, we can go further, and say that reading the word is not preceded merely by reading the world, but by a certain form of *writing* it or *re-writing* it, that is, of transforming it by means of conscious practical work. For me, this dynamic movement is central to the literacy process.

For this reason I have always insisted that words used in organizing a literacy program come from the word universe of the people who are learning, expressing their actual language, their anxieties, fears, demands, dreams. Words should be laden with the meaning of the people's existential experience, and not of the teacher's experience. Surveying what I call the word universe thus gives us the people's words, pregnant with the world, words from the people's reading of the world. We then give the words back to the people inserted in what I call *codifications*, pictures imaging real situations. The word *brick*, for example, might be inserted in a pictorial representation of a group of bricklayers constructing a house.

Before giving a written form to the popular spoken word, however, we customarily challenge the learners with a group of codified situations, so they will apprehend the word rather than mechanically memorize it. Decodifying or *reading* the situations pictured leads them to a critical perception of the meaning of culture by leading them to understand how human practice or work transforms the world. Basically, the pictures of concrete situations enable the people to reflect on their former interpretation of the world before going on to read the word. This more critical *reading* of the prior less critical *reading* of the world enables them to understand their indigence differently from the fatalistic way they sometimes view injustice.

In this way, a critical reading of reality, whether it takes place in the literacy process or not, and associated above all with the clearly political practices of mobilizing and organizing, constitutes an instrument of what Gramsci calls counter-hegemony.

To sum up, reading always involves critical perception, interpretation, and *re-writing* what is read.

I would like to close by saying that for these reflections on the importance of the act of reading I resolved to adopt the procedure I used because it was consonant with my way of being and with what I am capable of doing.

# 9

# THE POLITICS OF AN EMANCIPATORY LITERACY IN CAPE VERDE

Donaldo Macedo

Within the last decade literacy has taken on new importance as an issue among American educators. Unfortunately, the debate that has emerged has tended to recycle old assumptions and values regarding the meaning and usefulness of literacy. The notion that literacy is simply a matter of learning the standard language still informs the vast majority of literacy programs, and manifests its logic in the renewed emphasis on technical reading and writing skills.

I want to propose in this chapter that literacy cannot be viewed as simply the development of skills aimed at acquiring the dominant standard language. This view sustains a notion of ideology that systematically disconfirms rather than makes meaningful the cultural experiences of the subordinate linguistic groups who are, by and large, the objects of its policies. For the notion of literacy to become meaningful it has to be situated within a theory of cultural production and viewed as an integral part of the way in which people produce, transform, and reproduce meaning. Literacy must be seen as a medium that constitutes and affirms the historical and existential moments of lived experience that produce a subordinate or a lived culture. Hence, it is an eminently political phenomenon, and it must be analyzed within the context of a theory of power relations and an understanding of social and cultural reproduction and production. By "cultural reproduction" I refer to collective experiences that function in the interest of the colonizer, rather than in the interest of the oppressed groups that are the object of its policies. I use "cultural production" to refer to specific groups of people producing, mediating, and confirming the mutual ideological elements that emerge from and reaffirm their daily lived experiences. In this case, such experiences are rooted in the interests of individual and collective self-determination.

This theoretical posture underlies my examination of how the public school systems in the Republic of Cape Verde have developed educational policies aimed at stamping out the 75% illiteracy rate inherited from colonialist Portugal. These policies are designed to eradicate the colonial educational legacy which had as its major tenet the total de-Africanization of Capeverdeans. As Freire (1978) succinctly points out, colonial education

> was discriminatory, mediocre, and based on verbalism. It could not contribute anything to national reconstruction because it was not constituted for this purpose. . . . Schooling was antidemocratic in its methods, in its content, and in its objectives. Divorced from the reality of the country, it was, for this very reason, a school for a minority and thus against the majority. (pp. 13–14)

Before the independence of Cape Verde in 1975, schools functioned as political sites in which class, gender, and racial inequities were both produced and reproduced. In essence, the colonial educational structure served to inculcate the Capeverdean natives with myths and beliefs which denied and belittled their lived experiences, their history, their culture, and their language. The schools were seen as purifying fountains where Capeverdeans could be saved from their deep-rooted ignorance, their "savage" culture, and their bastardized language which, according to some Portuguese scholars, was a corrupted form of Portuguese "without grammatical rules (they can't even be applied)" (Caetano, p. 349). As a result, as Paulo Freire (1978) points out, "This system could not help but reproduce in children and youth the profile that the colonial ideology itself had created for them, namely that of inferior beings, lacking in all ability" (p. 14).

On the one hand, schooling in Cape Verde served the purpose of de-culturating the natives while, on the other hand, it acculturated them into a predefined colonial model. Schools in this mold functioned "as part of an ideological state apparatus designed to secure the ideological and social reproduction of capital and its institutions whose interests are rooted in the dynamics of capital accumulation and the reproduction of the labor force" (Giroux, 1983). This educated labor force in Cape Verde was composed mainly of low-level functionaries whose major tasks were the promotion and maintenance of the status quo. Their role took on a new and important dimension when they were used as intermediaries to further colonize other Portuguese possessions in Africa. Thus, colonial schools were successful to the extent that they created a petit-bourgeois class of functionaries who had internalized the belief that they had become "white" or "black with white souls," and were therefore superior to Africans who still practiced what was viewed as barbaric culture.

The assimilation process in Cape Verde penetrated the deepest level of consciousness, especially in the bourgeois class. For instance, with respect to becoming "white," I am reminded of an anecdote about a black Capeverdean so preoccupied with his blackness that he paid a well-respected white Capeverdean to issue him a decree proclaiming him white. The man jokingly wrote for him on a piece of paper "Dja'n branco dja," meaning "I have thereby been declared white."

After independence and in the reconstruction of a new society in Cape Verde, schools have assumed as their major task the "decolonization of mentality," as it is termed by Aristides Pereira, and which Amilcar Cabral called the "re-Africanization of mentality." It is clear that both Pereira and Cabral were well aware of the need to create a school system in which a new mentality cleansed of all vestiges of colonialism would be formulated: a school system that would allow Capeverdeans to appropriate their history, their culture, and their language. A school system where, according to Freire (1978)

> It was imperative to reformulate the programs of geography, history and the Portuguese language, changing all the reading texts that were so heavily impregnated with colonialist ideology. It was an absolute priority that students should study their own geography and not that of Portugal, the inlets of the sea and not Rio Tejo. It was urgent that they study their history, the history of the resistance of their people to the invader and the struggle for their liberation which gave them back the right to make their own history, and not the history of the kings of Portugal and the intrigues of the court. (p. 20)

Freire's proposal to incorporate a radical pedagogy in Capeverdean schools has met a lukewarm reception in Cape Verde. I want to argue that the suspicion of Capeverdean educators is deeply rooted in the language issue (Capeverdean vs. Portuguese) and has led to the creation of a neo-colonialist literacy campaign under the superficially radical slogan of eliminating illiteracy in Cape Verde. The difficulties of reappropriating Capeverdean culture have been magnified by the fact that the means for such struggle has been the language of the colonizers. I want to argue in this chapter that the present literacy campaign in Cape Verde concerns itself mainly with the creation of functional literates in the Portuguese language. No longer based on the cultural capital of subordinate Capeverdeans, the program has fallen prey to positivistic and instrumental approaches to literacy concerned mainly with the mechanical acquisition of Portuguese language skills (Bourdieu & Passeron, 1977).

Before my discussion of the politics of an emancipatory literacy program in Cape Verde, I want to discuss the various approaches to literacy. First I will briefly discuss those approaches which are derived from a positivistic school and are linked to the process of cultural reproduction. Then, I will analyze the role of language in the reproduction process. Finally, I will argue that the only literacy approach which would be consistent with the construction of a new

Capeverdean society is one rooted in the dynamics of cultural production and informed by a radical pedagogy. That is, the literacy program that is needed is one that will affirm and allow Capeverdeans to re-create their history, culture, and language and that will, at the same time, help lead those assimilated Capeverdeans who perceive themselves to be captive to the colonial ideology to "commit class suicide" (Freire, 1978).

## APPROACHES TO LITERACY

Almost without exception, traditional approaches to literacy have been deeply *ingrained* in a positivistic method of inquiry. In effect this has resulted in an epistemological stance in which scientific rigor and methodological refinement are celebrated while "theory and knowledge are subordinated to the imperatives of efficiency and technical mastery, and history is reduced to a minor footnote in the priorities of 'empirical' scientific inquiry" (Giroux, 1983). In general, this approach abstracts methodological issues from their ideological contexts and consequently ignores the interrelationship between the socio-political structures of a society and the act of reading. In part, the exclusion of social and political dimensions from the practice of reading gives rise to an ideology of cultural reproduction, one which views readers as "objects." As Paulo Freire (1978) has aptly stated, it is "as though their conscious bodies were simply empty, waiting to be filled by that word" from the teacher (p. 72). Although it is important to analyze how ideologies inform various reading traditions, in this chapter I will limit my discussion to a brief analysis of the most important approaches to literacy, linking them to either cultural reproduction or cultural production.

## THE ACADEMIC APPROACH TO READING

The purpose assigned to reading in the academic tradition is two-fold. First, the rationale for this approach "derives from classical definitions of the well-educated man—thoroughly grounded in the classics, articulate in spoken and written expression, actively engaged in intellectual pursuits" (Walmsley, 1981, p. 78). This approach to reading has primarily served the interests of the elite classes. In this case, reading is viewed as the acquisition of predefined forms of knowledge, and is organized around the study of Latin and Greek and the mastery of the great classical works. Second, since it would be unrealistic to expect the vast majority of society to meet such high standards, reading was redefined as the acquisition of reading skills, decoding skills, vocabulary development, and so on. This second rationale served to legitimize a dual approach to reading: one level for the ruling class and another for the dispossessed majority. According to Giroux (1983) "this second notion is geared primarily to working class students whose cultural capital is considered less compatible, and thus inferior in terms of complexity and value, with the knowledge and values of the dominant class." This two-fold academic approach to reading is inherently alienating in nature. On the one hand, it ignores the life experience, the history, and the language practice of students. On the other hand, it overemphasizes the mastery and understanding of classical literature and the use of literary materials as "vehicles for exercises in comprehension (literal and interpretative), vocabulary development and word identification skills" (Walmsley, 1981, p. 80). Thus, literacy in this sense is stripped of its socio-political dimensions; it functions, in fact, to reproduce dominant values and meaning. It does not contribute in any meaningful way to the appropriation of working-class history, culture, and language.

## THE UTILITARIAN APPROACH TO READING

The major goal of the utilitarian approach is to produce readers who meet the basic reading requirements of contemporary society. In spite of its progressive appeal, such an approach emphasizes the mechanical learning of reading skills while sacrificing the critical analysis of the social and political order which generates the need for reading in the first place. This position has led to the development of "functional literates," groomed primarily to meet the requirements of our ever more complex technological society. Such a view is not simply characteristic of the advanced industrialized countries of the West; even within the Third World, utilitarian literacy has been championed as a vehicle for economic betterment, access to jobs, and increase of the productivity level. As it is clearly stated by UNESCO,

> Literacy programs should preferably be linked with economic priorities.... [They] must impart not only reading and writing, but also professional and technical knowledge, thereby leading to a fuller participation of adults in economic life. (UNESCO, 1966, p. 97)

This notion of literacy has been enthusiastically incorporated as a major goal by the Back-to-Basics proponents of reading. It has also contributed to the development of neatly packaged reading programs which are presented as the solution to difficulties students experience in reading job application forms, tax forms, advertisement literature, sales catalogs, labels, and the like. In general, the utilitarian approach views literacy as meeting the basic reading demand of an industrialized society. As Giroux (1983) points out,

> Literacy within this perspective is geared to make adults more productive workers and citizens within a given society. In spite of its appeal to economic mobility, functional literacy reduces the concept of literacy and the pedagogy in which it is suited to the pragmatic requirements of capital; consequently, the notions of critical thinking, culture and power disappear under the imperatives of the labour process and the need for capital accumulation.

## COGNITIVE DEVELOPMENT APPROACH TO READING

While the academic and utilitarian approaches to reading emphasize the mastery of reading skills and view the readers as "objects," the cognitive development model stresses the construction of meaning whereby readers engage in a dialectical interaction between themselves and the objective world. Although the acquisition of literacy skills is viewed as an important task in this approach, the salient feature is how people construct meaning through problem-solving processes. Comprehension of the text is relegated to a position of lesser importance in favor of the development of new cognitive structures which can enable students to move from simple to highly complex reading tasks. This reading process is highly influenced by the early work of John Dewey and has been shaped in terms of the development of Piagetian cognitive structures. Under the cognitive development model, reading is seen as an intellectual process, "through a series of fixed, value-free, and universal stages of development" (Walmsley, 1981, p. 82). The cognitive development model thus avoids criticism of the academic and utilitarian views of reading and fails to consider the content of what is read. Instead, it emphasizes a process which allows students to analyze and critique issues raised in the text with an increasing level of complexity. This approach, however, is rarely concerned with questions of cultural reproduction. Since students' cultural capital, i.e., their life experience, history, and language, is ignored, they are rarely able to engage

> through critical reflection, regarding their own practical experience and the ends that motivate them in order, in the end, to organize the findings, and thus replace mere opinion about facts with an increasingly rigorous understanding of their significance. (Freire, 1978, p. 25)

## THE ROMANTIC APPROACH TO READING

Like the cognitive development model, the romantic approach is based on an interactionist approach with a major focus on the construction of meaning; however, the romantic approach views meaning as being generated by the reader and not occurring in the interaction between reader and author via text. The romantic mode greatly emphasizes the affective and sees reading as the fulfillment of self and a joyful experience. One writer praises

> the intimate reliving of fresh views of personality and life implicit in the work [of literature]; the pleasure and release of tensions that may flow from such an experience ... the deepening and broadening of sensitivity to the sensuous quality and emotional impact of day-to-day living. (Rosenblatt, 1949, pp. 37–38)

In essence, the romantic approach to reading presents a counterpoint to the authoritarian modes of pedagogy which view readers as "objects." However, this seemingly liberal approach to literacy fails to make problematic class conflict, gender, or racial inequalities. Furthermore, the romantic model completely ignores the cultural capital of subordinate groups and assumes that all people have the same access to reading, or that reading is part of the cultural capital of all people. This failure to address questions of cultural capital or various structural inequalities means that the romantic model tends to reproduce the cultural capital of the dominant class, to which reading is intimately tied. It is presumptuous and naive to expect a student from the working class, confronted and victimized by myriad disadvantages, to find joy and self-affirmation through reading alone. But more important is the failure of the romantic tradition to link reading to the asymmetrical relations of power within the dominant society, relations of power that not only define and legitimate certain approaches to reading but also disempower certain groups by excluding them from such a process.

I have argued thus far that all of these approaches to literacy have failed to provide a theoretical model for empowering historical agents with the logic of individual and collective self-determination. While these approaches may differ in their basic assumptions about literacy, they all share one common feature: they all ignore the role of language as a major force in the construction of human subjectivities. That is, they ignore the way in which language may either confirm or disconfirm the life histories and experiences of the people who use it. This becomes more clear in my analysis of the role of language in Capeverdean literacy programs.

## THE ROLE OF LANGUAGE IN CAPEVERDEAN LITERACY

The Capeverdean literacy programs have been plagued by constant debate over whether the language of instruction should be the native Capeverdean language or the official Portuguese language. Such debate, however, hides issues of a more serious nature which are rarely raised. This is in line with Gramsci's argument that,

> Each time that in one way or another, the question of language comes to the fore, that signifies that a series of other problems is about to emerge, the formation and enlarging of the ruling class, the necessity to establish more "intimate" and sure relations between the ruling groups and the national popular masses, that is, the reorganization of cultural hegemony. (cited in Donald, 1982)

Gramsci's argument illuminates the issue underlying the debates over language in Cape Verde, where there is still no agreement as to whether the native language is really just a dialect of Portuguese. Capeverdean educators repeatedly use the lack of orthographic uniformity for the Capeverdean language to justify their present policy of using Portuguese as the only medium of reading instruction. They raise the question of which dialect such an orthography should be based on. However, the most common argument is that Portuguese language has international status and therefore guarantees upward mobility for the Portuguese-educated Capeverdeans.

The sad reality is that while education in Portuguese provides access to positions of political and economic power for the high echelon of Capeverdean society, it screens out the majority of the masses who fail to learn Portuguese well enough to acquire the necessary literacy level for social, economic, and political advancement. By offering a literacy program conducted in the language of the colonizers with the aim of reappropriating the Capeverdean culture, these educators have, in fact, developed new manipulative strategies that support the maintenance of Portuguese cultural dominance. What is hidden in the language debate in Cape Verde is possibly a resistance to re-Africanization, or perhaps a subtle refusal on the part of the assimilated Capeverdeans to "commit class suicide."

The pedagogical and political implications of using Portuguese as the only medium of instruction in Capeverdean literacy programs are far-reaching and yet largely ignored. The reading programs in Cape Verde often contradict a fundamental principle of reading, namely that students learn to read faster and with better comprehension when taught in their native tongue. The immediate recognition of familiar words and experiences enhances the development of a positive self-concept in children who are somewhat insecure about the status of their language and culture. For this reason, and to be consistent with the plan to construct a new society in Cape Verde free from vestiges of colonialism, a Capeverdean literacy program should be based on the rationale that such a program must be rooted in the cultural capital of subordinate Capeverdeans and have as its point of departure the Capeverdean language.

Capeverdean educators must develop radical pedagogical structures which provide students with the opportunity to use their own reality as a basis of literacy. This includes, obviously, the Capeverdean language they bring to the classroom. To do otherwise is to deny Capeverdean students the rights that lie at the core of the notion of an emancipatory literacy. The failure to base a literacy program on the Capeverdean language means that oppositional forces can neutralize the efforts of Capeverdean educators and political leaders to achieve decolonization. Capeverdean educators and political leaders must recognize that

> Language is inevitably one of the major preoccupations of a society which, liberating itself from colonialism and refusing to be drawn into neo-colonialism searches for its own recreation. In the struggle to recreate a society, the reconquest by the people of their own world becomes a fundamental factor. (Kenneth, 1973)

It is of tantamount importance that the incorporation of the Capeverdean language as the primary language of instruction in literacy be given top priority. It is through their own language that Capeverdeans will be able to reconstruct their history and their culture.

The debate over whether the Capeverdean language is a dialect of Portuguese, a simplification of Portuguese, or a valid language, and whether it is a restricted or elaborated language, points to the issue of whether Portuguese is in fact a superior language. In a more important sense these linguistic categories rest on the technical question of whether the Capeverdean language is a valid and rule-governed system. Despite synchronic and diachronic analyses of the Capeverdean language (Macedo, 1977, 1982) the fact still remains that the Capeverdean language continues in a stigmatized and subordinate position. I want to argue that the Capeverdean language has to be understood within the theoretical framework that generates it. Put another way, the ultimate meaning and value of the Capeverdean language are not to be found by determining how systematic and rule-governed it is. We know that already. Its real meaning has to be understood through the assumptions that govern it, and it has to be understood via the social, political, and ideological relations to which it points. Generally speaking, the issue of systematicness and validity often hides the true role of language in the maintenance of the values and interests of the dominant class. In other words, the issue of systematicness and validity becomes a mask that obfuscates questions about the social, political, and ideological order within which the Capeverdean language exists.

If an emancipatory literacy program is to be developed in Cape Verde, in which readers become "subjects" rather than "objects," Capeverdean educators must understand the productive quality of language. Donald puts it this way:

> I take language to be *productive* rather than *reflective* of social reality. This means calling into question the assumption that we, as speaking subjects, simply use language to organize and express our ideas and experiences. On the contrary, language is one of the most important social practices through which we come to experience ourselves as subjects. . . . My point here is that once we get beyond the idea of language as no more than a medium of communication, as a tool equally and neutrally available to all parties in cultural exchanges, then we can begin to examine language both as a practice of signification and also as a *site* for cultural struggle and as a *mechanism* which produces antagonistic relations between different social groups. (Donald, 1982)

It is to the antagonistic relationship between the Capeverdean and Portuguese speakers that I want to turn now. The antagonistic nature of the Capeverdean language has never been fully explored. In order to more clearly discuss this issue of antagonism, I will use Donald's distinction between *oppressed* language and *repressed* language. Using Donald's categories, the "negative" way of posing the Capeverdean language question is to view it in terms of *oppression*—that is, seeing the Capeverdean language as "lacking" the Portuguese features which usually serve as a point of reference for the Capeverdean language. By far the most common questions concerning the Capeverdean language are posed from the *oppression* perspective. The alternative view of the Capeverdean language is that it is *repressed* in the Portuguese language. In this view, Capeverdean as a repressed language could, if spoken, challenge the privileged Portuguese linguistic dominance. Capeverdean educators have failed to recognize the "positive" promise and antagonistic nature of the Capeverdean language. It is precisely on these dimensions that educators must concentrate to bring forth an emancipatory literacy program which will demystify the Portuguese language and the old assumptions about its inherent superiority. Capeverdean educators must develop an emancipatory literacy program informed by a radical pedagogy so that the Capeverdean language will cease to provide its speakers the experience of subordination and, moreover, may be brandished as a weapon of resistance to the dominance of the Portuguese language.

## EMANCIPATORY LITERACY IN CAPE VERDE

In maintaining a certain coherence with the revolutionary plan to reconstruct a new society in Cape Verde, Capeverdean educators and political leaders saw the need to create a new school grounded in "a new educational praxis, expressing different concepts of education consonant with the plan for the society as a whole" (Freire, 1978, p. 13). In order for this to happen, the first step was to identify the objectives of the inherited colonial education. Next, it was necessary to analyze how the methods used by the colonial schools functioned, legitimizing the dominant values and meanings, and at the same time disconfirming the history, culture, and language practices of the majority of Capeverdeans. The new school, so it was argued, must also be informed by a radical pedagogy, which would make "concrete such values as solidarity, social responsibility, creativity, discipline in the service of the common good, vigilance and critical spirit—values by which PAIGC has been forged through the whole liberation process" (Freire, 1978, p. 43).

An important feature of the new educational plan in post-independence Cape Verde was the development of a literacy program rooted in an emancipatory ideology, where readers become "subjects" rather than mere "objects." The new literacy program needed to move away from traditional approaches which emphasize the acquisition of mechanical skills while divorcing reading from its ideological and historical contexts. In attempting to meet this goal, it purposely rejected the conservative principles embedded in the approaches to literacy I have discussed previously. Unfortunately, the new literacy program unknowingly reproduced one common feature of those approaches by ignoring the important relation between language and the cultural capital of the people whom the literacy program was aimed at. The result has been the development of a literacy campaign whose basic assumptions are at odds with the revolutionary spirit that launched it.

The new literacy program was largely based on Freire's notion of emancipatory literacy in which literacy is viewed "as one of the major vehicles by which 'oppressed' people are able to participate in the sociohistorical transformation of their society" (Walmsley, 1981, p. 84). In this view, literacy programs should be tied not only to mechanical learning of reading skills but, additionally, to a critical understanding of the overall goals for national reconstruction. Thus, the readers' development of a critical comprehension of the text, and the sociohistorical context to which it refers, become an important factor in Freire's notion of literacy. As he points out,

> The act of learning to read and write, in this instance, is a creative act that involves a critical comprehension of reality. The knowledge of earlier knowledge, gained by the learners as a result of analyzing praxis in its social context, opens to them the possibility of new knowledge. The new knowledge, reveals the reason for being behind the facts, thus demythologizing the false interpretations of these same facts. And so, there is now no more separation between thought-language and objective reality. The reading of a text now demands a reading within the social context to which it refers (Freire, 1978, p. 24).

Literacy, in this sense, is grounded in a critical reflection on the cultural capital of the oppressed. It becomes a vehicle by which the oppressed are equipped with the necessary tools to reappropriate their history, culture, and language practices. It is, thus, a way to enable the oppressed to reclaim "those historical and existential experiences that are devalued in everyday life by the dominant culture . . . in order to be both validated and critically understood" (Giroux, 1983).

The theories underlying Freire's emancipatory literacy have been, in principle, wholeheartedly embraced by Capeverdean educators. However, I must argue that, in practice, the middle class, especially teachers trained by the colonial schools, has not been able to play a radical pedagogical role. These educators have failed to analyze and understand the ways in which the colonizers used the Portuguese language to maintain class division, thereby keeping subordinate Capeverdeans in their proper place. I am reminded now of a friend in Cape Verde who, having intellectually embraced the revolutionary cause, is unable to perceive himself as still being emotionally "captive" to the colonial ideology. But when I asked him which language he most often uses in the office, he quickly answered, "Portuguese, of course—it is the only way to keep my subordinates in their place. If I speak Capeverdean, they don't respect me."

This view of language in Cape Verde is illustrative of the extent to which Capeverdeans are held "captive" by the dominant ideology which devalues their own language. Surprisingly, even Paulo Freire failed to completely convince Capeverdean leaders and educators of the importance of their native language in the development of an emancipatory literacy. Literacy programs in both Guinea-Bissau and Cape Verde are conducted in Portuguese, the language of the colonizer. In an illuminating discussion I had with Freire in the summer of 1982, he deplored this policy. He said, "The continued use of Portuguese as a vehicle of literacy education will only guarantee that the future leaders of Cape Verde will be the sons and daughters of the ruling class."

In essence, Capeverdean leaders and educators have not only failed to recognize the positive promise of Capeverdean language, but they have systematically undermined the principles of an emancipatory literacy by conducting literacy programs in the language of the colonizers. The result is that the learning of reading skills in Portuguese has not enabled subordinate Capeverdeans to acquire the critical tools "to awaken and liberate them from their mystified and distorted view of themselves and their world" (Giroux, 1983). Capeverdean educators must understand the all-encompassing role the Portuguese language played in this mystification and distortion process. Capeverdean educators must also recognize the antagonistic nature of the Capeverdean language and its potential challenge to the mystification of Portuguese language superiority. They must develop a literacy program based on the theory of cultural production. In other words, subordinate Capeverdeans must become *actors* in the reconstruction process of a new society.

Literacy in Cape Verde can only be emancipatory to the extent that it is conducted in the language of the people. It is through the native language that a Capeverdean "names his world," and begins to establish a dialectal relationship with the dominant class in the process of "transforming the social and political structures that imprison him in his 'culture of silence.' Thus, a person is literate to the extent that he is able to use his language for social and political reconstruction." (Walmsley, 1981, p. 84) The use of the Portuguese language in Capeverdean literacy programs weakens the possibilities for subordinate Capeverdeans to engage in dialectical encounters with the dominant class. Literacy conducted in Portuguese empowers the ruling class by sustaining the status quo. It supports the maintenance of the colonialist elitist model of education. This elite model of education creates, according to Freire (1978), "intellectualists and technocrats rather than intellectuals and technicians" (p. 75). In short, literacy conducted in Portuguese is alienating to subordinate Capeverdeans, since it denies them the fundamental tools for reflection, critical thinking, and social interaction. Without the cultivation of their native language, and robbed of the opportunity for reflection and critical thinking, subordinate Capeverdeans find themselves unable to re-create their culture and history. Without the reappropriation of their cultural capital, the reconstruction of the new society envisioned by Amilcar Cabral can hardly be a reality.

## REFERENCES

Bourdieu, P. & Passeron, J.C. *Reproduction in education, society, and culture.* Beverly Hills: Sage, 1977.

Caetano, J. *Boletim da Sociedade de Geografia.* 3 serie, n.d. Lisbon.

Donald, J. *Language, literacy and schooling.* London: Open University Press, 1982.

Freire, P. *Pedagogy in process.* New York: Seabury Press, 1978.

Giroux, H. A. *Theory and resistance: A pedagogy for the opposition.* South Hadley, Mass.: J.F. Bergin Publishers, 1983.

Kenneth, J. The sociology of Pierre Bourdieu, *Educational Review,* 1973, 25.

Macedo, D. Conceptualizing bilingual education for Capeverdeans in the United States, Second National Portuguese Conference, Providence, Rhode Island, 1977.

Macedo, D. Capeverdean orthography development in the United States. In Richard Wood (Ed.), *Language planning.* Texas: University of Texas Press, 1982.

Rosenblatt, L. The enriching values of reading. In William S. Gray (Ed.), *Reading in an age of mass communication.* New York: Appleton-Century Crofts, 1949.

UNESCO. An Asian model of educational development: Perspectives for 1965–1980. Paris: UNESCO, 1966.

Walmsley, S. On the purpose and content of secondary reading programs: Educational ideological perspectives, *Curriculum Inquiry,* 1981, II.

# 10

# TROPICS OF LITERACY

## Linda Brodkey

I have come to think of literacy as a social trope and the various definitions of literacy as cultural Rorschachs. By this I mean to draw attention not simply to the fact that every culture and subculture defines what it means by literacy (e.g., Heath, 1983, Scribner & Cole, 1981), and not even to the equally important fact that the history of the word "literacy" in a single society shows remarkable variation over time (e.g., Ohmann, 1985; Resnick & Resnick, 1980). Nor am I principally concerned in this chapter with ways that researchers have conceptualized literacy in order to study what John Szwed posits may well be "a plurality of literacies" extant at any given moment in a society (1981, p. 16). Yet, all these works, which explore historical, social, and cultural variation in literate practices, are critical to understanding that a nation can use literacy as a trope to justify or rectify social inequity. In this chapter, however, I explore the systematic expression of ideology, the tropics of literacy. Because all definitions of literacy project both a *literate self* and an *illiterate other*, the tropics of literacy stipulate the political as well as cultural terms on which the "literate" wish to live with the "illiterate" by defining what is meant by reading and writing.

Adult Americans, whose literacy has recently undergone intense scrutiny, provide a particularly dramatic example of what is meant by the tropics of literacy. While the sense that "illiterates" are irrevocably different from "literates" is perhaps most apparent in anthropology, where it is customary to use literacy to distinguish between traditional and modern societies (e.g., Goody & Watt, 1968), most definitions of literacy in industrialized societies presume that a similar distinction between orality and literacy obtains in the West (e.g., Ong,

1982). Moreover, when we move into the area of adult literacy, definitions usually specify which texts adults need to read, hence, the widely held notion of conventional literacy as "the ability to read, write, and comprehend texts on familiar subjects and to understand whatever signs, labels, instructions, and directions as are necessary to get along in one's environment" (Hunter & Harman, 1979, p. 7). And, even though in the last decade, conventional literacy in the United States has been redefined as functional literacy, Norvell Northcutt's widely cited study (1975) of the Adult Performance Level (APL) also assesses literacy as the ability to perform such literacy tasks as are considered essential to being adult: filling out job application forms correctly, for example, or understanding the check cashing policies in supermarkets.

The APL study sorted the adult population of the United States into three groups: APL 1 (adults who function in society with difficulty), APL 2 (adults who function in society but are not proficient), and APL 3 (adults who are functional and proficient members of society). Carmen Hunter and David Harman quote an official at the U.S. Office of Education to the effect that 23 million adults are at APL 1, and another 34 million at APL 2 (1979, p. 26). Needless to say, the literacy crisis referred to in the popular press uses statistics on that order, rather than the 5.2 million figure arrived at by a 1979 Census Bureau survey, and it is the higher figures that have been used to petition federal, state, and local government agencies and corporations for the funds necessary to launch and maintain adult literacy programs. Recently, the Bureau of the Census, working from data collected in a 1982 survey, has amended its earlier figure, and now reports that between 17 and 21 million adults are illiterate (U.S. Department of Education, 1986; "Over 12 Percent," 1986). By either measure, then, a staggering number of adult Americans are now deemed to be illiterate.

Many adult literacy programs prefer functional literacy to conventional literacy, since functional literacy stresses tasks that adults might well believe to be important to their day-to-day lives. In neither case, however, were the adults in question consulted, although the definition of functional literacy that Hunter and Harman stipulate in *Adult Illiteracy in the United States* means to take their interests into account:

> *Functional literacy:* the possession of skills *perceived as necessary by particular persons and groups* to fulfill their own self-determined objectives as family and community members, citizens, consumers, job-holders, and members of social, religious, or other associations of their own choosing. (1979, p. 7; italics in the original)

Let me emphasize here that my reservations about defining adults as functionally literate or illiterate in no way obviate the responsibility to provide literacy education to the adults who seek programs. Instead, my reservations arise out of a recent critique of the APL research design, in which Francis Kazemek

(1985) points out the remarkable fact that only adults in APL 1 were actually studied. In other words, while the functional literacy of the APL 1 population was tested, the literacy of the other two socio-economic groups was inferred from the data gathered on the population of APL 1. The implication is that the population designated APL 2 and APL 3 are members of the same social group, separated only by degrees of economic, educational, and professional success, while the individuals identified as APL 1 are a socially distinct group in virtue of their individual and collective inability to decode and comprehend the reading tasks designated by the APL.

As Kazemek's criticism suggests, there are not three but two populations being defined—us and them. Given that any definition of literacy invariably postulates an illiterate "other," at issue here is not so much the validity or reliability of the APL research design, but the alien, illiterate "other" projected by this particular definition of functional illiteracy. It is plausible, at least, to question whether the point of identifying functional illiterates is that there are adults who cannot read and write well enough to function in society, or that there are adults who do not apply for jobs, keep checking accounts, file with the IRS, take out insurance policies, and otherwise participate in the literacy practices that sustain late monopoly capitalism. Were everyone actually required to understand all these forms, I suspect that many of us now considered to be functionally literate would be reassigned to APL 1. For instance, I literally do not understand any of the literature sent me by the benefits office at my university.

I suspect that one important difference between the members of APL 1 and myself is that no one seems to expect me to understand the forms and policies. To wit, my university insures my life and my health, I insure my car with a friend of a friend, and I file my tax forms according to instructions from an accountant. This cadre of institutional and corporate surrogate readers, who are supposedly comprehending these important documents on my behalf, is available to all members of the middle class, many of whom use them more extensively, of course, than I do, and some of whom would also include lawyers and brokers in their reading circle. The point I'm making is really very simple. Functional literacy may be less a matter of decoding and comprehending such documents (since to do so requires specialized knowledge of law and economics as well as written language) and more the fact that I have ready access to the resources I need to use the documents. This is what separates the literate "us" from the illiterate "them."

In *Tristes Tropiques*, Claude Levi-Strauss tells a story about a tribal chief who, watching Levi-Strauss make notes while talking with members of the tribe, himself took to pretending to do the same in his interactions with the anthropologist, other chiefs, and members of his tribe. Levi-Strauss relates this anecdote in the essay called "A writing lesson." The lesson he says he learned, and the lesson he says he wants us to learn, is "the fact that the primary function of written communication is to facilitate slavery" (Levi-Strauss, 1973,

p. 299). The chief, argues Levi-Strauss, used writing to consolidate his power over the others. If we take this lesson in local, tribal politics home, he goes on to say, we will find that:

> the systematic development of compulsory education in European countries goes hand in hand with the extension of military service and proletarianization. The fight against illiteracy is therefore connected with an increase in governmental authority over the citizens. Everyone must be able to read, so that the government can say: Ignorance of the law is no excuse. (p. 300)

I have encountered similar though decidedly less hyperbolic claims about hegemony and literacy since first reading Levi-Strauss's essay (e.g., Donald, 1983; Olson, 1983). Among other things, these essays caution against presuming that adult literacy campaigns, adult literacy programs, and adult literacy students share a common understanding of what literacy may or may not do for adults.

Working with literacy educators and sitting on the boards of adult literacy programs, for instance, have taught me that not many of the people concerned are as circumspect about the putative, absolute value of literacy as Levi-Strauss. For instance, the *Philadelphia Inquirer* published an op-ed article, "Literacy has many happy returns," written by Ted Snowe, an active and informed corporate advocate for adult functional literacy. Snowe makes a compelling, if familiar, economic argument, a plea to the city to "invest" in literacy education and to the citizenry to volunteer as literacy tutors:

> Of course, not all people who can't read and write end up unemployed or on welfare. Nonetheless, hundreds of thousands of Philadelphians are locked out of the new economy [the information economy]. This year more money will be spent treating the symptoms of their unemployment—poverty, crime, drug and alcohol abuse—than will be spent treating one of the root causes—illiteracy. Taxpayers should be outraged at such an economically absurd system. (Snowe, 1985, p. 11-A)

In the course of his work, which includes tutoring as well as fund raising and advocacy, Snowe has seen the positive correlations between illiteracy and poverty, crime, and alcohol and drug abuse. He has reached the same statistically unwarranted, though plausible, conclusion that many other literacy advocates have, namely, that *their* illiteracy is a personal misery whose public consequences—unemployment, crime, and so on—cannot be abated without *our* assistance. Therefore, to fund literacy programs and tutor adults is to contribute to the stability of the new economy.

Snowe's is among the most effective arguments for adult literacy education because it identifies literacy as the solution to many of the social and economic problems to which large cities are subject. To the extent that unemployment can be attributed to illiteracy, however, those in APL 2 (adults who are functionally literate but not proficient) would be more likely to benefit from literacy instruction aimed at the new information economy than those in APL 1, for whom illiteracy is only one of many variables correlated with profound poverty. Moreover, the value of literacy is not absolute, but confounded by race and gender. For example, 15% of white male high school dropouts aged 22 to 34 live below the poverty line, compared to 28% of white females, 37% of black males, and 62% of black females (U.S. Department of Labor, 1983). Clearly, literacy is neither the only nor the most important variable operating in this social equation. It certainly looks as if some people, and particularly black women, need to be more educated than others just to survive.

The Philadelphia executive and the French anthropologist have both invested literacy with the power to change the lives of illiterates by changing their relationship to society. And, because in both cases literacy is identified as the agent (or agency) of social change, it is a trope in which to construct a variety of possible relationships between a society and its members. No matter that in one version functional literacy would enfranchise the illiterate poor, who are at once a danger to themselves and to us, while in the other, literacy allows a government to surveil its literate population. The tropes invariably tell us who we are by pointing out who we are not. The danger lies not in tropes, but in using the tropics of literacy as the sole explanation of the difference between us and them. As Michelle Fine, speaking about "solutions" aimed at urban dropouts, notes, "Targeting schools as the site for social change and the hope for the next generation deflects attention and resources, critique and anger from insidious and economic inequities" (1986, p. 407). Illiteracy does not explain massive unemployment any more than literacy explains bureaucracy.

If, as I have been arguing, literacy tropes invariably project a social relationship between the literate and the illiterate, the resounding failure of literacy campaigns in the industrialized nations of the West may well be a consequence of defining literacy as functional literacy. For, despite Hunter and Harman's generous definition, which focuses on "skills *perceived as necessary by particular individuals and groups* to fulfill their own self-determined objectives," most functional literacy materials define literacy conventionally as a set of reading tasks, and reduce reading to lockstep decoding procedures and multiple-choice comprehension questions. When considered at all, writing is likely to be defined as filling in the blanks and signing on the dotted line (e.g., Colvin & Root, 1976). Curricula designed from such materials define the functional illiterate as someone who needs to learn how to follow instructions. While individual teachers and students may well resist the curricula, and many community-based programs explicitly set out to do so (Fingeret, 1984, pp. 20–23), in this country literacy programs are funded because of a presumed relationship between illiteracy and unemployment. Hence, adult literacy materials and curricula are written from the perspective of what a literate society *believes* employed adults need to know. Very few programs are designed with the self-determined objectives of adult learners in mind, and fewer still with the goals of political empowerment advocated by Paulo Freire (1968).

Reports on successful literacy campaigns in the Third World usually document Freire's tropic of literacy as social and political empowerment. This trope of liberation, which limns a relationship of social reciprocity between the literate self and the illiterate other, emphasizes writing. In his article on "the Great Campaign of 1961" in Cuba, for instance, Jonathan Kozol (1980) mentions the 700,000 "letters to Fidel" housed in the Museum of Literacy. In their article on a vernacular literacy project at the College of the Virgin Islands in St. Thomas, Nan Elsasser and Patricia Irvine (1985) report that students used Creole to write summaries, essays, and research papers as well as letters to Creole authors and the student newspaper. Interesting, is it not, that while the Cuban government and teachers and students in St. Thomas can envision a nation of writers, the United States dreams only of a nation of readers?

When literacy means writing as well as reading, the illiterate other is projected as someone who "talks" back, which means that curriculum must provide grounds for a literacy dialogue. Let me illustrate what I mean by these grounds with an example from my own teaching. I recently taught a graduate course on Basic Writing, in which most of the students had never taught inexperienced adult writers. It happened that one student in the class, who was teaching an ABE class (primarily white, working-class women), wished to provide her students with an "authentic" reason to write. After a good deal of discussion, the teachers in my class decided to write the students in hers. For two months, the members of both classes corresponded weekly. By the second week, the teacher reported that while students had earlier tired of writing after five or ten minutes, they now asked to use the first half hour of class (which more often than not was extended to an hour) to write.

The letters her students wrote are intensely personal, a virtual catalogue of familial and neighborhood activities. The teachers soon learned to respond in kind so that within weeks they had exchanged a good deal of detailed information about their own lives and concerns. All successful instruction was by indirection. Students learned to format their letters, for instance, by simply reproducing the formats used by the teachers. Spelling was similarly taught and learned. Teachers simply used words that were spelled incorrectly in their responses, and when students wrote back many of those words were correctly spelled. I mention these aspects of the correspondence because literacy instruction was one reason for corresponding. As it turned out, however, the adult students taught us a great deal that had not been anticipated. Among other things: three out of ten were facing serious health problems; in two cases the primary providers had recently lost their jobs; and one woman had recently moved into a neighborhood where there is no supermarket within walking distance.

These grounds for dialogue are a consequence of interpersonal relationships established in the "literacy letters." That these issues were raised and discussed in the course of writing about their lives certainly confirms that adult Americans would be better addressed by a critical or radical literacy curriculum (Giroux, 1983) than by either a conventional or functional literacy curriculum. Functional literacy requires them to learn to read what we write—our tropes, our worlds, our politics. The letters remind us that in our eagerness to instruct, we forget that "illiterate" others also have tropes for literacy. Dialogic literacy would require us to learn to read the unfamiliar tropes in which they write their lives.

## REFERENCES

Colvin, R. J. & Root, J. H. (1976). *Tutor.* Syracuse, NY: Literacy Volunteers of America.

Donald, J. (1983). How illiteracy became a problem (and literacy stopped being one). *Journal of Education, 165*(1), 35–52.

Elsasser, N., & Irvine, P. (1985). English and Creole: The dialectics of choice in a college writing program. *Harvard Educational Review, 45,* 399–415.

Fine, M. (1986). Why urban adolescents drop into and out of public high school. *Teachers College Record, 87,* 393–409.

Fingeret, A. (1984). *Adult literacy education: Current and future directions.* Columbus, OH: ERIC Clearinghouse on Adult, Career and Vocational Education.

Freire, P. (1968). *Pedagogy of the oppressed.* New York: The Seabury Press.

Giroux, H. A. (1983). *Theory and resistance in education: A pedagogy opposition.* South Hadley, MA.: Bergin & Garvey.

Goody, J., & Watt, I. (1968). The consequences of literacy. In J. Goody (Ed.), *Literacy in traditional societies.* Cambridge: Cambridge University Press.

Heath, S. B. (1983). *Ways with words: Language, life, and work in communities and classrooms.* Cambridge: Cambridge University Press.

Hunter, C., & Harman, D. (1979). *Adult illiteracy in the United States: A report to the Ford Foundation.* New York: McGraw-Hill Book Company.

Kazemek, F. E. (1985). An examination of the Adult Performance Level project and its effect on adult literacy education in the United States. *Lifelong Learning, 9*(2), 24–28.

Kozol, J. (1980). A new look at the literacy campaign in Cuba. In M. Wolf, M. K. McQuillan, & E. Radwin (Eds.), *Language and thought / Language and reading* (pp. 466–497). Cambridge: Harvard Educational Review Reprint Series No. 14.

Levi-Strauss, C. (1973). *Tristes tropiques.* New York: Atheneum. (Original work published 1955)

Northcutt, N. (1975). *Adult functional competency: A summary.* Austin, TX: University of Texas Press.

Ohmann, R. (1985). Literacy, technology, and monopoly capitalism. *College English, 47,* 675–689.

Olson, C. P. (1983). Inequality remade: The theory of correspondence and the context of French immersion in northern Ontario. *Journal of Education, 165*(1), 75–98.

Ong, W. J. (1982). *Orality and literacy: The technologizing of the word.* New York: Methuen.

Over 12 percent of adults illiterate, census says. (1986, April 30). *Education Week,* p. 4.

Resnick, D. P., & Resnick, L. B. (1980). The nature of literacy: An historical exploration. In M. Wolf, M. K. McQuillan, & E. Radwin (Eds.). *Language and thought / Language and reading* (pp. 396–411). Cambridge: Harvard Educational Review Reprint Series No. 14.

Scribner, S., & Cole, M. (1981). *The psychology of literacy.* Cambridge: Harvard University Press.

Snowe, T. (1985, December 3). Literacy has many happy returns. *Philadelphia Inquirer,* p. 11-A.

Szwed, J. (1981). The ethnography of literacy. In M. F. Whiteman (Ed.), *Writing: The nature, development, and teaching of written communication.* Hillsdale, NJ: Lawrence Erlbaum Associates.

U.S. Department of Education. (undated). Update on adult illiteracy. [Factsheet in letter sent May 22, 1986].

U.S. Department of Labor, *Time of change: 1983 handbook of women workers.* Washington, DC: Government Printing Office, 1983.

# 11

# THE CONSTRUCTION OF SCHOOL
# KNOWLEDGE: A CASE STUDY

Jan Nespor

The knowledge taught and learned in schools is not "objectively" defined or "scientifically" validated. It is a social construction growing out of historical and structural processes, political conflicts, and human decisions. The outcomes of these processes, conflicts, and decisions—the curricula of schools and the authority accorded those who become the certified possessors of them—represent assertions about the nature of knowledge in the world. They also represent assertions about the relative abilities of individuals and groups to use that knowledge and justify their actions on its basis. In short, the curricula of schools embody institutionalized theories of culture.

This chapter examines the question of how the structure of curricular knowledge limits and channels the capacities of students to understand and act upon the world. In this respect the arguments depart from the agendas defined in previous programmatic and empirical studies of curricular knowledge (e.g., Goodson, 1982; Hammersley & Hargreaves, 1983; Williams, 1961; Young, 1971). These studies have tended to focus on the political and cultural conflicts through which different fields or subject areas gain institutional authority vis-à-vis other fields and subjects. Less frequently, they examine the internal construction of what counts as "knowledge" within particular fields of study (see Ball, 1982, 1983), or they study the ways in which knowledge

The research reported here was conducted with support from the National Institute of Education, Contract NIE-400-78-0600. However, the opinions expressed herein do not necessarily reflect the position or policy of the National Institute of Education, and no official endorsement by that agency should be inferred.

forms are differentially presented to students from different social backgrounds (Anyon, 1981).

⌐The focus here differs in that it concerns a fundamental and seemingly "neutral" skill—reading—and traces the connections between the skill as formulated in classroom activity, the wider social processes constraining classroom activity, and the value of the resulting "skill" as a cognitive tool.⌐The chapter takes as its point of departure one of the few theoretical frameworks that encompass all of the issues raised above—that of Pierre Bourdieu—and then explores the issues further through a case study of reading instruction in a postsecondary classroom.

## BOURDIEU'S MODEL OF THE ROLE OF KNOWLEDGE IN SCHOOLING

Bourdieu focuses on the fundamental problem of how mechanisms of symbolic domination and control maintain and reproduce existing social orders. His theoretical apparatus has at least three components: an assertion that cultural forms are essentially "arbitrary," a model of the roles of "cultural capital" and "habitus" in the transmission of culture, and an argument that schools help make arbitrary inequalities seem "natural" and inevitable.

### Arbitrariness and Cultural Conflict

For Bourdieu, the fundamental characteristic of culture is its "arbitrariness." This refers to the fact that definitions of social reality are social and cultural constructions which "cannot be deduced from any universal principle" (Bourdieu & Passeron, 1977, p. 8).

In one sense, this is merely a statement of anthropological relativism: culture is a social creation, there is nothing "necessary" or "inevitable" about the particular form or content it takes. However, for Bourdieu, cultural definitions of reality are not static or neutral creations of social groups as a whole. Rather, they are highly manipulable and malleable creations of institutions and agents of cultural production, and they serve mainly to create and maintain the legitimacy of dominant social groups. Thus, Bourdieu stresses the importance of a social stratum of specialists in the production of culture and the concomitant "*dispossession* of the lay population of the instruments of symbolic production" (Bourdieu, 1977d, p. 116). Social struggle is conceptualized as the struggle of classes or class factions to impose definitions of reality (which are "arbitrary" but unrecognized as such) that serve their own interests. These struggles take place both in the politics of everyday life and indirectly through the activities of specialists in symbolic production (e.g., artists and the like) (Bourdieu, 1977a, p. 115).

This is not an argument that more traditional conceptions of power based on wealth, control over the means of economic production, possession of state power, and so on, are false. Rather, Bourdieu is dissolving the distinction between different forms of "capital" (e.g., symbolic and physical capital) as sources of power. In his system, "capital" exists in many forms and can be converted or transfigured from one form to another form, each form having its specific effects. The particular importance of "symbolic capital," from Bourdieu's perspective, is that it masks its nature as capital and its origins in "material" forms of capital (Bourdieu, 1977b, p. 183). This is seen by Bourdieu as the fundamental process in the creation of the "legitimacy" of social orders. Symbolic power is "a subordinate form of power, is a transfigured, that is to say, misrecognizable, transformed and legitimated form of other kinds of power" (Bourdieu, 1977d, p. 117). But symbolic power must also establish its own legitimacy. That is, ideological and cultural forms must mask the fact that they themselves are "arbitrary." Bourdieu suggests that this is accomplished through the operations of the educational system.

### Cultural Capital and "Habitus"

The question of how individuals and groups accumulate symbolic capital or translate material capital into symbolic forms is answered in a complicated way by Bourdieu. One part of the answer is that groups can literally expend material wealth on the consumption of cultural goods, thereby acquiring "cultural capital." Attacking the Durkheimian view that the cultural heritage of a society is transmitted in a "harmonious" way as "the undivided property of the whole society," Bourdieu (1977c, p. 488) shows that different social groups spend different amounts of money and energy on different types of cultural activities (for example, professionals read more books and attend the theater more often than farmers).

Such differences in the consumption of culture are not treated as mere functions of differences in the economic capacities of social groups. Rather, Bourdieu argues that they depend importantly on the cultural and psychological capacities of different groups to "appropriate"—that is, to understand, appreciate, and use—symbolic goods. Although the cultural heritage of past generations is "theoretically offered to everyone," it is in fact available only to those who can "decipher" the "code" in which it is embedded (Bourdieu, 1977c, p. 488). Thus, the capacities to acquire cultural capital are differentially distributed in such a way that those groups already possessing a specific form of cultural capital are also most likely to accumulate more of it. The capacities to acquire culture are transmitted through two means: "habitus" and formal schooling.

Every individual, in Bourdieu's theory, is endowed with a "habitus," acquired unreflectively in the course of family life and everyday experience. It consists of a "system of lasting, transposable dispositions" functioning as a "matrix of perceptions, appreciations, and actions" (Bourdieu, 1977b, pp. 82–

83). That is, in their everyday experience of family and social life, individuals develop tastes, interests, interpretive skills, and the like that both direct their attention toward and allow them to appreciate and engage in certain kinds of cultural activities. However, "habitus" alone is not sufficient to insure cultural competence (Bourdieu, 1977c, p. 493). The school in particular is said to build upon characteristics acquired in the family context to produce groups of individuals who share similar cultural skills (mastery of the "codes" for appreciating and appropriating cultural goods) and similar sets of attitudes about knowledge and culture:

> It may be assumed that every individual owes to the type of schooling he has received a set of basic, deeply interiorized master-patterns on the basis of which he subsequently acquires other patterns. . . . The patterns . . . may govern and regulate mental processes without being consciously apprehended and controlled. It is primarily through the cultural unconscious which he owes to his intellectual training and more particularly, to his scholastic training, that a thinker belongs to his society and age—schools of thought may, more often than is immediately apparent, represent the union of thinkers similarly schooled. (Bourdieu, 1967, p. 343).

There is, however, nothing neutral about the kinds of knowledge distributed by schools or the means of knowledge transmission. Instead, school knowledge is said to most closely resemble the cultural capital of the dominant classes, and the established modes of academic instruction to closely resemble the modes of inculcation practiced by families of the dominant classes (Bourdieu, 1977c, p. 493). According to Bourdieu (1969) these close connections arise from the fact that the social significance of artistic or intellectual creations is determined by the agents and agencies who evaluate them and for whom they are produced. During the Middle Ages and into the Renaissance the Court and the aristocratic elite performed this role (Bourdieu, 1969, p. 90). With the industrial revolution and the breakdown of the aristocracy's cultural hegemony, the creators of intellectual goods became increasingly reliant on intellectual specialists or arbitrators of culture—and on institutions of cultural transmission such as the schools—as means of establishing the legitimacy of their creations (see Bourdieu, 1969, pp. 106–107).

Cultural producers thus compete for noninstitutional audiences and at the same time for institutionally distributed legitimacy and "consecration" (Bourdieu, 1969, p. 110). The social groups which at once constitute the most powerful faction of consumers or audiences and at the same time are the main participants in culture-transmitting institutions have a disproportionate influence over the types of cultural works that are produced and receive institutional legitimacy. Bourdieu argues that, at least in France, the dominant classes fulfill this role.

## The Transformation of Objective Probabilities into Subjective Expectations

Bourdieu argues that children from the dominant social groups, because they possess a "class habitus" that corresponds to the patterns of social interaction valued in school settings, and because they already possess forms of cultural capital that the school consecrates and transmits, do better in schools than children from lower-middle-class, working-class, or farming families. The school, by grounding its pedagogical methods on the assumption that all children possess the *same* cultural capital and habitus—or the equivalent assumption that school knowledge is neutral and objective relative to habitus and cultural capital—effectively "sanctions" initial cultural inequalities and transforms "*social* advantages or disadvantages into *educational* advantages or disadvantages" (Bourdieu, 1974, p. 36). The critical aspect of this process, according to Bourdieu, is that it makes social and hence "arbitrary" inequalities appear "natural" and inevitable. This is accomplished when the objective probabilities of agents' life chances are internalized as subjective expectations and aspirations. There is then a correspondence "between the objective classes and the internalized classes," between "social structures and mental structures" (Bourdieu, 1977b, p. 164).

In Bourdieu's scheme, the internalization of objective chances takes place through the medium of the "habitus." The habitus includes not only modes of perception and action, but also "attitudes towards cultural capital and educational institutions" (Bourdieu, 1974, pp. 32–33). These inherited attitudes and expectations are in turn based on "an empirical evaluation of the real hopes common to all individuals in their social group" (Bourdieu, 1974, pp. 33–34).

Working-class children are thus doubly disadvantaged in that they lack the cultural capital valued by the school and at the same time possess a habitus that discourages them from exerting themselves in school—a discouragement emphasized by parents who perceive that their children have little chance of scholastic success and who consider schooling itself to be of little potential value. Peer-group associations reinforce these attitudes toward schooling (Bourdieu, 1974, p. 35). The result, Bourdieu argues, is that the school's essentially "arbitrary" selection and sorting of students comes to seem natural:

> By awarding allegedly impartial qualifications (which are also largely accepted as such) for socially conditioned aptitudes which it treats as unequal "gifts," [schooling] transforms *de facto* inequalities into *de jure* ones and economic and social differences into distinctions of quality, and legitimates the transmission of the cultural heritage. (Bourdieu, 1974, p. 42)

Bourdieu thus makes three basic arguments. First, he suggests that the knowledge and cultural heritage transmitted by the school is neither "natural" nor neutral, but that it is instead an "arbitrary" creation of particular social factions. It follows, second, that different social groups or classes have different relationships to formal, school-based bodies of knowledge, and that the culture of the dominant classes is more closely aligned with school knowledge than that of the dominated classes. Finally, Bourdieu suggests that some and possibly all of the sorting and labeling of students that goes on in schools is based on students' possession of cultural capital.

Although this conceptual apparatus has considerable value as a framework for the study of institutionalized culture and knowledge construction in school settings, a number of critics have pointed out problems with the framework that limit its value as a general theory of social and cultural production and reproduction. It is obscure at key points (DiMaggio, 1979). It seems preoccupied with "high culture" to the exclusion of cultural forms produced by working-class or ethnic minority groups (Willis, 1981). It treats the "habitus" as a completely internalized generative structure and ignores the possibility that students creatively and strategically use and develop their cultural resources in opposition to the school. It neglects such important topics as the role of the state and the sexual division of labor (MacDonald, 1979–1980). In particular, the concept of the "transformation of objective probabilities into subjective expectations" is highly dubious (see e.g., Jenkins, 1982). Something very like it may occur: see in particular Ogbu's (1974) study of black American students' internalization of "job ceilings" and the resulting effects on their attitudes and performance in school. But far from making social inequalities seem "natural" and legitimate, Ogbu's students are articulately resentful of the state of affairs.

The object here, however, is not to develop a critique of the logical coherence or comprehensiveness of Bourdieu's theoretical positions. Instead, I want to take the theory and bring it into a "dialog" (Thompson, 1978) with a body of evidence as a means of learning more about both the theory and the empirical situation.

## ARBITRARINESS AND THE NON-NEUTRALITY OF KNOWLEDGE FORMS

Bourdieu's arguments about the social grounding of knowledge refer to the *content* of the culture transmitted through schools, and in particular to the knowledge forms most closely associated with what is called "high culture" in America—painting, sculpture, music, literature, and the like. It is much less clear how his arguments would apply to knowledge forms such as mathematics, physics, and the like, or to what are called "the basic skills"—for example, reading and writing. What I propose to do here is take "reading" as a kind of test case by means of which to examine the central issues and questions raised by Bourdieu, though from a rather different methodological and conceptual standpoint.

The peculiar status of literacy as a form of knowledge is by no means a virgin topic. Olson (1977), for example, argues that knowledge is "context-specific" (see also Lave, 1984; LCHC, 1982, 1983) and that different means of instruction are not alternative means to the same end, but different routes to different goals. In particular, he argues, the dominance of writing as the medium of communication in schools produces a situation in which "that which we call rationality and intelligence is not rationality in general, but mental procedures appropriate to the knowledge represented in formal texts" (p. 69). This "literate bias" of school knowledge functions to restrict access to knowledge to those students (primarily from the middle and upper classes) who enter the schools already acquainted with school-like literacy tasks and equipped with a positive attitude toward literate culture. By their reliance on written texts, schools "consecrate" a specific medium of culture. It is a medium, moreover, related to a specific type of cultural content: that which was embodied in the impersonal literate style formulated by European cultural elites in the 17th century (Olson, 1977).

This is of course not the only definition of "literacy" possible. Heath (1980, 1983), for example, has described black working-class communities in which literacy is used in ways fundamentally different from those espoused by schools. The difficulties that children from these groups experience in school reading classes stem not from a generic inability to read, but from the fact that the functions and uses of reading in school are different from those the children encounter outside the school. Lave's research on mathematics usage in grocery stores as opposed to school-like settings (Lave, 1984; Lave, Murtaugh, & de la Rocha, 1984) makes a similar point. Shoppers proficient in solving mathematics problems in everyday tasks had great difficulty solving analogous problems embedded in school-like tasks.

This leads us to an important point for amending Bourdieu's framework. It is not simply that dominant groups have cultural forms which they cause to be consecrated while the cultural forms indigenous to other groups are devalued, it is also a matter of a putatively unitary cultural form—like "reading"—being in fact highly differentiated but not recognized as such. The implications of this point are many. I explore them below through the analysis of an empirical case—a program of reading instruction in a community college.

## EVOLUTION OF THE AUTONOMOUS SKILL CONCEPTION

To make sense of reading instruction in any particular setting we must begin at a far broader level of analysis that will tell us something about how such settings have come about. This task is best begun by looking at changes in the uses and functions of "literacy" over time.

It has been argued that the social functions of literacy have moved through three broad phases in the West (Resnick & Resnick, 1977): first, a phase in which literacy corresponded to a set of highly complex problem solving skills restricted to a social elite; second, a phase in which literacy spread but the skill itself became highly routinized; and finally, a phase in which universal literacy became the accepted ideal but literacy became reified as an autonomous skill divorced from actual contexts of use.

During the first phase, which corresponded roughly to the period prior to the Reformation in Europe, one did not merely learn to read, one became a literate person. Reading and writing were not "skills" that could be taught indiscriminately to anyone, but a perquisite of elite status. One learned not just to "read," but to use written language for specific social purposes. The transmission of literacy remained a monopoly of the Church, a monopoly buttressed by the dominance of Latin as the medium of written communications as late as the 15th century (see, e.g., Febvre & Martin, 1976, p. 249; Steinberg, 1974, pp. 117–127).

Not surprisingly, the second phase in the evolution of literacy coincided with the breakdown of the Church's monopoly over written language. Publications in vernacular languages increased dramatically and pedagogical systems for learning to read without Church-based or formal instruction were promulgated (e.g., Strauss, 1981). As a result, reading spread beyond the boundaries of the elites into the peasantry and the urban masses.

In the course of its popularization, however, the nature of "reading" was transformed. Rather than being an integral part of a way of life, it acquired a very circumscribed meaning: it now referred primarily to the skills of learning to sound out and memorize a small set of familiar religious texts (Graff, 1978–1979, p. 3; Resnick & Resnick, 1977, pp. 372–374).

This simplified and ritualized use of literacy for religious purposes was the product of an era in which state structures were still relatively small, the locus of power was decentralized, and most material goods were produced and distributed locally. In short, the religious conception of literacy was particularly suited to precapitalist societies.

By the 19th century, however, industrialization created new systems of power and new lines of social demarcation. In Europe, urbanization and industrialization pressured dominant groups to search for means to integrate formerly isolated peasants and workers into national cultures. The situation in the United States, which is the focus of the discussion here, posed the additional problems entailed in coping with large numbers of non-English-speaking immigrants. Two complementary policies of social integration evolved: compulsory formal school administered by the state as an attempt to take over the socialization function from the family (Lazerson, 1971), and a new conception of literacy as a symbol of national identity.

This conception of literacy bore many similarities to the one that characterized the Reformation. Like the religious conception, it embraced very simplified notions of literacy skills. But where religious literacy had endorsed the sounding-out method of learning to read as a means of promoting the use of the vernacular and breaking the Latin-based dominance of the Church, the emphasis of the new "civic-national" literacy (Resnick & Resnick, 1977, p. 375) was on promoting and standardizing a national language. This emphasis entailed a pedagogical move toward an approach based on learning the "proper" phonemes of the language—the "right" American pronunciation (Robinson, 1977, pp. 46–47).

Literacy was thus no longer tied to any form of social practice—neither critical thinking nor religious worship. Instead, language itself became the focus of attention—not the use of language for any particular purpose, but the mastery of an idealized, reified form of "language" (see Heath, 1977, pp. 279, 281). The social definition of literacy shifted from one encompassing the use of reading and writing for specific social practices, to a conception of literacy as a set of "skills" divorced from use. Reading was accorded the status of an "autonomous skill": a skill that is presumed to be independent of its context and can thus be taught and learned without regard to the intentions, interests, or background knowledge of the learner.

In keeping with such a conception, the social contexts of literacy instruction underwent a crucial change. Literacy instruction, which had at first been part of an apprenticeship in certain forms of complex social activities and had later become part of a routinized form of social practice (religious observance), had now become routinized and embedded in a hermetic context: the public school. Formal literacy instruction was no longer grounded in everyday contexts of use (even of the ritualistic-religious variety). Instead, children were placed in particular institutional contexts whose sole function was to impart "skills" abstracted from contexts of use. Instead of learning to do things that entail reading and writing, one learned to "read" and "write" in courses designed to teach nothing but reading and writing.

## A CASE STUDY IN CLASSROOM READING INSTRUCTION

The remainder of this chapter explores the cognitive and social implications of the conception of literacy as an autonomous skill. The immediate focus of the analysis is a community college reading course. The analysis is drawn from a 12-month study that entailed observations in some 70 sessions of the reading classes, analyses of texts and tests, and repeated interviews with teachers and students in the classes (see Nespor, 1985, for a fuller discussion).

The course had three curricular components: one focused on pronunciation or "word attack," another on "vocabulary" or the memorization of word meanings, and the third on "reading comprehension." As this last component was considered by teachers and students to be most centrally concerned with "reading," it is the one I focus on here.

The comprehension component was organized around two sets of texts. One consisted of a collection of very short, artificially constructed "passages" accompanied by multiple-choice questions; the second was a group of novels and an anthology of excerpts from magazines, newspapers, and books.

The activity of reading and interpreting the artificial "passages" usually centered on finding their "generalizations" (and sometimes their "subject matter statements" as well). This was essentially a search and match operation. That is, the students searched for a sentence or phrase in the text that matched the categories defined in the text and emphasized by the instructor.

This was most obvious at the start of the semester, when students were required to look for "stated generalizations"—explicit summaries of the meaning of the text laid out in fully formed sentences. Their own paraphrases or interpretations of main ideas were not acceptable. This practice produced a situation in which the instructors, when asking their classes to identify the generalization of a passage, would be answered with a number (e.g., "the second sentence") rather than with a statement. Reading was operationally defined as the task of finding text fragments to fit the category systems.

Toward the end of the semester, along with the introduction of genuine texts (the anthology of articles and the novels), instructors usually introduced the idea of "unstated generalizations," that is, generalizations that students could formulate in their own words. However, the notion of unstated generalizations was usually introduced by means of exercises in which students were told to look first for stated generalizations and to construct generalizations in their own words only if they could not find them already explicitly formulated in print. Students usually responded by guessing for stated generalizations.

An example may help here. Students were asked to read the following passage, taken from a genuine text (Leonard, 1930, pp. 35–36):

> A serious man was Bacon, a master of the dialectic sleight-of-hand so much admired at the time, a reader of strange languages and curious about distant countries beyond the borders of Christendom. In these ways he was not unique. In one respect only he differed from the men of his time. He had little regard for authority. When he read in some ancient author that a vessel of hot water freezes faster than one of cold, he didn't accept this as an ultimate truth. He took two vessels exactly alike, filled them with hot and cold water, and set them outside in the street. When the cold water froze first, he didn't conclude that his eyes deceived him or that a devil was laughing down the chimney. He said the ancient author was mistaken or a liar. When a diamond-cutter told him that he broke diamonds in a mortar like anything else, he didn't call him a scoundrel, but concluded that Pliny knew as little about diamonds as he did about the tides.

The students were given the following assignment. After reading the passage they were to:

1. Decide if there is a sentence in the article that contains the writer's main thought [I.e., see if there is a "stated generalization"]
2. If there is not a sentence that contains the main thought—write your own sentence giving the main thought [I.e., give an "unstated generalization"]

The students were split into small groups of three and four to search for the generalizations. As they worked, the instructor moved from group to group monitoring their activities. When the instructor decided that the groups had finished analyzing the passage, she made the following statement to the class:

> In every piece of writing there's a main thought and it is supported by details. That's the secret of reading—recognizing the main thought and seeing how it's supported by details. Okay, now did you all find a sentence in the . . . article that contains the main thought?

One student volunteered, "First sentence." "The first sentence," the instructor repeated. "Okay, then you think the main idea was that Bacon was curious?" Another student disagreed with this and pointed out that the second sentence said Bacon's curiosity was not unique, so the first sentence could not contain the main idea. This student went on to say that the main thought was contained in the sentence "He had little regard for authority," and that the following statements merely exemplified Bacon's disregard for authority—they were "details" for this generalization.

The instructor endorsed this answer by choosing that point to shift the discussion into a more general vein. She read the first two sentences of the passage aloud, stressing the final sentence, and then explained that the author of the passage "lists all these characteristics that Bacon had, then he says that they were not unique. Then he begins to talk about the way in which Bacon *was* unique—in his lack of respect for authority."

The basic format of classroom instruction in comprehension lessons was thus for the instructor to allow time for reading, then go from student to student soliciting answers until a "correct" one was given. When a student succeeded in identifying the "main idea," the instructor would take over the discussion and explain how the rest of the passage fit in with the main idea. In short, the task was to sift through the sentences of the text—not reason about its meaning, importance, or validity—and to find a sentence that fit into the proper slot in the terminological framework and satisfied the teacher.

The Bacon example also provides a useful illustration of the way in which "genuine" texts were made "inauthentic" in classroom instruction (see Widdowson, 1978, p. 80). The "passage" itself is a paragraph pulled out of context. It was written as part of a book on the history of chemistry. In that context its function was *not* merely to highlight the unique characteristics of Bacon himself but to show his place in the evolution of "scientific thinking." When the passage is examined out of context its "main idea" has little to do with the functions or meanings it had in its original context. Thus one can learn little about Bacon or the history of chemistry from the passage (indeed, it is not entirely clear if the passage is about Francis or Roger Bacon). More importantly, insisting that a complete main idea can be found in each fragment of text distorts the nature and coherence of naturally occurring texts and sends ambiguous messages about how the latter are to be read. Is the student to go paragraph by paragraph through a text searching for discrete, paragraph-specific main ideas and generalizations? If so, how are these to be ultimately tied together? How in general are nonfiction texts longer than two or three paragraphs to be read? Such questions were never addressed.

When, in the course of the semester, students were finally required to construct "unstated generalizations," they essentially switched to a new kind of guesswork. The object now was to find a sentence or phrase (usually a paraphrase of a sentence in the passage) acceptable to the instructor. Instead of trying to interpret the passages critically or find some personal relevance or meaning in them, they began to guess at phrases that might satisfy the instructor. That is, they called out answers in classroom discussion until the instructor accepted one as correct or supplied the proper answer. Students "guessed" because it was the instructor who determined what an acceptable formulation of an "unstated generalization" would be. There were no "objective" or explicitly stated criteria for doing this. The instructor's interpretation was the one that counted, and no ambiguities, no multiple or conflicting interpretations were permitted. As one student put it:

> I was sure that they [some of his answers] were right, and I got a couple of them [marked] wrong. And I thought, why is it this way? And she [the instructor] said "Well, because I felt . . ." So you still have to formulate an opinion of what you think the teacher will feel.

Another student, referring to the other students in the class, said that:

> I think they're reading [the novel] hoping to find the answer that she [the teacher] wants 'em to have . . . . I don't think none of 'em are formulating their own opinions about it. I think that's important . . . These concepts should be on a one-to-one basis. If it fits for you that's fine, and if it doesn't it shouldn't be important.

To summarize, the instructors sought to focus the students' attention on certain aspects of texts by teaching them a framework of categories and terms. In order to make this framework generalizable across texts, the instructors focused on the frameworks themselves rather than on the meaning of texts in terms of the students' interests, knowledge, and beliefs. Focusing on the meanings of texts, the instructors felt, would amount to "teaching content" to students, and this, they felt, would result in the students not bothering to read for themselves. The consequence of this system was that the image of texts presented to the students was that of "autonomous," context-independent objects, with explicit and unambiguous meanings. Texts, as presented in the class, were objects into which authors had encoded precise meanings. As one instructor explained to her class, "The writer encodes his ideas and on the opposite end of the continuum, the reader decodes the ideas." From this perspective, the task of reading becomes one of deciphering exactly what it is that the writer intended to say. The skills of reading are presented as passive and receptive. The use of reading from the reader's point of view is presented as that of simply decoding the message. The uses of texts in terms of social activities that students might engage in were not considered.

This image of reading was reinforced by the task system of the classroom. Teacher-centered discussions focused attention on giving the teacher what she wanted rather than on the students discovering what they wanted from the text. The preoccupation with memorizing terminology, the definition of the comprehension task as the proper application of terms, the emphasis on uncovering a single unambiguous meaning in the text, the denial of multiple interpretations, and the lack of attention paid to the purposes or possible uses of the text—all of this created a vector of activity in which reading to construct meaning for oneself was subordinated to reading to find the portion of text that fit the category system. In short, in the absence of a framework of activities related to the students' experiences or interests outside the classroom, the only activity into which the reading skills could be integrated was the classroom-specific activity of finding the answer to satisfy the teacher.

## THE COGNITIVE CONSEQUENCES OF READING INSTRUCTION

The transference of skills across contexts is a very difficult individual achievement—that is, what people learn in one context (e.g., a classroom) often fails to have any impact on their action or thought in other tasks or contexts (Gick & Holyoak, 1980; Lave, 1984; LCHC, 1982, 1983; Schoenfeld, 1983). Critiques of curriculum definition and enactment such as the one developed in the preceding section thus stop short of a crucial question: *How* do such systems of instruction influence student cognition and practice? When such transference does occur, it is most likely to be a social achievement accomplished in one of two fashions (LCHC, 1983, p. 340).

First, the socially guided discovery of relationships between tasks encountered in different contexts is an important source of transference (D'Andrade, 1981). That is, people can explicitly explain and demonstrate to one another that problems in one context share important features with problems previously encountered and solved in another context. However, little of this sort of guidance seems to have taken place in the reading classes. No mention was made of the different kinds of texts or reading tasks that students might encounter in other classes or in reading situations outside the school.

A second means of transference takes place through language. People develop specialized lexicons or ways of talking about different contexts that encode their similarities. Again, the reading classes did little to provide the sorts of lexical cues that would have enabled students to transfer knowledge to different sorts of texts outside of the reading classes. Terms such as "main idea" and "generalization" would appear to be candidates for transcontextual application, but in the reading classes these were attached exclusively to short, artificial passages. In fact, they were usually associated with actual sentences in the text, so that finding the "generalization" became a matter of finding the most general sentence in the passage. Most importantly, interpretation or the construction of relevant meanings of texts in terms of one's own interests and needs—a type of activity that would be required for transference to take place—was explicitly proscribed.

In short, the social mechanisms by which students could learn to take the "skills" taught in the reading courses and transfer them to other contexts (either work or school) were not available in the reading classes. At the same time, the students couldn't simply ignore the courses or their requirements, if for no other reason than because the courses carried objective traces—grades—that went on the students' records and influenced their overall chances of academic success.

The students in the reading classes were thus in a position in which they needed to produce a set of products—worksheets, workbooks, tests, and so forth—in order to secure acceptable grades. From the instructors' point of view these products were part of a complex task system designed to increase the students' general capacities to deal with written texts. That is, the instructors acted on the basis of what has been called a "central processor model" of cognitive skills. The basic thrust of the model

> is to assume that experience operates on the current state of some central cognitive structures (perhaps characterized by stagelike features, perhaps characterized only by level). Each learning experience . . . contributes some increment in power (level, amount) to the central processing machinery that is then deployed to deal with individual performance tasks. (LCHC, 1982, p. 651)

Each product in the reading classes was intended to function as part of a process in which students acquired comprehension skills that would have general applications to any texts that they might encounter outside the classroom. Thus when students did exercises in the comprehension books they were supposed to be learning the skills of drawing generalizations and main ideas from text. When they took the tests they were supposed to be manifesting their understanding of the concepts and skills that the instructors had taught them.

But reading and other social-cognitive skills are attached to specific contexts of use, and most tasks in the reading classes (for example, answering multiple-choice questions about artificially constructed passages in workbooks) took place in micro-contexts unlikely to be found in the outside world. The one task that seemingly pertained to general literacy processes—finding the main ideas or generalizations of passages—was constrained by the fact that the students were not supposed to construct meaning from the text. They were, instead, to find the meaning embedded in a supposedly autonomous text. Since the students were proscribed from using their own notions of relevance, importance, or meaning, the norm of rationality in the classroom became the strictly "formal" or "instrumental" one (Habermas, 1972; Weber, 1964) of finding a main idea or generalization statement that would satisfy the teacher and get the reward (the grade) offered by the class task system. The "substantive" rationality of constructing a meaning of some relevance to oneself was subverted. Indeed, trying to make personal sense of the passages would have produced a poor grade. In order to perform their tasks appropriately in terms of the classroom norms of rationality the students had to "cognitively segregate" the activities taking place in the classroom from activities taking place in the rest of the world (Anderson, 1977, p. 423–427).

Cognitive segregation is not an uncommon finding of research on school knowledge. DiSessa (1982), for example, has shown that undergraduate students with training in physics frequently invoked "Aristotelian" conceptions of momentum (i.e., the idea that objects move in the direction they are pushed only so long as force is applied) when asked to explain motion in a non-physics-class setting. Schoenfeld (1983, 1984) reports similar findings: college students who were able to solve geometry proofs pertaining to a particular geometric construction acted like "naive empiricists" when asked to actually produce the construction. That is, they evaluated their efforts on the basis of how the construction looked rather than accepting or rejecting the construction on the basis of the proof. Schoenfeld concludes that for these students theories and proofs were a special kind of knowledge that was, as it were, deposited in a box marked "to be opened only in math class." In short, the students in these studies were able to use their school knowledge about physics and math in order to meet the task requirements of their school classes, but outside the school they perceived and interpreted the world in ways quite inconsistent with that knowledge.

The model of the reading classes developed here posits that similar processes of task-specific learning were taking place there. To make good grades, the students had to avoid "interpreting" or "constructing" personally relevant meanings from the text. They learned to segregate classroom tasks from other real world experiences and as a consequence acquired reading "skills" that had no functions or uses outside the classroom.

## LEARNING ABOUT READING

It would not be entirely true, however, to say that the students did nothing more than learn the routines necessary to do the work required for passing grades. This is true in the sense that what they learned from the tasks in the classes was how to carry out classroom-specific tasks and that the "skills" acquired in this fashion could not be expected to have useful applications in dissimilar contexts. But the students may have been learning more than that: they may have been learning how to define the task of reading itself.

Consider the discussion of the conditions necessary for the successful social transfer of cognitive skills. First, there is a need for explicit social guidance. That is, the relevance of skills used in one context to problems encountered in other contexts must be pointed out and explained in social interaction. Second, there must exist some sort of lexicon for linking problems embedded in different contexts. It has been argued that neither of these requirements were met in the reading classes with regard to the "skills" taught there. The teachers did not explain how the "skills" or categories presented in the classes related to texts or reading situations that students might encounter outside the classes.

On another level of analysis, however, there was a very powerful lexical item linking reading practices within the reading classes to reading practices outside the classes: this was the term "reading" itself. The reading classes, in effect, appropriated the term "reading" and asserted that the tasks and practices carried out in the classes constituted "reading" itself. In this sense, the students were clearly guided by the instructors to define "reading" as an activity made up of the types of tasks presented in the classes. Lave (1984) makes a similar point in her discussion of arithmetic skills. She found that the people she studied could perform math calculations quickly and accurately in their heads while shopping, but reverted to ineffective, half-forgotten procedures when asked to demonstrate their skills outside the everyday contexts in which they used them. Lave points to the "ideological character" of arithmetic, the belief among schooled adults that "school-taught algorithms are the only 'right way' to do arithmetic" (Lave, 1984, p. 22).

The point being made here can be stated succinctly: knowledge and skills are context-specific. Unless the connections between contexts are explicitly made in social interaction and make sense in practice, the skills people learn in classrooms will not be applied outside those contexts. By the same token, an office worker or factory worker may learn math or literacy skills on the job that will be specific and appropriate to their work (just as Lave's shoppers had learned math skills specifically tied to the activity of shopping). But within schools people learn to define practices such as "mathematics" and "reading" in specific ways that are linked to the types of tasks found in the school context.

Thus Lave's shoppers were quite proficient at arithmetic in the grocery store when they did not think of themselves as doing math. When they were explicitly asked to do "arithmetic" problems they shifted gears radically and tried to call up less effective practices learned in school. Similarly, the students in the reading classes were taught to attach a set of routines and procedures to the concept of "reading": they were taught a definition of reading specific to the school setting. Although they might go on to learn effective ways of dealing with written language in everyday settings, they were being taught that situations explicitly defined as "reading" were to be dealt with in terms of the skills laid down in the classes. "Reading" was thus presented as the activity, not of constructing meanings or using written texts for practical purposes, but of searching for fully formed and unambiguous "generalizations" supposedly embedded in the texts by their authors.

The students were thus taught, not to challenge or interpret texts, not to search for personal meanings or uses in them, but instead to treat them as complete and objectified entities. This segregation of "reading" from everyday life transforms the text into an entity which can no longer challenge the reader's own predispositions or opinions. It may be instrumentally useful, it may entertain, but it cannot engage one in dialogue or debate with the author. "Reading" becomes the arduous process of reconstructing someone else's monologue, and the only options presented are those of accepting it or ignoring it altogether.

## CONCLUSION

The arguments formulated above call into question the range of application of Bourdieu's notions about the relationship between culture and education. Bourdieu suggests that the content of educational curricula is closely related to the cultural capital that children of the privileged classes acquire at home. These children are thus advantaged when putatively identical educational opportunities are presented to children of all classes. The present argument focuses less on why some students as opposed to others succeed in school and more on the question of what schooling does to those who participate in it. The argument holds that for some curricular knowledge forms—specifically those concerned with fundamental skills such as "reading" or "writing"— school curricula have no genuine relationship to the cultural capital of any class, at least in the way Bourdieu would conceive such a relationship.

Instead, the school-specific task systems in which "reading" and "writing" are embedded operate to establish authoritative definitions of the skills themselves; they create "legitimate" versions of these skills and label students as competent or incompetent in their use. These labels and skill definitions persist even after students leave school and develop their actual reading and writing abilities in the course of the common, everyday activities they participate in as adults. This has several effects. First, it masks cultural inequalities. When the school labels two individuals equally "literate" and one goes on to a position or occupation in which complex reading and writing are part of everyday activity while the other moves into a position where written language use is highly routinized, the impression is created of an equality of skills where none exists. Work settings are defined as places where knowledge previously gained is put to use, not as educational environments in their own right.

Second, it masks the sources of social and economic inequalities by asserting that students who perform differently on school-specific literacy tasks are differentially suited to and differentially deserving of prestigious, well-paying, high-discretion work (when in fact the reading skills acquired in school settings have no direct bearing on social competence outside the school).

Finally, by defining occupations whose task systems resemble those of schools as embodying "educated" or "literate" activity, a false distinction between "mental labor" and "manual labor" is created. As an increasingly large body of work demonstrates, even the most seemingly routinized forms of work—industrial piecework, for example—require complex and sophisticated "working knowledge" for their performance. These forms of knowledge are not formalized or systematized, and the workers who use them may not conceptualize them as legitimate bodies of knowledge, but they are nonetheless forms of "mental labor" (see, e.g., Kusterer, 1978; Scribner, 1984; Singleton, 1978). The school, by defining particular forms of mental labor as mental labor per se lessens the likelihood that those in possession of nonschool forms will consciously reflect upon them and develop them. At the same time, by making the claim that the favored form or forms of mental labor are the only ones possible it limits the likelihood that those who possess them will challenge their limits or examine alternatives.

## REFERENCES

Anderson, R. C. (1977). The notion of schemata and the educational enterprise. In R. Anderson, R. Spiro, & W. Montague (Eds.), *Schooling and the acquisition of knowledge* (pp. 415–431). Hillsdale, NJ: Lawrence Erlbaum.

Anyon, J. (1981). Social class and school knowledge. *Curriculum Inquiry, 11*(1), 3–42.

Ball, S. (1982). Competition and conflict in the teaching of English: A socio-historical analysis. *Journal of Curriculum Studies, 15*(1), 1–28.

Ball, S. (1983). A subject or privilege: English and the school curriculum. In M. Hammersley & A. Hargreaves (Eds.), *Curriculum practice: Some sociological case studies* (pp. 61–88). London: Falmer.

Bourdieu, P. (1967). Systems of education and systems of thought. *International Social Science Journal, 19*(3), 338–358.

Bourdieu, P. (1969). Intellectual field and creative project. *Social Science Information, 8*(2), 89–119.

Bourdieu, P. (1974). The school as a conservative force: Scholastic and cultural inequalities. In J. Eggleston (Ed.), *Contemporary research in the sociology of education* (pp. 32–46). London: Methuen.

Bourdieu, P. (1977a). The economics of linguistic exchange. *Social Science Information, 16*, 645–668.

Bourdieu, P. (1977b). *Outline of a theory of practice*. Cambridge: Cambridge University Press.

Bourdieu, P. (1977c). Cultural reproduction and social reproduction. In J. Karabel & A. H. Halsey (Eds.), *Power and ideology in education* (pp. 487–511). New York: Oxford University Press.

Bourdieu, P. (1977d). Symbolic power. In D. Gleeson (Ed.), *Identity and structure: Issues in the sociology of education* (pp. 112–119). Driffield: Nafferton Books.

Bourdieu, P., & Passeron, J. C. (1977). *Reproduction*. Beverly Hills: Sage.

D'Andrade, R. (1981). The cultural part of cognition. *Cognitive Science, 5,* 179–195.

DiMaggio, P. (1979). Review essay: On Pierre Bourdieu. *American Journal of Sociology, 84,* 1460–1474.

DiSessa, A. (1982). On learning Aristotelian physics: A study of knowledge-based learning. *Cognitive Science, 6,* 37–75.

Febvre, L. & Martin, H.-J. (1976). *The coming of the book: The impact of printing, 1450–1800.* London: New Left Books.

Gick, M. & Holyoak, K. (1980). Analogical problem solving. *Cognitive Science, 12,* 306–355.

Goodson, I. (1982). *School subjects and curriculum change*. London: Croom Helm.

Graff, J. (1978–1979). Literacy past and present: Critical approaches in the literacy / society relationship. *Interchange, 9*(2), 1–29.

Habermas, J. (1972). *Knowledge and human interests*. London: Heinemann.

Hammersley, M., & Hargreaves, A. (Eds.). (1983). *Curriculum practice: Some sociological case studies*. London: Falmer.

Heath, S. B. (1977). Language and politics in the United States. In M. Saville-Troike (Ed.), *Linguistics and anthropology, GURT 1977* (pp. 267–296). Washington, DC: Georgetown University Press.

Heath, S. B. (1980). The functions and uses of literacy. *Journal of Communication, 30*(1), 123–133.

Heath, S. B. (1983). *Ways with words*. Stanford: Stanford University Press.

Jenkins, R. (1982). Pierre Bourdieu and the reproduction of determinism. *Sociology, 16*(2), 270–281.

Kusterer, K. (1978). *Know-how on the job: The important working knowledge of "unskilled" workers*. Boulder, CO: Westview Press.

Lave, J. (1984, April). *Experiments, tests, jobs and chores: How we learn what we do*. Paper presented at the annual meeting of the American Educational Research Association, New Orleans.

Lave, J., Murtaugh, M., & de la Rocha, O. (1984). The dialectic of arithmetic in grocery shopping. In B. Rogoff & J. Lave (Eds.), *Everyday cognition: Its development in social context* (pp. 67–94). Cambridge: Harvard University Press.

Lazerson, M. (1971). *Origins of the urban school: Public education in Massachusetts, 1870–1915*. Cambridge: Harvard University Press.

LCHC [Laboratory of Comparative Human Cognition]. (1982). Culture and intelligence. In R. Sternberg (Ed.), *Handbook of human intelligence* (pp. 642–719). Cambridge: Cambridge University Press.

LCHC [Laboratory of Comparative Human Cognition]. (1983). Culture and cognitive development. In W. Kessen (Ed.), *Handbook of child psychology, Vol. 1: History, theory, and methods* (pp. 295–356). New York: Wiley.

Leonard, J. N. (1930). *Crusaders of chemistry*. Garden City, NY: Doubleday.

MacDonald, M. (1979–1980). Cultural reproduction: The pedagogy of sexuality. *Screen Education*, No. 32 / 33, pp. 141–153.

Nespor, J. (1985). *The construction of knowledge in school settings*. Unpublished doctoral dissertation, Department of Anthropology, University of Texas at Austin.

Ogbu, J. (1974). *The next generation: An ethnography of education in an urban neighborhood*. New York: Academic Press.

Olson, D. (1977). The languages of instruction: The literate bias of schooling. In R. Anderson, R. Spiro, & W. Montague (Eds.), *Schooling and the acquisition of knowledge* (pp. 65–98). Hillsdale, NJ: Lawrence Erlbaum.

Resnick, D., & Resnick, L. (1977). The nature of literacy: An historical exploration. *Harvard Educational Review, 47,* 370–385.

Robinson, A. (1977). Reading instruction and research in historical perspective. In A. Robinson (Ed.), *Reading and writing instruction in the United States: Historical trends* (pp. 44–58). Newark, DE: International Reading Association.

Schoenfeld, A. (1983). Beyond the purely cognitive: Belief systems, social cognitions, and metacognitions as driving forces in intellectual performance. *Cognitive Science, 7,* 329–363.

Schoenfeld, A. (1984). *On belief and knowledge: Sophisticated students as naive empiricists.* Paper presented at the annual meeting of the American Educational Research Association, New Orleans, LA.

Scribner, S. (Ed.). (1984). *Cognitive studies of work.* Special Issue, *Quarterly Newsletter of the Laboratory of Comparative Human Cognition, 6*(1 & 2).

Singleton, W. (Ed.). (1978). *The analysis of practical skills.* Lancaster, England: MIT Press.

Steinberg, S. (1974). *Five hundred years of printing* (third edition). Harmondsworth: Penguin.

Strauss, G. (1981). Techniques of indoctrination: The German reformation. In H. Graff (Ed.), *Literacy and social development in the West: A reader* (pp. 96–104). Cambridge: Cambridge University Press.

Thompson, E. P. (1978). *The poverty of theory.* London: New Left Books.

Weber, M. (1964). *The theory of social and economic organization.* New York: Free Press.

Widdowson, H. (1978). *Teaching language as communication.* Oxford: Oxford University Press.

Williams, R. (1961). *The long revolution.* London: Oxford University Press.

Willis, P. (1981). *Learning to labor: How working class kids get working class jobs.* New York: Columbia University Press.

Young, M. (Ed.). (1971). *Knowledge and control: New directions for the sociology of education.* London: Collier-Macmillan.

——————————— 12 ———————————

# BENJAMIN'S STORY

## Jonathan Kozol

The airman is viewed as an information processing system with limited cognitive capacity. (Duffy, 1984, p. 41)

One of my oldest friends in Boston is a woman whom, for now, I will call Ellen.[1] She is forty-two years old. A descendant of three generations of nonreaders, she is perhaps the poorest person I have ever known. She is also a poet. I will return to this. Her background is unusual and, in one sense, symbolic. She is part white, part Mexican, part black. She might represent, within her lineage, an ethnic spectrum of America. Because she is my friend, it isn't easy to regard her as a symbol; but the symbolism seems too obvious to miss. She is, for certain, an explicit product of our nation's history.

One of Ellen's great-grandparents was a slave. Another was a migrant farmer. A third came to the United States from Scandinavia. Her grandmother was a sharecropper; her mother, a domestic maid. Ellen can read and write a little, but so poorly that the pedagogic world would have to call her semiliterate. Her oral vocabulary, however, is both searching and expressive. She sits with me in her kitchen often for long evenings and she "tells me poems." I write them down. Several have been published in fine literary journals. Nobody knows that this extraordinary verse has been composed by somebody who cannot read it.[2]

I wonder sometimes how much beauty, how many poems and stories like the ones she tells me, must be stillborn every year, each decade, in America. How much of our possible aesthetic wealth is annually diminished, lost forever? This would not appear in figures about GNP. Some of our citizens might think it should. But that is another story. It is Ellen's son whose story is important here.

Ellen has five children. Two of them were bused to a suburban school and learned to read quite well. Two others, who attended school in Boston, read and write only at marginal levels. The fifth one scarcely reads at sixth grade level. He is the second oldest. His name is Benjamin.

Benjamin is the only member of the family I do not know well. He was sent down South to live with his grandparents when he was in second grade. He did not return to Roxbury until he was nineteen. Since that time, he has appeared increasingly withdrawn, sometimes rebellious, but more often silently resistant to his mother's love. He was beaten as a child in the Boston schools. A scar on his forefinger is a cicatrix of bitterness that he too willingly restricts, constrains, conceals.[3]

Still a poor reader, he attempted for six months to find a job, had no success, then fell into a grim, depressive state. For over a year he sat at home, glued to the TV. Involved in constant travel during that most crucial year, I called some friends. They did their best to get him signed up in a literacy program. He seemed to be prepared to try it, but the waiting list was long. By the time he was admitted he had lost whatever spark of interest he had felt. The program, moreover, took place in a local school. He found this painful, showed up once or twice, then finally withdrew and settled once again into the same depression.

Stirred from slumber one night by a TV plug—"Go Army! Be a man!"—he went downtown and got himself enlisted. By the time that I returned to Boston, he had managed to squeak past a literacy exam, was given his orders, and sent off to Oklahoma.

It turns out, after cutting back on all the humane answers to the literacy crisis, the government provides one seldom-noted but heavily funded and distinctly "national" response which too many poor young men cannot turn down.

Those who are the children of illiterate adults, those who live their early years in single-parent families where the single parent is statistically most certain to be partially or totally illiterate, those who are obliged to go to the most underfunded and destructive schools—those, in short, who are most likely to be sent into the world without the educational resources to compete and to prevail within a print society—do have one last recourse in pursuit of literacy instruction. That recourse is the U.S. Army.[4]

Men whose literacy is very poor but good enough to win a GED and barely to get through some very simple tests can be admitted to the U.S. Army and will be provided, in the course of training, with a special brand of militarily effective competence. What is likely to be viewed as functional in military terms may be imagined without difficulty. Nor do we need to imagine, since we already know too well—both from the words of military specialists themselves and from the experience of thousands of young men like Benjamin—precisely what they learn and how they are indoctrinated to apply that learning in the service of an institution which depends on blind obedience, fosters functionally acquiescent consciousness, and cannot be expected to do otherwise in view of its mandated role in our society.

The soldier is "trained." It is explicit. This is war preparedness. It is not ethics or aesthetics. Soldiers are not burdened with the histories of Tacitus, the fears of Madison, the eloquence of Erik Erikson, of Emerson, Thoreau, or William James. Nor are they confronted with the metaphors of Melville, Robert Lowell, William Faulkner, Thomas Mann, or C. P. Snow. Neither a love of life nor the respect for beauty that a civilized and life-affirming social order can bestir is part of the curricular endowment that a military officer is hired to impart.

"The interests of the individual," writes Thomas Sticht,[5] one of the more knowledgeable observers of the military's literacy plans, "are subordinate to the goals and missions of the organization" (1984, p. 5).

We may think we can imagine both the "goals" and "missions" that he has in mind; most of us, I think, will be alarmed to see how far the vivid details may exceed our most uneasy fears.

According to Thomas Duffy, in a paper titled "Literacy Instruction in the Military" (January 1984),[6] "Armed Forces personnel must operate and maintain some of the most sophisticated, costly, and dangerous equipments in existence" (p. 17). Literacy, for this reason, "is perhaps more critical in the Armed Forces" than in any other sector of society.

Forty percent of all recruits who enter the armed forces every year read at eighth grade level or below. Many read at only grade school levels. The volume of technical documentation needed on the job in military service is extensive. "A single stack of all the documentation required to support the equipment" on a single nuclear submarine "would be higher than the Washington Monument" (p. 4). Over a million pages of reading matter "are required to support the operation and maintenance of the B-1 bomber" (p. 4).

In one instance, Duffy writes, technicians must refer "to 165 pages in eight documents . . . just to isolate and repair one fault in a radar system" (p. 5).

For these reasons, "there is a formal requirement in each service that personnel must use the technical documentation during all maintenance work. Failure to have the appropriate manual turned to the appropriate page can, and has, led [sic] to disciplinary action" (p. 5). Forty percent of new recruits cannot meet these minimal demands.

There was a time, writes Duffy, when education in the military was offered to meet broader purposes than those described above: "The instruction [of an earlier age] seems to have been offered for the good of the individual and society and not necessarily for the good of the service" (p. 8). This error, Duffy indicates, has been corrected.

By present guidelines, instructional courses in the military are provided through two different offices. One is labeled education. The other is described as training. "The training command . . . constitutes the bulk of the instruction. It is also the instruction that is judged as essential to the maintenance of military readiness" (p. 10). In order to be sure that new recruits are able "to deploy equipments," Duffy writes, it is the "training" factor, not the "education," which receives the burden of attention. Training is taken "during normal duty hours and is considered part of 'the job.'" Courses under the education command, in contrast, are "not considered essential to the job" (p. 10).

What, then, falls into the category termed essential?

It is essential, Duffy writes, "that everything needed to perform the job is taught but that there is no instruction on irrelevant or unnecessary topics or skills" (p. 18). In electronics training, for example, mathematics is restricted in two ways: "First, only that mathematics instruction deemed essential to successful performance in the electronics area is taught" (p. 19). Second, students "are not taught general mathematics nor are the formulas presented in abstract terms, e.g., $A = BC$" (p. 19). The purpose, he explains, is to spare the student "the extra burden of generalizing. . . ." This, he says, is viewed as "quite unnecessary" (p. 19).

Today, writes Duffy, literacy programs in the military have been rendered uniform in order to conform to the requirements described above. This is all the more important, he remarks, because "the move to the all volunteer force . . . was seen as greatly reducing the quality of personnel" (p. 26). Indeed, he says, "the percent of Army recruits in the lowest ability category [has] increased from ten percent in 1975 to 31 percent in 1981" (p. 26). The Department of Defense, to use his technocratic words, is suffering today from "decreased access to desirable individuals" in what he calls "the primary assession pool" (p. 26).

Illiterate and undesirable are treated as synonymous.

Even as late as 1983, despite all of the emphasis on mechanistic skills, education still appeared to have been getting in the way of basic military needs. The General Accounting Office reported, with disapproval, that "general literacy" was still pervasive in the U.S. Army programs and was undermining emphasis on "job-related" skills. The GAO recommended that these programs (educational, not "relevant") be "terminated."

Duffy feels convinced that military policy will henceforth be in line with this directive. The Navy, faced with the "undesirable" influx of "lower aptitude personnel" (the Navy's term), now guarantees that "content is specific to the . . . training area" (p. 35–36). The Army, quick to be attracted to the technological approach, now insists that 50 percent of its curriculum be "computer-based." Both the Army and the Air Force seem to have brought technological and fragmentized ("specific") skill instruction to a level that will satisfy the GAO.

The Army, according to Duffy, because it operates a number of small and isolated European bases, cannot afford to offer on-site literacy training taught by an instructor. Videodiscs and microcomputers therefore take the place of teachers. The computerized system, known as STARS, "has the positive feature," in the words of Duffy, that it can be used without instructors. The video material, suggestive of a kind of space wars fantasy that sounds a great deal like the content of the comic books and television programs aimed at fourth or fifth grade children, "provides strong motivational context." Duffy adds that these materials are "excellent," "enticing." Instruction is presented "in the context of the student [as] a member of a space team who have numerous tasks to perform" (p. 42). One of these tasks is the demonstration that "a time machine really works." The videodisc presents "the motivational context of the space ship and coworkers" (p. 42).

The desiccating jargon used repeatedly by Duffy in describing all these programs ("motivational context," "primary assession pool," "lower aptitude personnel") would not warrant our attention if it did not crystallize so well the values and the ethos of these military efforts. It is all the more disturbing because these, the jargon and the ethos and the shabby values, permeate civilian pedagogic discourse too. The language represents a perfect paradigm for the renewal of a disciplined, a punitive, a tightly stratified, and (most of all) obedience-based education system, structured to assure perpetuation of a fragmentized but useful population.

"The airman," in Duffy's words, "is viewed as an information processing system with limited cognitive capacity" (p. 41).

We might like to speculate how Jefferson or Tocqueville, Orwell or Bonhoeffer might respond to these extraordinary words. A dark voyage threatens to entice not just the soldiers in their isolated capsules of computer-based instruction in their European missile stations but the growing children and the semiliterate adults who live right here within our own hometowns.

C. P. Snow once asked a man about his taste in books.

"Books?" the man repeated. "I prefer to use my books as tools."

Snow seems to have reflected for a while on this answer. "It was very hard not to let the mind wander—what sort of tool would a book make?" He wondered aloud: "Perhaps a hammer? A primitive digging instrument?" (p. 13).

These are the questions which would not be asked in military circles. Books or manuals, lists of truck or missile parts, instructions for dismantling a gun— all of these are clearly viewed as useful tools. If they were not, they would be excluded from the body of instruction Duffy has described. They would then be viewed as "education" and would, for this reason, be in conflict with the guidelines of the GAO.

But Snow's speculations and his puzzlement might give us pause to ask if we can tolerate the "missions" and "objectives" that the military has in mind for those that it defines as undesirable and lower-aptitude personnel.

"Perhaps a digging instrument?"

If our government continues on its way, and if we cannot denounce the people who contrive these programs for the art of killing while they starve civilian programs for the art of life, who will there remain to use these instruments once military men have finished with their "space wars" and "deployments"? What of the rest of us? What of America? What of the world? Will there still remain a world for these robotic beings to inhabit? Who, then, will remain to do the digging?

There is something savage in this nation.

After absolute capitulation on a decent answer to the failures of the state and local schools, here is a military answer which is racist by selection and dehumanizing by intent.

Benjamin is done with basic training now. He wrote his mother a letter last month. It was his final week in Oklahoma. Since she reads so poorly, she called up and asked me to come over. It was an amazing document. He misspelled simple words like "freinds," "imposibble," and "terrifyed." His spelling was perfect, however, when it came to "weapons," "enemy," "deployment."

In June he was assigned to go to Europe. He was given two weeks off in order to come home to say good-bye. Ellen used a neighbor's phone. She wanted me to come for dinner. He was not unfriendly with me. He was distant. A cynicism I had never heard pervaded the entire conversation. He looked transformed: rigid and slim. He spoke of killing those he called "The Enemy" with macho jubilation.

"Could you do it?" I asked.

"A soldier does what must be done," was his reply.

Benjamin is at an army base in Germany today. He is part of a detachment which will be responsible for the deployment of cruise missiles.

Many of the sorrows of Illiterate America, and all the dangers of the neatly functional machine that any nation can produce out of the slag heap it has first created, are at stake in this—Benjamin's story. Illiteracy: created by decrepit schools staffed by exhausted and defeated teachers, passed down through generations of nonreading parents. Next: passivity, the TV tube, humiliation, and despair. At last, the all-American and patriotic answer: basic training, absolute obedience to flag and anthem, suspension of emotion in the face of death, a certain hedonistic joy—a punk-rock fascination—at the prospect of mechanical annihilation. Yet he cannot write a simple note of love in lucid words, correctly spelled, to a good-hearted mother who, in any case, can't read them.

Benjamin is functionally competent at last. One day he may have his chance to press the button that releases that long, trim, and slender instrument of death that he so much resembles. Is this the kind of literacy we want? Is this the best that Jeffersonian democracy can do?

In my recent book, *Illiterate America* (1985), I have argued otherwise. Whether the nation shares my faith remains a question to which I do not dare risk an answer.

## NOTES

1. Identifying details of Ellen's life and of her children's situation have been altered to protect their anonymity.

2. This story was recorded during August 1983. Since that time, Ellen has been spurred by her own courage and ambition to pursue aggressive programs of instruction, some of it essentially self-education; but she has also enrolled in classes in a setting which has given her strong motivation to succeed. One day before very long, she may be writing her own stories and producing finished works for publication without mediation from her friends.

3. "A scar on his forefinger . . ." This is a common souvenir of public education for the children who attended school in Boston in the 1960s. Many young adults in Boston's black community still bear those scars today. (See Kozol, 1967.)

4. Officially, the Army insists upon ninth grade completion, a GED or high school diploma, and ability to pass two written tests. Yet 27 percent of those who are accepted cannot read at seventh grade level (Laubach Literacy International, 1982.) Whatever the formal standards for entrance to the military, it is widely known that actual criteria for military service are pragmatically adjusted to absorb the needed number of recruits in any given year.

A relevant excerpt from the *Washington Post* (Omang, 1982): "The nuclear vigil has required expanded remedial reading and math courses for a record number of [military] recruits who read just barely above the fifth-grade level. The armed forces had 220,000 people in remedial math and reading courses last year, focusing on the words and computation needed in the nuclear era."

5. See Sticht (1984). Note that Sticht is not speaking here exclusively of literacy training in the military, but of literacy work conducted in several institutional settings: military, business, industry, etc. Nonetheless, his choice of words ("missions") and his long identification with the military sector indicate that military programs are, if not his exclusive focus, unquestionably foremost in his thoughts. (One would seldom speak of "missions" in discussion of a literacy plan devised for Polaroid or Citibank.)

Sticht has developed his views on literacy in the military in a number of publications. See, for example, Sticht (1982). Although I differ sharply with some of his views, I do not wish my criticism of the military programs in this chapter to be mistaken for a criticism of Sticht's positions. He is consistently more open, less constricted in his focus, and—above all—far less jingoistic than the mainstream organizers of the military's efforts.

6. This remarkable document merits close examination. Much of the most frightening material has not been included in my brief summation. Duffy tells us, for example, that the Army recently developed a "portable" literacy program which can be carried by the soldier in a briefcase. Two of its initial exercises are described as "Picture Battle" and "Word War." Both are taught by a voice-synthesized speech duplicator which speaks to the soldier from a hand-held computer. The "Handheld Tutor" (Duffy's term) is now being tested at Fort Stewart, Georgia. In fairness to the Army, it should be added that the paper uses the expression "whole man focus" in description of the Army's job instruction. How much of "the whole" (or what sort of "a whole") the Army has in mind is not made clear.

## REFERENCES

Duffy, T. M. (1984). *Literacy instruction in the military.* Pittsburgh: Communications Design Center, Carnegie Mellon University.

Kozol, J. (1967). *Death at an early age.* Boston: Houghton Mifflin.

Kozol, J. (1985). *Illiterate America.* New York: Doubleday & Company. *Laubach literacy fact sheet.* (1982). Syracuse, NY: Laubach Literacy International.

Omang, Joanne (1984). *Washington Post,* November 27, 1982.

Snow, C. P. (1964). *The two cultures and a second look,* New York: Cambridge University Press.

Sticht, T. (1982). *Basic skills in defense.* Alexandria, VA: Human Resources Research Organization.

Sticht, T. (1984). *Strategies for adult literacy development.* Unpublished paper, Applied Behavioral and Cognitive Sciences, Inc., San Diego, January 10, 1984.

## 13

# PETRA: LEARNING TO READ AT 45

### Pat Rigg

I met Petra Rodriguez almost two years ago. I was investigating the perceptions of literacy held by various groups of adults who were considered illiterate, and one of these groups was Spanish-speaking migrant workers. The person helping me interview people in the migrant camp suggested that we interview Petra because he knew that she had never been to school and could not even write her name. So one hot afternoon in late September, when Petra and her husband came back from a long day spent on ladders picking apples, D and I were waiting for them at their two rooms in the camp barracks. It was here that I first met Petra. She is a big woman, a little over five and a half feet tall, large bosomed and very handsome with strong white teeth and long black hair in a thick braid down her back. Her hands are big and calloused.

D acted as translator, since neither Petra nor her husband knew any English, and my Spanish is minimal. He asked if we could have a few moments of her time, and introduced me as *la profesora de la universidad*, someone interested in talking with people who did not read or write. Petra gave me a small smile and, because she knew and liked D, waved us graciously into the tiny sweatbox that served her, her husband, and her two sons as kitchen, dining room, and living room, all in one. Her husband took a towel and a bar of soap and went off to the

Thanks are due to Francis E. Kazemek for helpful suggestions which have been incorporated, and to Clara Villamizar for sharing her tutoring log. This chapter and the work it describes owe much to Shirley Brice Heath, whose articles and whose *Ways with Words* have been shining beacons. A previous version of this chapter appeared in *Literacy—Alphabetisation*, Volume 9, Number 2, published by the Movement for Canadian Literacy.

building which housed the communal showers and toilets. Petra apologized for still being covered with field dirt. She invited us to be seated on the bench that was pulled up to the table. I turned on the tape recorder, and D began asking Petra questions from the Burke Interview.

The Burke Interview is a set of questions designed to elicit a person's unarticulated and unconscious theory of reading. Since all of the questions assume that the person being interviewed reads to at least some extent, these questions are often irrelevant to someone who does not read or write at all. Discovering that irrelevancy was one result of the study.

At one point in the interview, D asked, "If you knew someone was having difficulty reading, how would you help him?" and after a long pause during which Petra looked at him searchingly, D asked, "Do you understand the question?" This is Petra's answer: "I miss not knowing how to read. People like you, who know how, should come to help me so I could learn some stories, at least how to write my name."

"But," D persisted, "you, how would you help someone who doesn't know how to read?"

"As I told you," she replied, "If I were like you who know how to read, I would be very nice to that person who doesn't know how to read. You know, there are a lot of people like that, right? Someone who already knows how to read is all the time saying, 'Why do you want to learn that?' and they don't care. They are all the time judging one because one doesn't know how to read, but one knows how to think in one's head."

I was struck by this woman's reply, by this woman herself. Of all the people we had interviewed, she was the first one to assert her right to literacy, and to demand help. She did it pleasantly, softly, courteously, but she did it. "People like you should come to help me . . . at least to write my name."

After D had asked all the questions on the Burke Interview, I told him, "Ask Petra if she has any questions for us."

Petra turned to me. Pausing after each sentence so that her words could be translated clearly, she said, "This is what I want to know: Why are you asking these questions? Are you trying to help those who can't read, or are you asking them to help yourselves?"

True, Petra couldn't read, but she could think in her head.

Before Petra asked her searching question, while we were still going through the Burke Interview, Petra gave a shrugging laugh to many of the questions and said, "*No se leer*. I can't read." Finally, I interrupted the interview: in very halting Spanish I said to her, "Yes, you can read, at least something."

"No," she shrugged and laughed a short laugh, "*Se nada*. I don't know anything."

I waved at a can of shortening and a box of rice on the small shelf over the sink: "D, tell her she must have read those labels, or she couldn't have bought the right things." D translated back to me, "She says she's memorized the look of the containers, but she can't read." I don't know why, but I was almost desperate to prove to this woman that she could read and, however little, was reading. I pulled a pad of paper in front of me and printed her name in block capital letters, saying "Petra Rodriguez" as I did so; then I wrote D's name and my own, saying each, and passed the paper to her. "Which one is yours?" She put her finger on PETRA RODRIGUEZ and looked at me inquiringly. Yes, I nodded, "You can read. Puedes leer."

We finished our interview, turned off the tape recorder, and packed up our tapes and pencils and paper, all but the paper on which I had written the three names. And I forgot about that paper.

Two months later, after the apple picking was over for the year and the migrants had moved on to Florida, D stopped by my place. "I saw Petra yesterday. Do you remember her? She and her husband and her two sons are staying here over the winter. Do you know what she has been doing? She kept that sheet of paper you wrote her name on, do you remember? She has been copying her name. Now she can write her name. She told me to tell you and to give you greetings."

I don't know if I can express clearly how moved I was by this, how important it was to me. By God, here was a woman who deserved whatever help I could find for her. Imagine, keeping that paper and tracing over and over, and then copying onto grocery sacks and similar papers, since there are no writing supplies in her household, the letters of her name, PETRA RODRIGUEZ. As it happened, I was just beginning to teach a class in adult literacy, and one of the assignments was to tutor an adult beginning reader. One of the students was from Colombia, a lovely Spanish-speaking woman. I introduced them to each other, and for the next four months, Clara tutored Petra, often with me present. Clara's log and the records I kept of our many talks with each other, about Petra and about our work with Petra, form the basis of this report.

## TUTORING PETRA: THEORETICAL BASES

Clara and I share a psycholinguistic view of reading, which means that any materials and any techniques we selected for Petra had to meet the following criteria: they had to be meaningful, and they had to be complete units of discourse, so that language would neither be fragmented nor without context. We also wanted materials and techniques that were interesting to all three of us. Clara and I share a view of what kind of teaching, what kind of learning we should strive for. That view had been expressed over a dozen years ago by Paulo Freire:

> The adult literacy process as an act of knowing implies the existence of two interrelated concepts. One is the context of authentic dialogue between learners and educators as equally knowing subjects. This is what schools should be—the theoretical context of dialogue. The second is the real, concrete context of facts, the social reality in which men exist. (Freire, 1970, p. 214)

## TUTORING PETRA: FIRST SESSION

For our first tutoring session, I drove Clara to Petra's trailer, No. 247, only a car width away from Nos. 246 and 248. Petra welcomed us warmly, extending her big rough hand to clasp each of ours in turn, and took us inside. An old television set was on, the images dimly discernible through the set's snow of static, the musical messages urging Petra, in a language she didn't speak, to buy products she could little afford. There was a small baby, a neighbor's son, whom Petra babysat every day, drowsing with a bottle half in his mouth, kept from rolling off the couch by two cushions. The rest of the furniture consisted of a table and chairs for eating. No books, no magazines, no sewing materials, no embroidery or knitting—Petra spent her days in this bare space.

Clara and I arranged our coats, books, papers, tape recorder, and selves as best we could, finally settling the three of us on the sagging couch, with Petra seated between Clara and me, so Clara could tutor and I could record and take notes. After some conversation in which Clara and Petra set up their schedule of meetings, Clara gave Petra a picture to look at and discuss. The picture, torn from an old magazine, shows a young, dark-skinned woman holding a baby, both of them obviously very poor; and on the wall above the woman and baby is a photo of a healthy, blonde, middle-class young woman beaming at her healthy, blonde baby. The contrast is a strong one. The dark-skinned woman could be Mexican. Petra and Clara discussed the picture a bit, and then Petra dictated and Clara wrote down this interpretation:

### POR FALTA DE DINERO

Ella se siente triste porque tiene muchos niños y porque ella no tiene trabajo. Pues no sabra leer tambien como yo. Pues ahora ya tiene que ensenarse ye tiene que estar diferente. Ya no tiene que estar igual como antes si ella se ensena porque ella ya va a saber leer, porque tiene que tener una maestra muy buena y ella la tiene que ensenar.

Here's an English translation:

### FOR LACK OF MONEY

She feels sad because she has a lot of kids, and she doesn't have a job. Well, she doesn't know how to read, just like me. Well, now she has to learn and she has to change. She is not going to be the same as before, if she learns. Because she is going to learn to read; because she is going to get a very good teacher and that teacher is going to teach her.

## TUTORING PETRA: MATERIALS

We used *Por Falta de Dinero* as reading material for the next months, rereading it over and over again to Petra. But of course, that was not the only material we found for her. At first, neither of us had many Spanish materials but then I made a trip to a Mexican bookstore in Chicago and Clara made a trip to Mexico City; both of us bought or begged material we could use with Petra. Clara begged a few children's readers, the primers that her host's children had used in first grade. She bought a great many magazines, including some Mexican equivalents of *Ladies Home Journal,* full of fashions, recipes, and advice to the middle-class housewife. I bought *fotonovelas,* which are the very cheap paperback version of TV soaps, complete with many close-ups of anguished faces—Should Mario tell Rosa that Linda spent the night with Arturo? And I bought a slim volume of prayers for specific saints' days, a book of riddles, and some tabloids, *La Alarma,* the Mexican equivalent of *National Enquirer.*

From a friend of mine who taught Spanish, I got some poems by modern Hispanic poets. Our combined collection of Spanish materials offered Petra a wide choice of reading material; she could select any of it for intensive study with Clara or for leafing through during the 10 minutes of sustained silent reading (which I will describe later) in each tutoring session. We also continued to elicit reading material with the language experience approach (Rigg, 1981). Petra wanted very much to communicate with a sister whom she had not seen in over two years, so she dictated a letter which Clara took down carefully, making a carbon copy so that she would have one for Petra's rereading after the letter had been mailed.

## TUTORING PETRA: TECHNIQUES

Typically, after Clara and Petra had reviewed previous language experience materials and produced new ones, they turned to commercially published materials. Usually Clara read these aloud to Petra, finger pointing as she did so, and then handed the book or magazine to Petra. Petra could look at the selection, ask Clara questions, and read whatever parts of it she could and wanted to. We encouraged her to do this reading silently, but she often read orally, sometimes only a word that was repeated several times, sometimes a phrase or sentence. Petra picked out a recipe for *Calabacitas en Libro* from one of Clara's Mexican women's magazines, a dish which looked really delicious in the picture accompanying the recipe. She and Clara worked over the recipe, using the procedure I've just mentioned. After some work, Petra could read the recipe, although she couldn't call off most of the words accurately; she reported the next week that she had taken the recipe home and tried it. She also said that she had a recipe of her own for *calabacitas* (zucchini), so she dictated that to Clara.

Petra's dictated recipe for *Calabacitas de Petra* made it clear that, through the processes of reading recipes and dictating a few of her own to Clara, Petra had learned the concept of recipe. This concept includes at least two important aspects: (a) consideration of the reader as someone who does not already know how to prepare this dish; and (b) knowledge of the format of recipes—ingredients listed first, with notes on measurements, then instructions on preparation. Six weeks earlier, when Petra first dictated a recipe to Clara, it had taken over 30 minutes to elicit vague directions for preparing tortillas; Petra's dictation of *Calabacitas de Petra* took half that time, and for a recipe many times more complicated than the tortillas.

The tutoring sessions included Clara's reading to Petra, something that Clara enjoyed and hoped Petra would too. This oral reading was often poems of modern Hispanic writers, especially Mexican and Colombian writers, and Clara also read prayers, short stories, and riddles. Petra seemed to enjoy hearing all of these, but it was the prayers and poems she wanted to read herself.

Clara's reading to Petra accomplished two things: It demonstrated to Petra the wide selection possible for her to choose from, and it demonstrated how written language sounds. The ways we talk and the ways we write use language differently, and to become literate one needs to become accustomed to the different conventions, structures, patterns, and intentions of different kinds of written discourse. Petra had received a few letters from her sister, and in dictating a letter of her own she showed that she knew what format a personal letter required. By working through recipes with Clara, Petra learned what structures were required by recipes. Clara and I found some written material—prayers and riddles—that was very close to structures Petra used in speech but we wanted her also to become accustomed to the sound of literary language.

Let me recap: The tutoring sessions began with each person reporting on her accomplishments since the last session. Then we looked over materials we had produced at previous sessions, rereading many. Then we produced new material using the language experience approach. Clara read aloud, and then we usually closed with 10–15 minutes of sustained silent reading. Sustained silent reading is, as the name suggests, a quiet time in which each person, teacher and student, reads something silently without interruption or questions (McCracken, 1971). I have two videotapes of Petra and Clara working together, each tape showing a period of sustained silent reading. In the first, Petra goes slowly, page by page, through a magazine, backwards. In the second, filmed six weeks later, Petra goes slowly through a *fotonovela*, forwards. When I drove her home after that second session, I asked Petra if she had understood the *fotonovela*. She smiled and nodded, "Yes, some."

## PROBLEMS: VIEWS OF READING

So far, this all sounds as though we had no problems, but we did. We faced two problems. The first problem was this: As I've said, Clara and I share a psycholinguistic view of reading. But Petra doesn't. Her view of reading differs from ours considerably. We think both the purpose and the process of reading are building meaning, using visual cues from the print and nonvisual cues from behind the eye (Goodman, 1975). We think the individual words don't matter much, that the reader should build meaning of the whole (the whole letter, the whole recipe, the whole riddle), and if interested, go back later and bother with the words. If Petra was concerned with words, though, we were certainly willing to accommodate our teaching to her concern. But Petra didn't seem concerned with words. She didn't seem concerned with the meaning of the whole, either. She wanted to get the letters right. When Clara was reading Petra's simple yet eloquent description, *Por Falta de Dinero*, aloud to Petra, Petra interrupted. "Is that a T?" she asked, pointing. Clara stopped, "Yes," and started reading again. Petra put her hand in front of Clara's and pointed again, "Is that an M?" "Yes." And so it went throughout the whole story. We received more information on Petra's view of reading when she showed us what she had decided to do as homework. She brought us a page of lined paper from her notebook on which she had very carefully copied a couple of lines from the dialogue in a *fotonovela*, laboriously drawing each block letter as perfectly as possible. There were no spaces between words, so that it looked rather like this:

ONTIENDOTAMBIEN
LA EMOCION
QUELOEMBARBABA
AQUELLAERALA
EXPLOESIONDEUN
JOVENLLAERALA
ASPIRACIONESVREA

We admired her printing, and then Clara asked her to point out or say any of the words she had copied, but Petra couldn't. She had not been aware of copying words, only of practicing her letters. Literacy meant drawing clear letters, and drawing one's name. Here is an excerpt from Clara's journal, written about this time:

> In today's lesson . . . I wrote a letter to her, pointing out her progress and interest in learning. I included the words: *trabajo, maestra,* and *ense nar* in my letter. I gave her my letter and asked her to identify three important words. She looked at it and concentrated on vowels and letters but couldn't figure out the words. So I gave her the cards [each word was written on a card] to match these words with the three important words in my letter. She couldn't do it. She just said, "Is this an A?" I chose this technique because I wanted to find out if she had grasped the idea of a word, but I realized that her concept is consonants or vowels.

A little after this, I read part of a prepublication copy of Ferreiro and Teberosky (1982). My reading about three- and four-year-olds' conceptions of literacy, especially about their frequent confusion of the terms *word* and *letter,* made me think perhaps we interpreted Petra's actions wrongly. Perhaps she did have the concept of *word, palabra,* but thought when Clara asked for "*tres palabras importante*" that she was asking her to point out letters. I still don't know if she had the concept and just confused the label, or not. At any rate, we knew that our theories of reading differed from hers, and we had to adjust our lesson plans accordingly. This adjustment was a continuous process, typical of the unarticulated negotiation that two adults go through when they combine their efforts to accomplish a task, with each having a different idea of how to go about it, but both being courteous.

Petra did begin to use the word *palabra* in the same sense as we did within the next three weeks, especially after a session in which Clara brought several food labels, kinds of food we knew were in Petra's cupboard, and asked Petra to select labels she could read (i.e., she knew what food those labels represented). Petra chose *sal* and *tomate* and Clara showed her, amongst all the print on the labels, just where SALT and TOMATO were. Then Clara wrote SAL and TOMATE on cards, one each, and asked Petra to create a sentence. "I like tomatoes. *Me gustan tomates.*" Clara wrote the sentence on the back of the TOMATE card. The rationale for this technique is that Petra can read the sentence because she knows what it means; from the sentence she can focus more finely on a word. I don't know if it was this technique that was responsible for Petra's growing ability in the next five or six lessons to identify specific words, indicating that she now had the same concept and the same label as we.

Writing her name was still Petra's major goal, and she was happy to practice that for self-imposed homework one week, coming to our meeting the next time eager to show us that she had written her name on the steno notebook and folder we had given her. "Now I can write my name on everything that belongs to me," she said proudly. We continued to adjust our instruction, admiring her well-drawn letters, including Mexican first-grade primers in the collection we offered her for reading material, and so forth. We believed it more important to maintain an Adult–Adult relationship (Vella, 1979) than to adhere rigidly to our psycholinguistic theory of reading.

## PROBLEMS II: SOCIAL-CULTURAL EXPECTATIONS

The second problem involved Freire's concept of *conscientization*, becoming critically conscious of oneself and one's situation. This problem proved more difficult to solve; indeed, we never did.

Petra lived five miles from Clara, and Clara had no car, nor does the town have a bus service. At first, I picked up Clara and took her to Petra's trailer, participating in the session myself as much as my little Spanish allowed. But I wanted Clara, who was my student, to feel independent and responsible. I also wanted Petra out of that trailer where the only reading material was the labels on food cans and detergent boxes and the TV screen. But getting Petra the five miles to the school where Clara had reserved a small room in the library meant that Petra's 18-year-old son, José, had to drive her. In other words, when José finished his English class, he had to drive five miles home, pick up his mother, drive her the five miles back, babysit his 10-year-old brother for an hour and a half, and, finally, drive everyone back home. José preferred to work on the family car, which only he knew how to drive or was licensed to drive, or to meet a couple of his buddies downtown. Petra was middle-aged; she was a female; most of all, she was his mother. José saw no reason for her to start reading and writing: better she stay home and make fresh tortillas for his arrival home from class.

After the third time Clara had waited an hour for José to bring Petra to the library, I learned to leave Tuesday and Thursday afternoons open, so that I could respond to Clara's frantic call: "José won't bring Petra again this afternoon; can you take me to her trailer? We have already missed one session this week!" Although Clara and I had plenty to say about José to each other, we never openly castigated him or complained about him to his mother. We were timid: We feared that José would never bring Petra if we made a fuss, and that Petra would acquiesce if José said that she should stay home and not attend any more tutoring sessions. We feared that she would slip back into that isolation, with no one all day every day to talk to except an infant and a TV gabbling in a foreign tongue. So we muttered to each other and dropped hints to José, to which he remained oblivious. Between ourselves, Clara and I condemned José for his selfishness, for his sexism, for his stereotyped view of what his mother should be and do. But I did not examine my own stereotypes of women, or of illiterates, or of Mexican migrants. In her first language experience story, Petra had said of the woman in the picture, "She is not going to be the same as before, if she learns to read." Petra gave us the lead we should have followed. Here was the topic for discussion, the theme that should have organized our materials and our sessions. We didn't recognize this theme or use this lead to create the authentic dialogue that could have increased our critical consciousness of ourselves and our situations. One of us was Petra's *maestra,* her teacher, a very special position; the other was *una maestra de la universidad,* a position deserving high respect. And we two *maestras* never asked Petra what changes she anticipated as a result of learning to read; we never investigated what changes in any of our households were caused by our attempts to become better educated.

Why didn't I share with Clara and Petra my memories of when, like Petra, I was "imprisoned" in a tiny trailer with squalling babies, no books, and no way to get out? We two *maestras* never mentioned any times in our own families when our menfolk had treated us shabbily; we two *maestras* never started even one discussion that might have freed all three of us to learn about ourselves and about each other.

And so that strong woman, who, still grubby from a day's hard labor picking apples, had talked about being able to think in the head; that woman who had faced *la maestra de la universidad* and asked, "Are you doing this to help people who can't read and write, or are you doing this for yourself?"—that woman followed our lead, let us pick the topics for our sessions, and was thrilled when she could read TOMATE and SAL.

## POSTSCRIPT

That's the story of Petra. I've shared it with people more than once, and each time I do, someone says, "You can't stop there." Sometimes, most of the time, someone wants to know what Petra is doing now, whether she is reading and writing. I report from my last visit with her that she is not reading, but is still writing her name on her possessions. Sometimes someone wants to comfort me, to convince me that I wasn't a complete failure with Petra: "After all, she did become literate as she defined literacy: she wrote her name." I do take some comfort from that, because I recognize now that it is Petra's definition of literacy, not mine, that is important for her. And sometimes someone asks, "What did you learn?"

A great deal. I've already indicated how I learned to adjust my lessons to Petra's theory of reading, even though hers contradicted mine. Much more important, I learned how strongly literacy development is affected by immediate social context. As an academic, I had read and talked about how one's literacy development is affected by the people with whom one most closely associates, and by the assumptions and expectations held by those people. Petra showed me what that really meant. It meant José's inability to remember that his mother had a reading lesson that day; it meant Petra's quiet acceptance of being forgotten and waiting for a ride that never came. The context of Petra's family, especially the assumptions held by her son as to what was proper for a Mexican mother, almost denied her any literacy training; the unexamined assumptions held by her tutors (Clara and me) prevented her from using literacy in a liberating way. Petra knew she was literate when she wrote her name; she knew she was illiterate when she leafed through a women's magazine while we watched. Like everyone else, Petra is literate in some situations, not in others. Like everyone else, Petra's perceptions of herself as literate or not are strongly affected by the social situations she is in and by the way the people around her—family and teachers—perceive her literacy.

It's important to remember the larger political and economic contexts in which Petra lives, because they too affect her literacy. She has always been a migrant fruit-picker; it is improbable that she will be able to leave this life, even with reading and writing. More, the terribly exhausting work, the rotten living conditions, the low pay she receives—all affect how much reading and writing she can do.

Probably the clearest way I can show how Petra changed my teaching is to describe a recent visit I paid to a woman I've been meeting with recently. Jane grew up in California, and had at least eight years of school; she's 40 now and has never held a job, nor does she want to. Like Petra, she can write her name, but I have never seen her read or write anything else. The last time I dropped by Jane's tiny apartment for coffee and chat, I brought with me and read to her Lucille Clifton's poem "*Good Times*" (in Clifton, 1969, pp. 10), and we talked about what "good times" meant to us. Then Jane said something about her three daughters that I wrote down for her to keep and show the girls:

A GOOD LIFE

I hope my daughters have a good life.
I hope that they can get somethings for theyself.
And I hope they get a good man for theyself.
That's what I mean by a good life.

Jane

That's what I mean by liberatory literacy lesson, using reading and writing to understand ourselves, and to enlarge our lives.

## REFERENCES

Clifton, L. (1969). Good times. In L. Clifton, *Good times* 10. New York: Vintage Books.

Ferreiro, E. & Teberosky, A. (1982) *Literacy before schooling*. Portsmouth, N.H. Heinemann.

Freire, P. (1970) The adult literacy process as cultural action for freedom. *Harvard Educational Review, 40* (2), 205–225.

Goodman, K. S. (1975) Behind the eye. *Reading process and program*. Urbana, IL National Council of Teachers of English.

McCracken, R. A. (1971) Initiating sustained silent reading. *Journal of Reading, 14* 521–524, 582–583.

Rigg, P. (1981) Beginning to read in English the LEA way. In *Reading English as a second language, moving from theory: Monograph 4 in language and reading*, 81–90. Indiana University, School of Education.

Vella, J. K. (1979) *Learning to listen: A guide to methods of adult nonformal education*. University of Massachusetts: Center for International Studies.

# Part IV

---

## LITERACY, HISTORY, AND IDEOLOGY

# HOW ILLITERACY BECAME A PROBLEM (AND LITERACY STOPPED BEING ONE)

### James Donald

I will start, polemically, with Lenin. "An illiterate person stands outside," he insisted; "he must first be taught the ABC. Without this, there can be no politics; without this, there are only rumors, gossip, tales, prejudices, but no politics" (Grant, 1964, pp. 29–30). Lenin was the first political leader to initiate a mass literacy campaign, and his analysis was sophisticated. Literacy was not, as so often, promoted here as a means of improving economic efficiency, but as a prerequisite for full political membership in a society. Literacy was not taken solely for an individual ability to read and write, but was seen as a necessary condition for particular forms of social and cultural organization. When a colleague suggested to Lenin that, under the old order, illiteracy at least stopped the minds of workers and peasants from being corrupted by bourgeois ideas, he drew a perceptive distinction: "Illiteracy was compatible with the struggle for the seizure of power, with the necessity to destroy the old State apparatus. Illiteracy is incompatible with the tasks of construction" (Hoyles, 1977, p. 20).

In the language of present-day sociology of education, this could perhaps be restated as a contrast between working-class *resistance* against an imposed culture and the struggle for *hegemony*, the project of bringing class fractions into a political alliance.

That duality, however expressed, is what this chapter is about. In particular, I want to examine how it operated in the conflicts and negotiations around language, literacy, and popular schooling in England during the nineteenth century. The point of doing so is to draw out how *illiteracy* was constituted as a problem, and how state-provided education came into being (in part) as a solution to that problem. In doing so, I hope to suggest how the State operates ideologically to secure the consent of the governed. In this process, language and literacy are crucial. Just how crucial is indicated in this comment by Gramsci:

> Each time that in one way or another, the question of language comes to the fore, that signifies that a series of other problems is about to emerge, the formation and enlarging of the ruling class, the necessity to establish more "intimate" and sure relations between the ruling groups and the national popular masses, that is, the reorganisation of cultural hegemony. (1975, p. 2346)

The formation of the ruling class, the establishment of intimate relations between ruling groups and "national popular masses," the reorganization of cultural hegemony—these are the coordinates for my brief history of literacy in England.


## VICIOUS BOOKS

The publication of Tom Paine's *Rights of Man* in March 1791 stands emblematically at the start of that history. "From above," from the perspective of a bourgeoisie politically nervous in the wake of the American and French revolutions, it seemed to embody what Webb, in his classic study *The British Working-Class Reader 1790–1848* (1955), called "the challenge which a literate working class presented to its betters" (p. VII). "From below," in contrast, Paine's combination of a popular liberalism, which was atheist, republican, democratic, and fiercely anti-aristocratic, with an assertion of the rights of the "free-born Englishman" appeared as a powerful point of ideological and political cohesion. It set the tone for the radicalism of those artisans who over the next half-century gave expression and identity to the English working class.

The speed with which Paine's book was distributed now seems remarkable. By 1793, it was alleged that 200,000 copies were in circulation. By some estimates, when Paine died in 1809, the total circulation had gone as high as 1,500,000—at a time when the total population of the British Isles was no more than 16,000,000. Even allowing for some exaggeration in these figures, they do indicate that the ability to read was already quite widely diffused. This therefore tends to confirm Laqueur's argument (1976) about the cultural origins of popular literacy in England. Starting from the strikingly large number of people who could read and write in preindustrial England, he claims that the penetration of literate forms of communication into many aspects of everyday life—including legal and economic relations, politics, Protestant religion, and recreational forms of literature—meant that literacy was already commonly valued as necessary for full participation in the popular culture. What changed at the end of the eighteenth century was not the number of people who could read and write (the rise in literacy rates was marginal) but the perception of literacy. It became a crucial tactic in emerging working-class political strategies.

This in turn provoked the English ruling bloc into quite new interventions into the sphere of culture.

The first response to *The Rights of Man* was something like panic, a hasty recourse to the traditional repressive powers of the state in an attempt to stamp out the "alarming discontents actively propagated by seditious publications" (Webb, 1955, p. 40). The use of repression mounted throughout the 1790s as radical publications became more widely available. *The Rights of Man* was banned as seditious libel in 1793, and Paine himself was driven into exile. Harsh legal action against publishers and booksellers culminated in the transportation of the leaders of the Edinburgh Convention, a meeting of radicals from all over England and Scotland, and in the suspension of Habeas Corpus in 1794. Further acts in 1795 limited the holding of public meetings and extended the scope of high treason. As a result, the radical self-education societies that had flourished earlier in the decade (of which the London Corresponding Society was probably the most famous) began to disappear. The final blow came in 1799 with the Corresponding Societies Act, which outlawed the groups and also imposed strict control by Justices of the Peace over the printing trade.

At the same time as this repression sought to silence opposition, however, it is possible to detect in embryo a more sophisticated ideological response which saw the need to engage in a battle of ideas. In the House of Commons the Prime Minister, William Pitt, called for "a great deal of activity on the part of friends of our constitution, to take pains properly to address the public mind, and to keep it in that state which was necessary to our present tranquillity" (Webb, 1955, p. 40). Subsidized responses to Paine—often in the form of scurrilous attacks on his character—were widely distributed. Perhaps most symptomatic of this emerging ideological strategy, though, were the writings (some in her own name, some anonymous) of Hannah More. Her most popular antireform tract was *Village Politics Addressed to All the Mechanics, Journeymen and Labourers in Great Britain, by Will Chip, a Country Carpenter,* in which a silly radical mason is trounced in argument by a solid blacksmith. More had been the moving force behind the *Cheap Repository Tracts* in the mid-1790s, which were designed to counteract French Revolutionary ideas. She also became involved in popular education, setting up Sunday schools in the Mendip area in the late 1790s. For this she was criticized by some of her Tory allies. "I allow of no writing for the poor," she protested in response. "My object is not to make them fanatics, but to train up the lower classes in habits of industry and piety" (Simon, 1960, p. 133).

What are we to make of Hannah More? Her concern with popular literacy does not reflect a sudden growth in the ability to read among the working class. The threat she saw lay in the conjunction of this already existing competence with a number of other factors—with the increasing urbanization of the working class, with new techniques of printing, publishing, and distribution that made widespread circulation feasible, and, above all, with a new popular, radical political discourse. But she saw literacy not only as a threat to political stability, but also, in certain institutional forms, as a new means of regulation and discipline, a new way of intervening to shape the "habits" and character of the people along particular lines. Her strategy certainly needs to be set in the context of Evangelicalism alongside those of William Wilberforce, Bishop Barrington and his Society for Bettering the Condition of the Poor, John Bowdler and his Society for the Suppression of Vice and Encouragement of Religion, and the Society for the Promotion of Christian Knowledge. These crusades represented in part a vigorous response to the failure of more traditional forms of Anglicanism to capture the popular imagination. But, I think, they also embody a new conception of the power of the state. They did not merely seek readjustments to the centralized institutions that constitute the formal political regime, but proposed an insistent and insidious modification of the everyday forms of the exercise of power. Their strategy was not just to hold in check the natural viciousness of the working class and to silence radical opposition through legal sanctions. Instead they were trying to devise institutions and techniques that would produce new forms of consciousness *for* the working class. In other words, their aim was to establish the intimate and secure relations between rulers and ruled that Gramsci perceived in struggles around language. Rather than calling for repression, the Evangelical response was *hegemonic* in attempting to exert moral and intellectual leadership over the subordinate classes.

The clash between the coercive and hegemonic strategies also points to another of the problems which Gramsci said were signified by the question of language: the formation and enlarging of the ruling class. During this period, the political clout of the urban, industrial fraction of the bourgeoisie was increasing at the expense of the rural landowners. This meant changes in the forms of social control—broadly, a shift from ties of tradition, birth, and faith to new conceptions of rationality and knowledge. The split is vividly illustrated by the debates within the Tory party about the bill for establishing parish schools proposed in the House of Commons in 1807 by Samuel Whitbread, the liberal Whig leader. The traditionalists, enraged by the threat to their bucolic idyll from newfangled urban ideas, remained convinced that popular literacy and schooling would open the floodgates to Painite revolt. The classic statement of this position came from Davies Giddy, the president of the Royal Society.

> However specious in theory the project might be of giving education to the labouring classes of the poor, it would, in effect, be found to be prejudicial to their morals and happiness; it would teach them to despise their lot in life, instead of making them good servants in agriculture, and other laborious employments to which their rank in society has destined them; instead of teaching them subordination, it would render them factious and refractory, as was evident in the manufacturing counties; it would enable them to read seditious pamphlets, vicious books, and publications against Christianity; it would render them insolent to

their superiors; and in a few years, the result would be, that the legislature would find it necessary to direct the strong arm of power against them. (Simon, 1960, p. 132)

Although Whitbread's bill was lost in the face of such squirarchical opposition, other Tories besides Hannah More saw the potential of schooling as a means of molding popular consciousness. Among the most interesting was Patrick Colquhoun, a London magistrate and a polemicist for an organized police force who amassed often-lurid statistics to demonstrate the extent and gravity of the threat posed by the "labouring classes." He was, for example, one of the first people to make correlations between illiteracy and criminality. Even more prescient were the solutions he proposed. He argued that the new urban proletariat had to be policed, not just through repression, but through a broad strategy of surveillance, regulation, and training. He set out his ideas in his *New and Appropriate System of Education for the Labouring People* (1806):

The higher and noble aim of preventing those calamities which lead to idleness and crime, and produce poverty and misery, by guiding and properly directing the early conduct of the lower orders of the community, and by giving a right bias to their minds, has not, as yet, generally attracted the notice of those who move in the more elevated walks of society.... The prosperity of every state depends on the good habits, and the religious and moral instruction of the labouring people. By shielding the minds of youth against the vices that are most likely to beset them, much is gained to society in the prevention of crimes, and in lessening the demand for punishment.... It is not, however, proposed by this institution, that the children of the poor should be educated in a manner to elevate their minds above the rank they are destined to fill in society, or that an expense should be incurred beyond the lowest rate ever paid for instruction. Utopian schemes for an extensive diffusion of knowledge would be injurious and absurd. (pp. 11–12)

Colquhoun shared with Giddy a concern to keep the poor in "the rank they are destined to fill in society"—and he shows himself a true Tory in wanting to achieve this at "the lowest rate ever paid for instruction"! Where he differed was in his perception that in a period of social transformation, the old political ties were no longer adequate. What was needed was active leadership in guiding and directing the subordinate classes, in giving a right bias to their minds— more intimate and secure relations, in other words.

In arguing for new forms and institutions of social discipline, Colquhoun was not merely a precursor of the increasingly active role of the state in organizing and managing popular culture. He also prefigured new modes of social investigation and understanding that redefined the problem of "the poor." Although he still saw the social hierarchy as a matter of destiny, in explaining criminality and fecklessness in terms of incorrect childhood socialization he paved the way for an attribution of class differences to the social or psychological *inadequacies* of the poor, and specifically of working-class families

(Donzelot, 1980). New techniques for the exercise of power went hand in hand with new ways of defining the problem, with new forms of knowledge.

## A RIGHT BIAS TO THEIR MINDS

To detect the contours of new political tactics in Colquhoun's prescriptions does not mean that the appropriate techniques of administration came forth fully formed. What we can perceive is the emergence of new ways of thinking and new objects of thought. The shape eventually taken by institutions of popular schooling was hammered out in a series of political and ideological conflicts. The institution for which Colquhoun himself had particularly high hopes was the monitorial school developed by Dr. Andrew Bell, Bell's Free School in Orange Street, Westminster. Its appeal was not simply that it seemed to provide a cheap and efficient means of indoctrinating the children of the laboring poor, but that it subjected them to a regime of constant surveillance, inspection, and regulation. The youngest pupils were to be taught by older pupils acting as tutors, with an elite of the eldest being appointed monitors—themselves responsible to the master or mistress who sat like a spider in the middle of this web. Colquhoun described it thus:

> The province of the master or mistress is to direct the whole machine in all its parts. . . . It is their business to see that others work, rather than work themselves. The master and mistress, from their respective chairs, overlook every part of the school, and give life and motion to the whole. They inspect the classes one after another; call upon the monitors occasionally to bring them up, that they may specifically examine the progress of each pupil. (p. 16)

The details of the technique were largely derived from colonial experience—Bell had pioneered it in Anglican schools in India—but it also had affinities with Colquhoun's proposals for a police force that would saturate the working population. We are clearly in the intellectual and political universe of Jeremy Bentham's *Panopticon,* the institutional means of subjecting a population through the consciousness of perpetual scrutiny and inspection (Foucault, 1977, pp. 200–209). This perhaps is the clue to the appeal of the monitorial schools. Contrary to the usual assumption that they were no more than a cheap and nasty spin-off from the factory system, they were taken by Tories, Whigs, and Utilitarian Radicals alike to be an appropriate administrative and institutional system for the controlled diffusion of popular education. By subjecting their pupils to constant surveillance and rational discipline, they would provide a vehicle for shaping the very consciousness and subjectivity of the subordinate classes.

In fact, however, the monitorial schools proved both ineffective and unpopular. In part their failure was the result of internal tensions and contradictions. The rivalry between the Anglican Dr. Bell and his nondenominational counterpart, Dr. Lancaster, although often conducted at the level of petty bickering, reflected a deeper political division. Lancaster, vociferously supported by Utilitarians like James Mill, Henry Brougham, and Francis Place, was first in the field and promoted a view of literacy that offered both reading and a limited degree of writing. This embodied a Methodist conception of personal responsibility for interpreting the Scriptures as a guide to conduct. As I have already indicated, this was too radical for the Evangelical Tories. To them the idea that laborers and their children could have anything to communicate in writing was at best absurd and at worst downright dangerous. All they wanted from pupils was the ability to read written instructions and selected passages from the Bible. The London showcases of both factions remained atypical, and there are horrendous accounts of how poorly run, tedious, and brutal many of the schools were. It is hardly surprising that the radical journalist William Cobbett should have dismissed this "Bell and Lancaster work" as "Heddekashun," the very opposite of true learning.

The fundamental reason for the failure of the schools, though, was a lack of political imagination. Intimate and secure relations between the ruling groups and the national popular masses cannot be imposed; they have to be *negotiated*. That perception is at the heart of any hegemonic strategy. The monitorial schools failed because they took no account of the existing educational culture of the "subordinate classes" or of the remarkably successful intellectual and moral direction being given to their struggles *from within*. Nor were the more perceptive bourgeois ideologues—especially among the liberals and radicals associated with the Whigs—slow to learn these lessons. In 1819, for example, the Utilitarian publisher Charles Knight reasserted the need not only to control but to direct the thoughts and actions of the working population. "There is a new *power* in society," he wrote, and he warned that contemporary journals like Cobbett's *Political Register* and T. J. Wooler's *Black Dwarf* had "combined to give that power a direction. The work must be taken out of their hands" (Simon, 1960, p. 132).

## A NEW POWER IN SOCIETY

What was this "new power" that men like Knight wanted to usurp? In developing recognizably hegemonic strategies, the ruling bloc was in fact responding—in a process of trial and error—to the success of often self-educated radicals who had provided popular movements with intellectual leadership as well as political organization. The creation of a radical culture from the 1790s onward was not a spontaneous working-class reaction to social changes brought about by the industrial revolution. As the title of E. P. Thompson's magisterial history of *The Making of the English Working Class* suggests, the class was not predetermined by its location in the relations of production: it had to be *constructed*. This involved an alliance spanning working-class, artisan, and lower-middle-class groupings, drawn into coherence around a new cultural identity forged from Paine's *Rights of Man*, from Cobbett's speeches and writings, and later from Chartist newspapers—*The Northern Star* in particular. It is only as part of this *bricolage* that radical educational strategies in the first half of the nineteenth century can be understood. What we would now specify as politics, education, literacy, journalism, and recreation were still bound inextricably together. Their division into separate institutions was one effect of the ruling bloc's new techniques of power.

The radical artisans and laborers had educational goals which were utopian and libertarian rather than administrative and disciplinary. As Johnson has shown in his essay "Really Useful Knowledge" (1979), this led to a dual strategy. Because this fraction saw knowledge and literacy not only as valuable in themselves but also as means to political emancipation, they were acutely aware of the partiality and poverty of most forms of official and philanthropic education that were being provided. They were therefore quite combative in their resistance to them. At the same time, they also developed their own institutions, their own ways of teaching, and their own distinctive educational content. (It is to the last that the "really useful knowledge" of Johnson's title refers: the term was also used in conscious parody of the Society for the Diffusion of Useful Knowledge, a lavishly subsidized effort by Brougham and his colleagues in the 1830s to publish wholesome works that would win working-class and petit-bourgeois readers away from more radical or sensational literature.) These educational forms often remained informal, haphazard, and ephemeral, responding to local needs at a particular time rather than creating alternative systems. That is not to say that counterinstitutions did not develop—the secular Sunday schools and the Owenite halls of science were notable examples—but what remains striking, certainly up to the 1830s, is the diversity of broadly educational activities. The common strategy underlying them all seems to have been the creation of an autonomous class culture and the formation of a recognizable class identity. Led by the radical artisans, the working class found a *voice*, a position from which to negotiate in political and cultural conflicts and exchanges. (The coherence of this voice was, of course, imaginary, and it was also one among several.) In this, they were probably helped more than hindered by the ham-fisted attempts by the state to suppress the radical press, for these both highlighted the polarity between the classes and made the state itself the object of ridicule. (Thompson, 1968.)

This independent strategy Johnson calls "substitional." He contrasts it with "statist" strategies, which have centered on agitation for the provision of educational facilities and for the more active and equitable intervention of the state to regulate such matters as the length of the working day, children's employment, and child health. Indeed, it was during the campaigns to limit working hours through the factory acts during the 1840s that the cultural and practical difficulties of sustaining autonomous educational initiatives became inescapably apparent. At the same time, optimism about the political prospects of the Charter or of Owenite social regeneration waned; by 1851, the remnants of the Chartist movement accepted the principle of agitating for democratically controlled state education. (Johnson, 1981, pp. 28–30).

The cross-class alliance that had created the literate radical culture earlier in the century had by now broken up. The artisan class fraction which had provided its intellectual and political leadership between 1790 and 1850 became increasingly defensive and concerned to protect itself from below as much as from above. The resulting political, economic, and ideological changes brought a realignment in which "the political" and "the cultural" were decisively sundered. The defeat of Chartism, Stedman Jones (1974) has argued, put an end to the sustaining conviction that the economic and political order brought into being by the industrial revolution was a temporary aberration.

> Working people ceased to believe that they could shape society in their own image. Capitalism had become an immovable horizon. Demands produced by the movements of the pre-1850 period—republicanism, secularism, popular self-education, co-operation, land reform, internationalism, etc.—now shorn of the conviction which had given them point, eventually expired from inanition, or else, in a diluted form, were appropriated by the left flank of Gladstonian liberalism. The main impetus of working-class activity now lay elsewhere. It was concentrated into trade unions, co-ops, friendly societies, all indicating a *de facto* recognition of the existing order as the inevitable framework of action. (p. 499)

The radicalism that had fostered the intellectual culture of the century's earlier decades now shifted its focus to a labor movement concerned primarily with industrial relations and parliamentary representation. A new alliance between the "labour aristocracy," the radical urban bourgeoisie, and the nonconformist churches found its political home within one wing of the Liberal Party. In the educational agitations of the 1860s this alliance produced the Education League, which, as McCann (1970) has shown, provided much of the impetus behind Forster's 1870 Education Act. This act set up a national system of elementary Board schools and irreversibly established the state as the main provider of mass education.

Alongside this political realignment, and helping to make it possible, there were a number of cultural changes. The sort of social investigation pioneered by Patrick Colquhoun was developed and transformed after 1830 by social reformers like Sir James Kay (later Kay-Shuttleworth). The nature of the social problem confronting the state came to be defined less as the political threat posed by an organized proletariat (although Kay-Shuttleworth did argue explicitly that only by education "can the workman be induced to leave undisturbed the control of commercial enterprises in the hands of capitalists" (Simon, 1960, p. 357) and more in the terms of the emerging social sciences of psychology and sociology. They assembled an image of a working class held in subordination by its own natural inadequacies—including illiteracy—and so requiring the amelioration that only the state could offer. In the sphere of popular publishing, as James shows in *Fiction for the Working Man* (1973), the 1830s saw a marked shift away from educational and political works towards more sensational periodicals and fiction—which were then quoted as further evidence of the depraved tastes and condition of the poor. This development was followed in the second half of the century by the rise of the new commercial, mass-circulation press, which effectively marginalized the traditional forms of radical journalism. In short, the autonomous political and educational organizations of the working class were supplanted by state education and a commercial entertainment and information industry.

By 1870 the social relations identifiable as a coherent popular culture had been profoundly transformed. Before the defeat of Chartism the radical working class and its allies had created a distinctive voice through educational activities, journalism, political agitation, and self-organization. In terms of the duality I posed at the start, that battle had been waged *for* hegemony, *for* political power. The remarkable achievement of the English state—and especially of the strategy formulated by Disraeli—was to disentangle the various threads of this radical cultural and political movement, and to deal with each of them in isolation from the rest. The state offered real political and material concessions on suffrage, on education, and on welfare which were imposed on it by the struggles of the subordinate classes—but always with the effect of breaking apart the carefully nurtured *identity* created by the radicals and the Chartists. Thus although there were later attempts to create autonomous working-class education (especially during the socialist revival during the period between 1880 and the 1920s), the limits of opposition were now effectively defined by the state. On the one hand, political agitation focused on demands for improved provision and access. And on the other hand, the permeation of the power of the state into the very fabric of working-class experience led to a culture (or counter-culture) based on working-class *resistance* to schooling.

## STANDARD ENGLISH

How is the question of literacy related to this new political settlement? In *Keywords*, Williams points out an important ambiguity in the concept of literacy itself. The term *literacy* was only coined late in the nineteenth century, although *illiteracy* had existed earlier. The confusion is perhaps clearest in the adjectival form *literate*. Whereas *literature* has shrunk from meaning anything and everything that has been printed to meaning only certain prestigious forms of imaginative writing, *literate* retains connotations not only of the ability to read and write, but also of the condition of being well read (Williams, 1976, pp. 150–154). If we consider this ambiguity in the light of Lenin's remark about the illiterate person "standing outside" and also the strenuous attempts to control the radical press and the spread of working-class reading in England during the nineteenth century, then the political stakes of struggles around literacy become clearer. The question is not just access to written matter in general, but the access of specific social groups to specific types of literature—in both the broad and narrow senses.

Again, this takes us back to the "question of language" and the "series of other questions" which Gramsci took it to signify. Writing in a context where Italian as a national language maintained only the most fragile hegemony, undermined on one side by a tenacious variety of dialects and on the other by the continuing hold of ecclesiastical Latin, he was especially concerned with the role of language in producing (rather than reflecting) the categories of "the nation" and "the people." A national language, in short, was a precondition of the formation of a progressive social-cultural identity for the popular classes—the sort of class identity constructed by the radical educational movements in England during the early nineteenth century, which had been made possible by the country's early linguistic integration, fairly widespread popular literacy, and developed technologies of printing.

Equally, though, Gramsci said the institution of a single national language was crucial to "the formation and enlarging of the ruling class." In *Education, Class Language and Ideology (1979),* Bisseret suggests that the French bourgeoisie, like the English working class, only found its voice in the process of struggle—in this case against both the old aristocracy and the popular masses.

> Historically, dominant language and dominated language established themselves as such through relations of class antagonism. . . . The forms imposed by grammarians from the sixteenth and seventeenth centuries were unconsciously chosen and codified by the bourgeoisie as being suitable to express and shape its identity as the rising class. The rising class became the social referent for the gradual reorganization of signifiers. Once the bourgeoisie had gained political power, through its practices (including its linguistic practices), it constituted itself as the dominant class and the "others" as the dominated one. It set up its own language habits (sign of its supposed natural superiority) as an absolute standard. (p. 67)

Why was this linguistic change necessary for the development of a capitalist economy and a bourgeois state? The French case has been studied in some detail by Balibar and her associates (Balibar & Laporte, 1974). They argue that the displacement of regional and class dialects by a codified, uniform French was an economic, legal, and ideological necessity. It contributed to the formation of capitalism by enabling commodities to circulate freely within a *national* market. It allowed the wage-labor relationship between capitalist and worker to be codified as contracts between ostensibly free and equal subjects. But above all it was necessary for the exercise of the state's political role. Through the national language the national state attempts to organize people's processes of thought by forging a "national-popular" identity. This does not take place solely at an ideological level; as we have seen, it is one determinant of the institutional forms in which the state provides education. Nevertheless, it is important to examine the ideological formation that makes such a strategy possible.

The premise here is that language is politically important because of its ideological power—its meanings shape our perceptions and our experience of the world. Our consciousness is formed by the languages we encounter, where and when we encounter them, and our relationship to them. These relationships are possible because language actually constructs places for "I," "me," and "you" within the symbolic world it signifies. We become social subjects as we enter culture. We enter culture by learning language. The Soviet linguist Volosinov has put it this way:

> Consciousness takes shape and being in the material of signs created by an organized group in the process of its social intercourse. The individual consciousness is nurtured on signs; it derives its growth from them; it reflects their logic and laws. The logic of consciousness is the logic of ideological communication, of the semiotic interaction of a social group. If we deprive consciousness of its semiotic, ideological content, it would have absolutely nothing left. (Volosinov, 1973, p. 13)

Individual consciousness, in short, is a "social-ideological fact." It is not individual in the sense that "individual" is opposed to "social"; nor is it like a blank sheet of paper waiting for experiences to be written on it. Volosinov insists that consciousness and experience can have no existence outside of, or prior to, a culture's codes for classifying knowledge, representing reality, and positioning subjects. "It is not experience that organizes expression, but the other way around—*expression organizes experience*. Expression is what first gives experience its forms and specificity of direction" (p. 85). Political struggles around language therefore involve the attempt to control these codes, to generate certain meanings rather than others, literally to define a society's common sense. The problem for dominant groups is to tie down the potential plurality of meanings that language can produce, to control what Volosinov calls its multiaccentuality: "The ruling class strives to impart a supraclass, external character to the ideological sign, to extinguish or drive inward the struggle between social value judgements which occurs in it, to make the sign uniaccentual" (p. 23).

How this goal might be achieved is suggested by Bisseret's (1979) observation that during the sixteenth and seventeenth centuries the "rising class became the social referent for the gradual reorganization of signifiers" (p. 67). She is referring to a decisive historical shift in the European conception of language. Previously, it had been assumed that the grammar of language reproduced the natural order of things in the world. By the end of the seventeenth century—by the time John Locke wrote on language in his *Essay concerning Human Understanding* (1690), for example—this had given way to the view that what gives language coherence was not a cosmic hierarchy but the relation between its internal structure and the logic of the human mind (Cohen, 1977). Thus, the older linguistic view was secularized and there was a new emphasis on the central category of the individual human subject.

This "subject" was not simply an abstraction of an essential, timeless humanity. On the contrary, it was Man—quite literally the white, bourgeois male—that was established as the point of reference around which linguistic codes came to be organized. In fact, it came to appear as if the definition of other social categories through their differences from this ideological norm were required by the structure of the language, the organization of society, or even "human nature." Man, the individual legal-political subject, nominally free in the statements he chooses to utter, was in fact a representation of only one class's self-definition: the patriarchal bourgeoisie's. The previous linguistic diversity gave way to a single system of signs, the national language, organized around a single hidden referent. This introduced antagonistic new relationships to language for different social categories (and not just classes, as Volosinov and Bisseret perhaps imply.) To be bourgeois and male was simply to be. Anything else was to be *different*, and this had to be marked linguistically.

The introduction of a single national language actually shifts the nature of linguistic difference from one of variation to one of antagonism. It produces a split between a language of power and languages of nonpower. It defines the axes of domination and subordination along which social categories and subjectivity are produced and reproduced. In short, it creates the conditions for establishing the intimate and secure relations of cultural hegemony.

How such linguistic shifts tie in with literacy and schooling—at least in France—has been explained by Balibar (Balibar & Laporte, 1974; Balibar, 1974). At the same time as it imposed a uniform language during the Revolutionary period, she argues, the bourgeoisie also took over and transformed the elite schooling system inherited from the *ancien régime*. In doing so, it preserved for itself a second language which marked its cultural superiority. This was reproduced through the concentration on studying *literary* texts, forms that exceeded the simple communicative function of everyday language. This tendency was reinforced later in the century by the establishment of a national education system divided along class lines. Whereas the children in secondary schools were offered some conceptual framework for understanding how language works, the sons and daughters of "the people" were instructed in primary schools to learn mechanically the formal rules of the language. Just as the juridical equality between legal subjects turns out to be illusory given the different positions of worker and capitalist in the relations of production, so the apparent equality of French speakers in relation to the national language conceals a class-based inequality. The bourgeoisie—the class that is the language's hidden referent, in Bisseret's terms—experiences that language as its own. The subordinate classes, in contrast, have the language imposed on them through the education system; they are, quite literally, not at home in it. They experience it as an external discipline, and as an exclusion from a superior, lit-

erary language. Thus, literary texts actually help to maintain bourgeois dominance in language.

This, then, is the hidden history of the ambiguities apparent in the notions
of *literacy*, *literate*, and *literature*. Of course, Balibar's analysis should not be
imposed on the English case in a procrustean way, since the struggles leading
to the institution of a national language and of a national education system in
England took quite different forms (Doyle, 1982). Nevertheless, the underlying cultural strategy does seem to have been similar. Take, for example, the
thinking behind what became the *Oxford English Dictionary*, initiated in 1860
and taking over half a century to complete. The aim of this "very text of texts"
(as Davies has called it) was to *fix* the language, to render the sign system of
*standard* English uniaccentual. For Richard Chenvix Trench, the driving force
behind the *OED*, the dictionary represented a political and moral duty: "The
care of the national language I consider at all times a sacred trust and a most important privilege of the higher orders of society" (Aarsleff, 1967, p. 245). The
project was part of a strategy for winning cultural hegemony by constructing a
history and an identity for "the nation" and "the people."

> If the great acts of that nation to which we belong are precious to us, if we feel
> ourselves made greater by their greatness, summoned to a nobler life by the
> nobleness of Englishmen who have already lived and died . . . what can more
> clearly point out their native land and ours as having fulfilled a glorious past, as
> being destined for a glorious future, than that they should have acquired for
> themselves and for those who came after them a clear, a strong, an harmonious, a
> noble language? (Cited in Aarsleff, 1967, pp. 245–246)

In his article "Education, Ideology and Literature" (1978), Davies argues
that the "standard English" fixed by the *OED* did not become fully hegemonic
until the latter half of the nineteenth century, when it was incorporated into
the fundamental routines of compulsory universal education. And, like Balibar,
he finds in its formal specifications and its prescriptive standards of spelling,
grammar, and pronunciation, this language the language of *literature*. This
conception of literature was itself produced as the term's reference narrowed
down to aesthetic, imaginative writing, and particularly to the body of such
writing within the national language. This new connotation had emerged during the 1860s and 1870s when,

> faced with a crisis of ideological dominance, and unable to resort either to the
> classics or to a science increasingly feared as the voice of a soulless materialism,
> education *discovered* and therefore *created* literature as the principal material and
> object of its institutions and practices. (Davies, 1978, p. 7)

Davies puts the case polemically: the main point is that literature is never just a
description of certain types of text, but an *evaluation*. The literary canon,

taken as a whole, embodies and preserves standard English. "Literary ideology," often institutionalized as literary criticism, lays down the practical criteria for making these judgments, for dividing the literary from the nonliterary, and for setting up a hierarchy of aesthetic and moral values. Nor does it discriminate only between texts: it also sorts out people. Those who "appreciate" literature have taste, refinement, judgment. Those who don't are, in a sense, illiterate, spiritually deficient, and in need of compensating education. Once again, literature is used to pass off a class-based training as if it were a natural aptitude.

## LITERACY, HEGEMONY, RESISTANCE

I said in the introduction that an implicit theme of this chapter is the distinction between concepts of *hegemony* and *resistance*. Through a case study of the radical literate culture in England during the first half of the nineteenth century, I have tried to suggest the centrality of hegemony to the formation of popular-democratic political alliances as well as to the organization of relations between ruling and subordinate blocs. And in terms of the emerging system of state education, I argued that its institutions, pedagogy, and dispositions of knowledge were effective *ideologically* only to the extent that they won consent to their definitions of common sense. True, they were backed up by the legal coercion of compulsory attendance, but the important point is that the state, as Poulantzas has argued, "also acts in a positive fashion, *creating, transforming and making* reality" (1978, p. 30).

How does this relate to resistance? The best work from this perspective (for example Willis, 1977; McRobbie, 1978) shows how pupils negotiate the experience of schooling by bringing into play other categories and criteria from their cultural repertoire. These forms include rejection of curricular forms of knowledge in favor of "street wisdom," refusal of the dependency and submission of adolescent pupildom, a preference for an active and subversive *practice* over book learning, an orientation toward adult destinies (but in a mode of manual labor, unrelated to school), adult sexuality, and, in the case of girls, romance and marriage (Johnson, 1981, p. 27). The question that I am concerned with, though, is how such resistance might fit into a coherent cultural strategy. Certainly, it can undermine many of the overt ideologies of schooling. But the rejection of the "literate" culture of the school may actually reproduce the two networks of bourgeois education (Baudelot and Establet, 1971): instrumental, imposed forms of knowledge on the one hand, and an idealist rationalism on the other. These are, of course, intimately allied with the distinct forms of literacy identified by Balibar and Davies. For the individual, therefore, resistance can mean being cut off from what Bourdieu and Passeron (1977) calls *cultural capital*. Politically, the implication seems to be that resistance—like illiteracy for Lenin—may be "incompatible with the tasks of construction."

Ideological struggle, according to Willemen (1978), involves two necessarily simultaneous moments:

1. the undermining, displacing of specific ideological configurations and / or discourses within them, in order to change determinate discursive regimes, to change the balance of forces within institutions, within ideologies; and

2. the production or the supporting of other sets of discourses, other subject productions in ideology, other imaginary unities which will allow or contribute to the political project (itself an imaginary unity) presiding over the struggle. (p. 68)

The second aspect is clearly hegemonic—not liberating an essential working-class (or black or women's) voice, but *constructing* ideological points of identity around which alliances can be formed. The first would certainly involve resistance. But, I think, it should also involve the systematic deconstruction of the existing disposition of knowledges and competences—theoretical work on literacy and ideology, for example, but also *teaching*.

## REFERENCES

Aarsleff, H. *The study of language in England, 1780–1860*. Princeton: Princeton University Press, 1967.

Balibar, R. *Les Francais fictifs*. Paris: Hachette, 1974.

Balibar, R., & Laporte, D. *Le Francais national*. Paris: Hachette, 1974.

Baudelot, C., & Establet, R. *L'Ecole capitaliste en France*. Paris: Maspero, 1971.

Bisseret, N. *Education, class language and ideology*. London and Boston: Routledge and Kegan Paul, 1979.

Bourdieu, P., & Passeron, J. C. *Reproduction in education, society, and culture*. London and Beverly Hills: Sage Publications, 1977.

Cohen, M. *Sensible words*. Baltimore: Johns Hopkins University Press, 1977.

Colquhoun, P. *A new and appropriate system of education for the labouring people*. London: J. Hatchard, 1806.

Davies, T. Education, ideology and literature. *Red Letters*, 1978, 7, 4–13.

Donzelot, J. *The policing of families*. London: Hutchinson, 1980.

Doyle, B. The hidden history of English studies. In P. Widdowson (Ed.), *Re-reading English*. London: Methuen, 1982.

Foucault, M. *Discipline and punish*. London: Allen Lane, 1977.

Gramsci, A. *Quaderni del carcere*. Turin: Einaudi, 1975.

Grant, N. *Soviet education*. London: Penguin Books, 1964.

Hoyles, M. (Ed.). *The politics of literacy*. London: Writers & Readers, 1977.

James, L. *Fiction for the working man*. London: Penguin Books, 1973.

Johnson, R. Really useful knowledge. In J. Clarke, C. Critcher, & R. Johnson (Eds.), *Working-class culture*. London: Hutchinson, 1979.

Johnson, R. *Education and popular politics*. Milton Keynes, England: Open University Press, 1981.

Laqueur, T. The cultural origins of popular literacy in England 1500–1850. *Oxford Review of Education*, 1976, 2, 255–275.

McCann, P. Trade unions, artisans and the 1870 Education Act. *British Journal of Educational Studies*, 1970, *18*, 134–150.

McRobbie, A. Working class girls and the culture of feminity. In CCCS Women's Studies Group, *Women take issue: Aspects of women's subordination*. London: Hutchinson, 1978.

Poulantzas, N. *State, power, socialism*. London: New Left Books, 1978.

Simon, B. *Studies in the history of education: The two nations and the educational structure 1780–1870*. London: Lawrence & Wishart, 1960.

Stedman Jones, G. Working-class culture and working-class politics in London, 1870–1900. *Journal of Social History*, 1974, *7*, 460–508.

Thompson, E. P. *The making of the English working class*. London: Penguin Books, 1968.

Volosinov, V. N. *Marxism and the philosophy of language*. New York: Academic Press, 1973.

Webb, R. K. *The British working-class reader 1790–1848*. London: Allen and Unwin, 1955.

Willemen, P. Notes on subjectivity. *Screen*, 1978, *19*, 41–69.

Williams, R. *Keywords*. London: Fontana, 1976.

Willis, P. *Learning to labour*. Farnborough, England: Saxon House, 1977.

# 15

# HEGEMONIC PRACTICE: LITERACY AND STANDARD LANGUAGE IN PUBLIC EDUCATION

### James Collins

Richard Ohmann has recently characterized literacy in a remarkably concise fashion:

> Literacy is an activity of social groups, and a necessary feature of some kinds of social organization. Like every other human activity or product, it embeds social relations within it. And these relations always include *conflict* as well as cooperation. Like language itself, literacy is an exchange between classes, races, the sexes, and so on. (1985, p. 685)

In this chapter I will try to draw out the implications of such a view—that literacy is an activity which "embeds social relations" of "conflict as well as cooperation." Beginning with the work of Michel Foucault on the institutionalization of particular discursive practices, I will briefly trace the historical

This chapter has endured a long gestation period and acquired a correspondingly long list of debts. For their comments and questions I would like to thank audiences at a public lecture given under the auspices of the Language and Literacy Division of the UC Berkeley School of Education, April 24, 1986, and at the invited sessions on "Language and Political Economy," American Anthropological Association Annual Meetings, December 6, 1986, Philadelphia. Individuals I would like to thank for their oral and written comments on various drafts include Richard Bauman, Adrian Bennett, Jonathan Church, John Comaroff, Jane Hill, Benjamin Lee, Hugh Mehan, Leo Rigsby, Brian Street, Francis Sullivan, Fiona Thompson, and Susan Wells. Their queries and caveats have informed my thinking on the matters discussed, even when they have not resulted in changes in the text. Editors at the *Journal of Education* have improved the prose. An earlier version of this study appeared as Working Paper No. 21 of the Center for Psychosocial Studies (Chicago).

development of social conceptions of literacy in the United States and England. That history reveals what is all too often missing in Foucault's accounts—a direct motive in class conflict for the institutional shaping of discourse. Turning then to discuss the particularly effective linking of literacy and linguistic prescriptivism, I will note ways in which work by Antonio Gramsci and Pierre Bourdieu helps us to think about these matters, whether viewing them as historical process or contemporary practice. Ending on a critical note, I will try briefly to explore some of the difficulties of wedding studies of language to accounts of social reproduction, using the notion of literate tradition as an exemplary case of just this dilemma.

When we think about literacy, we face a number of paradoxes. Presumably linked to an increase in mental abilities, communicative resources, and general social powers, literacy has for most of world history been the special property of small socio-political elites which have, when necessary, fiercely guarded that property. Presumably linked to social mobility and betterment, literacy seems elusive for the general population; witness the recent alarms over mass illiteracy in this country and Britain. The alarms are sounded not simply out of altruistic concern for the less fortunate, but because modern literacy is closely tied to conceptions of social, political, and economic order. In particular, in the modern era, literacy is associated with the rise of nation states, with the "linguistic unification" which often accompanies the political and economic centralization found in the nation state, and with the formation of public educational systems. These last show in stark relief the association between symbolically valued literate traditions, mechanisms of social control, and the shaping of what gets called "literacy" as a field wherein power is deployed in particular discursive practices.

## THE INSTITUTIONALIZATION OF DISCURSIVE PRACTICES

### Foucault on the Examination

Foucault (1975) presents an important analysis of the school as an element in a tutelary complex, as a site of control realized through surveillance and discipline. Building upon the Foucauldian account, various analysts have characterized the school as a central element in a new system of industrial recruitment, one in which the systematic observation of symptomatic data serves as the primary means of controlling and establishing knowledge about given populations (Apple, 1982; Lasch, 1984). At the heart of this system has been the examination, a mechanism that linked a certain exercise of power (surveillance and judgment) to a certain formation of knowledge (documentary accumulation of symptomatic data). As Foucault says, the examination

> combines the technique of an observing hierarchy and those of a normalizing judgement. It is a normalizing gaze, a surveillance that makes it possible to qual-

ify, to classify and to punish. It establishes over individuals a visibility through which one differentiates them and judges them. That is why, in all the mechanisms of discipline, the examination is highly ritualized. In it are combined the ceremony of power and the form of the experiment, the deployment of force and the establishment of truth. (1975, pp. 184–185)

The rise of the examination, as part of a process of gaining knowledge and control over populations, transformed schooling in the 17th and 18th centuries, and that transformation crucially depended on the uses of literacy. As Foucault has shown, the examination itself arose during a period of increasing documentation of individuals. In various institutions of "therapeutic" control—hospitals, prisons, and schools—the procedures of examination were part of a system of intense registration and of documentary accumulation. As he phrased it: "The examination that places individuals in a field of surveillance also situates them in a network of writing" (p. 185). In the school this "network of writing" is found in the records which define the aptitudes of individuals, situate their level and abilities, and indicate the possible use that might be made of them.

This process of examination and documentary accumulation was extended with the development of mass schooling in the 19th century and increased in extent and depth with the ascendancy of the testing paradigm in 20th-century educational systems. Concern with *literacy* has been central to this history, and some of the characteristics of the institutionalization of discursive practices concerning literacy can now be outlined. It has involved a defining of normal or acceptable literacy versus other, unacceptable, non-normal forms of literacy. Literacy has thus been stratified, with divisions between the literate, subliterate, nonliterate, and so forth. This coopted or official literacy has shaped "local" practices, such as the initial teaching of reading and writing in actual classrooms, as well as guided the more general bureaucratic documentation (Foucault's "network of writing") of standardized texts and tests and their accumulation, which, in turn, inform and constrain the daily classroom practices.

A brief glance at the histories of public education and literacy in England and the United States will show the general shaping of literacy as part of the rise of elite-controlled mass education. Those histories present an interesting progression from nonschooling (and perceived social disorder) to schooling (seen as the inculcation of a moral order as well as a transmitter of useful, controllable knowledge). They show that the definition of what is and what is not literacy is never a purely technical but always also a profoundly political matter.

## The Creation of Schooled Literacy in England and North America

Donald (1982) has described the vigorous popular literacy which existed in early 19th-century England, a literacy which was both a continuation of earlier cultural tradition and also a result of the political ferment of the time. There were, for example, numerous small presses and correspondence societies; Tom Paine's *Rights of Man* sold over 1.5 million copies in a population of just over 17 million. Donald also describes how middle-class reformers such as Hannah More explicitly decried the dangers of this radical, subversive literacy and proposed the school as an alternative. The school meant mass compulsory education, a controlled site where selected teachers could inculcate in the children of the lower orders a moral discipline appropriate to the status quo. In this setting, mass literacy could be carefully guided by the right kind of readings (a political course in Dick and Jane we might say). By the end of that century, with mass education firmly in place, we find commissions lamenting mass illiteracy and laying the blame on various "cognitive deficiencies" prevalent among the lower classes.

We find a similar history in the United States and Canada. The social unrest of the early 19th century led to a call for systems of public education, of "mass" schooling, which were to instill a moral order along with "useful knowledge." Led by middle-class reformers and liberal members of the industrial bourgeoisie, this movement resulted in a system of public schooling explicitly designed to prepare workers for the new industrial order. That is, schools became sites for the socializing of populations, both immigrants and the native-born, to the emerging class-divided industrial societies of 19th-century Canada and the United States (Nasaw, 1979).

Literacy plays an interesting role in this development, as ideology and as linguistic practice. In a study of the social definition and organization of literacy in 19th-century Canada and United States, Harvey Graff (1979) examines the putative relation between literacy and social mobility. Using statistical data to critique the official view that literacy promotes social mobility, he shows that family and ethnic background were far more effective predictors of social position, throughout the century, than was literacy. Literacy did account for differences among the native- or English-born Protestant population, but accounted for very little difference among the Irish Catholic or other immigrant or nonwhite populations. What is important, however, is the linkage that official pronouncements drew between literacy, schooling, and social mobility, a point to which we return below.

Whether in England or North America, class conflicts and tensions motivated the creation of institutions of public education. These became the locus of social discipline and social promise. We see in this history a transformation of literacy: from a plurality of scriptal practices embedded in a commonplace working-class culture of political dissent, to a unified conception and execution, centered on the school, with deviations from the school norm attributed to deficiencies and deviations in working-class homes, communities, and minds. The end result of this process is what Jenny Cook-Gumperz (1986) has aptly called *schooled literacy*—a universalistic literacy, context-independent and functionally general, evaluated by tests under prior assumptions of differential achievement. This literacy has slowly become *the* norm for all literacy. Encompassing and redefining, it has turned a prior diversity of literate practices into a stratified literacy, driving a series of wedges into popular cultural practices and traditions.

## A FORM OF HEGEMONY: STANDARD LANGUAGE LITERACY

This universalistic literacy constitutes a strong ideological control or domination, the sources of which are quite interesting. Mobilizing a consensus without (extreme) coercion, universalistic literacy allows dominant groups to appropriate popular practices and traditions. More particularly, it lets them transform subaltern literacies into a general literacy, purportedly universal yet controlled by elites, held out as a universal ideal yet stratified and unequally available. In short, such literacy contributes to that "direction without domination," or domination without overt coercion, that Gramsci (1971) called "hegemony" and Bourdieu and Passeron (1977) "symbolic domination."

There are several major reasons why literacy in the standard language has this hegemonic capacity. One is the relation between the political processes of national integration and the standard language, especially strongly emphasized in the nationalism of the 18th–20th centuries. Another is the link between literacy, schooling, and the ideal of individual social mobility. Finally, there is the way in which a literate tradition and schooled literacy achieve a particular kind of indexical fixing of texts, both their production and their comprehension. Examining these reasons in some detail will allow us to appreciate the problematic status of the notions of hegemony and symbolic domination, a subject upon which I focus in the Conclusion.

### National Integration and Standard Languages

It has long been known that standardization of languages accompanies movements for political autonomy, in particular movements for national autonomy and consolidation. Indeed, it is a commonplace of linguistics that those entities called "languages" are usually *standard languages*. That is, they are institutionally imposed ways of speaking, associated with classes and groups which exercise dominant power in particular political structures, typically nation states. The centralizing institutions of modern nations—universal education and military service, massive bureaucracies of the economy and government—bring about a linguistic unification in that one way of speaking becomes the *explicit* norm for conducting business and displaying competencies (in short, it becomes the standard) (Bloomfield, 1933; Bourdieu, 1982; Gumperz, 1968).

That literacy is tied to the standard dialect is perhaps as it should be, for in the case of English arguments can and have been made that the literary dialect, or at least the orthography, represents an abstraction of core features of lexicon and phonology; it permits, in principle, the widest transmission of messages, the widest communicability (O'Neal, 1980). The literary dialect, however, is never merely an orthographic norm for representing lexico-phonological structure. In moments of insurgent nationalism, such as those which swept Europe in the 19th century, it becomes a tool of mobilization, a principle of identity, a means of constructing communities imagined or imaginable (Anderson, 1983). In secure and consolidating nationalisms, it often becomes the "subtext" for standard language prescriptivism, that prescriptivism in which a class dialect is imposed in the name of imparting the literary standard.

As Raymond Williams (1961) has noted, in 17th- and 18th-century England there was a decisive shift in conceptions of the standard. Where once it was viewed as simply a literary dialect, a written code, it became a prescription for all linguistic practice, for regimenting speech as well as writing or reading.[1] In the United States, as in England, there has been a clear link between literacy and standard language prescriptivism. Shirley Brice Heath (1980) has described a shift from a more pluralistic concern with the literary dialect as a tool for writing, common in the early 19th century, to a more authoritarian prescription of the standard as norm for all correct usage, whether spoken or written, found later in the century. This latter generalized prescriptivism, in which the standard came to be viewed as symbol of nationalist authenticity, occurs during the period of national consolidation in the post–Civil War United States, a time when stringent monolingualism also became the official language policy of the emerging empire (Heath, 1977).

The general issue, however, is that linguistic unification and standardization is always *imputed* as well as real, counterfactual as well as factual (Bakhtin, 1981; Heath, 1980). The result of political centralization, the rise of great cities, and the stabilizing of literary norms in the service of print-capitalism, language standardization is an undeniable aspect of life in modern nation states. Yet it is also an official representation, an official definition of speaking practices (as good and bad), an attempt to impose a class dialect on an always complex array of social dialects. The standard *qua* ideal is not an illusion, or simple play of power, yet it is part of a system of class hegemony, of ruling-class legitimation. A partial truth which is the official truth, it is an attempt to universalize the particular and class-bound, an attempt which has various sources of strength and points of tension or weakness.

### Literacy and Mobility

One source of support for language standardization has been the perceived link between standard language, literacy, and social mobility. As literacy became the province of the school, it also became progressively linked to ideals of social mobility, throughout the 19th and 20th centuries in the United States and Britain.

The ideal of mobility hinges on the belief that there is equal opportunity in education and, through education, opportunity for social mobility and a more equitable society. This view encapsulates a number of partial truths,[2] and contains a number of egregious distortions, as critics have been quick to point out.[3] But the germane point is that the idea of mobility through literacy and education remains persuasive, despite radical arguments to the contrary or the historical experience of most people. If we ask why this should be so, several answers suggest themselves. Perhaps the most basic is that ideas about mobility correspond in the educational and economic realm to ideas about (electoral) democracy in the political realm. By defining the political universe and the realm of possible participants narrowly enough, parliamentary democracy seems to work: the people elect "their" government. By defining the relevant measures of educational success and the relation between educational attainment and social position narrowly enough, social mobility seems to work: we succeed through our "own" efforts, as represented by the match of education and job.

Whatever the possible criticisms, the relevant point for our argument is that there *is* a perceived relation between literacy and social mobility. That perception dates from at least the preceding century. Working with 19th-century materials, Graff (1979) has argued for the existence of a "moral economy of literacy." In this period, literacy was officially valued as a means to broad social and cultural participation, but more particularly as a putative means to higher-status employment.[4] Along with this valuation, however, there was also the actual stratification of literacy, a symbolic good whose unequal distribution was achieved through an emerging system of differentiated educational institutions.

If the 19th century presents us with a moral economy of literacy, in which a stratified transmission of skills coexists with an ideology of literacy as self-improvement, then the 20th century confronts us with an increasingly "technocratic economy of literacy," in which a persisting stratification of skills coexists with an ideology of literacy as technical capacity and marketplace worth. The engine of this process has been an emerging Late or Monopoly Capitalist political economy which has extended contradiction-ridden procedures of centralization and control to diverse areas of social life. As part of this process, in 20th-century North America (and England) an educational testing paradigm appropriated literacy, defining it as a precisely measurable assemblage of technical skills (Ohmann, 1985). These skills supposedly exist independently of any particular context or use; their possession has come to define educability in general (Cook-Gumperz, 1986) and, correlatively, fitness for an increasingly complex technical economy. The 19th-century concern with moral uplift and civic participation has been replaced by a more basic concern with technical adequacy, as defined by standardized tests.

However, just as critiques of electoral democracy can point to the (hidden) class bias in party structures, election procedures, and the major nonelectoral institutions of the state, so also a critique of the link between literacy and mobility can point to class biases in the discursive practices through which literacy is enacted and defined. Such biases and impositions are not the result of a simple elite conspiracy to mystify and dominate. They arise from those complex processes, discussed by Marx, through which the ideas and conventions of a ruling class come to seem "universal," that is, natural and self-evident.

For example, for the middle classes of western capitalist democracies, schooling has been a central element in *their* historical experience of economic mobility and widening political-cultural participation. Hence their faith in this institution, which they genuinely view as "progressive" (at least when properly controlled). The rise of testing also presents complexities. Alongside its obviously manipulative and exclusionary motivation, testing seems to spring from a basic desire in our political-pedagogic culture for objective, disinterested modes of evaluation. Popular movements, such as the U.S. civil rights movement, or the English labor and civil rights activities of the 1960s, often spur the development of testing. The initial goal is to overcome obviously prejudicial forms of evaluation and selection, but proponents later discover that the new "objective measures" conceal a bias in instrument or implementation.

## THE INDEXICAL FIXING OF LITERACY

I would like to suggest that schooled literacy achieves a "social magic" of definition and deception. It uses yet disguises biases of text, curriculum, and classroom practice by evoking the literate tradition in ways which discriminate against those who have the least exposure to that tradition. It does so by treating aspects of the tradition which are the most tied to particular class-based varieties of language as symptomatic indices of skill, ability, or proficiency in general.

### Indexicality and the Literate Tradition

The notion of *indexicality* provides a way of talking about this imposition of the "literate tradition" in a reasonably precise fashion. Briefly put, indexicality is a mode of signification, and indexical meaning is meaning which attaches to a sign form by virtue of an understood copresence between the form and its object (Peirce, 1932).[5] Indexical meaning is "contextual meaning," but only if we have a rich and robustly *cognitive* view of "context." Indexical relations are not matters of simple correlation, of static copresence between speech forms and the contextual surround; they involve also the cognitive dimension of awareness or salience. (This point is also made by, among others, Gumperz, 1982; and Silverstein, 1976.)[6]

An early and consistent demonstration by ethnomethodologists was that all language was indexical—that is, required some context for its interpretation. The relevant or pertinent context may of course differ, and the account of dominant (or school) and dominated (or working-class) language suggested by

Basil Bernstein has been reinterpreted along precisely these lines. As John Gumperz (1972) argued over a decade and a half ago, the difference between Bernstein's "restricted" and "elaborated" codes (1975) was largely a matter of what was necessary for their interpretation, that is, of what each "code" index-ically presupposed. In the case of elaborated codes, they presupposed the syntax and lexicon found in grammars and dictionaries, that relatively codifiable aspect of language. In the case of the restricted code, it was a knowledge more specific to particular situations, perspectives, and social groups, that non-lexicalized and non-syntacticalized mixture of tradition, shared experience, and local expression, which escapes the lexicographer and the grammarian yet is so vital to meaning-making.

In their analysis of language, education, and social reproduction, Bourdieu and Passeron (1977) have reframed these polar contrasts in terms of bourgeois and working-class language. The former, they say, is characterized by distance from topic, *literary* allusion, ambiguity, and irony; the latter by directness, sub-jective closeness to topic, nonliterary allusion to the immediate situation of speaking and understanding, and the figuring of experience through the language of local narrative and proverb (see also Bourdieu, 1982). This dichot-omy, as with elaborated/restricted, grossly over-simplifies. Its value lies in seeing that all language is indexical, requiring some context for interpretation, but that the presupposed or presupposable context differs. For "bourgeois" language it is the literate tradition; for "working-class" language it is more local traditions, ways with words less directly tied to the markets and institu-tions of print.

But what are we to make of notions like "the syntax and lexicon found in grammars and dictionaries," or Bourdieu's even more general "literate tradi-tion"? I think we are to make of them a set of indexical contexts, evoked in par-ticular institution-bound discursive practices, some deployed in situations of face-to-face evaluation, some embedded in a technology of text-evaluation; some reducing to direct type-token comparison,[7] some raising the problem of how approved or prescribed text form is successfully evoked in speech or writing.

### The Literate Tradition and Face-to-Face Evaluation

In developing this argument, let us turn first to situations of face-to-face evaluation, in which the literary dialect serves as the indexical reference point for the evaluation of speech. That the literary dialect does serve as such a refer-ence point has been discussed in various works (see Bloomfield, 1933; Havranek, 1964 [1932] on Czech; Williams, 1961 on "Standard English").[8] One of the various forms which that evaluative relation takes is revealed in the organization of reading instruction.

Reflected in this organization we typically encounter the idea that reading consists of Standard English pronunciation. Graff's (1979) study of the organization of literacy in the 19th-century school provides a useful historical perspective on the matter. Graff describes the selection of texts for their middle-class bias in subject matter, and, more interestingly, he describes instructional techniques. He shows that a pervasive institutional definition of literacy, especially for working-class and immigrant minority students, was of literacy as the "reading aloud" of text, rather than say silent reading with scanning ahead and behind to answer questions. What Graff argues, quite plausibly in my view, is that this allows a cooptive definition of literacy—enacted in classroom practices—as pronunciation of spelling norms of dominant groups, a definition and practice that permits the open surveillance and public devaluing of nonstandard varieties of speech. Such conceptions and practices are common in contemporary public education in the United States, as quantitative and ethnographic studies of reading instruction have shown (Collins, 1986; Labov, 1972; Piestrup, 1973; Rist, 1970).

In gauging the significance of this enduring emphasis on reading as pronunciation, a point to bear in mind is that most recent work on English orthography has insisted on the *abstractness* of standard orthography, that is, that there is—and should be—only an indirect relationship between orthography and pronunciation (O'Neal, 1972, 1980). A second matter worth remembering is that despite the certainties of prescriptive doctrine, there is no accepted body of research showing the effects of nonstandard speech, qua structure, on learning to read or write, when these are viewed purely as cognitive activities (Gibson & Levin, 1975).

However, in a quantitative study of dialect use and teacher styles, Ann Piestrup (1973) has shown that teacher *attitude* toward nonstandard speech does affect educational performance. In particular, the study shows that teachers who were assiduous in correcting nonstandard speech were usually ineffectual with urban minority students—indeed, they were least effective with students who spoke the strongest vernacular. One reason is that dialect correction often detracts from the business of reading. Some of the ways in which this works can be seen in following examples.

Example 15.1 is taken from Piestrup's study and is a portion of a longer transcript illustrating how diverse corrections of speech disrupt the process of reading. The correction has nothing to do with the misrecognition of words, a common problem with novice literates, but rather concerns final t / d deletion, a stereotypic characteristic of Black English Vernacular. As we see, attention is focused on pronunciation of the final "t" in "what." Ironically, most colloquial styles of English delete a t / d in this environment—in clusters before a following noncontinuant (for example, most readers of this journal would pronounce "coldcuts" as [kolkats] rather than [kold'kats]). Given Piestrup's general findings that dialect correction was frequently irrelevant for reading task, it seems that suppression of nonstandard speech is being carried out (in this example, through insistence on hyper-correct spelling pronunciation) to the detriment of a larger concern with reading.

**Example 15.1**
**Correction of Vernacular (From Piestrup, 1973, pp. 96–97)**

| 1 | T | All right, class, read that and remember your endings. |
|---|---|---|
| 2 | CC | "What did Little Duck see?" |
| 3 | T | What*t*. |
| 4 | CC | "What did Little Duck see?" |
| 5 | T | I still don't hear this sad little 't'. |
| 7 | CC | What did — What did — What — |
| 8 | T | What*t*. |
| 9 | T&CC | "What did Little Duck see?" |
| 10 | T | OK, very good. |

Example 15.2 is taken from fieldnotes and transcripts of an ethnographic study of reading groups which was conducted in Berkeley in 1979–80 (as part of the School Home Ethnography Project; see Collins 1986 for fuller description). Here we see how a combination of dialect difference—whether one says *I'll* with a diphthong [ayl] or monophthong [a:l]—is confounded with a decoding problem—recognition of the apostrophe and its purpose. The confounded correction occurs early in the lesson, later during the middle, and finally, in a long and confusing exchange, near the end.

**Example 15.2**
**Cumulative Confusion of Dialect Correction and Reading Instruction (from fieldnotes)**

Initial correction early in lesson:

| 1 | T | Go on Clancey | |
|---|---|---|---|
| 2 | CL | "Debbie looks out | 'It looks like |
| 3 | T | | keep plugged in (to other student) |
| 4 | CL | [la:k] a day for the park.' " | ... |
| 5 | Cx | | Where are we? |
| 6 | T | Go on | |
| 7 | CL | " 'Ah^y | Ah'll [a:l] be out.... |
| 8 | T | | *I*'ll |

....

| 1 | T | Go on... say "*I:*'ll" | |
|---|---|---|---|
| 2 | CL | Ah'll | Owl [a:l]..." |

3    T            not Al, *I'll*

4    CL           'I'll [aᵛl] wait for Ann' ."

Subsequent correction with different reader:

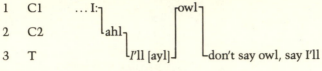

1    C1           ... I:

2    C2           ahl

3    T            *I'll* [ayl]            don't say owl, say I'll

4    C1           I'll..     come.

5    T                 come     okay

Major multi-party correction near end of lesson:

1    C1           Oh, forgot this line: 'I [a:] will come

2    C2           ... I will come

3    C3           ... Ahl come

4    C4           ... Ah' uhl come

5    T            (returning from distraction away from group) I want

6                 Wally to tell me what the very last line says

7    W            I will come.

8    T            My book doesn't say that

9    C4           I: uhl

10   C5           Owl

11   T            My book says "*I:'ll*"

12   C2           "I:ll"?

13   T            What does your book say? (directed at other than W)

14   C1           I'll

15   C5           Owl

16   C3           Ah'll

17   T            Not ahl, *I'll*

18   CC           I:

19   T            Say "I"

20   CC           I    [ay]

21                Ah [a:]

22   T          Say "I: uhl" [ay..əl]

23   CC         I: uhl

24              a'll [aɛl]

25              ah: uhl [a:..əℓ]

26   T          Not 'ah', 'I'

27   CC         I

28              Ah

29              Ae

30   T          What's your book say? (directed at new student)

Such exchanges illustrate what can only be called a regimenting of reading as standard pronunciation. In this case there is ample confusion, and no little frustration, though this is difficult to indicate on a transcript, and the potentially useful lesson about the function of apostrophes in orthography is lost in the melee.

The final example, (15.3), is from a comparative study of reading groups and social background I conducted in Chicago in 1981 (see Collins, 1987a for fuller discussion). It is interesting in a slightly different way from the previous examples. The apparent "error" results from a metathesis process common to Black English Vernacular. The student reads and the teacher corrects in line two.

We should note that the student does not seem to understand the correction. Instead, she mimics the teacher's stress pattern. That the student does not interpret the teacher's utterance as a correction of consonant sequence but rather of stress is consistent with other dialect perception studies, showing that young dialect speakers systematically turn features of Standard English into their vernacular in translation and mimicry tasks (Labov, 1972).

These examples have been selected to make a point: it is linguistic *stereotypes* which form much of the basis of prescriptive ideology. That is, prescriptivist practice seizes on that which is most salient—departures from the spelling norms of the standard—whether in a text being read or simple talk. Insisting on spelling pronunciation is a particularly efficacious way of imposing the standard on speakers of other varieties: The phonological segments of the literary dialect serve as a constant template or reference point upon which to

**Example 15.3**
**Correction of Vernacular (from Collins, 1986, p. 186)**

1   C          "... for goodness sake why?" aksd Olive⌐
                                                        |
2   T                                                   Lasked

3   C          *aksd* Olive Owl.

focus the novices' attention. The attention given to linguistic difference varies, of course, according to the shifting interactional conditions of classroom lessons (see Collins, in press, for discussion), but prescriptivist practice, basic to educational institutions and their view of people and language, nonetheless works a subtle discrimination. A definition of literacy as "reading aloud" is not merely a technical display and evaluation of skill, but rather a socially inculcated orientation toward literacy, with demonstrably differing effects on various classes and groups in society.

The literate tradition, or written language, also influences the assessment of other types of spoken language. One of the main thrusts of Sarah Michaels's early work on classroom interaction (1981) was to show how implicit expectations about written language enter into judgments about *spoken* language (see note 8) and result in classroom processes ultimately as inegalitarian as overt prejudice. Michaels's work, since replicated in other studies (see Michaels & Cazden, 1986), compared teacher–student interaction between teachers and students from different class and ethnic backgrounds, during first-grade "show and tell" narrative sessions. She found that teachers had an *implicit* discourse model—that of a topic-centered expository essay. When students' narrative performances did not match this model, interaction during the events was strained, and teacher evaluations were negative. Covering not just discourse form, but also presumed cognitive abilities, these evaluations had long-term implications for students' placement in ability groups. A brief contrast of the narrative types is provided in Table 15.1.

Michaels argued, correctly I think, that the narrative events served as an "oral preparation for literacy," as a practice ground for developing, in collaboration with a teacher, a literate style of spoken discourse. That is true, however, only when they work, when the classroom interaction is successful. But interactional "success" requires many things: minimally, a match between the teacher's implicit assumptions and the children's habitual ways of speaking; optimally, a measure as well of that trust and regard which seems to underpin much successful pedagogy. As reported, Michaels's sharing time events represent prime examples of an "implicit pedagogic message" (Bourdieu & Passeron, 1977), which only those with prior (domestic) familiarization will receive.

**Table 15.1**
**General Features of Narrative Types (summary of Michaels, 1981)**

| *"Literate style"* | *"Oral style"* |
| --- | --- |
| Single topic focus. | Topic-chaining. |
| Prevalence of topicalizing constructions. | Lexical and syntactic parallelism. |
| Prosody matching sentential units. | Prosody matching phrasal and rhetorical units. |

A suggestive reanalysis of Michaels's material by James Gee (1985) makes the same sociopolitical point and an interesting semiotic observation: the so-called "literate" style shows the functional dominance of *topic*, while the "oral" style shows the functional dominance of *message form*, with the poetics of repetition and parallelism guiding the interpretive process.[9] It seems thus that the direct prescriptivism of imposed spelling pronunciation—in which the visual representation provides an indexical token of a presumed standard phonological *type*, against which any particular reading can be evaluated as sufficient or insufficient token—is part of a more general literate bias in which the *types* are far more difficult to specify. The expository model of these studies is precisely an ideal of *written text*, for which it is difficult to specify exact replication, and whose general principles may be acquired through subconscious familiarization rather than learned through overt, conscious instruction.

## The Literate Tradition and Technologies of Text Evaluation

The evaluation of particular narrative performances as like or unlike this ideal type raises the problem of authorized language, as does the organization and evaluation of reading aloud. In both cases, the question is how particular discursive forms evoke the blessings of legitimate (in this case, literate) language. In the case of reading aloud, we can argue for a direct type / token comparison between pronunciation and written text; in the case of classroom narratives, for a less direct but persistent imposition of tacit expectations about textual form. There are other ways, however, in which a selective literate bias is involved, not in face-to-face interaction, but in a more general demarcation of the literate and nonliterate. This latter demarcation is achieved with what might be called *textual technologies*—those linguistic forms and conventions which become part of a non-interactional mechanism for producing and evaluating texts.

As a reasonably direct example of such a "technology," consider first the skewing of vocabulary knowledge found in educational materials. Much of the argument about education and mobility rests on a fundamental assumption of the educational testing paradigm: that examinations are based on materials made suitable for all students. As has been often noted in the decade-long controversy over testing, however, putatively value-free tests often incorporate class and ethnic bias (Hall & Freedle, 1975).

A corollary of this bias in *tests* is a bias in the construction and evaluation of *texts*. One recent study showing such effects is particularly interesting. In a quantitative study of class and ethnic differences in typical lexicon, Bruce, Rubin, Starr, and Liebling (1984) have shown that standard instruments for evaluating reading-text complexity, such as readability formulas, skew existing differences in lexical knowledge by selecting for those already known by middle-class speakers.

**Table 15.2**
**Intersections Between Categorical Groups' 732 Most Frequently Spoken Words (adapted from Bruce Rubin, Starr, and Liebling, 1984, p. 471)**

|  | Groups | Intersections core vocab. | Distinctive 1st, not 2nd | Distinctive 2nd, not 1st |
|---|---|---|---|---|
| Class | MC1, WC2* | 707 | 182 | 196 |
| Race | Black1, White2 | 688 | 203 | 179 |

*: MC = Middle-Class
   WC = Working-Class

In this study they found differences in aggregate vocabulary when comparing groups of 5-year-old children belonging to different social class and racial groups. More importantly, however, they found areas of "distinctive vocabulary," that is, sets from one social group of typical and frequently used vocabulary which were unused or infrequently used by other groups. Table 15.2 compares differing class and racial groups for their most frequently used vocabulary and for overlap with other groups.

We may note that there is considerable overlap between vocabulary, but the black group contains the largest number of distinctive vocabulary items (203) followed by the working-class group (196). That is, these groups had the highest number of distinctive word types which were not in frequent use by other groups.

There is not merely difference by race and class, however. Standardized readability formulas—lists used to assess the difficulty of texts—overly select for particular categories. Three such instruments are compared in Table 15.3, which shows how many words of a group's distinctive vocabulary occur on a particular list.

**Table 15.3**
**Number of Readability Formula Words Appearing in Distinctive Vocabularies of Class and Race Groups (Bruce et al., 1984, p. 472)**

| Group | Spache 1040 | Dale 769 | Spache Added 365 |
|---|---|---|---|
| MC | 75 | 62 | 19 |
| WC | 63 | 47 | 23 |
| Black | 63 | 51 | 18 |
| White | 81 | 53 | 34 |

Again we see a pattern of class and race inclusion and exclusion. As Bruce et al. observe, the differences are significant, even when adjustment is made for differences in total vocabulary and number of distinct, frequently used word types. Readability formulas are used to establish, among other things, the grade level of particular reading texts, and the findings point to a language bias built into the formulas. A text ranked by either of these three formulas would under-rate the difficulty of the text (measured as "commonness" of words contained) for working-class and black readers. Ironically, reforms to eliminate cultural bias in such formulas have only introduced greater skewing against working-class and minority speakers.

As a more complex example of such technologies, consider the skewing to-ward a particular literate form expected in writing assignments. It is unlike the case of readability formulas, in which the specification of literateness and the relevant criteria are tightly bound to a calculus for determining "difficulty" that is, in turn, based on a definition of "typical" lexicon. Rather, what seems to be operating in writing assessment is a looser prescription of depersonalized syntax and lexical "explicitness."

There is a relevant history to this prescriptive technology, a history which shows a different selective mobilization of the literate tradition. Evelyn Wright (1980) has discussed how "School English," a particular codification of middle-class usage, was organized in the late 19th and early 20th centuries. Justified on grounds of clarity and correctness, "School English" featured im-personal sentences and an expository paragraph format, together with sanc-tions for approved pronouns, verb forms, and "misused" phrases. When initially developed it served as the basis for recitation (that is, for disciplining spoken language) as well as for the assessment of written language. An authori-tative set of maxims which have served as basis for various codebooks on usage in educational settings, "School English" stipulates depersonalized language and expository prose formats as the ideal of organized thought in language.

The effects of "School English" can be discerned in Michaels's and other classroom studies, but they can also be found in the assessment of *writing*. In a study of a remedial writing program at a large urban university, Francis Sullivan (1985) compared graders' holistic rating with text characteristics. Es-says written by students in the program were analyzed sentence by sentence, using a taxonomy of *given / new* information.

Sullivan found that a particular construction type accounted for much of the variation in raters' assessment.[10] That construction was the *contained in-ferrable*—a complex noun phrase in which information inferrable from the head noun was explicitly stated in the complement. Examples are such as the following: "The Russian revolution *of 1917*"; "The students *of the school*"; "The censorship *of books and movies*." In each case the information contained in the *of* clause—1917, the school, books and movies—is easily deducible from general knowledge of those entities denoted by the head noun.

Such constructions often create overly explicit texts, providing information which any educated reader presumably knows. They violate, for example, the preference scales proposed by Ellen Prince (1981) on the basis of her survey of general writing samples. But contained inferables seem to be preferred in this writing test situation, for they correlate positively with higher ratings. Alerting readers who are also raters that the novice writer is aware of the need to be redundantly explicit, they belie any claim that mere informational adequacy is primary in evaluation of written text. Overly precise, such constructions secure positive assessment; the construction types which presuppose more of the reader, common in other types of writing, are negatively assessed. The findings suggest that in formal situations the safest assumption is that verbosity—elaborate presentation of unnecessary information—is the preferred mode of discourse.[11]

These matters point to a general problem in communication, whether oral or written: the question of audience. That issue has been settled in a particular way, however, by "School English" and by the implicit emphasis on expository prose models found in school-based literacy events. It should be noted that, as with Michaels's study, we are talking about subconscious principles. They can often only be gotten at by circuitous routes: by indirect elicitation of participants' assumptions and close conversational analysis in Michaels's case; or by analysis of aggregate decision data concerning text features and rater responses in Sullivan's case. Yet such principles, such implicit preferences, are brought to bear in evaluating the discourse of those groups that are least likely to have them. Rarely part of an explicit pedagogy, such principles are employed in that tacit matching of conventions for a "literate" style, whether in speech or writing, which forms so large a part of educational assessment.

In all the cases above, we deal with an indexical fixing of literacy: a social definition of reading which judges against the voices of popular classes; an assessment of early narrative which selects against "oral" narrative logics; a formulation of "readability" which selects *for* the typical lexicon of particular classes and races; and, finally, a formulation of "School English," discernible in the aggregated response to placement essays, which is more a matter of social style than necessary content. The various cases represent a cumulative determination of privileged criteria and reference points, both overt and covert, for defining and imposing literacy. That determination parallels the appropriation of possible literacies found in the history of public schooling, only now "on the ground," in the specifics of classroom interaction and the technologies of text evaluation.

## CONCLUSION

I began this chapter by arguing for a particular shaping of literacy, as conception and practice, within the more general compass of an institutional development that was itself driven by class conflicts. The legitimacy of standard language literacy seems a composite of three diverse developments operating at distinct levels of sociopolitical and discursive generality: the association of language with national unification, the association of literacy with mobility, and the indexical fixing of an authoritative literate tradition. In these developments educational institutions have increasingly been called upon to mediate the tension between class-divided societies and the ideals of democratic opportunity; that mediation has taken particular forms, forms in which literacy, as symbol and practice, has figured as a primary cultural medium.

Schooled literacy, technically homogenized and effectively stratified, has come to occupy the place that virtue held in an earlier, more religious age. As with much religion, we see a historical appropriation of a valued symbolic realm by particular groups. Schooled literacy and its indexical enactibles would seem to be exemplary instances of Bourdieu's symbolic domination (1977) and Gramsci's hegemony (1971). The preceding analyses have therefore concentrated on the processes through which the selective and class-based are presented as a universal measure.

There are problems, however, as critics have pointed out, with the notions of symbolic domination and hegemony. Neither Bourdieu nor Gramsci satisfactorily characterizes the strength or internal articulation of the reigning consensus, nor do they identify where effective points for opposition or resistance might lie. Bourdieu's account of social reproduction, for example, requires at least a *recognition* of the authoritative norms for conduct in society, if not an overt allegiance. Social reproduction, however, may not require a consensus with regard to dominant values or norms. Maintaining existing social relations in advanced capitalist societies may depend instead upon a pervasive *fragmentation* of the social order (Jameson, 1984; Thompson, 1984). Rather than primarily fostering adherence to orthodox values and official standards, it may be that the contemporary school contributes most to social reproduction by proliferating divisions between members of a social formation. This service is performed in complex complementarity with that restructuring of family, community, and nation wrought by international capital and its divisioning of labor.

The relevant point is that simple opposition to the established order does not suffice. Unsatisfied with Gramsci's formulation of hegemony, we may ask, with Perry Anderson (1977), what are the fulcrum points for a genuine popular and working-class political or cultural hegemony? Oppositional attitudes by themselves do not generate a coherent alternative view or provide a basis for political action; and the social basis of such alternative views remains unclear in the writings of Gramsci and his many commentators (for example, Mouffe, 1979; Salamini, 1981). More pointedly, we might ask what is the leverage point for a challenge to ruling class legitimacy, as organized in formal institutions, outside of some general challenge or alternative state power, or some effective decoupling of the usual symmetry between formal institutional legitimacy and economic dominance (as in the informative Catalan case described by Woolard, 1985)?

An apt study of the dilemma of consensus and opposition, if not its solution, is provided by Paul Willis's classic ethnography of a working-class English high school (1977). This study persuasively argues that social reproduction occurs even though the rebellious working-class "lads" achieve a limited critique of the fierce individualism and spurious mobility offered by contemporary schooling. The "lads" wind up in harsh industrial jobs with agency and insight: they reject the school and "choose their fate," so to speak. Their rejection involves, among other things, the avoidance of school work, itself part of a larger rejection of formal language—of any distanced, considered, working with language, of reading, writing, and "all that."[12] One reason for the "lads'" rejection of school language is of particular interest: such language is part of the "mental work" of the school, and the students' critique of the school involves an inversion of the usual valuation of mental over manual labor. They valorize manual labor, while making other problematic symbolic associations including male vs. female and white vs. non-white. But rejecting considered language, in shaping a rebellion which excludes women and racial minorities, the "lads" fail to find any other, more encompassing principle of opposition.

It may be that hegemony and symbolic domination operate, not as a unified system of beliefs and values imposed on a population from above, but rather, as John Thompson has proposed of ideology, "through a complex series of mechanisms, whereby meaning is mobilized, in the discursive practices of everyday life, for the maintenance of relations of domination" (Thompson, 1984, p. 63). Such a formulation, which would allow us to escape from a strict consensualist model, still leaves us with the task of specifying mechanisms through which ideology is deployed and hegemony secured.

Foucault's account of examinations in the disciplining institutions of our societies suggests one mechanism, though that account needs to be grounded in some historical analysis of how class tensions shape institutions. Bourdieu's (1982) and Gramsci's (Salamini, 1981) analyses of standard languages, fully consonant with that sketched above for English, suggest additional mechanisms, located in class and regional rivalries; in Bourdieu's account we gain additional insight into the primary association of standard language literacy and social mobility. Counterposed to the unifying tendencies of standardization is the heterogeneity of language, an inherent social dialect diversity (Bakhtin, 1981). But an account of this diversity cannot rest on general allusions to social differentiation (*pace* Bakhtin). Nor can an account of the role of formal institutions in encompassing and excluding that diversity ignore the contradictions, based on class and other social divisions, that this encompassing and stratifying unification engenders. More capacious accounts of linguistic hegemony, of symbolic domination, need to find the institutional and extra-institutional loci of the unifying and disintegrative tendencies in language. The tension between official representation and counter-representation, official pronouncement and subversive counter-movement, needs to be carefully worked out, to be located vis-à-vis some account of social domination in class societies. Analyses of that domination must confront the potent linkage of nationalism, language standardization, and schooled literacy that informs contemporary definitions of language and schooling. By studying the historical formation of those definitions, as well as the text-based discursive practices in which they are enacted and confirmed, we may gain a better appreciation, in intellectual and political terms, of the issues which confront any critique of or resistance to discursive domination.

## NOTES

1. Of this period Raymond Williams has written:

The class-structure of England was now decisively changing, at the beginning of a period which can be summed up as the effort of the rising middle-class to establish its own common speech. By the nineteenth century, after many important changes, this had been achieved, and it is then that we first hear of "Standard English," by which is meant speech: a very different thing from the written "standard" established so much earlier. Indeed, its naming as "standard," with the implication no longer of a common but of a model language, represents the full coming to consciousness of a new concept of class speech: now no longer merely the functional convenience of a metropolitan class, but the means and emphasis of social distinction. (1961, p. 220)

2. Formal equality of opportunity depends on important rights which do exist in our society—for instance, the universal right to education, including minimum provisions for the education of all children, and certain legislative guarantees against discrimination. Furthermore, social mobility *is* linked to education. The education system acts as a labor-power selection device, or a device for rationing class privilege, but the result is the same: the more education, the better the job opportunities (Lasch, 1984; Ogbu, 1978).

3. Criticisms include the following. Historically, discriminatory job ceilings have restricted the opportunities of women and minorities regardless of education (Ogbu, 1978), and class background remains a greater determinant of adult social position than education (Bowles & Gintis, 1976). In addition, social mobility may exist without altering fundamental social relations. We may have a highly stratified, inegalitarian society, although there is limited movement of individuals through social positions, and that movement is tied to educational credentials (Apple, 1982; Bourdieu & Passeron, 1977; Nasaw, 1979). In short, formal rights do not guarantee substantive conditions.

4. In a recent study of this 19th-century ethos, Lee Soltow and Edward Stevens have written:

An ideology of literacy carried forward from the eighteenth century and associated primarily with the spiritual well-being of individual and community alike had been further developed within the contexts of nationalism and the ethic of economic self-improvement. Collectively, literacy clearly was considered part of the social cement which helped to guarantee social stability and adherence to cherished social and political norms. The function of literacy was seen as integrative; its value was to be assessed in terms of social cohesion. Individually, literacy was one attribute which helped to make the good man, that is, it was part of being virtuous, and the better man was the man who could improve his skills in reading and writing. (Soltow & Stevens, 1981, p. 85 [cited in Cook-Gumperz, 1986, pp. 31–32])

5. There have been developments of the Peircean doctrine in sociology and linguistics. Early work by Aaron Cicourel demonstrated that indexical relations and contextual knowledge are essential to social reasoning of diverse kinds (1973). In linguistics, classic statements are Roman Jakobson (1971) and Emile Benveniste (1956). Papers by Michael Silverstein (1976, 1985) have broadened and systematized this tradition, applying the concept of *index* in analyses of various social anthropological problems.

6. This issue of cognitive orientation or focus, central to most accounts of indexicality, raises the problem of contextual indeterminacy, that is, that each interpretation and meaning is unique because tied to a potentially infinite set of contextual aspects. See Collins (1987b), Hanks (1984), and Silverstein (1980) for attempts to deal with this issue in light of commitments to general social and communicative analysis.

7. One way of confronting the problem of unique contexts and meanings, of contextual indeterminacy, is by distinguishing between indexical *types* and *tokens*. Types are by definition general and correspond to sociolinguistic *rules of use*, that is, to general statements of how speech forms are associated with contexts of speaking within some understood, reconstitutable system of social action. Tokens are by definition nongeneral or unique and correspond to language use or "parole," that is, to unique, real-time communicative events.

8. Many years ago, Leonard Bloomfield insightfully characterized linguistic prescriptivism in the United States as essentially a matter of imposing implicit notions of writing on speech:

> The popular explanation of incorrect language is simply the explanation of incorrect *writing*, taken over, part and parcel, to serve as an explanation of incorrect speech. It is the writing of every word for which a single form is fixed and all others are obviously wrong. It is the spelling of words that ignorant people, or better, unlettered people, do not know. It is writing that may be done carefully or carelessly, with evident results as to correctness. (Bloomfield, 1964 [1927], p. 392)

9. The difference between focus on topic versus message form can be seen if we compare the sections drawn from two narratives analyzed by Gee as part of an elaboration and follow up of the original work on narrative styles (Gee, 1986). In the first we see a classic topic / comment structure:

```
        TOPIC:      ...  we have this park near our house
        COMMENT..        it really stinks
        ---
but     TOPIC:      ...  me and my friend Sarah were over there
        COMMENT:...      we were playing on the swings
```

In the second we see a structuring which relies on parallelism, reported speech, and sound effects (that is, on message *form*):

```
all right,  | I got this thing
            | MY ear's     all buggin me        an everything
            | MY ear   was all buggin me
and         | I         was     cryin
            | I         was all:                 oooh, oooh
            | I         was     doin all that
and         | MY mother put alcohol on          though
```

(Adapted from Gee, 1986, pp. 17–19)

10. A more interpretive approach, analyzing apparent warrants for claims, was used to judge texts which departed from the typical text type / rating profile (Sullivan, 1985, chapter 3).

11. This state of affairs has been pointed out by reanalysts of Bernstein's work, as well as by Bernstein himself in later restatements (Bernstein, 1975; Bourdieu, 1982; Ohmann, 1982).

12. As Willis says:

> What delivers group force into the concrete form of the specifically cultural ... is importantly a deflection from the dominant mode of signification—language—into antagonistic behavioral, visual and stylistic forms of expression....
>
> Words created under bourgeois sway in their determinate conditions cannot express what did not go into their making. Part of the reaction to the school institution is anyway a rejection of words and considered language as the expression of mental life. The way in which these creative insights are expressed, therefore, is one of expressive antagonism to the dominant bourgeois mode of signification—language. In a real sense, for the working class the cultural is in a battle with language. This is not to reduce the cultural to anti-abstract behavior. It is to posit it, in part, as an antagonistic way of expressing abstract and mental life centered, not on the individual subject, but on the group; not on provided language, but on lived demonstration, direct involvement and practical mastery." (1977, pp. 124–125)

## REFERENCES

Anderson, B. (1983). *Imagined communities*. London: Verso.

Anderson, P. (1977). The antinomies of Antonio Gramsci. *New Left Review*, No. 100, pp. 5–80.

Apple, M. (1982). *Power and education*. London: Routledge & Kegan Paul.

Bakhtin, M. (1981). *The dialogic imagination*. Austin: University of Texas Press.

Benveniste, E. (1956). The nature of pronouns. In M. Halle, H. Lunt, H. McLean, & C. von Schoonveld (Eds.), *For Roman Jakobson* (pp. 34–37). The Hague: Mouton.

Bernstein, B. (1975). *Class, codes, and control, 1*. New York: Schocken Books.

Bloomfield, L. (1933). *Language*. New York: Holt and Rinehart.

Bloomfield, L. (1964 [1927]). Literate and illiterate speech. In D. Hymes (Ed.), *Language in culture and society* (pp. 391–396). New York: Harper & Row.

Bourdieu, P. (1982). *Ce que parler veut dire*. Paris: Fayard.

Bourdieu, P., & Passeron, J. C. (1977). *Reproduction in education, society, and culture*. London and Beverly Hills: Sage.

Bowles, S., & Gintis, H. (1976). *Schooling in capitalist America*. New York: Basic Books.

Bruce, B., Rubin, A., Starr, K., & Liebling, C. (1984). Sociocultural differences in oral vocabulary and reading material. In W. Hall, W. Nagy, & R. Linn (Eds.), *Spoken words* (pp. 466–481). Hillsdale, NJ: Lawrence Erlbaum Associates.

Cicourel, A. (1973). *Cognitive sociology*. New York: Free Press.

Collins, J. (1986). Differential treatment in reading instruction. In J. Cook-Gumperz (Ed.), *The social construction of literacy* (pp. 117–137). New York and Cambridge: Cambridge University Press.

Collins, J. (1987a) Using discourse analysis to understand access to knowledge. In D. Bloome (Ed.), *Literacy and schooling*. Norwood, NJ: Ablex.

Collins, J. (1987b) Conversation and knowledge in bureaucratic settings. *Discourse Processes, 10,* 303–319.

Collins, J. (in press). Socialization to text: Structure and contradiction in schooled literacy. In M. Silverstein & G. Urban (Eds.), *Decentered discourse*. New York & Cambridge: Cambridge University Press.

Cook-Gumperz, J. (1986). Schooling and literacy: An unchanging equation? In J. Cook-Gumperz (Ed.), *The social construction of literacy* (pp. 16–44). New York and Cambridge: Cambridge University Press.

Donald, J. (1982). Language, literacy and schooling. *The state and popular culture, 1* [a unit in the Open University course on popular culture]. Milton Keynes: The Open University.

Foucault, M. (1975). *Discipline and punish*. New York: Random House.

Gee, J. (1985) The narrativization of experience in the oral style. *Journal of Education, 167,* 9–36.

Gee, J. (1986). Commonalities and differences in narrative construction. Unpublished ms. B.U.

Gibson, E., & Levin, H. (1975). *The psychology of reading*. Cambridge: MIT Press.

Graff, H. (1979). *The literacy myth*. New York: Academic Press.

Gramsci, A. (1971). *Selections from the Prison Notebooks*. New York: International Publishers.

Gumperz, J. (1968). Linguistics: The speech community. In D. Shills (Ed.), *International encyclopedia of the social sciences, Volume 9*. New York: Macmillan & Free Press.

Gumperz, J. (1972). Introduction. In J. Gumperz & D. Hymes (Eds.), *Directions in sociolinguistics* (pp. 1–26). New York: Harper & Row.

Gumperz, J. (1982). *Discourse strategies*. New York and Cambridge: Cambridge University Press.

Hall, W., & Freedle, R. (1975). *Culture and language: The Black American experience*. Washington, DC: Hemisphere.

Hanks, W. (1984). The evidential core of deixis. *Chicago Linguistic Society, 20,* 154–173.

Havranek, B. (1964 [1932]). The functional differentiation of the standard language. In P. Garvin (Ed.), *A Prague School reader in esthetics, literary structure, and style* (pp. 3–16). Washington, DC: Georgetown University Press.

Heath, S. (1977) Language and politics in the United States. In M. Saville-Troike (Ed.), *Linguistics and anthropology* (Georgetown University Round Table on Languages and Linguistics) (pp. 267–296). Washington, DC: Georgetown University Press.

Heath, S. (1980). Standard English: Biography of a symbol. In T. Shopen & J. Williams (Eds.), *Standards and dialects in English* (pp. 3–31). Cambridge, MA: Winthrop.

Jakobson, R. (1971 [1957]). Shifters, verbal categories and the Russian verb. In *Roman Jakobson selected writings, Volume 2* (pp. 130–147). The Hague: Mouton.

Jameson, F. (1984) Postmodernism, or the cultural logic of Late Capitalism. *New Left Review,* No. 146, pp. 53–92.

Labov, W. (1972). *Language in the inner city*. Philadelphia: University of Pennsylvania Press.

Lasch, C. (1984). *The minimal self*. New York: Norton.

Michaels, S. (1981). Sharing time: An oral preparation for literacy. *Language in Society,* *10,* 423–442.

Michaels, S., & Cazden, C. (1986). Teacher / child collaboration as oral preparation for literacy. In B. Schieffelin & P. Gilmore (Eds.), *The acquisition of literacy: Ethnographic perspectives* (pp. 132–154). Norwood, NJ: Ablex Publishing Corporation.

Mouffe, C. (1979). Hegemony and ideology in Gramsci. In C. Mouffe (Ed.), *Gramsci and Marxist theory* (pp. 168–204). London: Routledge & Kegan Paul.

Nasaw, D. (1979). *Schooled to order.* New York and Oxford: Oxford University Press.

Ogbu, J. (1978). *Minority education and caste: The American system in crosscultural perspective.* New York: Academic Press.

Ohmann, R. (1982). Some reflections on language and class. *College English, 44,* 1–17.

Ohmann, R. (1985). Literacy, technology and monopoly capital. *College English, 47,* 675–689.

O'Neal, W. (1972). The politics of bi-dialectalism. *College English, 34,* 433–438.

O'Neal, W. (1980). English orthography. In T. Shopen & J. Williams (Eds.), *Standards and dialects in English.* Cambridge, MA: Winthrop.

Peirce, C. (1932). The icon, index, and symbol. In C. Hartshorne & P. Weiss (Eds.), *Collected papers of Charles Sanders Peirce, Volume 2* (pp. 156–173). Cambridge: Harvard University Press.

Piestrup, A. (1973). *Black Dialect interference and accommodation of reading instruction in first grade.* Monograph No. 4, Language Behavior Research Laboratory, University of California Berkeley.

Prince, E. (1981). "On the Inferencing of Indefinites-this NPs." Elements of Discourse Understanding. In A. K. Joshi, B. L. Webber, & I. A. Sag (Eds.) NY: Cambridge.

Rist, R. (1970). Student social class and teacher expectations: The self-fulfilling prophecy in ghetto education. *Harvard Educational Review, 39,* 411–450.

Salamini, L. (1981). *The sociology of political crisis: An introduction to Gramsci's theory.* London: Routledge & Kegan Paul.

Silverstein, M. (1976). Shifters, linguistic categories, and cultural description. In K. Basso & H. Selby (Eds.), *Meaning in anthropology* (pp. 11–50). Albuquerque: University of New Mexico Press.

Silverstein, M. (1980). The three faces of function: Preliminaries to a psychology of language. In M. Hickman (Ed.), *Proceedings of a working conference on the social foundations of language and thought* (pp. 1–12). Chicago: Center for Psychosocial Studies.

Silverstein, M. (1985). Language and the culture of gender: At the intersection of structure, usage, and ideology. In E. Mertz & R. Parmentier (Eds.), *Semiotic mediation* (pp. 219–259). New York: Academic Press.

Soltow, L., & E. Stevens (1981). *The rise of literacy and the common school: A socioeconomic analysis to 1870.* Chicago: University of Chicago Press.

Sullivan, F. (1985). A sociolinguistic analysis of the distribution of information in university placement-test essays. Unpublished PhD dissertation, University of Pennsylvania.

Thompson, J. 1984. *Studies in the theory of ideology.* Berkeley: University of California Press.

Williams, R. 1961. *The long revolution.* London: Chatto & Windus.

Willis, P. (1977). *Learning to labour.* London: Routledge & Kegan Paul.

Woolard, K. (1985). Language variation and cultural hegemony: Toward an integration of sociolinguistic and social theory. *American Ethnologist, 12,* 738–748.

Wright, E. (1980). "School English" and public policy. *College English, 42,* 327–342.

# 16

# POPULAR LITERACY AND THE ROOTS
# OF THE NEW WRITING

## John Willinsky

Something of a small revolution has broken across the language arts at both the elementary and secondary levels. Over the last 10 years, writing has gradually nudged reading from the center of the language program in the schools. In more and more schools, writing shares the emphasis with reading in language arts and English classes, whether students are taking their first steps across the blank page or composing their first response to the works of Shakespeare. Through this new approach many more students stand to have in literacy both an *expressive* and an *interpretative* skill. The writing crisis of the seventies has produced a strong response in this decade. Theodore R. Sizer (1984), in a hard-hitting look at American education, has come to the conclusion that "writing should be the center of schooling," and the new pedagogies aim to implement this same notion on a widespread and popular basis. From the Bay Area Writing Project to Graves and Murray's work at the University of New Hampshire, this new emphasis on writing has taken a number of original forms for the classroom, beginning with pre-writing conferences and cooperative editorial settings and moving to student publishing and bookbinding (Myers & Gray, 1983; Stock, 1983). The strategies are drawn from the careful study of both professional writers and faltering students; these lessons are finding a surprisingly widespread application from the first grade to the college level.

But beyond the myriad strategies, what I find curious and want to pursue in this chapter is the richness of parallel and precedent in the history of literacy

The author wishes to thank Carl Braun for his helpful comments on an earlier draft of this chapter.

contained in these current practices. Much of what seems new in writing programs today has its immediate roots in educational experiments which took place earlier in this century, principally through the progressive movement in education (Brand, 1980). But there are also striking similarities between today's efforts and much earlier patterns of popular literacy which predate the emergence of public schooling and which flourished in quite different social and historical contexts.[1]

There are three principal parallels between popular literacy and the current writing programs which deserve to be considered. The first is a sociability of the literary enterprise, in the sharing of the printed word, which has always been a part of the popular life of the written word. The second is the approach of putting expression ahead of correctness, an approach that harks back to the nonstandardized beginnings of English literature and popular writing. The third is the emphasis on performance and publication; in seeking to make every student a writer, and a self-published one at that, the new programs are populist in a way that parallels the early history of popular literacy.

The historical continuity is not to be wasted. Out of an examination of these earlier developments in literacy there can be found a number of practical classroom suggestions for the enrichment of current writing programs. In fact, taking more directly from the historical artifacts of literacy can provide a rich model for advancing students' work. The illuminated medieval manuscript book is one instance worthy of emulation in student publishing, the easily produced chapbook folded from a single sheet of paper is another, and the small literary magazine of this century is yet a third. But more than a historical curiosity of some practical value, these parallels also raise questions about the function and purposes of writing on a popular scale. The fact is that popular literacy has not been well received historically because of the very power and pervasiveness of its message. One unrecognized promise of this new wave in writing instruction is its potential challenge to the normal bounds of the public voice; in this way it stands to address certain critical theories of education, such as found in the work of Pierre Bourdieu (1974) and Harvey Graff (1979), who have linked the school's approach to literacy to the reproduction of social class. Looking back over the historical development of popular literacy strongly suggests that reading and writing nurture more than the cognitive processes of individuals; these skills tend to reverberate soundly through the body politic. A consideration of these parallels brings to the fore the overlooked political and social implications of an active popular literacy. It raises the fundamental question of why we would have so many take up the pen.

## SOCIABILITY

The first parallel I wish to draw is between a new sociability and spirit of cooperation in the modern writing classroom and the historical and ongoing blend of oral and literate cultures which this sense draws on. The years of that

quiet time set aside for weekly writing and recopying have passed in the inno-
vative classroom. The enforced privacy of literacy, made painful in full classrooms of friends who were not to share their creative excitement, has given
way to a spontaneous commingling and testing of what has been found and created. The precedents for this sharing of the written word go back to the ancient Greek drama festivals and the Platonic dialogue—to the birth of
Western theater and philosophy. They are continued in the medieval literacy
of St. Augustine, who found it remarkably strange for his master to read without moving his lips, as if to keep to himself what he was reading. It only took
one or two accomplished readers in every village and town to share the latest
texts and tales to be found; during the Reformation, Martin Luther is reported
to have been repeatedly surprised at how fast and how far his tracts traveled.
Beginning in the 12th century, an age of European literary revival, the culture
of Europe became increasingly an indistinguishable blend of oral and literate
traditions (Stock, 1982). Literacy served the sociability of language: Before the
printing press and for some time afterward, "literary compositions were 'published' by being read aloud; even 'book' learning was governed by reliance on
the spoken word" (Eisenstein, 1979, p. 11). The oral primacy of the written
word was actually maintained until the latter part of the 19th century. This was
a century when "reading" in McGuffey's popular *Eclectic Readers* meant a
training for public speaking, when Charles Dickens's public readings were a
sensation (Ong, 1980).

In classrooms now, children are to be heard acting out or chanting from
books which play on the patterns in language; they shortly create their own
variations on the themes (McCracken & McCracken, 1979). In the older
grades, the spoken and dramatized word includes the sharing of drafts, impromptu skits, the staging of interviews, and the accompanied celebration of
the students' work (Burgess, 1984). Yet the roots of this engagement are not
simply in the past. A contemporary precedent for this thirst to perform and
play out language has also existed for some time only a few blocks from the
school and the neighborhood of Dick, Jane, and Spot. In black communities
this verbal playfulness is sung out in ways that have until recently meant nothing but trouble for the children from these homes. Shirley Brice Heath's recent
study of a black and a white community in the Carolinas (Heath, 1983) makes
clear the strength of this elaborative approach to language in the black
community.[2] But what makes this parallel with the classroom appear stronger
is that the other community she investigates—white, working or lower middle
class—provides what struck me as a fair representation of the older and still
common conception of language in the schools. Among the white families,
"the written word limits alternatives of expression"; in the black community,
"it opens alternatives" (p. 235). The idealization of reading in the white community, which seldom spends any time with books, does seem to have traces of
the old school of teaching about it. In the black community, on the other hand:

[They] read aloud to anyone who wants to listen on the plaza, report what they have read, ask for interpretations of written materials by the group, and enjoy stories which invariably ensue from a report of something read.... There is no space or time assigned for reading; its occurrences follow the flow of daily social interactions and decision-making in the community. (p. 232)

Now I would not want to idealize the nature of literacy in this one community: Books and bedtime stories were not to be found in their homes and the children were doing poorly in school. Heath points out that the reason the children were not performing well was not so much that their English was different from that of the teacher, but because their *approach* to language differed, flowing without the same regard for propriety. Heath includes in the book an interesting section on her work with the teachers in the area, both to increase their sensitivity to the differences and to help them prepare these black youngsters for the school life ahead. Ironically, she seems unaware that a number of new writing pedagogies are taking the approach to language cited above, as part of daily social interactions, to be a promising starting point for reaching, rather than challenging, the child's outlook on the life of the word.[3]

I am tempted to speculate optimistically about this trend in the teaching of writing, daring to suggest that by embracing what might be termed a popular blend of literate and oral cultures—and clearly one with common features across the centuries—the new programs are in a position to extend the democratic mandate in public education. Whether such optimism will continue to be warranted remains a particular challenge to the writing pedagogists. Traditionally, this public and social free-form approach to literacy and culture has been targeted for eradication through scheduled and disciplined forms of education—from the public schools of Horace Mann to the preschool hour of Sesame Street. Here, in the new push to creative writing, participation and performance are the vibrant themes, themes which are older than the schools and still in many instances fighting for a certain legitimacy in the classroom.

Taking up forgotten aspects of popular literacy also strikes me as an eminently sensible approach to our perennial literacy crisis. The ongoing crisis reflects traditional patterns of economic and cultural distribution (the poor are not as strong readers) combined with increasing rates of participation in public education (standards are falling as the percentage of students who remain in school increases). Yet only a few of the new proposals seem to recognize that, though all students could stand to write better, the distribution of a facility in writing is still a social issue and one which the new programs are in a strong position to address. The new writing programs seem capable of extending the reach of literacy by engaging more students actively in literacy practices— students who would otherwise have found the struggle with the blank page not worth the risk of marks or identity lost.

If the historical parallels are sometimes lost to sight, teachers of the new writing also seem to overlook the potential to be found in that contemporary blend of literate and oral cultures known as "the media." Teachers could go further in tapping the central place of the media script in our lives, from the McDonalds' commercial to the evening news, from Masterpiece Theater to the music video. These scripts provide interesting instances of work in a constant state of revision up to the final moment of production and of writing with a place for collaboration and multiple contributions. The new hi-tech literacy is still a sociable one. Like the medieval manuscript, the broadside, and the chapbook, it offers an artifact of literacy, in this case a contemporary artifact that lends itself to classroom and student production. The media script has the added bonus of being a highly lucrative field, which means it adds a vocational and functional aspect to the program.

In spite of this spirited advocacy on my part, I am not blind to the intellectual cost of explicitly taking up aspects of oral popular culture. The price has been most perceptively calculated by Walter Ong in his deliberations on the differences between orality and literacy (1980). He describes how oral cultures, whether Homeric or adolescent, have as their cultural thrust the effort to be "with it," to "get into the act," to participate and take up the celebration of the heroes and wisdom held in common. Ong points out how Plato was among the first to realize that an oral culture had little place for analysis or for the sort of critical questioning he would encourage in the pursuit of the good; to ensure a conversion to such a reflective state in his republic he banned the (oral) work of the poet. Popular literacy and culture have been equally disparaged as too taken up with sentimentality and sensationalism, with bad taste dressed up in bad form. While in our modern, blended approach to writing instruction, the temptation is to simply get "with it," the possibility remains of encouraging a move to getting "at it" in a critical way.

## NONSTANDARDIZED USAGE

The second parallel I wish to point out in seeking the roots of the new writing is a historical resistance by many English writers to standardization and regulation of the language, a resistance which was gradually overcome by concerns with correctness and propriety in language. The public school system in its traditional efforts at fostering literacy has been notorious for, though not notoriously efficient at, enforcing propriety before all else. The new writing programs have been challenging these convention-bound ways, but not for the first time. In the Renaissance and the early days of the printing press in Europe we find the historical precedent to the modern classroom cum writing studio (Graves, 1982) with writing going on in the child's own language of invented spellings and creative grammars, finding its way into publication and, in the later grades, of personal reflections and responses (with only a slight decrease in invention).

Gutenberg's invention of moveable type and an improved ink touched off a number of events which directly improved the state of literacy in Europe.

Hand in hand with the Reformation it brought the Bible before the people in their native language, and generally brought about an elevation of the European vernacular languages (Kahane & Kahane, 1979). But as well as the printing press developing a market for sacred texts, beginning with indulgences as well as the Bible, a plethora of profane publications were soon finding their way about the countryside. As reading was still a public and sociable enterprise, these works had a distribution and influence far beyond the ranks of the fully literate. Yet for our purposes, it is well to remember that in both sacred and profane texts the vernacular languages still lacked a good deal of standardization in such matters as spelling and other conventions. Literacy and mass publication preceded conventions in print and the standardization of the European languages.

Ivan Illich (1979) has described the situation in 15th-century Spain in which people began learning to read in a dozen dialects as printers and peddlers brought the book trade to the Iberian peninsula. The spread of this "wild untaught vernacular literacy," as he terms it (p. 61), demonstrated that printing does not necessarily require a standardized composition, a schooled mother tongue, or a silent and private literacy. The parallel can be seen between this headlong plunge into literate culture then and modern-day programs in which a concern with standardized grammar becomes "the last step," as Peter Elbow (1981) describes it.

Not surprisingly, then as now, such unconventional forays into print were treated with suspicion from some powerful corners. In Spain, the official complaint soon arose that the people had begun to "waste their time on novels and stories full of lies" (Illich, 1979, p. 38). Illich describes the gradual taming of this unlicensed literacy in Spain by Queen Isabella's adoption of a governed and official Castilian, replete with a Latin-based grammar textbook to guide it. The national language, promoted as a "consort of empire" (p. 35), was intended to exercise linguistic control by ensuring that all could understand the messages of officialdom, even if they could not use the same language to return their sentiments. Illich has described this move to standardize the language in political terms: It "established the notion of ordinary language that itself is sufficient to place each man in his assigned place on the pyramid that education in a mother tongue necessarily constructs" (p. 45). This is an issue addressed by today's writing programs which attempt to lessen the sole focus on mastery of the standard language as the threshold point of communication—even as they promote editing strategies to ease students into its use. The new programs tend in this way to shake up, though not topple, Illich's pyramid.

A similar historical move to take hold of English and create a standard was resisted in England in the Elizabethan era. Writers of that period chose to raise the status of their language, in relation to the prestige tongues of Latin and French, through eloquence rather than subscribing to a prescriptive grammar modeled on that of Latin. A strong example of the Elizabethan position is found in Philip Sidney, who in his *An Apology for Poetry* made the proud claim for English:

> Nay truly, it hath that praise that it wanteth not grammar: for grammar it might have, but it need it not; being so easy of itself, and so void of those cumbersome differences of cases, genders, modes and tenses, which I think was a piece of the Tower of Babylon's curse, that a man should be put to school to learn his mother tongue. (Sidney, 1970, p. 85)

During Sidney's time, without benefit of an apparent grammar or systematic spellings, writers found what R. F. Jones has described in his *The Triumph of the English Language* as "a short cut to literature without caring whether the language was ruled or not" (1953, p. 215). In those days when Shakespeare was playing for the people in the pit and literature in the English language flourished, a corresponding increase occurred in popular literacy. This growth in literacy among the common people was accomplished for the most part on an informal basis within families and communities; as a result the level of literacy reached as high as 60% among men in the larger towns of southern England by the 17th century (Laqueur, 1976).

The spirited resistance to formalized grammar which Sidney expressed was eventually to take the form of political opposition to proposals that England adopt an official language academy comparable to the Italian *Academi della Crusca* (established in 1582) and the *Academie Francais* (established in 1659). The effort to establish an English counterpart began in the late 17th century and was supported by Daniel Defoe and Jonathan Swift among others. As Defoe put it, "The Work of the Society shou'd be to encourage Polite learning . . . and advance the so much neglected Faculty of Correct Language, to establish Purity and Propriety of Stile" (Defoe, 1961, p. 59). But the proposal failed, as it did later in the young United States when it was raised by John Adams and others (Baron, 1982). Though the movement for an academy faltered, the fight continued for a regulated language. Those who felt that an ungrammared English was a danger and a disgrace pressed ahead with strong advice for the improvement of the language, basing their claims on the model of the classical languages, on both national and male chauvinism, and on a certain consistency in the language. By the end of the 18th century, what Sterling Leonard (1962) has identified as "a doctrine of correctness in English usage" had effectively, if not legislatively, taken hold, giving English the grammar Sidney had once disparaged. The doctrine was based on a prescriptive grammar, developed for the most part by retired schoolmasters and clergymen; it was intended "to enable us to judge every phrase right or not," in the words of Robert Lowth, a leading grammarian of the day (cited by Myers, 1966, p. 225).

I have dealt with these historical developments, if only sketchily, to raise this decisive split in language attitudes—favoring either a natural or a prescribed development for the English language—a split which continues to be played out in the schools and in the press. My concern here is with the public schools, which from the beginning, and with few exceptions, have taken up the doctrine of correctness as their very mandate. They enact the "curse" which Sidney foresaw of children being schooled in their mother tongue through the rigors of instruction in grammar, a practice introduced as morally uplifting in the last century and still defended today despite a half century of research proving its inability to facilitate writing.[4] Progressive experiments early in this century (Cremin, 1956) partially interrupted this public-school tradition and the new pedagogies in writing offer the possibility of laying it to rest.

## PUBLICATION AND PERFORMANCE

The historical split which I have been describing over the regulation of the language had been between educated parties, the one citing Horace ("Usage is both the rule and norm of speaking") in favor of following naturalized patterns in the language, and the other taking Horace's Latin as the very model of the well-governed tongue. It should also be recalled that on the side of the resistance to regulation, and opposed to such advocates as Defoe and Swift, there developed a long literary tradition encompassing such notables as Lawrence Sterne and Gertrude Stein. Their creation in literature has fully and delightfully played against these doctrines and standards, as if art could best flourish in the cracks and disruptions of convention. But insofar as I am arguing that the new writing is borrowing heavily from traditions of popular culture rather than a strictly literary one, I would like to focus here on another sort of resistance to convention in the development of literacy. Here we begin to consider the encouragement of publication and a public voice which has become a major concern of the new pedagogies in writing. In an unrecognized alliance of interests, popular literacy has in some ways been carrying on its own class action against prescription and formality across Europe. However, this promising growth area in literacy has met with less than unbridled enthusiasm among the educated classes.

In Spain, Illich (1979) reports that the complaint against the shallow and sensational works of popular literacy emerged as early as the beginning of the 16th century. In France, a certain danger was recognized in the fact that the common people were "active users and interpreters of the printed books they heard and read, and even helped to give these books form. . . . Oral culture and popular social organizations were strong enough to resist mere correction and standardization from above" (Davis, 1965, p. 225). In England, the rush into print also took an explicit political turn as the pamphlet and the broadside became the broadcasting vehicles of choice: Two thousand pamphlets were published, for example, in the heady year of 1642 on the eve of the Puritan Revolution (Stone, 1969, p. 99). Popular literacy was not only uncultivated in a manner which offended finer sensibilities, but was also notably subversive, both religiously—here Ginzberg (1980) provides a fascinating and deadly instance—and politically. The political subversion was especially frightening to the genteel classes. E. P. Thompson in his history of the working class has recorded a number of such improprietous letters from the early 19th century:

> I Ham going to inform you that there is Six Thousand men coming to you in Apral and then We Wil go Blow Parlement house up and Blow up afour hus/ labring Peple Cant Stand it No longer/dam all Such Roges as England governes but Never mind Ned lud when general nody and his Harmey Comes We Will soon bring about the greate Revelution then all those greate mens heads gose of. (1963, p. 784)

Widespread reading and writing skills were simply not always welcomed: They repeatedly gave voice to an independence of spirit and thought within a class which, as many of their betters viewed it, had no need for literacy in the first place. The British instances of its suppression range from an act of 1543 forbidding women and men under the rank of yeoman to read the English Bible, to the use of the stamp acts in the 18th century to constrict the press (Innis, 1951; Williams, 1961). Lawrence Stone has described "the terrible spectre of a literate, politically minded working class" which faced the respectable classes: "Should a Horse know as much as a man, I should not like to be his rider," Bernard Manville quipped in his *Fable of the Bees* (1726, cited by Stone, 1969, p. 85). The schooling of the working class from 1780 to 1850 has been described by Richard Johnson in terms of a crisis in hegemony over who would control the education of workers' families. The institution of philanthropic mass schooling was initiated, not as a measure against widespread illiteracy among the working class, but against their control of their own education through private Chartist and Owenite schools (Johnson, 1976, pp. 50–51).

Literacy has been both feared as a source of sedition among the masses and used against their potential for disturbance. During the 19th century, as an instance of literacy's intended part in pacification, the Mechanics' Institutes, of which there were 500 established by 1850, introduced lectures on literature. Margret Mathieson writes, "Literature was included in the instruction, on the grounds that its study would protect the young workers against the corrupting effects of seditious political material and the sensational products of the cheap press" (1975, p. 17). Harvey Graff (1979) found in his study of a 19th-century Canadian city that literacy had little impact on the individual's economic future and chances of social mobility; he concludes that literacy and public education were promoted as one aspect of a middle-class desire for greater control and domestication of the growing urban and indigent laboring classes. Reading, writing, and arithmetic were intended to make them civil rather than unleash any expressive urges which many advocates of public education felt were already too visible in the streets of the burgeoning cities.

That may seem the distant and unenlightened past. We may consider that in these liberal times, freedom of expression is an entrenched right which cannot be restricted and that the power of the written word is open and encouraged for all. Yet David Street reports that the British Arts Council refused grants to one current adult literacy project "on the grounds that the work produced in this way was not 'literature,' and complaints by at least one Member of Parliament that the content of students' own materials was too politically radical" (1984, p. 15). The power and the politics of the word remain a contested area and yet one not fully realized by those heavily engaged in exploring the writing process. The question of the subversive and outspoken as a part of the history of popular literacy has been sidestepped by the advocates of the new writing even as they provide the students with many of the same vehicles—pamphlets and broadsides—which once carried disturbing messages.

This shift in status for the literacy of the student is part of the radical change offered by the new programs. It is a shift which addresses the critical-theorist argument that schools, rather than opening up the path of social mobility on the base of merit, have rewarded and certified the linguistic traits which the middle class bring to the classroom. Students coming to the school without this linguistic and cultural background are described by Bourdieu and Passeron (1977) as lacking what the school cannot provide; they are taught, in essence, that these gifts which they do not possess determine their place in the world. These are serious charges and yet are to a certain degree borne out by the century-long statistics on the schools' limited contribution to social mobility (Mare, 1981). The new programs in writing cannot effect a revolution in educational promise. But they do hold out the possibility of altering the inequity to some degree because they address the crucial role which language plays in this certification of ability and gifts. For example, the new writing programs do not lend the same weight as previous programs to separating out those who have brought a certain standard of literary language and culture from home; they provide opportunities for students to make their own way into literacy. More importantly, the new approaches to writing stand to turn around the common scorn for any mother tongue which is other than the standard and help in that way for more students to gain a stronger sense of their own voice.

There is undoubtedly a romantic bent to my reading of both the history of literacy and the potential of the new wave in writing. But it bears a hearing in the face of the more isolated concerns with writing expressed by the swell of new methods in which, for example, the "expansion of learning," and paradigm shifts to process models are the principal points of intellectual excitement (Donovan & McClelland, 1980; Haley-James, 1981). More recently, Miles Myers has stated his fear that writing instruction risks becoming "a hodgepodge of gimmicks without a foundation in theory" (in Myers & Gray, 1983, p. 3); but he sees the resolution for this in adherence to the three psychological paradigms—processing, distancing, and modeling—which he believes dominate the field. The missing question, it strikes me, is whether the encouragement of the written organization of thought and feeling simply constitutes a cognitive capacity without context or moral imperative—a rhetoric without commitment.

The corollary to this question is: If we lack commitment to anything beyond the art of writing and learning, do we expect the same from our new writers? More to the point, are we prepared to face, to aid and abet through the new programs, the voicing of deeper and less comforting sentiments—of the sort, for example, which now find rancorous expression through spray-bomb graffiti and new wave music or, in a quieter fashion, through Harlequin romances and *The National Enquirer.* The history of popular literacy, which I believe the new programs are drawing from, also holds out this other prospect—radical, sensational, and shallow by turn—for the place of literacy in people's lives. The new wave in writing must be prepared to address the substance of this literacy, to address what it wants from this renewed enthusiasm for the written word. Yet we seem in the current discussion of writing to hold naively to an innocent and neutral search for improved performance in what should amount to a certain (reasoned) outspokenness.

Stirring the students' thirst for newsstand literature, rock lyrics, or spray-bomb slogans may not be a particularly strong danger for the new programs as they embrace the ways of popular literacy. Teachers have too little respect for these forms to give them active encouragement, though tastes for them have developed well enough in the past without this approval. More importantly, the active literacy to which these students will be introduced differs radically from previous programs both in what counts as literacy and in what students are expected to do with these abilities. The new programs encourage the students as both writers and editors; the students begin to publish and distribute their work on an informal basis; independence of voice, topic, and technique is fostered. The new programs in writing invite a more active participation in the use of the word. Thus I see this outspokenness—rather than, say, the increased consumption of paperbacks—as the most important and intriguing consequence of embracing and encouraging popular literacy.

In times not too distant, these skills and attitudes distributed on a popular basis sent shivers among the propertied classes; in the 19th century this literacy produced the *Poor Man's Guardian*, the Unstamped Press, the Chartist Movement, and countless anonymous ballads all with a similar thrust—the ability to write is the ability to name, to sing out against, inequity (Hampton, 1984). This time the schools are actively arming the young, encouraging them to take up the pen, and yet at the same moment seem oblivious to the historical importance of this act. Too often the fact that a student writes becomes no more than a means of proving just how well the new program works.

What, then, do I envisage from a better-informed new wave? Up to this point, I have overlooked a number of the more radical literacy advocates working on the margins of the field. They have taken this outspokenness as their starting point and thus they provide instances of what I am suggesting is implied by a history of the word. Paulo Freire is a leading example. A political self-consciousness is the point of his moral and pedagogical strength in promoting literacy among adults. He has worked to "enable the people to reflect on their former interpretation of the world before going on to read the word. The more critical *reading* of the prior less critical *reading* of the world enables them to understand their indigence differently from the fatalistic way they sometimes view justice" (Freire, 1983, p. 11). This is, then, a concern for literacy *in situ;* reading is neither instrumental nor an end in itself, but is the moment of stirring reflection which then provokes a re-reading of the world.

Freire's work with Brazilian and African adult literacy programs may strike teachers as distant from their concerns; closer to their work in the schools are the experiences of Ira Shor and Chris Searle. Shor (1977) has described how he assisted his students in re-imagining their world through the drawing up of new constitutions for the nation, marriage contracts for the family, and curriculums for the schools. The students were part of an experiment in open admissions at the City University of New York, which, though short-lived, represented a popularizing approach to extending literacy. Chris Searle (1977) has compiled a collection of works by his early adolescent students who wrote out the nature of their own world and soon moved on to the nature of the larger world, which they came to realize was very much tied to their experiences—to the way people were treating each other in their inner-London neighborhood. But these instances remain exceptional, drawing on the commitment of their instructors. If the other new and lively writing programs are going to become part of the mainstream of public education, we must encourage a discussion of what we expect and what we would have of this widespread literacy. At the forefront of this discussion should be those who have been so instrumental in elevating the place of writing in the curriculum to an active partnership with reading.

## CONCLUSION

Over the course of this chapter, I have introduced an abbreviated history of literacy with a focus on how its populist roots point to strengths in the new wave in writing. I have discussed a few practical suggestions, from illuminated manuscripts to TV scripts, which emerge as classroom ideas from this history. Yet I feel compelled to return to the larger question of the purpose of writing. I raise this otherwise absent issue because I have begun to wonder whether the political implications have been ignored to ensure a ready acceptance in today's conservative climate, or whether these implications are indeed unintended and no longer relevant to educators. The history of popular literacy strongly suggests that the issues will emerge of their own accord however ill-prepared educators are to recognize them. It should, at the very least, test their commitment to the encouragement of widespread and open literate expression. I raise the question because writing is surely more than a means of enhancing learning in the abstract or facilitating success in college. The student's voice, as it moves and on occasion disturbs, must be taken more seriously than that, or we stand to trivialize this promising introduction to the powers of literacy.

## NOTES

1. My conception of popular literacy is taken in part from Thomas Laqueur's article "The Cultural Origins of Popular Literacy in England 1500–1850" in which he colorfully sets the field in his opening sentence: "For all its maypoles and rough music, its bear baitings and St. Monday drunks, its ancient feasts and more ancient folkways, the popular culture of seventeenth and eighteenth century England was fundamentally literate." (1976, p. 255).

2. Heath gives a convincing description of this elaboration on a text using one woman's prepared prayer and what she in fact produced in conjunction with the congregation (pp. 209–211); I use the term "elaborate" fully aware of how it will for many readers reverberate back to Basil Bernstein's unfortunate and influential division of the world into elaborate and restricted code speakers.

3. English teachers' recognitions of this issue have been most cogently put in "The Students' Right to their Own Language" (1974), which was a position paper adopted by the Conference on College Composition and Communication, an affiliate member of the NCTE. That this acceptance is still a controversial position among English teachers is indicated by Sledd (1983).

4. Baron (1982) reviews the moral imperative of grammar in the last century; Davis (1984) provides a current defense if for somewhat different reasons; and Lyman's (1929) work gives an indication of how long the debunking has been going on.

## REFERENCES

Baron, D. (1982). *Grammar and good taste: Reforming the American language.* New Haven: Yale University Press, 1982.

Bourdieu, P. (1974). The school as a conservative force: Scholastic and cultural inequalities. In S. Eggleston (Ed.), *Contemporary research in the sociology of education.* London: Methuen.

Bourdieu, P., & Passeron, J. C. (1977). *Reproduction in education, society and culture* (R. Nice, Trans.). London: Sage.

Brand, A. G. (1980). Creative writing in English education: An historical perspective. *Journal of Education, 162,* 63–82.

Burgess, T. (1984). Diverse melodies: A first year class in a secondary school. In J. Miller (Ed.), *Eccentric propositions: Essays on literature and the curriculum.* London: Routledge and Kegan Paul.

Cremin, L. (1956). *The transformation of education: Progressivism in American education 1876–1957.* New York: Vintage.

Davis, F. (1984). In defense of grammar. *English Education, 16,* 151–164.

Davis, N. (1965). Printing and the people. In N. Davis (Ed.), *Society and culture in early modern France.* Stanford: Stanford University Press.

Defoe, D. (1961). An essay on several projects. In S. Tucker (Ed.), *English examined: Two centuries of comment on the mother tongue.* Cambridge: Cambridge University Press. (Original work published 1702)

Donovan, T., & McClelland, B. (1980). *Eight approaches to teaching composition.* Urbana, IL: NCTE.

Eisenstein, E. (1979). *The printing press as an agent of social change.* Cambridge: Cambridge University Press.

Elbow, P. (1981). *Writing with power.* New York: Oxford University.

Freire, P. (1983). The importance of the act of reading. *Journal of Education, 165,* 5–11.

Ginzburg, C. (1980). *The cheese and the worms: The cosmos of a sixteenth-century miller* (J. Tedeschi & A. Tedeschi, Tedeschi,Trans.). Harmondsworth: Penguin.

Graff, H. (1979). *The literacy myth: Literacy and social structure in the nineteenth century city.* New York: Academic Press.

Graves, D. (1982). *Writing: Teachers and children at work.* Exeter, NH: Heinemann.

Haley-James, S. (Ed.). (1981). *Perspectives on writing in grades 1–8.* Urbana, IL: NCTE.

Hampton, C. (1984). *A radical reader: The struggle for change in England, 1381–1914.* Harmondsworth: Penguin.

Heath, S. B. (1983). *Ways with words: Language, life, and work in communities and classrooms.* Cambridge: Cambridge University Press.

Illich, I. (1979). Vernacular values and education. *Teachers College Record, 81*(1), 31–76.

Innis, H. (1951). *Bias of Communication.* Toronto: University of Toronto Press.

Johnson, R. (1976). Notes on the schooling of the English working class, 1780–1850. In R. Dale et al. (Eds.), *Schooling and capitalism: A sociological reader.* London: Routledge and Kegan Paul.

Jones, R. F. (1953). *The triumph of the English language.* Stanford: Stanford University Press.

Kahane, H., & Kahane, R. (1979). Decline and survival of Western prestige languages. *Language, 55*(1), 183–199.

Laqueur, T. (1976). The cultural origins of popular literacy in England 1500–1850. *Oxford Review of Education, 2,* 255–275.

Leonard, S. (1962). *The doctrine of correctness in English usage: 1700–1800.* New York: Russell and Russell. (Original work published 1929)

Lyman, R. L. (1929). *Summary of investigations relating to grammar, language and composition.* Chicago: University of Chicago Press.

MacCracken, M., & McCracken, R. (1979). *Reading, writing and language: A practical guide for primary teachers.* Winnipeg: Peguis.

Mare, R. D. (1981). Change and stability in educational stratification. *American Sociological Review, 46*(1), 72–87.

Mathieson, M. (1975). *The preachers of culture: A study of English and its teachers.* London: George Allen & Unwin.

Myers, L. M. (1966). *The roots of modern English.* Boston: Little, Brown.

Myers, M., & Gray, J. (Eds.). (1983). *Theory and practice in the teaching of composition: Processing, distancing, and modeling.* Urbana, IL: NCTE.

Ong, W. J. (1980). Literacy and orality in our times. *Journal of Communication, 30,* 197–204.

Searle, C. (1977). (Ed.). *The world in a classroom.* London: Readers and Writers.

Shor, I. (1977), *Critical teaching in everyday life.* Montreal: Black Rose.

Sidney, P. (1970). In F. Robinson (Ed.) *An apology for poetry.* New York: Bobbs-Merrill. (Original work published 1595)

Sizer, T. J. (1984). *Horace's compromise: The dilemma of American education.* Boston: Houghton Mifflin.

Sledd, J. (1983). In defense of the students' right. *College English, 45,* 667–675.

Stock, B. (1982). *The implications of literacy: Written language and models of interpretation in the 11th and 12th centuries.* Princeton, NJ: Princeton University Press.

Stock, P. (Ed.). (1983). *Fforum: Essays on theory and practice in the teaching of writing.* Upper Montclair, NJ: Boynton and Cook.

Stone, L. (1969). Literacy and education in England 1644–1640. *Past and Present, 42,* 69–139.

Street, D. (1984). *Literacy in theory and practice.* Cambridge: Cambridge University Press.

Students' right to their own language, The. (1974). *College Composition and Communication, 25,* 1–32.

Thompson, E. P. (1963). *The making of the English working class.* Harmondsworth: Penguin.

Williams, R. (1961). *The long revolution.* London: Chatto and Windus.

# INDEX

# ABOUT THE EDITORS AND CONTRIBUTORS

ADRIAN T. BENNETT is working at the Literacy Assistance Center in New York City on the development of a curriculum to train displaced bilingual garment workers to become educational paraprofessionals.

LINDA BRODKEY is Associate Professor of English at the University of Texas at Austin, but in the fall of 1992 she will be Director of the Warren College Writing Program at the University of California, San Diego. She is the author of *Academic Writing as Social Practice* and numerous articles on writing and literacy.

JAMES COLLINS is Associate Professor of Anthropology at State University of New York at Albany and a linguist who has done extensive research on the politics of literacy and on American Indian (Tolowa) language and culture. His articles, chapters, and reviews have appeared in numerous journals and books. His book, *Literacy in Context: Social and Linguistic Education Possibilities*, is forthcoming.

JAMES DONALD is Lecturer of Educational Studies at the Open University in England. He was previously a teacher and editor of *Screen Education*, and is presently an editor of *Formations*, a journal which focuses on cultural theory and history.

PAULO FREIRE is Professor Emeritus of Education at the University of Sao Paulo in Campinas, Brazil, and has recently retired as Secretary of Education in Sao Paulo. He is the author of *Pedagogy of the Oppressed, Education for Critical Consciousness*, and *Literacy: Reading the Word and the World* (with Donaldo Macedo).

JAMES PAUL GEE is Professor of Linguistics at the University of Southern California. His books include *The Social Mind: Language, Ideology, and Social Practice, Social Linguistics and Literacies: Ideology in Discourses* and *Fundamental Concepts in Linguistics* (forthcoming).

PERRY GILMORE is Associate Professor and Chair of the Department of Education and Director of the Language and Literacy Project at the University of Alaska, Fairbanks. Her research interests include sociolinguistics and educational anthropology with a special focus on language and literacy acquisition and narrative development.

HENRY A. GIROUX is currently Professor of Education and Renowned Scholar-in-Residence at Miami University, Ohio, but in the fall of 1992 he will assume the position of the Waterbury Chair in Secondary Education at Pennsylvania State University. His books include *Ideology, Culture and the Process of Schooling, Theory and Resistance in Education, Education Under Siege* (with Stanley Aronowitz), *Teachers as Intellectuals, Schooling and the Struggle for Public Life*, and *Postmodern Education: Politics, Culture and Social Criticism* (with Stanley Aronowitz).

JONATHAN KOZOL is the author of *Death at an Early Age, The Night is Dark, Free Schools, Illiterate America*, and most recently, *Savage Inequalities*. He has taught at Yale University and at South Boston High School.

DONALDO MACEDO is Associate Professor of English and Director of the Bilingual/ESL Graduate Studies Program at the University of Massachusetts at Boston. He has published extensively in the areas of linguistics, language acquisition, literacy, and creole studies. His latest work includes *Literacy: Reading the Word and the World* (with Paulo Freire).

SARAH MICHAELS is Associate Professor and Chair of the Department of Education at Clark University and Director of the Literacies Institute, a consortium of universities, research institutions, and public schools created in 1988 with a grant from the Andrew W. Mellon Foundation. She has published widely in the areas of sociolinguistics and literacy.

CANDACE MITCHELL is Assistant Professor of English at the University of New Hampshire. She has published and edited numerous articles on the subject of literacy.

JAN NESPOR is Associate Professor of Curriculum and Instruction in the College of Education at Virginia Polytechnic Institute and State University. His research interests are in the areas of anthropology of knowledge, curriculum, and learning processes.

PAT RIGG has a small consulting business, American Language and Literacy, in Tucson, Arizona. Author of several articles about literacy in both first and second language, she is co-editor of *When They Don't All Speak English* (1989).

MICHÈLE SOLÁ teaches Spanish and is Director of Public School Outreach Program at Manhattan Country School in New York City.

KATHLEEN WEILER is Assistant Professor in the Department of Education at Tufts University. She is the author of *Women Teaching for Change* (Bergin & Garvey, 1987).

JOHN WILLINSKY is Director of the Centre for the Study of Curriculum and Instruction at the University of British Columbia and the author of *The Well-Tempered Tongue, The New Literacy,* and *The Triumph of Literature*.